D0948975

The Sword and the Scepter

The Sword and the Scepter

THE PROBLEM OF MILITARISM IN GERMANY

Volume I:
THE PRUSSIAN TRADITION
1740-1890

By GERHARD RITTER

Translated from the German by HEINZ NORDEN

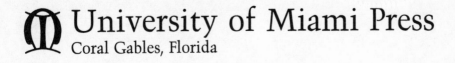 University of Miami Press
Coral Gables, Florida

Translated from the third, revised edition, 1964 version, published under the title *Staatskunst und Kriegshandwerk: Das Problem des Militarismus in Deutschland, Erster Band: Die altpreussische Tradition (1740-1890)* by Verlag R. Oldenbourg, Munich. Copyright 1954 by R. Oldenbourg Verlag, Munich.

Copyright © 1969 by University of Miami Press

SBN 87024-127-3

Library of Congress Catalog Card Number 68-31041

Designed by Bernard Lipsky

Manufactured in the United States of America

To my valiant wife

Contents

The Sword and the Scepter

Preface to the First Edition

T HIS BOOK is the fruit of the upheavals, in soul and mind, of the Second World War. No other generation has ever been confronted to so profound a degree with the vital problem of whether the demoniac forces of unrestrained warfare can be held in leash and by what means. For us Germans, moreover, this challenge took on special form: What were the historical elements that allowed our people to become abject followers of a militarist more extreme than the world had ever known, a maniacal personality that made the good name of Germany the horror and bogy of Europe?

Originally planned in 1941 as an essay within the context of a more comprehensive work, this writing grew under my hands into a voluminous book. Since I was not content with the printed sources, I made several trips to Berlin and Potsdam in 1942 and 1943, to consult such depositories as the Hohenzollern Family Archives in Charlottenburg, the Secret Prussian State Archives in Dahlem, the Army Archives in Potsdam, the Army Library (formerly the General Staff Library), and the Library of the Army Archives. The heads and staffs of all these institutions treated me with the utmost courtesy. Materials I was unable to deal with thoroughly on the spot were dispatched to me at Freiburg, despite the prevailing war stringencies, for use in the University Library. Some of the material was in photostat form, and I was able to have part of the rest copied here. One source not readily accessible during the war was the Political Archives of the Foreign Office. Even there I might have gained access with the aid of the Army High Command, had my academic obligations left me time to take the necessary steps in time, i.e., before the great aerial bombardment of Berlin began. Looking back, I consider it something of a miracle that I was able to utilize all these historical documents at the last possible moment, so to speak. Only a small part of the material I sought—including the bulk of the papers of King William I—had by then been taken to places of safekeeping. Today everything has either gone up in smoke, like almost the entire Army Archives, or been lost otherwise, including, it would seem, large parts of the Hohenzollern Family Archives; some has been taken abroad, like the papers of Roon and Schlieffen, now in Washington, and the Army Library, supposedly shipped to Russia; and some of the material is inaccessible because of the zonal division.

In the Charlottenburg and Dahlem archives I found the papers of Adjutant General Edwin von Manteuffel—his aide-mémoires for William I during the army conflict; large parts of his correspondence with Roon, William I, Alvensleben, and Prince Frederic Charles; and the handwritten minutes of the Army Committee of the Prussian Diet of 1860-1861. These sources provided unexpected insight into the political background of the quarrel over the army appropriations from 1860 to 1866, a subject viewed too long through the semiofficial eyes of Heinrich von Sybel, who toned down his presentation after the fact.

In the Potsdam Army Archives I scanned the files of the Military Cabinet, the War Ministry, and the General Staff. The first-named, insofar as they relate to "Mobilization and Operations 1866 and 1870-1871," are especially important to the debate between Bismarck and Moltke during the French campaign. This lode has meanwhile been mined also by A. O. Meyer and Stadelmann.

In the War Ministry files I took note of everything affecting the organization of the various military authorities, their access to the sovereign, and their respective jurisdications. This includes especially general and other staff work from 1817 to 1914, personal reports to the sovereign and other reports and cabinet decisions from 1817 to 1890, and campaign plans from 1862 to 1864.

In the General Staff Archives I studied primarily the secret journal of the Chief of the General Staff from 1869 to 1914, in order to gain a concrete picture of his relations with other Reich authorities. I obtained access to certain items of correspondence noted in it, which were of special interest to me. Next I studied the "Correspondences and Negotiations Concerning Political Matters, Operations, etc., from March 4, 1865, to June 22, 1866," a very instructive collection in respect of General Staff relations with the War Ministry and of Moltke's political orientation in 1865-1866. These too have meanwhile been drawn on by others. I examined, further, old files on General Staff organization from 1814 to 1831, files concerning military attachés from 1853 to 1918, and finally the long and very impressive series of deployment plans Moltke prepared against the event of war. W. Foerster, President of the Army Research Institute on War History, was kind enough to supplement these by allowing me to examine his copies of the deployment plans by Waldersee for 1890, by Schlieffen for 1891, 1892, 1894, 1897, 1898 to 1900, 1899, 1902, 1905, and

1912, by the younger Moltke for 1911 and 1913, and by Ludendorff-Moltke for 1912. During my American visit in 1953 I was able to supplement this material still further from the papers taken from the Potsdam Army Archives and now in the National Archives at Washington. I was able to locate—and have microfilmed—Schlieffen's various drafts and final copies of his operational plans from 1905 to 1912.

I hope to be able to publish in the not too distant future part of the historical documents that have come into my possession in this way. I owe a sincere debt of gratitude to the Freiburg Science Society, which helped me to defray part of my traveling and copying expenses.

About half the manuscript was finished by October, 1942, and formed the substance of a public lecture during the winter semester of 1942-1943. Its continuation to the end of the present first volume was completed by late summer of 1944, under the impact of the furies of war that were then reducing to utter ruin the Germany of my youth, the Germany of the Bismarckian Reich with all its political and intellectual traditions.

After the War it seemed at first as though there would never be any hope of publishing such a book in Germany. In addition, I was assailed by new organizational, scholarly, literary, and political obligations to a degree that would have overwhelmed even the most tenacious worker. Still, once the worst postwar emergency was over—i.e., soon after 1948—I proceeded to rewrite the first volume and to prepare and write the second, which is to include a review of the problems of militarism in the rest of Europe.

I hope to complete this volume shortly. I am encouraged by an awareness that in the new and unexpected situation of our country my book may have a role to play that is not without significance. I am grateful to my publishers, Oldenbourg, for mustering the courage not to delay further presenting to the public this volume, complete in itself. Readers interested in acquainting themselves with the further course of my thinking may do so in outline by reading my essay, "The Problem of Militarism in Germany," in Volume 277 (1954) of the *Historische Zeitschrift*.

I am indebted to many friendly hands for assistance in typing and proofreading, especially to Mrs. Tilla Feist.

I dedicate this work to my wife, whose contribution to it was incalculable during our enforced separation in the last dreadful war winter of 1944-1945 and whose valiant support during the worst months of my life was to me the greatest human help of all.

Freiburg i. Br., December, 1953   GERHARD RITTER

An Afterword to the Second and Third Editions appears on p. 323.

Introduction

THE PROBLEM of militarism is the question of the proper relation between statesmanship as an art and war as a craft. Militarism is the exaggeration and overestimation of the military, to a degree that corrupts that relation. Militarism is encountered whenever the pugnacious aspects of diplomacy are one-sidedly overemphasized and the technical exigencies of war, real or alleged, are allowed to gain the upper hand over the calm considerations of statesmanship.[1] Viewed in this light, "militarism" appears as the diametric opposite of "pacifism"—taking that term to mean an attitude renouncing resort to arms on principle and in all circumstances, i.e., at best acknowledging conflict by word, by purely intellectual means.

Yet this opposition, however clear it may be in theory, cannot be translated into practice. The realities of history record many militarist states, while radically pacifist states are seen only exceptionally, and even then but fleetingly. Without an adequately secured system of universal supranational law a national policy of radical pacifism could be maintained only at the risk of self-destruction; and survival is the basic instinct of all living things and of states as well.

Hence militarism has a much better claim to political realism than pacifism, which—at least from our present experience—carries political weight not as a general policy put to the practical test, but rather as an ideology that may be widely professed on an individual basis and thereby serve to erode a country's military potential. There are, to be sure, "peace-loving" governments, side by side with "militarist" ones; but there are none that can be called "pacifist." A predilection for peaceful settlements, moreover, cannot be described as extreme in the sense of a fundamentally bellicose orientation. It is rather an indispensable element of true statesmanship.

Accordingly, the problem of militarism cannot be made plain without a picture of what the proper relation between statesmanship and war should be. We have spoken of war as a craft rather than an art, although the conduct of war is indeed as much an art as is the government of states, and in no way inferior. (Awareness of this is reflected in the fact that successful generals usually rate many more public monuments than successful statesmen!) Yet it is part and parcel of sound public order that the military function remain subordinate to over-all government. The Prussian military theoretician Clausewitz 120 years ago reduced this to a formula that has since been unendingly reiterated: War is the continuation of diplomacy by other means.

He was stating nothing new. The principle had long been recognized by monarchial governments and their ministers. War was purely a profession, a craft. Armies were to be regarded merely as instruments of statecraft, to be used as sparingly as possible, and only for very definite, clearly delimited ends. The essence of militarism is best understood in the reversal of this formula in the twentieth century by General Ludendorff and his ilk. "Politics subserves the conduct of war," runs the brusque statement; or even: "Sound policy is the continuation of war by other means in peacetime."[2] This was the theory on which Adolf Hitler subsequently based his policy—with the devasting consequences that are all too well known.

A long road had to be traversed before this reversal was effected, and it is our object to trace its main stages. But first the problem of militarism—i.e., the question of the proper relation between statesmanship as an art and war as a craft—requires discussion at greater length. Quite evidently it is not enough to say that war is to be regarded merely as a means of diplomacy. This is no more than a truism—if diplomacy is viewed solely as a struggle for power.

It is a fact that military history offers numerous instances of vehement quarrels between political and military leadership in wartime, between government and army high command. We read of the conflict in Athens over the Sicilian Expedition of Alcibiades; of serious disputes, both in Rome and in Carthage, during the Punic Wars; of Prince Eugene's fights with the War Council at the Vienna Court; of objections to Metternich's policy of appeasement by Blücher's headquarters; of serious disagreements between Bismarck and Moltke; and of even more serious ones between Ludendorff and Bethmann Hollweg that shook the government to its foundations—to cite but a few of the better-known examples.

How explain all these conflicts if diplomacy (as a struggle for power) and war are basically one and the same thing? Are they nothing more than "misunderstandings," owing to poor jurisdictional demarcation, conflicting ambitions, lack of political and military skill? One would have to draw this conclusion, from a reading of traditional military history which deals out praise and reproof with the greatest assurance and usually judges that the best solution is to combine government and generalship in one hand. But is this not even more of a truism? It is true that outwardly the soldier king seems to solve the conflict, especially if he is a great captain and at once a statesman of genius like Alexander, Caesar, Frederic the Great, or Napoleon. But who can say whether within these men the same conflicting elements that are usually embodied in different personalities may not be at war with each other? Above all, when that happy union is absent, whose claim has absolute priority in war? Or can there be no such priority, on principle, everything depending upon the whims of history?

To pose the question is to point a finger at the fact that of the two opposing concepts, diplomacy and war, only one is unequivocally definable—namely, war, the clash of arms. Diplomacy is not a clear-cut thing, despite the efforts of theoreticians in the service of National Socialism to equate the "concept of diplomacy" outright with the "friend-foe relation," the element of fighting. If this equation were valid there should be no existential conflict between state and army leadership, and recorded instances of such conflicts would have little historical interest. They would be at best examples of human failure, of lack of political sense; and history would offer us nothing but the monotonous specta-cle of endless struggles for power among states.

But diplomacy is in truth not a clear-cut thing. It carries a dual meaning with which the mysterious demoniac quality that hovers over all political history is closely associated—as is the infinite, inexhaustible variety of actual political life, of the true history of states.

Wherever the state makes its appearance in history it is first of all in the form of a concentration of fighting power. National policy revolves around the struggle for power: the supreme political virtue is a ceaseless readiness to wage war with all its consequences of irreconcilable enmity, culminating in the foe's destruction, if necessary. In this view political and military virtue are synony-mous—*andreia, virtus,* manliness, valor, will power, a disposition to take clear-cut action, a sense of dedication, rigid self-discipline and, where necessary, discipline imposed on others, a sense of honor that is instantly aroused, a resolve to carry every conflict to its ultimate conclusion whatever havoc that may wreak.

So powerful can this destructive drive be that in the heat of battle the moral standards without which an orderly society is impossible, without which there can be no rule of law or peace, are severely shaken. The vehemence of this force increases with the violence of the action, the unleashing of passions, the imminent danger of destruction for the contending parties. Fighting for one's life, one is little inclined to pay heed to the conventions of civil life. All is fair in war: every ruse is permissible. The application of brute force is limited only by considerations of its countereffects, the permanent destruction it may bring on, not least in the moral values of the participants. Such considerations, at the very

least, are far more effective than those of humanity and law. A similar law of
nature holds outside war as well. In the great power struggles among nations, as
in their internal partisan strife, what restrains public men from completely
ignoring the civil conventions is far less a sense of the moral force of those
conventions than fear of endangering their own power, reputation, and credibility. For command of moral trust is a power factor of the first order.

In any event, the ethics of war, first detailed with unequivocal, relentless, and
even brutal clarity by Machiavelli,[3] are altogether different from those of
peaceful society. Indeed, in large measure the two are diametrically opposed.
Yet fighting power is not the whole of the state, whose ends are not nearly so
simple and clear cut as those of an army. Real conflicts between military and
political policy are never confined to jurisdictional disputes between soldiers
and statesmen, nor can they be solved by technical or organizational measures
such as "unified leadership" or "close liaison" between military and political
command. No, such conflicts tend to reach into the very heart of the political
sphere.

For even more than to prevail in war, it is essential to the idea of the state to
be the guardian of peace, of law and order. Indeed, this is the highest, the proper
end of policy—to harmonize conflicting interests peaceably, to conciliate national and social differences, to establish law on a firm foundation, to promote
human welfare, to overcome selfish private and class goals by education in
public service and civil integrity to the end of creating true national and
international communities.

From this point of view, an altogether different set of mainly political virtues
is deemed to be in the public interest—strict law-abidingness, social responsibility, mutual assistance, a willingness to compose differences. Manliness may have
been one political ideal of ancient Greece, but so were justice, moderation, and
piety; and the ancient Roman philosophy of Sallust placed *moderatio* and the
justum imperium beside *virtus* and *audacia* as cardinal virtues. Politics as "the
art of the possible," moreover, is always dependent on the skillful conciliation
of conflicts, the harmonization of interests, if there is to be a true political
community of people living together in tolerable conditions. Theory is of little
use in achieving these ends. The problem always has to be solved in practice.

Historically there have been very different solutions, in keeping with the
basic orientation of the statesmen concerned and the objective situation in
which they found their countries. There have been stormy times that knew no
peace, when decaying orders left only a legacy of chaos from which new power
centers formed with difficulty, in savage ferment; times dominated by ruthless
soldiers and power-hungry politicians, like the feud-ridden late middle ages in
Germany and the incipient Renaissance in Italy. In such times military ability,
the *virtù* of Machiavelli, is everything, and the peaceful work of the legislator is
held in disdain. The only thing that is sought, admired, grasped with the ruthless

mailed fist is the success of the moment. None is concerned with the smoking ruins, the destruction of moral, spiritual, and material values in the fighting, so long as power for conquest prevails. At such times there is no true conflict between sword and scepter, for politics is all struggle and nothing but struggle.

But once the chaotic ferment has quieted and given birth to a new order, that order strives to perpetuate its dominion. The peaceful elements in political life re-emerge and seek to confine the instincts of war. War becomes an exceptional state instead of the rule. Instead of its heroism being admired, its bloody shambles is recognized for what it is, a national disaster.[4] If it becomes unavoidable every effort is made to curb its internal dynamics, to shorten it, to limit its aims, to streamline and humanize it as much as possible, or at least to confine its horrors to a strictly limited number of preferably professional combatants, to prevent the unleashing of murder and rapine by strict military discipline. These are times when statesmanship displays its greatest zeal, to keep war instincts even in the midst of crisis from getting the better of calm political reason as expressed in terms of a permanent peaceful order.

That is the time when real conflict arises between political and military command. The army may demand commitment of every resource to achieve final victory, while the statesmen begin to calculate whether such a commitment is still worthwhile. Or the army may insist on draining its triumph to the dregs, while the statesmen seek to conciliate the enemy by generous treatment, to make a friend for tomorrow of the foe of yesterday. Or the strategists may counsel against neglecting any occasion to destroy the enemy forces, while the statesmen may fear destruction of permanent values, undesirable political side effects, the stiffening of the enemy's resolve against peace. Or the generals may wish to trust only in the tested, tangible, and visible effects of physical force, while seasoned politicians prefer to operate with psychological warfare or diplomatic efforts which, while less certain, are also less costly and risky. In general terms such conflicts arise whenever immediate military ends fail to coincide with political goals—which, however, may very well include impressive successes in the field.

These conflicts take on their full gravity only when both considerations are accepted with equal seriousness—the need of the struggle for power and the restoration and preservation of an enduring peaceful order. Neither in high policy nor in high strategy is there a set of ready-made rules and regulations, a patent solution that can be learned and taught, any more than there are convenient rules in private morality that prescribe the proper conduct in every crisis—whether or not the demands of self-preservation outrank those of altruism, brotherly love, and society. Conscience alone, from its irrational depths, can resolve these conflicts. The realities of moral life are made up almost exclusively of such conflicting claims, as shown by daily experience.

And what is true of the individual is repeated at a higher level in the life of the state. Here the stakes may be the lives of millions, yet every crucial decision ultimately amounts to a risk taken without rational certainty about the demands of the hour; and rather than being taken on rational grounds these decisions seem to stem usually from political instinct—or perhaps it is more accurate to say that they are based on the total character of the men who have to make them, on whether they incline more to armed action or to peaceful construction.

The statesman, in any event, is forever torn between the demands of concentrated fighting power and those of peaceful and enduring order, as between Scylla and Charybdis, and must seek a firm footing between the two. One might even say that his historic stature depends directly on his taking both claims with the utmost seriousness—the need for the struggle for power as a means to create and preserve an enduring peaceful order as the ultimate goal—on his bridging them in action rather than evading them.

This at least is true of the great states of history, especially the great continental powers whose situations and traditions permit no escape into neutrality in foreign affairs. Noncombatant neutrality, a pure policy of law and welfare—these have been vouchsafed only certain marginal and insular states which, owing to special circumstances, were able to maintain themselves beyond the sphere of great power decisions. Citizens of the great powers envy this exemption, unattainable to them. Within their countries true statesmanship can exist only when the sense of power, the readiness to wage war, is combined with a determination to maintain order.

This ideal, alas, is the rare exception and history is full of attempts at evasion. The devout provincial sovereigns of Germany in the sixteenth and seventeenth centuries, for example, desired only to be peaceful rulers, free of military ambition, content to care for their patrimony and the eternal salvation of their subjects. But if we fail to note any conflict between a policy of war and peace here, it is only because these petty principalities, huddling under the protection of the Holy Roman Empire, had no real power. They were only partially states in the modern sense. For the rest they were little more than large personal estates. They certainly never intruded into the sphere of high policy.

The reality of history is just as barren of the extremist military ruler—with no sense whatever for the tasks of enduring peaceful order—as it is of the purely peaceful prince. True, there have been political activists for whom other affairs of state came far behind the concentration of fighting power—one need think only of Charles XII of Sweden, of Louis XIV, and above all of Napoleon. It is no accident that Napoleon's extreme activism with its demoniac unleashing of military power on a grandiose scale elicited an equally monomaniacal antagonist, Metternich, the great champion of order conceived of in purely static terms and the founder of the most durable peace our continent has known since the middle ages.

Yet the limitations of his achievement are plainly seen. He sought to preserve a form of law and order which the passage of time itself was undermining from within. New vital forces were arising and the dynamic militant policy of Bismarck did them far better justice. In Bismarck's person both elements were joined in a rare combination—the will to power and the striving for an enduring peaceful order, national self-assertion, and a sense of European responsibility. Yet even here the mixture can scarcely be called ideal, for there can be no question that Bismarck's combative will power was much more strongly developed than his sense of law and justice. In domestic affairs particularly he shows up as the lordly aristocrat, forever locked in a battle for power with the political parties. He never knew how to harness their ambitions to the service of the nation, replacing partisan strife with a higher integration of forces. But when one takes a close look at the heroes of history, one finds no ideal figures; and despite everything the phenomenon of true statesmanship may be studied in Bismarck to better effect than in almost any other figure in our history. After Hitler, the most extreme of all activists and militarists, we Germans have become doubly aware of that fact.

The strongest impression from such a study is the tremendous importance of *Staatsraison*—that higher political wisdom without which no state can truly flourish. [5] Properly understood—and considered apart from the special historical coloration the term took on during its origin in the sixteenth and seventeenth centuries[6]—such political wisdom is neither mere skill in grasping the advantage of one's own side nor a mere appreciation of "reasons of state," the inexorable necessities of political life. Nor is it a transition from the natural or primitive pursuit of power to a more idealistic conception of law and culture, a mere rationalization of the power struggle serving to enlighten blind power instincts. A policy is not necessarily statesmanlike, informed by true political wisdom, merely because it proves itself particularly shrewd and adaptable, i.e., an effective means of practical power politics, in the sense of a clever opportunism capable of correctly assessing the needs of the moment, or because it employs particularly effective methods in the struggle for power. Nor does statesmanlike conduct imply the idealistic pursuit of cultural ideals that power is to subserve.

A statesman in the higher sense never allows his inalienable responsibility for creating, preserving, and securing a true and therefore enduring order of society to be diluted by the passions, triumphs, and emergencies of the power struggle. For that reason it is germane to statesmanlike thinking to remain forever aware of the unique character of any war situation, to realize that there are limits that cannot be transgressed without risk of destroying enduring moral values beyond repair, without alienating and dehumanizing the very combatants. A statesman in the higher sense is a leader who even in the heat of battle never for a moment neglects to ask himself what the real issue is, how the world is to look afterward. What is the new order toward which we are drifting? Unless the struggle is to be perpetuated, it must lead to a new communal order—not only among the states but among the classes and individuals of each state—an order with a chance of enduring. That chance accrues only to the kind of order that is viewed as a society based on true morality, not one that is foisted on the people. It must be seen to be sound, in keeping with the actualities of life, the true national and social needs, and the balance of power. In the proper sense, therefore, higher political wisdom turns out to be moral reason. It has two aspects: clear, statesmanlike insight into the realities of the situation, the sure political eye without which no political task succeeds; and an unfailing awareness of moral responsibility that is not drowned out by even the fiercest din of battle.

It is this true political wisdom that can in practice overcome the insoluble antinomy of power struggle and peaceful order, for the power struggle then becomes only a means to create an enduring peaceful order. Political wisdom alone invests the diplomatic power struggle with moral justification, not considerations of "culture" and "cultural ideals," vague concepts quite unsuitable for the comprehension of political problems. It is true that political wisdom is never clear enough and strong enough to hold down all the blind, intemperate, destructive passions of the combatants. Indeed, there is no social order that would meet all the criteria of true justice, if only for the reason that life keeps moving ahead; hence law and order cannot prevail forever, for new claims stand against old, the natural interest of one against that of the other. But this lesson from history is no more than what experience teaches us about the kind of human inadequacy that marks all life. Great political power struggles bring home to us with particular clarity the fact that life forever moves on the borderline where the human will and human capacity collide with superhuman forces, with the powers of destiny that often defy control.

When we now look back at the starting point of our consideration of the subject, we see that any proper analysis of the many conflicts between state and army leadership necessarily leads us into the central problem of policy in general. It would be very tempting to trace the history of such conflicts within the total context of history. A comparison of analogous events occurring in the several states of Europe should reveal their innermost structure to our eyes. But first things first. An analysis of our own Prussian and German past has priority. German readers of today need scarcely to be told how urgent this task is. It goes to the very heart of our political self-examination; and the present study, begun and in its first major part concluded during the Second World War, never pursued any other aim. It sought to help answer the question that gnawed at us even then: How did the German people, for centuries among the most peaceful nations of the West, come to be the terror of Europe and of the world, acclaiming a violent adventurer who will live on in history as the destroyer of the old order of Europe? The origins and growth of what is today called Prussian militarism were to be laid bare, unhampered by ingrained prejudices rooted in our national history—but also without the prejudices which a foreigner, proceeding from altogether different political premises, might naturally be expected to bring to them.

Militarism is one of the vaguest and hence most confusing catchwords of our day. The distinction between the military profession proper and militarism is being more and more obscured. It is not appreciated that they differ as much as do character and truculence, steadfast and enlightened self-assertion and headlong recklessness, loyalty and slavish submission, genuine power and brute force. We have already discussed the kind of militarism implied in the subtitle of this book—military extremism that falsifies policy because it completely misreads the essential and foremost purpose of all social order.

This is what we set out to fathom: how was the proper relation between statesmanship as an art and war as a craft almost completely reversed in Germany; or to put it another way, what was the road that led from political war to warlike politics? It is a road that at the same time led from a professional army to a nation in arms. Both are closely associated, but, as will be shown, they are not the same. There is a difference between an armed and a militarized nation.

Today the German people have surrendered all their traditions, even that of a nation able to defend itself. Unlike 1918, many today look on our military past as a haunting nightmare from which they would escape forever. Others wince as they look back on so many blunders in our history. Still others may ask whether it is still worthwhile for us today to discuss statesmanship and war in the historical sense, since in the age of world powers, mass democracy, and the atom bomb, both political wisdom and the craft and profession of war have changed so completely that the concepts and standards prevailing in the nineteenth century and at the beginning of our own seem obsolete. War itself seems to have become unsuited as an instrument of high policy, now that its destructive power has reached the point of threatening all life. We may well ask whether there can any longer be a statesmanship able to control the demons of war once they have been unleashed.

Yet precisely because this may be true, a historical analysis of what led us into this abyss is doubly necessary. We do not know what the future will bring; but we plainly sense that we are living in an iron age in which the world is haunted by a specter of war more terrible than at any time in history. After the great European wars of the past, occurring each time during the early part of the eighteenth, nineteenth and twentieth centuries, there was always hope that enduring peace might be achieved. Today mankind is farther away from such hopes than ever.

All this, in my view, lends special urgency to our theme. Without insight into history there can be no true understanding of the present and its problems. Such insight cannot be gained by politically oriented journalism but only by careful and patient examination of the original sources.

1

The Era of Absolute Monarchy and Professional Armies — The Christian Concept of the Duties of Rulers and the Power Politics of Frederic the Great

FOR CENTURIES, ever since the end of the middle ages, the mass of the German people lived out their lives in impotent principalities where the glories of war and military ambition had little meaning. Hence they occupy a very peculiar position within the total development of Europe. The great wars with which Turks and Frenchmen constantly assaulted the frontiers of Germany were in the main the concern of the imperial house and the great European potentates—although the Holy Roman Empire did occasionally muster defensive contingents from its petty and not-so-petty lieges. It is true, furthermore, that the Thirty-Years' War stirred the ambitions, venturesomeness, and power hunger of even minor German princelings; but this gave rise to no enduring power structure of any consequence.

Later on members of the German high aristocracy who entertained a thirst for military action commonly sought service under one of the great powers of Europe, preferably the house of Hapsburg, their native heritage usually offering them insufficient scope. After the ancient feudal musters ceased to be adequate, waging war became a luxury far too expensive for the modest revenues from provincial domains, apportioned by penny-pinching rural estates. Often there were scarcely enough funds to defray the cost of even a small unit for guard and parade purposes. Even such substantial sovereigns as Frederic William I of Brandenburg, the Great Elector, and his successor, the first king of Prussia, were unable to maintain their standing armies or have them take the field without foreign subsidies.

Over and above these financial stringencies the devout German sovereigns in earlier times entertained moral and religious reservations regarding any effort to reach out for power. The medieval Christian doctrine of the proper duty of princes retained its authority for a very long time in Germany, enjoining the prince to preserve peace and justice and to resort to war only on the morally justifiable grounds of pure self-defense. The Reformation emphatically confirmed this doctrine. It is true that Luther's preachments were far from pacifist in the sense of radically renouncing the maintenance of just claims. Quite the contrary, "A sovereign and overlord," he exhorted the authorities, "is not a private person but must live for others, serve them, protect them, defend them"; and it may indeed come to pass that "the office placed upon his shoulders compel him to wage war. . . . In that event go to it with might and main, show that you are men of mettle. War is not waged by thinking about it. It is a serious business that dulls the teeth of even the proudest, fiercest, and most defiant fire-eater, leaving him scarcely able to bite into fresh butter."[1] But that held good only for self-defense, when a neighbor forced a prince to protect himself, heeding no offers of peaceful settlement. Any other war violated God's law.

And indeed—at least during the second half of the sixteenth century—we note many instances when German principalities sought to prevent hostilities by invoking legal aid from the Holy Roman Empire, or from voluntary arbitrament. Feeble as was the power of the Empire, so long as its organs functioned at all it helped to turn the military feuds of German principalities into peaceable litigation.

We have much eloquent testimony for every century since the Reformation on how these traditions shaped the views of the German sovereigns about the relation between diplomacy and war. The Saxon councilor Melchior von Osse, for example, in his famous political treatise of 1556, "God-fearing, Wise, Reasonable and Righteous Government and Justice," earnestly cautions princes against any striving for "pagan" war glory "which commonly gives rise only to manslaughter, murder, arson, rapine, violation of women and girls, and disaster to rich and poor alike, let alone that it often hinders or even extirpates religion, lays waste the pulpit, dissolves order and discipline and encourages among young people an insolence that is but slowly mastered."

Moltke later on was to credit war with "bringing out man's noblest virtues that would otherwise slumber and fade away—valor and self-abnegation, obedience to duty and the willingness to stake one's life."[2] But at the time of which we speak war was still considered the great moral despoiler and national disaster which the honorable prince must seek to avert by all means. It was his proper task to provide for the common need and welfare, to promote the physical and spiritual weal of his subjects—by stern justice, careful husbandry, moral supervision in the Christian spirit, the maintenance of churches and schools, and the preservation of the teachings of the faith in all their purity.

Almost exactly a century later much the same thing was said by Veit Ludwig von Seckendorf, Lutheran chancellor of Duke Ernest the Pious of Gotha, in his *Der Teutsche Fürstenstaat.* Here the state appears as the enlarged personal estate of the prince who guards it from foreign avarice, seeks to augment his revenues, all the while carefully protecting traditional corporate rights and fulfilling his obligations as the emperor's liege. He resorts to arms only in the last extremity; and even when he sees himself attacked in his well-established rights, he will think thrice before risking bloodshed, "seeing that the same is a dangerous thing, to be treated with care, and that our times especially, call for gentle means." This was soon after the Thirty-Years' War.

Yet by the time this was written, the high tide of the confessional church was already ebbing. A new breed of princes was rising, much hungrier for secular glory and even prepared to subordinate religious faith to political expediency—an example was the ambitious Duke Ernest Augustus of Lüneburg-Hanover. The great dream of these German princes was to rival the splendor of the court at Versailles, and that required military spectacles. If money for such purposes was lacking, one petitioned for subsidies in the service of the great potentates of Europe, seeking to advance one's own interests as much as possible by skillful maneuvering among the various power groupings. Elector Max Emanuel of Bavaria strove all his life to acquire some foreign royal crown and would even have traded his Bavarian heritage for such a privilege. To advance his ambitious designs he did not hesitate to ally himself with France, thereby bringing the rigors of a European war upon the countries of South Germany. Frederic Augustus II, elector of Saxony and hereditary head of the royalist Protestant party, unhesitatingly abjured his Lutheran faith to gain the will-o'-the-wisp of the Polish crown; and as king of Poland he allied himself with the Muscovites and Danes to fight against Protestant Sweden.

The political rise of the Electorate of Brandenburg-Prussia proved more durable than the successes of these ambitious men, some of whom soon met with failure while others proved to have followed mere show and glitter. Even under the Great Elector Brandenburg's extremely cunning foreign policy was supported by a carefully cultivated army. Yet precisely in this case, we see with particular clarity how tenaciously traditional views on the relation of war and diplomacy were held by German princes even at this new stage. It was the proud boast of Frederic William I, the soldier king of Potsdam and creator of the army of Frederic the Great, that he was no longer a "king for hire" *(roi mercenaire)* in the service of foreign courts but could fight *nach eigener Conniventz* (at his own convenience). He inspired his army with a spirit of relentless effort in the service of the state power, initiating a revolutionary change in German territorial policy from which the new type of Prussian and German was to emerge. Yet in the section of his testament of 1722 dealing with foreign policy the best he could recommend to his successor was a cautious see-saw policy that would seek to extract modest advantages from the military entanglements of the great European powers—"for whoever holdeth the balance in the world will always have some profit for his lands, daunt his enemies, and be respected by his friends." He also cautioned urgently against hasty, frivolous, and "unjust" wars:

The welfare of a regent is that his land be well peopled; that is the true wealth of a land. Let your armies march abroad and your excises will not bring in one-third as much as when the army is at home. The prices of things will drop, for the estates will not be able to pay their levies properly, which leads to total ruin. In the name of God I implore my dear Successor never to start an unjust war nor to be the aggressor; for God hath forbidden unjust wars; and ye shall have to render account for every man who falleth in an unjust war. Consider ye that the judgment of God is severe; and if ye read history ye will see that unjust wars never turn out well.[3]

Such were the ideas still held by the father of Frederic the Great on the relation of diplomacy and war. The ruler's proper task was to see to the "peopling" of his country, to guard its economic welfare. War was at best a hazardous venture that might ruin the meager government revenues. It was important to preserve the country's peace and security by "adroit friendship and alliance . . . with the great rulers," especially the emperor and the Russian czar. At the same time one must show a martial bearing by strong armaments, uphold a good reputation, and decently support the "just pretensions" of the ruling house.

Thus it was diplomacy rather than war that was the crucial instrument of high policy, although the king himself confessed that the "sharp practices and skulduggery" of the diplomats were not at all to his liking and chilled his spine. A new element as compared with the practice of the earlier German princelings was his large army—too large, the neighbors thought—organized at great effort and constituting a formidable weapon of policy. It gave great impetus to self-assurance and occasionally encouraged bluffing in place of timid self-containment. But the bluff seldom worked; and in any event, the fundamentally peaceable disposition remained intact.

From this tradition of centuries there suddenly and unexpectedly leaped in meteoric trajectory the military genius of King Frederic II, the first to carry the grand style of European power politics into the world of the petty German principalities.[4] It was he who first put the Prussian army on the road to military glory. Only under him did it begin to become known as the best army in the world.

And how did he justify his decision to invade and occupy the Austrian province of Silesia in peacetime, without prior negotiations with the Vienna cabinet? "At my father's death I found all Europe at peace. . . . The minority of the youthful Czar Ivan made me hope Russia would be more concerned with her internal affairs than with guaranteeing the Pragmatic Sanction. Besides, I found myself with highly trained forces at my disposal, together with a well-filled exchequer, and I myself was possessed of a lively temperament. These were the reasons that prevailed upon me to wage war against Theresa of Austria, queen of

Bohemia and Hungary. . . . Ambition, advantage, my desire to make a name of myself—these swayed me, and war was resolved upon."[5]

Thus wrote the youthful king in 1742, directly after concluding his First Silesian War. Frederic indeed trivialized the claims of his dynasty to parts of Silesia. His own cabinet minister, von Podewils, who tried to demonstrate these claims to the world with great care and detail, he damned with faint praise as a "worthy charlatan," in an excess of high spirits.[6] It would seem at first blush that the Teutonic traditions of royal honor, loyalty, and fair play had been thrown overboard with considerable frivolity. Be that as it may, Frederic did set all Europe in motion, and he spent the rest of his life in a steadily more difficult struggle to maintain the fruits of his first swift campaign of conquest. For seven long years it seemed he had brought only perdition on his house and country. In the familiar words of an English ambassador, the whole Prussian state had become "an armed camp in the midst of peace."

War seemed to have become Prussia's proper element. Peace was no more than a breathing-space for mustering new forces against the enemy without, by the aid of an administration tailored to the demands of war. The judgment passed on this irksome state by its German contemporaries, roused from their tranquility, was along such lines. They viewed it as a soulless instrument in the hand of a violent, infidel, cynical despot, forcing his subjects under the brute discipline of the corporal's stick, disturbing his neighbors with his recruitment and impressment, and thus ultimately threatening the freedom of all Germans. Fear of the harsh compulsion of this militarism echoed into the days of Bismarck's creation of the German Reich, especially in South Germany.

The contrast between the old Germany and the new, between Weimar and Potsdam, continued to play a major part in anti-German propaganda in the twentieth century. Germany in the age of petty principalities—cosmopolitan in temper, peace-loving, fond of philosophy, given to poetry and reverie—was again and again favorably compared with the latter-day German spirit of Potsdam, militant and brutal, bent on conquest and rulership. And all these characterizations seemed to be corroborated beyond question when Hitler came to power and, in a familiar histrionic scene, described his government to the world as the legitimate heir of the spirit of Potsdam and himself as the true standard-bearer and consummator of the policy of Frederic the Great. Neither at home nor abroad did any of his historical myths find as much credence as this one, the authority of which seems unshaken to this day.

If the myth were true, however, the whole question asked in this book and the examination to be conducted in it would be superfluous. We should simply be dealing with a continuation into the twentieth century of the methods of war and the policy of Frederic the Great. To trace these in detail would be an undertaking of little point, for all we should encounter would be the same monotonous and repulsive spectacle of crude power politics and one-sided belligerence.

German historians, to be sure, can point to the fact that King Frederic by no means appeared to his contemporaries purely in the light of a warlord, conqueror, and disturber of world peace. He was admired throughout Europe—including particularly France and England—as the past master of a cold and rational brand of statesmanship and above all as an enlightened, progressive, and hard-working monarch, the founder of a modern sensible rule of law. At times he was actually lionized as the champion of West European culture against the hereditary Catholic house of Austria and all the powers of reaction. He was forgiven his Silesian adventure all the more readily since the cabinet policy of the age did not yet recognize moral sensitivities and national reservations against the conquest of neighboring provinces. Indeed much of Europe was then embroiled in colonial power struggles on which were to hinge the future of whole continents. The sharp moral condemnation of Frederic's policies is of recent vintage, stemming in part from much later experiences in which Europe was exposed to the warlike vigor of the Prussian state.[7]

All this, of course, has not been overlooked; but Prussian historians have been at pains to emphasize that Germany needed a firm core of power to overcome its traditional weakness in foreign affairs and that it owed this new power structure to the Prussian king. They pointed out that no state sets out on the road to greatness without sacrifice and that there was no other way than forcible conquest for Brandenburg-Prussia to break out of its narrow and petty obscurity into European recognition.

Hence, inside Germany, patriotic veneration of Frederic has always primarily revolved around his genius as a soldier. His great historic achievement was thought to be the unswerving courage with which he maintained himself and his domain against all his enemies. Again and again he served as an inspiration when the country was in trouble (after the defeat by Napoleon at Jena and after the two world wars, for example) and the people's sense of dedication had to be stirred. Thus the single aspect of military hero worship has come more and more to the fore. The time would seem to have come for correcting this one-sided picture and reinterpreting Frederic the Great in the light of his own age, without the prejudices of later times.

The first question we must ask ourselves is whether it is at all correct to look on Frederic as the representative of a fundamentally militant activism, a man for whom political action consisted solely of a display of fighting energy. Did he completely relinquish the ideal of the just and peaceable father of his country to which so many of his predecessors zealously adhered, or did he merely supplement it, so to speak, by employing his power more boldly and ruthlessly?

His earliest surviving political utterance, a confidential letter written to his equerry von Natzmer in February, 1731, when he was under arrest in Küstrin as Crown Prince, points the way to the right answer.[8] He saw with astonishing clarity the geopolitical verities dictating the foreign policy of Brandenburg-

Prussia. It was a land of the middle, stretching across central Europe, cut up into many pieces, a kingdom of mere border strips (as Voltaire was later to put it), clearly dependent on maintaining good relations with its neighbors. This meant that it had to remain forever in a state of timid impotence, hopelessly on the defensive in every conflict, since it could be attacked from several sides at once. "Yet in matters of grand policy he who does not advance must retire." A ruler possessed of creative imagination would not rest content with such a situation. He will "necessarily" (i.e., without respect for the customary chances of dynastic ties) put himself in possession of such provinces as will round out his patchwork domains. Initially it was an open question whether this must be done by military means. As before, the preservation of peace seemed a most desirable goal—but only if the king of Prussia "were able to maintain a peace solely from a sense of justice and not from fear," for he would no longer be impotently exposed to danger but "cut a good figure and play an important part among the great of the world" and "be able to wage war emphatically whenever the honor of his house demanded it. . . . For he would have nought to fear but the wrath of heaven, nor have reason to fear that so long as the fear of God and a sense of justice prevailed in his land over irreligion, partisan strife, avarice, and selfishness. My goal for the Prussian state is that it should rise from the dust in which it has lain and bring the Protestant faith to full flower in Europe and the Holy Roman Empire, that it become the refuge of the oppressed, the protector of widows and orphans, the supporter of the poor, and the terror of the wicked."

Clearly Frederic's vision was that the king of Prussia should occupy a position like that of the head of a great power; but this position of power was to serve him to govern in peace and justice, to cultivate law-abidingness and the fear of God in his country, to prove himself the champion of the true faith, of widows and orphans, and of all who were oppressed. We note with much surprise that the ideals of Protestant sovereignty and Christian chivalry lived on in full strength and were taken for granted in the wishful dreams of the nineteen-year-old heir to the throne. Unfortunately the Christian guise was soon to wither and drop away under the hot light of the French philosophy of enlightenment. But the ethical ideals of chivalry remained—of a just and humanitarian regime that nevertheless put its trust in its military power and, having compensated for the ill-favor of its geographic situation by rounding off its territory where essential, was to become the one German state that could secure the peace.

Even the most resolute power drive, unafraid of risking the test of war, is not at all the same thing as a true and innate fighting spirit which is actually at the heart of the steady struggle for power that proves so exhausting to the art of statesmanship. There are traces of Machiavelli, theoretician of militant power politics, of a doctrine of government that transcends the mere techniques of political in-fighting. He suggested a need for *virtù ordinata,* a kind of political efficiency that proves itself in the wise ordering of a state of law rather than by strength and skill in the conquest of power.[9] However, in the total context of Machiavelli's writings these hints are almost buried beneath a truly demoniac emphasis on the militant politician's absolute need to surrender all impeding reservations, to ignore all law and morality.

This was precisely the point at which Crown Prince Frederic leveled his criticism, in his *Antimachiavelli* of 1738 in which he showed himself an apt disciple of humanitarian political philosophy from Locke and Fénelon to Voltaire. The work has often been belittled as the immature product of a youthful enthusiast. Its political moralizing has been held up against the harsh realities and "Machiavellian" methods of Frederic's own later policies of alliance and war. It is quite true that the book has a dash of naive, though reasonable, optimism that is blind to Machiavelli's innermost purpose and the demoniac forces at work in the sphere of politics. Yet the King would probably have had no reason to renounce even a single sentence of what the Crown Prince wrote on the relation of politics and war.

"To uphold the law is a ruler's first duty," Frederic states in his first chapter. It is for this very end that people (according to the general view of natural law) instituted thrones and Italian *principini,* "preference was given to the somber glory of the conquerors—their sensational deeds of grandeur that compelled respect—over the milder virtues of justice and mercy." But in our own enlightened age "we are cured of the madness of encouraging and even celebrating the cruel and savage passions that aim only at world upheaval and the destruction of thousands of lives. Justice is enthroned above us all and we will have nought of heroic conquest and military genius when they threaten us with perdition. . . . A manful spirit, a clear head, a wealth of experience, power over the minds of people—these are traits that will find admiration even on their own in a conqueror. They are misused only by those who are obsessed with malice and power. True glory accrues only to him who puts forward every effort to maintain the law and becomes a conqueror only by necessity rather than his own ungovernable temperament" (Chapter 3). All this is little more than a primitive schoolbook exposition in the style of the kind of political philosophy preached by Fénelon, to whom explicit reference is made (Chapter 7). Yet we note that conquest is not condemned as such but only when it "threatens disaster" or stems from an "ungovernable temperament" rather than "necessity."

And indeed the notion of the ideal prince takes on a personal tinge as soon as Frederic comes to speak of a ruler's military duties. "Every last consideration obliges him to take personal command of his troops and to be the first one in his army as at his court. . . . How great the glory of a prince who wards off foreign conquest with skill, intelligence, and valor, whose audacity and ability triumph over the designs of powerful enemies!" (Chapter 12). Hence the ruler must earnestly study the craft of war, must learn how to lay out a camp, maintain discipline, and keep supplies moving up. He must bear the hardships of the field, make up his mind swiftly, and ever think ahead. On the other hand he must guard against the narrow mind of the professional soldier. A king must be neither a petty drill sergeant nor a strutting braggart. Indeed "a prince fulfills only half his destiny when he devotes himself solely to the craft of war. It is wrong that he be a soldier and nothing else. . . . Rulers are primarily judges. When they are generals, it is but in a subsidiary role" (Chapter 14). They must be ever mindful that forcible conquest is not the only way by which their domains can grow, but that there is another way that promises no less success, the way of "hard work." Among the most important of a ruler's duties is the planned cultivation of the economy (in the mercantilist style) as well as the advancement of science and the fine arts (Chapter 21).

One can see plainly how these two ideals stand side by side: the brilliant successful field captain and the great patron of the arts and shepherd of his people. For the time being humanitarian sensibilities were still most strongly to the fore. How happy would the world be if it could do without the "cruel, fateful, hateful" arbitrament of war! But there are no judges to decide whether the conflicting claims of kings are just, and thus justice and the liberties of the people can in many instances be protected only by force of arms. These are the cases of "just war," and they are enumerated in full keeping with ancient Christian-Occidental tradition—including even wars of aggression, although these may be fought only in defense against a great power growing to giant proportions, i.e., in defense of the liberties of the people.

"All negotiations among states naturally have but one aim, the peace and welfare of the land. To this focus all the paths of statesmanship must ever converge." Moderation in war aims is always indicated, together with the greatest economy in risking life and limb of soldiers. "War is such an abyss of misery, its issue so uncertain, its consequences for a country so devastating that a ruler cannot consider the risk too carefully. . . . I am convinced the hearts of kings would be wrenched could they but see the plight of the people in all its horror"—the oppressive burden of taxation, young people dying by the thousands, the sufferings of the maimed, the tears and despair of widows and orphans. "No tyrant has been able to commit such atrocities in cold blood. A prince who begins an unjust war is crueler than a tyrant. . . . In sum, the wardens and rulers of the world cannot consider each single step carefully enough. They cannot be parsimonious enough with the lives of their subjects, for these are not to be looked upon as their serfs but as equals, indeed in some respects as the real sovereigns" (Chapter 26).

It is on such a note of humanitarian exhortation that the work ends. In the literary circle of Rheinsberg it was taken to represent a kind of government program of its author. That its pathos is genuine is quite beyond doubt. Every line glows with the young prince's desire to help usher in a new and better age in which the sun of reason would triumph over the somber hate and power instincts of crude barbaric ages.[10] This was the great hope that dominated the whole century of the Enlightenment. Nor did anything change when the King soon afterward noted from his own experience that "ambition and the desire to make a name for myself" were stronger than the assiduously acquired ideal to be the peaceful shepherd of his people. Frederic knew himself to be utterly free of any hateful or predatory instinct directed against the house of Hapsburg or his chivalrous antagonist Maria Theresa. His ambition moved on a higher level; and he thought himself amply justified by the vital need of his country "to rise at last from the dust where it has lain," as he put it in his youthful letter of 1731. As early as 1738 he had written in a pamphlet that it was "a firm principle of rulers to enlarge their domain in the measure their power allows."[11] Here, however, he attributed this to the ever-present demoniac powers of ambition and unrestrained human passion, and he added a vigorous exhortation to princes to bethink themselves of their mission as guardians of the welfare of their people.

After his experiences in the First Silesian War he was compelled to confess that the practical statesman could never quite escape the welter of lies, violence, and disloyalty that dominates the sphere of high policy, unless he were willing to have others exploit his magnanimity for their own advantage.[12] "Machiavelli," he said in 1752, "insists that an unselfish power caught between selfish ones must inevitably perish. I am afraid I must admit he was right." Yet this realistic conclusion by no means pushed him into somber resignation. To be sure, no active statesman could survive without a certain measure of violence and guile. Yet in the end all depended on using both in moderation. "Princes must be necessarily possessed of ambition, but their ambition must be wise, temperate, and illuminated by reason."[13] Frederic himself was convinced that compared to other rulers he behaved in "rather highminded fashion" during the Silesian War, "and even though the general custom subjugated my reason, my heart was not spoiled." In the end there was always as a last resort the appeal to later centuries when "an age still more enlightened will grant sincerity the place that is its due."[14]

What enabled Frederic the Great to reconcile within himself the humanitarian obligations of the peaceable ruler with the militant ambitions of the war hero was his unshakable faith in the shining victory of reason. He was aware that when it came to the test his ambition and power drive were curbed by insight and reason, by political wisdom. Hence he was able to cultivate both a genuine belief in humanitarianism and an equally genuine ardor for military laurels. Caesar the conqueror and Marcus Aurelius the philosopher-emperor of peace were two heroic images closely conjoined in his mind. After all, had not Voltaire, literary apostle of the great humanitarian movement of the age, written the history of the soldier king, Charles XII of Sweden, in terms of a heroic epic? True, the book concluded that what kept the Lion of the North from becoming a great statesman was his thirst for honor, glory, and vengeance, unreasonable passions all. Charles was a unique figure rather than a truly great man, and "princes should learn from his life that peaceful and happy governance stands high above even the greatest measure of honor and glory."

This prototype of the pure fighting man was much on Frederic's mind when he was still Crown Prince; and like Voltaire he reached the conclusion that one-sided exaggeration had transformed the military virtues of this great adventurer into dangerous vices.[15] In Frederic's view Charles was ill suited to serve as a model even in the military sense, for nowadays the art of war required more than mere bravery and physical prowess. It called for military knowledge, an ability for shrewd calculation. "Today guile wins over force, art over valor. A general's brain has more influence over the success of a campaign than the arms of his soldiers. . . . Bravery without intelligence is nothing, and in the long run a calculating head will always win over the most daring swashbuckler." A "calculating head" meant not merely a general in command of the newer techniques of strategy, but a cool and reasoning statesman who knew how to keep the passions of war in leash and who always fixed his eye on the objective national interest. These were the very qualities Charles XII lacked. In Frederic's mind humanitarianism and sober political wisdom were closely associated. Both implied curbing the passions, the instincts of hate, the pure fighting will.[16]

These views did not remain mere theory. The life story of Frederic II shows at every point that he was just as seriously concerned with the welfare of his subjects as with limiting his own power goals. Despite his military ambitions he was anything but a "soldier king" in the sense of a blind daredevil or crude ruffian. Time and again he bitterly complained that fate had compelled him to spend the best years of his life amid the din of arms and the bloody trophies of war rather than at Sanssouci in converse with his beloved Muses.[17] (In fact he spent no more than ten of his forty-six years as king in the field!) In his letters and verse epistles from the field he was ever passionately cursing the bloody trade of the soldier; and he was deeply shaken by his grim impressions of the battlefield.

What a strange spectacle he offers, this commander who after his day's work at war declaimed long scenes from Racine in his tent and was moved to tears by them; who by candlelight in a crude peasant cottage labored away on elegies and sonnets in French, celebrating his own heroic and tragic adventures or bemoaning the impending doom of his country. How strangely all this departs from our wonted picture of the manly warrior! A secret well of human sensitivity that could find no other outlet was here clamoring for clandestine expression.

Somehow it never swerved this king and commander from his cold, clear, and objective decisions, but this was not because his nature was at heart Machiavellian. It was the result of a continuing struggle for iron self-discipline.

The ideals of peaceful and humanitarian governance were more than mere passing moods with Frederic. They were extremely active in motivating him. Recognition and assessment of this element is rendered difficult, for thoroughgoing aristocrat that he was and out of touch with the common people, he often displayed an arrogant and cynical contempt for them. Yet his administration was as singleminded as those of any of the petty Christian princes had ever been in its effort to secure for his subjects the highest measure of welfare compatible with the meager resources of Old Prussia and the limited means of a strictly authoritarian regime.

Prussia is the last country one would have been justified to charge with exploiting the people for the benefit and glamour of the court or with wasting government funds generally. This was much more than mere theory. In his secret political testaments, intended solely for his successor, Frederic insisted over and over that the regime of the Prussian king could and should be mild since he reigned over a hard-working people of amiable disposition, from whom no serious internal resistance need be feared. Quite at odds with Machiavelli's counsel, the king was to encourage by reward rather than deter by punishment, seek to lighten burdensome government imposts as much as possible, always be mindful that he was but the first servant of the state, and to devote his whole life to that service which should be his sole guiding star. In short he must be a man of honor *(honnête homme)*–"the welfare of his people must be close to his heart for it is inseparable from his own."[18]

We are familiar with the actions that stemmed from this resolve. For decades, with unflagging application, Frederic II concerned himself with the "peopling" and "melioration" of his country, with promoting trade and commerce, and with improving the school system and institutions of learning. It is true that he did this not so much for his subjects as such, but above all on behalf of the state and its military striking-power. Yet the state did not mean an end in itself to the king,[19] any more than did the enhancement of state power or the acquisition of military laurels. Both aspects served only to create the outward prerequisites for a grander, fairer, richer future for the country as a whole. It is no accident that in Frederic's Political Testament of 1752 justice and sound finances are mentioned among the four "main pillars" of good government—mentioned, together with social and economic welfare and the church, *ahead* of the tasks of foreign policy and war. The Prussian militarist state may have made harsh demands on its subjects but its architect clearly pursued a vision of law and culture. That is why he placed a clear-cut limit upon the expansion of governmental intervention, a limit that was never to be exceeded—the limit of law and toleration.

Even the defense and foreign policy of the state of Frederic the Great shows, on closer scrutiny, the same system of strictly rational self-limitation. Everything within that state ran in accordance with carefully calculated rules—finances, diplomacy, the army. As Frederic himself put it, they were to be directed from a central point "in clear-cut extension, shoulder to shoulder, like the team of four horses drawing an Olympic chariot"; and so, too, the claims of war were to be held within the firm limits of political expediency.

Frederic's contemporaries were accustomed to a far lower level of military effort, and to them his limits seemed excessively generous. Today we should probably consider them relatively narrow. Compulsory military service did not in practice extend beyond a quota of peasant sons and journeymen artisans. Even that manpower reserve Frederic exhausted to the ultimate only reluctantly and hesitantly, under the lash of the Seven-Years' War. This was forced upon him by economic considerations, especially the inexorable claims of agriculture, which also compelled him to recruit abroad about one third of the troops he required. From a military point of view this was a highly undesirable and even dangerous expedient, although for political and economic reasons Frederic might have wished to man his companies with foreigners to the level of two thirds. The commercial middle class and the professions were exempted from the draft in principle. If the king had paralyzed their work, excise taxes, the most important source of government revenue, would have declined. Even in peacetime there must not be too much interference with peasant labor on the estates or smallholds; hence soldiers were furloughed for most of the year, and the two "drill months" were timed before or after main harvest time, whenever possible.

When crops were poor and grain became scarce, military stockpiles were thrown on the market to keep prices from rising excessively. Indeed these army supplies, like the trade outside guild limitations, permitted soldiers in their spare time to fatten their meager pay, were carefully integrated with mercantilist state policy. The clear-cut distinction between peasants and artisans subject to call-up, exempted middle class, and privileged aristocracy (which as a general rule provided the officers' corps) accorded closely with the social order of the old three-corporation state. There was not the slightest thought of altering that order by such a measure as mobilizing all classes equally.

Plainly the military monarchy of Frederic the Great, which appeared to his contemporaries as a militarist state pure and simple, lagged far behind the "total militarization" of modern continental mass states. Not even in wartime was it ever truly an "armed camp" compared with later times. Frederic entertained no notions of a "nation in arms," any more than he was familiar with the concept of "total war" embracing all spheres of life. On the contrary, he was particularly proud of his ability to wage war in such a fashion that the "peaceful citizen in his home remains quiet and undisturbed nor would even notice that his country were at war but for the war dispatches. . . . The husbandman tills his fields under the protection of the noble guardians of the fatherland. The law is upheld in the courts. Trade flourishes and all professions are pursued without hindrance."[20] War as an instrument of power policy was to be wielded by wise statesmanship only with the greatest care, even while it was being waged in the field with the fullest effort. Vital peaceful interests must be spared as much as possible. That also meant that war had to be waged without passion.

The lower the heat of passion, the greater the influence of political and economic considerations even on the details of warfare. At a later date the military establishment, seeking to assert its own destructive autonomy, might reject such interference as "irrelevant," but this was certainly not true in the age of cabinet war.[21] In coalition wars especially it was customary for war plans to be negotiated through diplomatic channels among the several courts, often for months on end, allowing full play to the special political and economic interests of each ally. The preponderance of such interests explains in part the strategy of maneuver and attrition practiced in the eighteenth century. The paralyzing influence of the Vienna court's War Council on the Austrian armies in the War of the Spanish Succession was notorious, as was that of the *Betaalsheeren* of the Dutch estates on the generalship of the princes of Orange.

King Frederic enjoyed the advantage of combining political and military war leadership in his own person. But precisely for that reason it never occurred to him to exclude political considerations from his military planning. He was more boldly aggressive than most of his contemporaries. Threatened and exposed on several sides at once and short of funds and manpower, he was impelled to strike swiftly and vigorously, indeed sometimes almost recklessly. For these reasons he has been viewed as an exceptional figure within his era, anticipating the "strategists of annihilation" of later ages.[22] But as we shall show, the mark of those strategists is that they know only one war aim, the application of physical force to render the enemy utterly defenseless; and they vigorously resisted any interference with this policy of destruction, from political motives. From this point of view Frederic was certainly not a strategist of annihilation. On the contrary, closer examination of his campaigns shows that his strategy was by no means "absolute" or "total." It was indeed limited in two directions. Frederic was under the constant necessity to resort to diplomatic methods when the desired issue could not be forced by purely military means; and he was ever ready to content himself with partial successes, in hopes of weakening the enemy's resistance even without destroying him outright, or for that matter exhausting his own resources to the last.

His very first invasion of Silesia, seemingly dictated by unrestrained ambition and blind defiance of every political caution, was actually the product of carefully calculating the political opportunities. Frederic would scarcely have ventured on this operation but for his firm conviction that one of the two Western powers, England or France, would soon join his side for reasons of high policy. He was further convinced that his virtually unarmed adversary could be overrun with ease, that the opposing leader, a helpless woman, was incapable of serious and tenacious resistance while her husband, from faraway Lorraine, would be unwilling to offer any. Indeed, Frederic was hopeful of being able to persuade Maria Theresa to renounce Silesia voluntarily, by guaranteeing to support her against attack from any other source.

Both these calculations proved deceptive: the Austrian enemy at Mollwitz showed himself to be exceedingly dangerous; and instead of the expected anti-Austrian alliance an anti-Prussian one seemed for a time on the verge of forming. Frederic therefore let the war virtually fall asleep for many months, from April, 1741, until the late autumn (i.e., the season most favorable for military operations) in order to secure better political backing by diplomatic negotiation. When he finally succeeded in persuading the French to break with Vienna and advance their armies against Upper Austria, while at the same time the Anglo-Russian counteralliance also broke up and Saxony and Bavaria rose against Maria Theresa, the cause of the Hapsburg queen seemed indeed lost.

And what did the Prussian king do then? Did he advance vigorously to administer the *coup de grâce?* No, in deepest secrecy he met with Neipperg, commander of the sole army the Austrians were then still able to field, and at Kleinschnellendorf castle he advised Neipperg how he might best attack Prussia's allies. Frederic concluded a politico-military agreement that granted the Austrians safe retreat from a highly dangerous situation while giving the king nothing he did not already hold quite firmly—surrender of the fortress of Neisse and undisturbed winter quarters in Upper Silesia. In return he pledged to confine his claims to Lower Silesia in the impending peace negotiations.

From a purely military point of view all this can scarcely be justified. The motive may have been in part a certain impatience to reach a rapid conclusion without another winter campaign. Against the newer theories, however, it must be maintained that Frederic, without compelling need, deprived himself of the opportunity to carry the campaign to a clear-cut military decision. In the light of present-day views of strategy, some of Frederic's clauses seem very odd: an agreement to feign a siege and bombardment of Neisse and to continue pseudo-skirmishes among outposts, in order to deceive Prussia's allies!

There were political considerations behind all this, of course. Frederic was afraid that Saxony might draw too great an advantage from the war and that his French ally might become too willful and demanding. It was better to allow Maria Theresa to regain her breath. The whole style of Frederic's Silesian strategy becomes clear from this incident. It was still quite in the style of cabinet war—with clear-cut and limited aims, carefully calculated risks, an almost capricious switching of alliances, the most parsimonious use of resources, a great deal of diplomatic bluff, and constant attempts at deception.

Frederic's campaigns until 1745 were accompanied by a continuous game of alliances, offers of alliances, and treaties that were renewed as quickly as they were withdrawn. The war aim was not at all the destruction of Hapsburg power but the possession of Silesia and the creation of an independent and prestigious position within the Holy Roman Empire and toward France as well. Victory in battle brought the king of Prussia the greatest political renown and was therefore indispensable; but diplomatic skill and the ruthless exploitation of momentarily favorable political situations also served his purpose. It was his ambition to outdo all his fellow players in such tricks, but apparently he went too far, seriously hurting his reputation abroad. Three times in quick succession he took his allies by surprise with premature peace treaties. He did not at all desire to fight the war to the complete exhaustion of his enemy but only up to a stage that might suit Prussia's "political convenience."

"The art of war is like any other art, useful when properly practiced, harmful when misused." As late as his Political Testament of 1768, which sums up his whole life's experience, Frederic clung to the doctrine that only a "just" war was justifiable—i.e., one demanded by inexorable vital political needs—while any other war was "culpable."[23] "Henceforth I shall attack not even a pussy-cat," he insisted after the Peace of Dresden in 1745, "—unless it be to defend myself." And seven years later he was still declaring that he now desired to move at last to a "system of preserving peace," so long, that is, as this "were possible without violating the majesty of the state. . . . It would be unseemly for us to recommence the war. A brilliant deed like the conquest of Silesia is like a book. The original is successful but imitations keep losing in effectiveness." All Prussia's neighbors had now been startled into alertness. "My life is too short to lull them back into security."[24]

In the "political reveries" of his 1752 Testament he did ponder what other acquisitions might be useful in enlarging Prussia at some future date: Ansbach-Bayreuth, Mecklenburg, Saxony, Polish Prussia, and Swedish Pomerania. Saxony could be conquered by war only if circumstances were particularly favorable. The others might be gained by diplomacy, treaty, or succession. But he himself described these plans as mere "chimeras," giving no more than a general direction to a Prussian policy of acquisition for the next generation or perhaps only the one after that. For the foreseeable future the European situation was too unfavorable to afford him an opportunity for their realization; and he firmly declined to become an adventurer like Charles XII.

Latter-day historians have tried in vain to represent Frederic's strike at the outset of the Seven-Years' War as a kind of repetition of his inspired coup of 1740, only this time directed against Saxony rather than Silesia. Yet this final crucial test of the power of his state was elicited not by a headlong urge for conquest but from concern to secure, defend, and salvage Prussia's position as a great power. The need was to break a dangerous encirclement that was closing about the country. The fact that Frederic sought to protect Prussia's position through a preventive war, always a questionable tool of policy, necessarily suggests that political reason was clouded by military considerations.

We know today that the political results were disastrous and that the war helped materially to bring about the Grand Alliance. Yet almost immediately diplomacy put a spoke in the wheel of militarism. Prussian diplomacy spent precious weeks in desperate but fruitless efforts to foil the hostile coalition at the last moment, losing Frederic the tempting opportunity to attack and defeat his main adversary while that enemy was still on an unarmed approach march. Again, much time was spent on the complete occupation and exploitation of Saxony for purely politico-economic considerations. The campaign of 1756 ended without a decisive success.

The attempt at surprise invasion was made only the following spring, on the urgent counsel of Field Marshal Schwerin and General Winterfeldt. Frederic himself, guided by political considerations, had originally planned a more defensive approach. In keeping with whatever might be the results of his negotiations with the coalition powers and his English ally, he was prepared to distribute his troops along several fronts. Yet in the end he decided to ignore his apprehensions concerning subsidiary fronts and concentrate the full force of his armies upon delivering a major blow against his main enemy.[25]

In the campaign of 1757, up to the battle of Prague, his strategy reached the point at which it most resembled Moltke's methods. Indeed in militancy and sheer force this war greatly exceeded earlier campaigns. There was no scope left for political escapades. Prussia was defending its very life as a state against the united great powers of the European continent. Chivalrous fencing over limited war aims had suddenly turned into a life-or-death struggle.

Yet so uneven a struggle could not be won by military means alone. The very size, cumbersomeness, and heterogeneous structure of armies at the time prevented their deployment for the kind of blow of destruction Napoleon was to achieve in a later age. Frederic was quite clear on this point, as is seen from all of his military manuals. Directly following the disastrous day of Kolin we see him recommencing his diplomatic efforts to loosen the encirclement. A thousand different channels were utilized between battles and during the winter lulls to sound out the possibilities of political understanding and equable settlement with Maria Theresa's allies, to spot and if possible widen hidden rifts in the coalition. Going through the long series of volumes of "Political Correspondence" for these war years, with their marvelous jumble of political and military documents that show the king functioning at one and the same time as commander-in-chief, chief of staff, and head of the diplomatic service, one gains the liveliest picture of the unbroken connection between political and military leadership—the one always supplementing the other, though in the end political considerations always tipped the balance. And in the end it was a political rather than a military event that brought Frederic salvation, the death of the Czarina

Elizabeth and the resulting defection of Russia from the Grand Coalition.

And yet the king owed his final success not to political chance but to his indomitable fighting spirit, the powers of endurance inherent in his character. But for these soldierly qualities he would have sought his "convenience" long before that fortunate event of 1762, as the compromisers advised him to do, sacrificing Silesia altogether or at least large areas of Silesia as well as of the Rhineland. He rejected these importunities, thus maintaining his position as the founder of Prussia's role as a great power.

Still, he often came perilously close to transcending the limits of political reason. In England the "stubbornness" he then displayed was severely criticized. It was a kind of stubbornness, however, in no way comparable to that of Hitler who in 1944-1945 deliberately sacrificed Germany's future—citing the example of Frederic the Great, though in fact his only motive was to prolong his already clearly doomed regime.

As for Frederic, his ultimate success shows him correctly anticipating that his enemies would exhaust their resources and that he could win by sticking it out; and even in success he remained detached, governed by cool political reason. He never allowed himself to be misled into falsifying the meaning of his defensive war through fanciful new plans of conquest. He had thoroughly fathomed the limits of his power in bitter experience, and he was most carefully intent on avoiding exposure to further external dangers for his country.

For several decades he concentrated all his energies on strengthening the internal resources of the monarchy by methodical constructive work. The great acquisition of his old age, the province of West Prussia, was gained by purely diplomatic methods; and when, in the last years of his life, he decided to take the field once again to preserve the balance among the major German powers, his Bohemian campaign of 1778 provided the last historical example of a pure cabinet war of maneuver, with diplomacy achieving far more than military action.

In the history of Frederic the Great, war and diplomacy seem to merge into complete unity; and in the violent struggles between German statesmen and strategists during the following century he was always looked on as a shining example. This was amply justified, for Frederic never allowed the diplomat's pen to forfeit what the sword had won nor military ambitions to destroy the finely spun webs of diplomacy.

Yet when one examines his life more carefully one notes that the façade of a resolute royal will concealed tremendous tensions necessarily stemming from the irreconcilable conflict between political and military ambitions. Indeed at times one can hear the violent explosions. At the very outset of his reign the twenty-eight-year-old ruler's experienced generals and ministers regarded his Silesian enterprise, to be launched without any diplomatic preparation, as an extremely risky adventure. Frederic railed against them: "When ministers speak of politics they are on ground they know, but when they speak of war it is like an Iroquois Indian speaking on astronomy."

During the war, his loyal minister Podewils grew afraid of the European conflagration his young master was about to unleash, and he shied away from a military alliance with unreliable France against the imperial house. "I have reason to be very dissatisfied with you," said Frederic, "and unless you undo the mischief you have done I want you to know that there are plenty of fortresses in my land in which to intern ministers who act against their master's will."

Soon afterward Frederic himself grew uneasy about the French alliance; and the fact that he concluded the convention of Kleinschnellendorf without consulting his minister points to a secret uncertainty about what he ought to do. This, however, was primarily a matter of military and political expediency. The deeper-reaching conflict was between militant will power and the desire for glory on the one hand and a policy of peace and welfare on the other. It was a conflict that permeated Frederic's whole personality. At times the immense burden of responsibility for his people grew to almost intolerable proportions; and in his darkest hours the king more than once was driven to the verge of suicide. Ultimately, he had to carry these inner conflicts alone, without any chance of sharing them with responsible councilors, leading figures in politics, or the army, who might lighten the burden in open discussion. This is what turned him into the solitary recluse, the "guest of stone" among men, appearing to his fellows all too easily as the cold soulless embodiment of "state reason."

Yet it was this very political wisdom and it alone that constantly enabled him to strike a balance between the claims of diplomacy and war, between a peaceful policy of welfare and a militant policy of power; and it is this balance that is characteristic of the reign of Frederic the Great. The hopes, longings, and expectations of the masses did not yet depend on the ruler's political and military decisions. They did not restrict his mobility, his capacity for adapting himself to the changing political constellations. Wars could still be begun and waged—and broken off, if necessary—without whipping up the passions and hatreds of the multitudes. When the king lost a battle, the motto at home was *Ruhe ist die erste Bürgerpflicht* (the citizen's foremost duty is to keep calm)—as a high German bureaucrat put it in the dark days after Jena; and when the king won a battle, he cared little for the applause of his subjects. He alone determined the size of the effort his people would be asked to make in the interest of maintaining and expanding the national power.

Times were bound to change. Frederic marks the farthest limit of almost three hundred years of absolutist development. Three years after his death a revolution in the European order was to begin, completely changing all the external and internal premises of his style of government and along with them the relation between politics and war.

2

Rational Strategy and War Policy in the Rococo Age – The Goddess of War Tamed

I T WILL now have become plain just what the appearance of Frederic the Great meant in the development of our problem. So long as the policy of the German princelings had been to pursue essentially the peaceful goals of maintaining hereditary power and property and domestic welfare, the perpetual struggle between peace and order on the one hand and objectives that could be won only by the exercise of power on the other had scarcely risen into view within their domains. It was only with Frederic the Great that this antinomy became a problem that could profoundly affect that ruler's whole life. Yet he managed to muster the resources to get the better of it—not without a certain degree of vacillation, to be sure, especially when he was new to the job—without seriously shaking his royal self-assurance, which was based on a firm faith in the power of reason. In subsequent times, this faith was not to be taken quite so much as a matter of course. Once the tremendous dynamics of modern mass warfare were unleashed, it was far harder to maintain the primacy of calm political reason over the passions of war. The difficulty was to be measurably aggravated when responsibility for supreme command was divided among professional soldiers and professional politicians, each running separate but coordinate areas. This development was to contribute, soon after Frederic's death, to the enormous complication of the machinery of modern war and the modern state. Ultimately, when it sifted from the sphere of the rulers down into the broad mass of the ruled, this conflict was to have devastating consequences, splitting nations at war into two groups no longer able to communicate effectively with each other. This was to be the end result of developments from the eighteenth century to the eve of the First World War.

Yet we must guard against viewing this development along too straight a line. Things might have turned out very differently, but for the intervention of a foreign power into German life, the great juncture of the French Revolution, and the wars that followed in its trail. It seemed at first as though the Prussian warrior king was to remain an altogether unique phenomenon, his dominion sinking back into peaceful quietude upon his death. Only six years after that event, as shown by the campaign of 1792, the army of Frederic the Great was already in decline. The austerity of his administration gave way to an era of humanitarian reformers, the Beymes and Menckens who tinkered with many acts of amelioration and improvement, in the spirit of an enlightened and sensitive age.[1] In the field of foreign affairs, after a brief period of bustle under Frederic William II, the country all too quickly lapsed into a purely passive and unconditional neutrality.

And the effect of Frederic on the other German principalities? Beyond any doubt it was very strong—not merely in Austria where Joseph II was his ardent admirer while Leopold of Tuscany turned into the very model of an "enlightened" monarch, eager for reform. His influence was particularly felt at courts far too powerless even to dream of emulating Prussia's "military style of government," let alone of rivaling its military laurels. Yet this effect was inherently ambivalent, a blend of often ecstatic hero worship and unconcealed jealousy and fear on the part of the weak. Often there was an added element: vehement dislike of a regime that made such demands, exacted such sacrifices.

Court Councilor Friedrich Carl von Moser of Hesse-Darmstadt sang Frederic's praises as "a spirit who defies description." His pamphlet, "Master and Servant" (1759), was the most widely known "mirror of princes" of this enlightened century, and most typical of the mood of the age. "He is king among the heroes," wrote Moser. "His mind rises above the earth, he turns upon his own axis like the sun, shines in his own light, shares her heat and her spots. His are the dimensions of a great spirit, and centuries to come will study his stature and nature with the utmost care. . . . I feast upon his deeds, often trail him to fathom his secret ways, but the eagle soars at heights inaccessible to birds of lesser feather. . . ."[2]

But, adds Moser immediately: "He demands the space of a colossus. . . . I can think of no being more exalted than the King. More's the pity for us that he does not have a world to himself." Frederic is extolled as "the savior of Teutonic freedom" from "the despotism of the Viennese court." But "the Prussian—court, cabinet, and constitution—is like the famed sword of Scanderbec—useless without Scanderbec's arm." The military style of government is a system "to make monarchies great, while impoverishing small countries."

No doubt similar thoughts were entertained in all the small and middle-sized states. Frederic and his glory were admired; but there was awe of the cost in comfort and happiness Prussian militarism was believed to exact from all estates. Wieland, ruling over his literary circle in Weimar, once wrote in a thoroughly unpolitical but equally arrogant vein: "King Frederic is a great man, but God preserve us from the good fortune of having to live under the big stick that is his scepter."

The enlightened statesmen of neighboring Hanover were fond of finding new and complacent terms for comparing the virtues of their traditional corporate government with Prussian "despotism" that "has learned its great profession on the parade-ground," and "destroys everything that cannot keep to rank and file . . . that stems from ancient local custom, rooted in the peculiar character of the inhabitants of a given region—destroys it in favor of rules and commands on every hand. . . . It is pervaded by a sense of grandeur based on oppression."[3] The conservative spirit of traditional German particularism and corporate govern-ment, accustomed to more casual forms of restraint, resisted the tight reins, mechanization, and centralization of the kind of bureaucratic regime indispens-able to the exercise of power in a modern state.

The successes of the system of Frederic the Great nevertheless were too overwhelming not to invite imitation. A footling game of "playing soldiers" after the Prussian model ensued at many German courts, in barrack-yards, drill-fields, and parade-grounds; the frustrated ambitions of petty German despots sought gratification, to the horror of their nonmilitary ministers and all too often to the ruin of modest exchequers. Friedrich Carl von Moser sharply condemned this military foolishness, which he knew from bitter experience with his own sovereign, to whom he kept recommending in vain a "quiet, patriarchal style of government. . . . To keep the clock of government going steadily and in time," he wrote,[4] "is the meritorious albeit unpretentious task of the wise and settled man." Surely this was true for the entire world of petty states.

The course of the Seven-Years' War had indeed shown the participants in the "Imperial War" against Prussia, including the middle-sized courts, the absurdity of their military effort. All that they brought back from their inglorious campaigns was wreckage. And since Europe was now enjoying three decades of relative calm, if not completely undisturbed peace, the German military despots were finding it impossible to secure subsidies from abroad. During this period the troops of the South German imperial components, Bavaria and Württem-berg in the lead, deteriorated to such an extent that not even the English would hire them for the colonial wars in India and (after 1775) America.

Other petty sovereigns of the Holy Roman Empire like those of Hesse-Cassel, Brunswick, and Ansbach had better luck with selling their soldiers for service in America, although they thereby brought odium on themselves even from their contemporaries. None condemned these "cattle markets" more severely than Frederic the Great, who regarded the usage as the basest degradation of the profession of soldiering. To posterity it seems more than anything else the last and most extreme symptom of the degeneracy of German princes and their tradition of paternalism. Here was the clearest manifestation of the complete obsolescence of this world of petty states. They had sunk so low that they did not shrink from thus abusing the loyalty of their sturdy subjects or from hiding beneath a guise of political alliance what was in fact no more than an outright business transaction.

Fortunately for the German people the sense of duty had not decayed in this measure among all the German princes. Quite the contrary, it was at this very time receiving new impetus under the inspiration of European humanitarianism. Frederic II gained followers not so much as a war hero, but rather as a sovereign of peace, as the "sublime Antimachiavelli";[5] and the fervent reformist zeal of Joseph II found perhaps even more disciples. It was in the field of internal government reform that the example of Frederic exerted its strongest effect. In Germany as throughout Europe in these last, comparatively peaceful decades of the *ancien régime,* the Enlightenment reached its highest peak of self-assertion, progressive optimism, and zealous "do-goodism."

During the Seven-Years' War the Frankfurt professor, Thomas Abbt, had extolled Prussian patriotism, praising "death for the fatherland" as the highest test of manly virtue, in the spirit of ancient moral and political philosophy. But for the quiet decades that followed 1763, that patriotism seemed inappropriate if not indeed dangerous. Characteristic of this sentiment is an academic address the Prussian Minister of Justice and Cultural Affairs von Zedlitz delivered in 1777 in which he described the patriotic passions of the war years as an "unnatural state of affairs," indeed as a "veritable disease of the imagination," useful only in times of emergency. In peacetime, patriotism should be tolerated as a "gentle passion," in the form of good citizenship and devout loyalty toward the sovereign. At that useful level it should be cultivated in the public schools.[6]

All this was quite in keeping with the humanitarian mood and rational needs of the time. Many well-meaning petty sovereigns had become ambitious to be thought of as progressive and enlightened. The old Christian paternalism had found a new contemporary guise. Ordinances from on high soon began to drip with protestations—in elegant Rococo style—of how dearly the sovereign loved his subjects and admonished them to undying gratitude for their good fortune in having so enlightened and philanthropic an overlord. Monarchs were wont to pose either as the natural guardians and stern teachers of their people, holding them by wise legislation to a rational economy, or as liberators from an outmoded feudalism, seeing to it that everyone should "come into the undisturbed enjoyment of the fruits of his work and ingenuity." The ostensible role of the enlightened monarch was always that of an unselfish benefactor bent on putting the public weal above considerations of power, just as it had in the age of confessionalism. Only that the emphasis was now on popular enlightenment rather than on preserving the pure faith, and that the economic goal was skill and hard work rather than mere honesty and respectability. A particularly impressive incarnation of this unbroken princely tradition was the patriarchal figure of Margrave Charles Frederic of Baden, who preached the doctrines of both religion and the new physiocrat economics as guidelines for proper living to his "free, affluent, civilized, Christian people," as he called them.[7] It was a tradition that was to last into the age of revolution.

It was also a poor seedbed for military pride and virtue, this peaceful and humanitarian world of German states, proud of its rationalism and on top of that quite powerless in foreign affairs. Had not even the Seven-Years' War shown that the great continental powers could not really do one another serious harm with the means of power then at their disposal? Had not warfare itself been proved to be quite pointless? Indeed, had not the aging King of Prussia seemingly been anxious to bury his ambitions as a conqueror for good and all? The foreign policy of his closing decades was purely defensive, cautiously moving in Russia's wake. He seemed to fear nothing more than new conflict with the eastern powers. Against the restless power drive of Joseph II he mobilized all the old trappings of the imperial constitution with its privileges and guarantees. Resort to arms he eschewed as long as he could, even when armed conflict had become inevitable.

The halting and inglorious "Potato War" of 1778 was the very paradigm of a war of maneuver in which the full forces were never risked because the political aims did not seem to make it worthwhile—and that was how the conqueror of Silesia rounded out his brilliant military career! It really seemed as though "reason" had at long last tamed the genius of war, as though the time had come when moral insight and rational methods would curb if not eliminate altogether the irrational element of war, child of blind chance and mindless passion.

This was the very direction in which the general trend of the European Enlightenment had long been moving. The new political philosophy of West Europe—nurtured with criticism of absolute monarchism, and in France, especially, with opposition to the exaggerated political ambitions of Louis XIV—was decidely antimilitarist in character and for the most part utopian and pacifist as well.

In Germany these antimonarchist tendencies were absent, while in many of the petty states armed forces played virtually no part. Hence the blasts directed against standing armies by critics like Fénelon, Montesquieu, and Voltaire had met with little response. As the criticism of men like Rousseau, Quesnay, Helvetius, and Holbach grew more strident, Frederic the Great defended the standing army, Prussian style, with his pen. It was the indispensable backbone of a mercantilist economy, relieving the peaceful bourgeoisie of danger and military challenge, he said; and major German parliamentarians like Justi and Büsch were on his side.

Even in German literature, especially the literature that came from the petty courts, the antiwar and antimilitarist spirit made more and more headway after the middle of the century. The leading lights of the new German national literature shared in this trend, from Justus Möser to Herder, Kant, and the young Fichte. The details are not our proper concern here, nor is the medley of motives: humanitarian indignation over the brutalities of mercenary armies, traditional methods of recruitment, and the bloody atrocities of the battlefield; physiocratic reservations about the productive sterility of professional soldiers; vague romantic notions and hankerings about the ancient Germanic system of a militia-like defense; above all, considerations drawn from natural law of the "barbarous rationale" of a worldwide state of affairs in which relations among nations could be settled only by brute force—leading in turn to ever new proposals for a league of nations to preserve perpetual peace, in the style of the Abbé de St. Pierre. This literature culminated in Kant's writings on peace which, however, were guided exclusively by considerations stemming from the philosophy of law rather than by humanitarian sentiments. Kant even kept alive a sense of the beauty of military valor, its "inner dignity," its "loftiness." He knew that his project of "everlasting peace" had no validity as a political proposal for the present, but only as an ideal task mankind had to solve by "approximation progressing into the infinite."[8] Lesser spirits knew no such reservations, though there was an element common to all, the passionately earnest endeavor to control the irrationality of brute force as much as possible, to gain acceptance of the need to seek an order of permanent peace even while the passions of war were raging.

Much of this was to endure for a long time, some of it to this day. There had already been a great step forward when the crude mercenary armies of the seventeenth century, in the habit of destroying peaceful life without rhyme or reason, were supplanted by the disciplined professional armies of absolute monarchy, used with considered economy and supplied in orderly fashion from their own depots. The customs of war had become far more humane; they were now slowly being brought under a fixed juridical system. International treaties had begun to regulate such matters as the treatment, exchange, and ransoming of war prisoners; the surrender of fortified places; medical service in the field; the care of enemy wounded; billeting systems and war booty; renunciation of unnecessarily cruel missiles. The first comprehensive compendia of military and general international law came into being (Emmerich von Vattel, Christopher Konrad Wilhelm Friderici, Johann Jakob von Moser, and Georg Friedrich von Martens, among others), and they contributed on their part toward humanizing warfare. The ultimate goal was to hold the terrors of war to such narrow limits that the peaceful citizen would scarcely know there were such things.

Frederic the Great, as we have seen, was proud of having achieved it in large measure. An admirer praised his brother Henry for having managed to wage war so humanely that "farmers were able to till and harvest between the opposing sentinels and loaded wagons passed through the picket lines without being bothered by patrols."[9] It was an accepted rule late in the eighteenth century that private intercourse among citizens of hostile states proceeded with little or no interruption in time of war. It must be borne in mind, of course, that war in that age was generally conducted by an aristocratic class which felt itself joined by common bonds that transcended national and political boundaries.[10]

More remarkable is the fact that fighting forces were restrained by strict martial law from requisitioning, plundering, and marauding even in emergencies. As late as the Prussian resistance to Napoleon in 1806 it could happen that soldiers had to freeze and go hungry in camps pitched in the open, while trees and fences and even great piles of firewood might have provided them with ready-made fuel and the bursting barns and larders of nearby villages and towns could have furnished them ample provender. Down into the Napoleonic era there are examples as well, astonishing to the modern observer, of how the traditions of honor and chivalry endured among the officers' corps.[11]

Hostilities conducted without passion wherever possible, on the principles of calm political reason—this was the ideal that governed the craft of war as well. We are familiar with the great advances made in careful war-planning during the age of rationalism, from Maurice of Orange, Turenne, and Montecuccoli to Frederic the Great himself. What had indeed once been a primitive craft was now elevated to the level of a science, to well-developed theories of strategy and tactics.

From our study of Frederic the Great we are further familiar with the numerous obstacles a system of impressed mercenary armies places in the way of free initiative in the field. Scanty provincial exchequers limited the numbers of available troops, turning them into treasures to be carefully husbanded. The recruitment of foreigners in order to spare one's own subjects greatly increased the risk of desertion, paralyzing operations at every step. The effect extended down into battle tactics with their system of rigid lines; and another associated element was the strict and almost compulsive depot supply system which further shackled the strategic initiative, complicating especially the preparations for great battles of annihilation and favoring a mere strategy of maneuver. The main goal now became to cut off enemy supply and communication lines, and the greatest demonstration of the general's art was to secure his own "operational base." Together with the humanitarian considerations that were rife in the late eighteenth century, this strategy served to emphasize even more one-sidedly the rational element in military theory. It was even possible now to consider the supreme military achievement to be the winning of a war without any major bloodshed.[12]

Here the triumph of technical virtuosity was blended with the victory of humanitarianism. Bellona, the furious goddess of war, was to be rendered tractable, tamed like a kitten on the hearth. The Englishman Lloyd exalted a thorough knowledge of scientific and topographic factors as the philosopher's stone in strategy: "Whoever understands these things is in a position to initiate military operations with mathematical precision and to keep on waging war without ever being under the necessity to strike a blow."[13]

The rational elements in warfare are far easier to develop in matters of fortification and defense than in plans for the offensive. Self-defense, moreover, is easier to justify in moral terms than aggression. We can scarcely be surprised, therefore, that a marked preference for defensive warfare emerged. A false hope was indeed entertained that the world would become much more peaceable once smaller states were protected by solid defense works against the aggressive designs of their more powerful neighbors. It was in this spirit that Count William of Schaumburg, Scharnhorst's teacher, wrote in his *Mémoires pour servir à l'art militaire défensif:* "To wage war on the offensive means to serve the evil passions while to dedicate oneself to the defensive means to consecrate oneself to the welfare of mankind."[14]

The main thing, in any event, was to turn warfare into a precisely calculable procedure, an instrument of policy that could be wielded with reason. Map-reading and the study of terrain, "key positions" and favorable lines of oper-ation—these became the preoccupation of scholarly soldiers and the general staffs composed of them; and in a practical sense this may have been all to the good. Yet in these doctrines the most important instrument of war, the army and its leaders, appear only as a soulless tool working by purely mechanical laws.

Time and again, moreover, learned theory showed a tendency to degenerate into rigid doctrine, as seen even on the eve of the war of 1806 in the studies and memorials of Prussian General Staff officers such as Christian von Massenbach, Julius von Grawert, Karl von Phull, and Georg Venturini. There were some curious excrescences to the new science of "military mathematics," a combina-tion of geometric deployment tactics with theories of geology and terrain and of strategic maneuver. In the mocking words of von der Goltz: "A true strategist of that period considered himself incapable of leading three men across a gulley unless he had a table of logarithms."[15] Even so clear-sighted and progressive a reformer as the military writer Heinrich Dietrich von Bülow lost himself in outlandish mathematical doctrines, according to which the success of an oper-ation was essentially contingent on its being mounted at an "operative angle" of at least $60°$ and preferably more than $90°$.

Many people hoped that war would ultimately eliminate itself, having become a pure, universal science by means of mathematical equations that ruled out chance and the fortunes of war. Others like the widely read Berenhorst sought to reach the goal by the opposite route—through proof that war was chaotic and wholly irrational, subject to blind chance. War was senseless, they argued, and belonged to a barbarous stage in the history of mankind that must be overcome by enlightened thought.

3

The Revolution in Warfare and War Policy— Napoleon and Clausewitz

THE CENTURY of the Enlightenment drew to a close amid hopes that a time of "everlasting peace" was about to begin; but never were such hopes more cruelly disappointed. The French National Assembly of 1789 reveled in the proud confidence that the victory of liberty over the despotism of kings would put an end to war, hellish creature of dynastic ambitions. Article 6 of the Constitution of September 3, 1791, solemnly declares: "The French nation renounces the initiation of war for purposes of conquest."

Even so clear-sighted a statesman as Mirabeau who knew very well the risk of chauvinist passions in a parliamentary assembly proclaimed with pathos on August 25, 1790: "Perhaps the moment is not far off when liberty will acquit mankind of the crime of war and proclaim universal peace. . . . Then shall passion no longer tear asunder the bonds of brotherhood with bloody conflict, then shall the covenant of mankind be fulfilled." And as late as January, 1791, he spoke of the pleasing prospect that "the frontiers of all realms shall be wiped away to the end of making all mankind one family. . . . An altar shall be erected to peace from all the instruments of destruction that cover Europe."

In actuality serious tensions were then already in the making between revolutionary France and the conservative courts abroad, and only a year later they were to bring on an endless chain of wars over Europe. The nature of these Wars of the Revolution was presaged by Brissot's thundering rhetoric in the Jacobin Club: "A people who have conquered liberty after ten centuries of slavery need war. They need war to safeguard liberty. They need it to cleanse liberty of the vices of despotism. They need it to banish from their midst those who would despoil liberty. . . . We must revenge ourselves by destroying this bandit horde."

Civil wars of frightful cruelty, mounting to ever-greater heights of savagery, had to establish the political unity of the nation by force, to secure its religious and general cultural uniformity. Meanwhile, the need for resistance to European reaction held the whole life of the nation in thrall, the struggle rising in intensity the longer it lasted, the wider its fronts extended, from the Channel Coast to the Mediterranean. The Revolution could maintain itself only by total mobilization, by a merciless marshaling of all the country's forces. All the political and military efforts, all the sacrifices in blood and wealth that absolute monarchies had ever exacted from their subjects, pale before the intensity of this struggle. Everyone was accounted a traitor who dared assert the country's economic welfare against the demands of the war, let alone invoke the rights of private property, civil interest, and individual liberties that had but recently been praised so loudly and affirmed so solemnly. Tens of thousands of heads had to be lopped off by the guillotine to assure the complete solidarity of the French nation. The result was a triumph of political activism such as Europe had never seen before.

It also meant a radical shift in the prevailing relation between politics and war. True, the civilian commissioners of the new popular government always maintained their political hegemony over the military—indeed they did so with extreme ruthlessness. In time they consigned to the block every last "political" general from the old royal army who did not escape abroad. But the war policy of the revolutionary governments was no longer determined by the sober *raison d'état* of the old cabinet system in which welfare considerations played a large part, which firmly set itself only limited war aims tailored to the available military resources, and which constantly adapted the intensity of operations to a rational concept of efficiency. There was instead a passionate desire for victory governed by militant ideals like "national honor" and the moral justice of the cause rather than by political opportunism; and this motivation grew stronger during the struggle, setting itself ever-broader goals with growing military success.

The question of whether complete commitment is worthwhile, once so vehemently discussed, loses importance when the protagonist is impelled by the passionate espousal of a cause and when, as in the case of a modern popular government, the resources that can be mobilized are almost inexhaustible. An added element is that a modern people's war requires a tremendous propaganda machinery to take full effect. If they are to follow the call of their country, the masses must be indoctrinated with militant hatred by every available means. Emigrés encountered in battle had to be cut down ruthlessly. More than three hundred prisoners of war were massacred in this way. Later on this happened to more than eight thousand Spaniards, on order of the Convention; and Robespierre threatened the same fate to the Anglo-Hanoverian troops.

Thus was the ruthlessness of the civil wars translated to the external enemy.

And once ignited, hatred of this intensity is appeased only by total triumph, when the foe is utterly humiliated or destroyed—or when one's own side is completely exhausted. A popular government that yields before this point is reached, that rests content with half-success—with a view toward a peace that promises to endure, for example—will be discredited especially among the most zealous patriots and will invite the suspicion of needlessly betraying vital national interests.

Such was the fighting style of a new period in history, perhaps the most important and certainly the most enduring heritage the Great Revolution has bequeathed to modern political life. This new dynamic of political militancy soon prevailed, heedless of the libertarian ideals of the liberals and Girondists, and it has survived to this day with undiminished vigor. Compared with it the old cabinet-style warfare seems a mere clashing of Rococo foils, lacking in ultimate purpose, a game played according to carefully established rules.

Continual internal disorder and corruption prevented France during the Revolution proper from deploying its full national fighting power abroad. In any event, the 1790 and 1791 pledges never again to cross the country's historic national borders bent on conquest were very soon forgotten. Historic borders soon became "natural" frontiers which in turn became extremely elastic. Following the reorganization of the mass armies by Carnot, France's military power threatened all the neighboring countries like the floodwaters of a dammed-up river. Once the inspired leader had been found in Napoleon, who mastered both diplomacy and generalship with the same innate virtuosity, that power burst its dams and swept over all Europe.

Napoleon has been called the heir of the Great Revolution and at once its tamer—and rightly so. But what he tamed was not really the revolution of the barricades, the Reign of Terror of the Jacobin activists—that had been in effect broken with the fall of Robespierre. It was rather the anarchic liberalism of a bourgeois society that had, with its panic fear of the guillotine, also lost all respect for the sovereignty of the state, sighing only for relief from the oppression of the new tyranny. It hoped above all for an end to the constant alarums of war and for the establishment of an enduring new European peace. So overwhelming was the French people's longing for peace that even the victorious General Bonaparte had to conform to it outwardly when he returned to Paris after the successful conclusion of the campaign of 1797 and, in order to enhance his popularity, posed as a peacemaker and champion of lasting civil order. Actually his guns had, as early as 13th Vendémiaire, helped to insure the victory of the Convention's war party over the bourgeois pacifists—the same party whose coup d'état of 18th Fructidor he supported and helped execute.

Napoleon chose to rise to power as a partisan of the Montagnards, the most radical imperialists and warmongers. German historians, nursing the national-ist resentments of their people long after the Wars of the Liberation, kept on representing him as the heir and perpetuator of the Montagnard policy of conquest, as the incarnation of the "ravenous conqueror." Only toward the end of the last century, when the German nation began to revel in a sense of its new-found power and security, was the scene set for that controvery among historians over the "Napoleonic problem" in which certain German and French scholars made common cause in an attempted vindication of the Corsican. It was not from unrestrained ambition and thirst for power, so went the theory, that Napoleon had hurled Europe into ever new wars. A mighty destiny had forced his hand—true, a destiny that he as a man of titanic will had readily accepted. The issue forced on him was to bring to a conclusion the struggle with England, in effect a struggle of the whole Continent against the island empire.

It is not our task to settle this controversy here. In numerous separate discussions, the quarrel revolved again and again around the question of whether English or French militancy and power politics bore the greater share of responsibility for blocking a durable peace in Europe. As was to be expected, the original source material offers no unequivocal answer to such questions. Can posterity and even contemporaries ever determine in detail the degree to which great political decisions are governed by personal pugnacity or reasons of state, free initiative or the pressure of objective circumstance?

The latitude for free decision is always very small in the sphere of grand policy. There is, to be sure, not a single moment in Bonaparte's history in which his fighting spirit cannot be justified by reference to some compelling motivation, some concrete need for maintaining or expanding his power. No statesman of stature ever starts a war from sheer caprice.

An altogether different question is whether Napoleon's over-all policy pursued the military success of the moment or an enduring peace in Europe. There was no delay in posing it—indeed it was unequivocally answered not only by his own contemporaries but by Napoleon's most experienced collaborator in the field of foreign policy, his minister and grand dignitary, Talleyrand. This talented diplomat employed all his political skill in efforts to end the state of constant war. He sought to enlist his lord and master's support for his attempts to find channels of reconciliation that might restore the classic balance of power on which the art of diplomacy subsisted in the eighteenth century. When he failed again and again, he did not shrink from committing a kind of diplomatic high treason in an effort to keep Napoleon from expanding his power further.[1]

The contrast between the two statesmen typified with almost classic clarity the antinomy that is our absorbing subject here—the conflict between a policy of war and one of peace. From Talleyrand's point of view Napoleon was the first transcendently great incarnation in modern history of Machiavelli's ideal hero[2]—the man of limitless action, of will power pure and absolute; the great parvenu owing allegiance to no traditional order and hence never quite enlisting the kind of faith in the durability of his power that would have legitimized his exercise of brute force; the man whose conduct kept on challenging the whole world, which saw in him a perpetual threat to peace.

It would be doing Napoleon an injustice to ignore his earnest efforts at such legitimization, not only by joining his house to one of the ancient hereditary dynasties of Europe but by a kind of creative recasting of the whole West— comprehensive simplification of national boundaries, replacing a long-obsolete feudal system by more appropriate constitutions and codes, construction of a body of legislation of impressive scope and clarity, improvement of communications and political institutions over wide areas. It is certainly true that Napoleon's work was far from being wholly destructive. It did, however, fly in the face of the innermost life of old Europe. The continent's political and cultural pluralism simply would not bow to the command of one man. Above all Napoleon never really made people believe that an enduring peace in Europe was his ultimate goal.

For a man of his character and destiny there could be no halting or withdrawing from the constant struggle for new and sensational military success. To restrain himself and follow the wise counsel of a Talleyrand would have meant giving up his whole cause.[3] Crucial to the total outward effect he left on his time and on posterity is the blind militancy of his will. As he once remarked to Metternich, he did not "give a hang about the lives of a million people."[4] He was viewed as one who was as indifferent to the welfare of those he governed as he was to the ideal of nationalism—France was not his homeland. Even the ideals of the Great Revolution were in the end no more to him than a means to expand and buttress his personal power.

Even Napoleon's strategy appears as the very epitome of resolute militancy, compared with the kind of warfare practiced in the period that preceded him. He did not at all owe his victories to the invention of ingenious new strategic devices or to improved technical means. He was not even a trained strategist within the framework of the war philosophy of his time. Prior to St. Helena he engaged in virtually no studies of military history or strategic theory, reading for the most part books on history, moral philosophy, and politics.

To the learned maneuver strategists of his time his style of warfare seemed at first crude and artless rather than inspired.[5] What gave him his great advantage over all his enemies was in essence his tremendous offensive impact. Heedless of the refinements of strategy, he kept his forces together to deliver the decisive blow at the crucial place. He banked on speed, conducted his operations with an astonishing audacity that paid little attention to rearward lines of communication. To be at the focal point of decision with superior forces, to keep strong reserves always available, to aim his entire campaign at a decisive battle of annihilation, to pursue the beaten enemy to the point of complete rout—these were the elements that gave a new and greatly simplified aspect of overwhelming dynamism to Napoleon's generalship.

These were the methods by which the new unified national mass armies raised by the Revolution were put to the fullest use. And hand in hand with this new style of warfare went a corresponding new style of diplomacy. Here too power was concentrated to the utmost degree. The new diplomacy owed its greatest triumphs to the aggressive use of bluff and intimidation, terrorizing the enemy to the point of paralysis; but it also wielded the weapons of deception and blandishment with sovereign mastery, ignoring laws and treaties with little compunction.

It took the monarchial cabinets of old Europe an unconscionably long time to realize that they were up against a totally new and dynamic form of power struggle, in the face of which their traditional political and military methods were bound to fail. The history of the so-called Wars of the Revolution and of the Napoleonic campaigns of conquest drives home the utter inadequacy of the carefully husbanded financial and military resources that had worked in the past. It was like trying to hold back an avalanche with flimsy wooden fences. Unable even to make common cause, they were buried one by one.

Their military weakness was in keeping with their political naiveté. Until after Jena and Auerstädt there was no real understanding of the character of the new style of warfare.[6] Yet the crucial error, as Clausewitz clearly saw,[7] was made in the political rather than the military and strategic sphere. It lay in the erroneous estimate of the immense advantage in power which France, inwardly renewed, possessed over old Europe. Technical and strategic tricks were of no avail here. The only thing that would have served was a marshaling of forces of comparable strength and spontaneity.

The most important change that was needed was to replace that soulless, time-honored power instrument, the thoroughly venal professional army, with a whole nation in arms. More than that, the whole relation between politics and war had to change. Political action had to achieve a degree of militancy hitherto unknown. What was at issue was no longer mere rational planning for war, strategic utility, prudent insight. Here was something utterly irrational, calling for a moral act. The fact that this moral decision was first made in Prussia—which had been most deeply humbled and where the traditions of Frederic the Great lived on—exerted a crucial influence on the further course of German and European history. And it is no accident that it was a Prussian officer who was the first to grasp the full meaning of the great juncture that had come for Europe's war history with the appearance of Napoleon.

Long before Jena one sees in the letters and study notes of young Carl von Clausewitz the maturing of a new political approach that distinguishes him sharply from the intellectual world of the eighteenth century. What strikes one immediately is his passionate dedication to historical-political questions. He declares himself unable "to avert my gaze, to be anything at all apart from

fatherland and national honor. Everything I am or might be I owe to these two
earthly gods and without them nothing would be left of me but an empty shell
without meat or juice."[8] Yet his patriotism was much more than mere sentiment; it was pre-eminently a living quest for the interrelationships of grand
policy. The Concert of Europe was to him no longer a mechanical "system of
checks and balances," but a perpetual struggle, the result of a continual "moral
endeavor."[9] He did not view the state, as did enlightened and educated people
in the eighteenth century, as the sum of utilitarian considerations, a rational
institution to secure individual interests; nor did he regard it as the product of
creative forces slumbering within the people, in the Romanticist sense. To him
the state meant the deliberate and forceful mobilization of the common
national will—a proud and militant will that jealously defends its freedom,
indeed that stakes its very survival on "freedom and independence."

In Clausewitz's eyes a nation existed only where this vital will asserted itself.
True, he nurtured a lingering awareness of the universal tasks confronting the
European community;[10] but when romantic idealists used this as an excuse for
the impotence of their own country he thought it so much idle chatter. What
preoccupied him above all was the question of how great was the innate vitality
of the great nations, the political activity of their governments.[11] In sharpest
contrast to the idealism of a Schiller, for example, he disputed that a people
could, by means of arts and sciences, "ranson themselves from slavery of foreign
rule. . . . Rather must they hurl themselves into the furious elements of struggle,
staking a thousand lives against a thousandfold gain in life."[12] Poetic art and
science strive for values beyond time, but politics deals with the here-and-now,
and "since the working span of citizens is limited, they must lose no time nor
rest content with an uncertain goal of salvation in a distant future. . . . Time is
yours; whatever it will become, it will become through you!"[13] Individual
self-assertion is not enough. A nation "must live in freedom and in an aura of
fear. Unless these conditions are met, pride—whether individual or national—
will soon vanish."[14]

The militant character of the state is here emphasized more uncompro-
misingly than anywhere else in the literature of the period of regeneration.
Political life is viewed as the unceasing application of will power. This was a
natural reaction of the German mind to the devastating experience of witnessing
the utter impotence of the realm. As the young Hegel wrote at this time: "A
mass of people may call themselves a state only when they join in the common
defense of all their possessions . . . in active struggle."[15]

Like Hegel and Fichte, Clausewitz discovered Machiavelli during these years,
gaining deeper insight into the essentially demoniac character of power from
this champion of political activism. He declared it to be the duty of statesmen to
sacrifice their own morality for reasons of state when necessary, instead of
"sacrificing the state to their own righteousness," which would mean to act

selfishly, "to regard oneself as the end, the state only as a subordinate element."[16] He inveighed against the political moralists who lost all faith in a coming time of greatness over their carping at German faults and weaknesses.

Above all Clausewitz saw that political calculation is never sufficient to reach truly great decisions. He thrust ahead into the ultimate depths of political insight with the recognition that politically responsible action always entails risk, that it means choosing among uncertain alternatives, the best of which can be assigned no more than a high degree of probability. Everything depended on someone mustering the courage to discard some of the possibilities lest he become mired in a "labyrinth of alternatives. . . . Hence ordinary people, at times of great crisis, act reasonably only when they have reached the pinnacle of despair and see no other way out but a daring leap. This then gives them courage, unity, and energy. But all this ingenuity vanishes when remote possibilities arouse foolish hopes."[17] Bitter need is the best taskmaster of action.

An altogether new light is cast on war from this starting point. "War, great dangers, great disasters can lift simple people above their ordinary existence, whether or not they are compelled to forfeit their peacetime interests." War is the surest means of wrenching a nation from miserable weakness, replacing "cold cunning" with the "consuming fire" on which everything now depended. "Great ends are the soul of war."[18] "Peace is the covering of winter snow beneath which slumber [the forces of regeneration] . . . slowly growing stronger. War is the heat of summer that brings those forces to swift fruition and maturity."[19]

The bourgeois reformers of Prussia staked everything on improvement in internal affairs. Clausewitz the soldier watched them not without skepticism. He agreed that such improvements were necessary, indeed indispensable to the future of Germany. "But to wait for this always slow process of rebirth in the hour of need . . . seems absurd to me." In the long run everything depended on the inspiring deed, on instant action, on the leader's capacity for great resolve. "What was left of this militant [Prussian] spirit a bare six years after the death of Frederic the Great?"[20] The crucial cause of the defeat of the Prussian army leaders in 1806, in Clausewitz's view, was that despite their rectitude, conscientiousness, and academic knowledge they lacked the peculiar kind of military genius that lies in the willingness and strength to make decisions in pursuit of large and simple goals.[21]

This very defeat must now become the goad to dynamic regeneration. Will power thrives only under strong stimulation. Only in crisis does man transcend himself, surmount his natural sloth and cowardice. "A wide area for the deployment of forcible means opens up in wartime, and if I were to open the innermost secrets of my soul, I would say that I favor means of the utmost forcefulness. I would lash this lazy brute into bursting the chain its cowardice and pusillanimity have allowed to fetter it. I would let a spirit abroad in

Germany that would serve as a powerful antidote to extirpate the plague from which the whole spirit of the nation threatens to wither and die."[22]

War as a means of discipline, as the most effective spur to the nation's political education, as a method for hardening its militant power drive—these were altogether new ideas, of which even Machiavelli was quite innocent.[23] The eighteenth century had indeed, in Kant's philosophy, managed to acknowledge that war was a mainspring in "developing to the highest degree all the talents that serve culture"; and furthermore that "when it is conducted in good order and with scrupulous respect for civil rights it partakes of sublimity, while ennobling the spirit of the people waging it in such fashion, in proportion to the dangers to which they are exposed and the valor they display." A long peace, on the other hand, merely serves to foster the "mercenary spirit," and with it selfishness, cowardice, and flabbiness.[24]

Such praise, on esthetic rather than moral grounds, apparently applied only to involuntary wars of self-defense, however, and even then only when such wars were waged along strictly "humanitarian" lines! Hence this approach did not at all fly in the face of the general condemnation of war as a barbarous and mindless means of unenlightened policy.[25] Clausewitz was not concerned with moral questions, let alone cultural or esthetic, but with a specific political problem, how to transform what was no more than an area sharing a common culture into a determined political entity, a confident and militant nation-state jealous of its freedom and its reputation.

That such a question could be posed at all and debated with such passion while the problem of the moral justification of war vanished completely from the scene seems to us a symptom of the great change—one is tempted to say the Copernican Revolution—that was approaching in German intellectual history. Until this time German cultural life had occupied itself largely with speculations in the fields of theology and philosophy and with esthetic subjects. But under the shattering impact of political disaster a sharp turn began toward questions of history and politics, together with a deliberate reorientation from cosmopolitanism to nationalism, processes which Friedrich Meinecke has exemplified by tracing the development of the greatest German minds from Humboldt to Hegel and Ranke.

Within this intellectual movement Carl von Clausewitz occupies a place quite out of the ordinary. The primary element he brought to it was the pride and confidence of the soldier, the Prussian officer who knew very well that it was solely by military achievement that the Prussia of Frederic the Great had risen in the world and was able to survive. There was no need for circuitous thought to reach the goal of clear-cut national awareness. The very fact of the military defeat, bound to be interpreted by a professional soldier as a burning personal humiliation, challenged Clausewitz to ponder its deeper causes, and he brooded over the subject while a prisoner of war in France. In his comparison of the

Germans with the French Clausewitz found that it was precisely certain virtues of the German national character which made it so difficult to rally that nation determinedly for purposes of political power. Among them were the lack of restraint of the German mentality, the difficulty of influencing it, its propensity for thoroughness and theoretical speculation, its cold objectivity, its unswerving allegiance to principle, "the variety and originality of its individuals . . . the constant striving for a higher, self-selected goal."[26]

The vain and superficial French, on the other hand, were much easier "to weld into a uniform whole," forming an instrument obedient to political purpose. The Germans lacked the easily ignited national ardor of their neighbors, the "healthy prejudices" (!) without which there can be no national self-awareness. The Germans were too fond of argument and self-criticism. While the French were wont "often to lose themselves entirely in public opinion," the educated German put very little stock in public opinion, indeed defied it outright, a virtue that could turn into a serious political hazard if not an evil.

One sees quite plainly that for the sake of political advantage, the passionate patriot Clausewitz was prepared to allow the wealth of German culture to dry up and grow shallow. And it was precisely the base instincts and passions of man that were to be harnessed to the nation's power drive.[27] The idealistic nationalism and moral pathos of Fichte were as foreign to Clausewitz as was the Teutonic ardor of romantic patriots or Humboldt's effort to foster national regeneration through enhancing the spiritual forces of Germany.

Clausewitz was more sympathetic to Stein's notion—and Gneisenau's too—that the Germans must be schooled in politics "by being given a lawful share in government," but such phrases occur only very occasionally; and Clausewitz mustered only a limited interest in the complex and painstaking work of army reform to which Scharnhorst, his revered teacher, devoted the best efforts of his life. His revolutionary temperament urged him on more directly and impatiently than all the others to military action in place of mere organization, preparation, and education.

Yet Clausewitz was anything but a mere expert, a technician of the military craft. As shown by his poetic and expressive language alone, his was a truly creative mind, richly endowed, open to all the sensations of nature, the full wealth of the human spirit. All in all he represented a most curious and rare combination of philosophical contemplation and impatience for action, of cold, lucid intellect and passionate sensitivity—a reflective spirit who ardently longed for heroic deeds with an ambition that was never to be fulfilled.

He was, therefore, virtually predestined to cast the essence of the Prussian military spirit into a literary form none had found before him. It is true that his impetuous drive to swift action, his belief in the absolute priority of foreign affairs over domestic considerations, the purely militant goals he set for diplomacy—that all these stemmed from a rather one-sided view of political life, the view of a soldier, not a statesman. But if it was one-sided it was also touched with genius. Clausewitz grasped the urgent need of the historic moment with absolute assurance.[28]

His approach was in fact much broader. What Clausewitz was the first to comprehend was the fact that Germany's exposed position, wedged between powerful nations, compelled it to adopt a policy of extraordinary militancy. He responded much more acutely than many of his contemporaries to the glaring contradiction between Germany's international impotence over the centuries and its overflowing wealth in material and spiritual resources. Full awareness of this contradiction dawned on the Germans only under the oppression of alien rule, the rule of Napoleon; and this brought on the great spiritual turning-point of which we have already spoken. It was brought on by the disaster of the moment, not by any "tradition of Frederic the Great." That tradition had been buried if not supplanted in Prussia by a mild brand of humanitarianism as early as the turn of the century.

The world of new ideas arose from the depths of national defeat—the idealism of the German renewal, a movement of exceptional spiritual richness. As a political event it was superimposed on the process of German emancipation from the rationalism of Western Europe that had been going on for decades. This fateful coincidence was to have far-reaching consequences. Down into our own days it served to alienate us deeply from the culture of Western Europe, maneuvering us into a special position inside Europe.

Carl von Clausewitz found a predominantly soldierly formulation for the political program of the "German Movement": A great nation, to maintain its stature and character, must "live in freedom and inspire awe."[29] His *Protestation* of 1812, with which he sought to justify the entry of Prussian officers into Russian service, and his great manual *On War* took on almost classic significance for nineteenth-century Germany. It was no accident that Clausewitz's name rang out loudly only in Germany.

His *Protestation* of 1812[30] is by far the purest and most powerful expression of the new spirit of militancy that inspired the patriots of 1812-1813. Among other things it contains a virtual catalogue of political virtues and vices, a brief summary of the new militant political ethic, so to speak. Clausewitz solemnly rejected everything that might buffer the iron necessity of a life-and-death struggle, or that might tempt man to evade it—such things as the "frivolous hope" for a favorable chance; languid inaction while blindly waiting what the future might bring; "unworthy servility and flattery" to appease tyrants: "false resignation" and "unreasoning distrust" of one's own capacity; "culpable neglect of duty" toward the general good; and above all cowardly submission and the "shameless surrender of the country's and people's honor, of the personal dignity of man." What he pledged instead was to shed the last drop of blood for life's freedom and dignity; to put king and country above all else; to regard their preservation as a "most sacred duty"; to "meet danger with manly courage, calm and firm resolve, and full awareness"; to be prepared to make the "supreme sacrifice" without fear or false cunning, free of all selfishness, inspired by the "glorious struggle for freedom and the dignity of the fatherland."

Sentiments of this kind went far beyond the civil obedience of the time of Frederic the Great. They anticipate that everyone under arms will regard the cause of the state as his own. But beyond this grandiloquent profession of faith the *Protestation* includes a detailed consideration of the political and military situation. Nor does it seek to evade the question of whether Prussia still had the physical and technical resources to extricate itself from the alliance with France against Russia and to maintain itself in a life-and-death struggle.

Nothing shows more clearly than this section how greatly the times had changed. Not a trace is left of the shrewdly calculating spirit that dominated eighteenth-century statesmen. True, Clausewitz appears to be undertaking a coolly rational examination of the advantages and disadvantages of an alliance with France. Yet his heroically militant sentiments shine through every line, ultimately carrying the day over rational argument. His resolve to accept the greatest risks was unshakable.[31]

The basic premise for his whole approach is that the demoniac irrationality of Napoleonic policy made any true alliance illusory, leaving only the alternatives of self-immolation and implacable struggle. What characterizes Clausewitz particularly is that he faced the problem without any moralizing. He did not view Napoleon as a "monster," as a "satanic" figure, but as a soldier of titanic dimensions. "How can a state at all practice moderation when it pursues vast ends with vast means, when its every breath means new violence? For such a state moderation would be as foolish as would be a faltering spirit in other circumstances." As things were, there could be no advantage in a policy of conciliation. The conflict between its advocates and those who favored struggle was reduced to the moral plane. "Great things can never be accomplished without courage and resolve, for danger is ever-present. Contrary to a widely held view, diplomacy is not always synonymous with the cowardly use of deception. . . . Man is bound to turn evil when compelled to shed his blood for a cause he despises."

In the face of such a moral dilemma, difficulties counted for little. When we are summoned by the categorical imperative of duty all considerations of expediency are silenced. "Resolve must grow from the necessity for a solution, not its ease." Here we have the underlying thought of the many plans for rebellion with which patriotic Prussian officers and ministers kept besieging their king after 1808. Moral force, they insisted, must make up for what the country still lacked in material means.

The gloomy resolution with which Clausewitz formulated this thought is reminiscent of the attitude of Freiherr vom Stein in 1808, but differs in that Clausewitz forewent all moral condemnation of the enemy. His was an ice-cold resolve, remote from the triumphant optimism of a Gneisenau as well.[32] The element common to all these patriots is a heroic fighting will; they were prepared to dare even the seemingly impossible, which they hoped to achieve against all opposition by sheer moral effort. Here is soldierly tradition at its best. It guided the Prussian-German armies to many victories—and far beyond. When it became a political maxim, as it did at the end of the First World War and during the Hitler era, it led inexorably to perdition.

For the soldier's supreme virtue may become irresponsible recklessness in the statesman. Historical research has long since established that the patriots of 1808 and 1812 greatly overestimated the immediate danger that threatened the Prussian state from Napoleon.[33] And we shall have to consider further on why their plans for revolt appear politically premature, indeed altogether faulty in conception. What matters here is to follow the awakening of the new militant spirit without which a revolt in Germany could not even have been set in motion.

One thing is certain: whether or not the patriots of 1808 grasped the political realities of the situation, they correctly understood a most essential element, the power of Napoleon's will which permitted of no compromise except at the cost of German freedom. It is their historic achievement to have met this untamable force head on with an equally resistless pursuit of freedom. In so doing they triggered a political movement that deliberately translated the new style of warfare to Germany, meeting the Corsican's ruthless use of French national power with an equally ruthless deployment of German national power.

Clausewitz's book *On War* later provided a comprehensive theoretical elucidation of this new war style. Because it summarized the experiences of the Napoleonic era it became the bible of German military science.

To appreciate the novel character of this important book it is not really necessary to give an analysis of its tactical and strategic doctrines.[34] Its spirit becomes amply clear as early as the chapter entitled "The Genius of War" (Book 1, Chapter 3), in which Clausewitz memorably outlines the essential qualities of the great captain. It represents a radical break with eighteenth-century views of the kind of "methodical" generalship that relied on mathematical certainties, indeed with the whole idea of a "craft of war" characterized by clear-cut skills that could be learned by academic methods. What constitutes true mastery is not command of technical tricks and learned strategic theories, but a combination of spirit and character. The quality most important in a military leader is the ability to reach final and unambiguous decisions even under the shadow of danger, even when the elements to be considered are no longer clearly defined.

More than any other human activity "war is the domain of chance." In no other field is rigid and specious dogmatism more out of place, is the "mathematical method" as fruitless. The great general is the precise opposite of a specialist, anything but a mere technician. Neither is he, to Clausewitz, a man whose sole qualification is a tremendously aggressive will. Rather, what characterizes him is a harmonious combination of powers, the kind of equilibrium between reason and will power found only in men of true greatness. There were plenty of swashbuckling fire-eaters even among less civilized peoples, but they never produced "a truly great general, and only rarely anyone deserving to be described as a military genius, for that takes a degree of intellectual development not to be expected among the uncivilized."

The great names in generalship all fall into times when civilization had reached a higher level; and the leadership qualities with which Clausewitz deals are never seen in terms of ordinary endowment and brute vigor of a kind even the average man may possess but always as the expression of a superior intellectuality.

Courage is not mere bravura, but the pluck to act responsibly, the expression of genuine fervor. Reason is not mere common sense, but the ability to grasp and master obscure and unexpected situations instantly with instinctive assurance. Resolution is not mere effrontery but superiority of the spirit in the face of urgent doubt, even in positions of supreme responsibility where ordinary courage fails. Presence of mind is not mere habit—it springs from a deep inward balance of the mind. Energy is not mere will power but the capacity of a superior mind to stick it out, to overcome the countless inner frictions of the war machine, especially in situations that look desperate, "when the whole inertia of the mass presses upon the leader's will." This kind of vigor must be combined with the noblest sentiment, "the soul's thirst for glory and honor," ambition that reaches for the highest laurels. Firmness must be buttressed by understanding, becoming stalwartness. Strength of mind and soul must be such as to withstand the most vehement storms of passion, "obeying the dictates of reason" even under the impact of overwhelming events and preserving perfect self-control, possible only when pride and human dignity are developed to the highest level. These virtues cannot manifest themselves in their finest and most effective form in phlegmatic and indolent persons. It takes the kind of man who, "while not easily swayed, is profoundly sensitive, with deeply hidden passions," who, while not of outright sanguine temperament, bears the same relation to that temperament as embers do to the flame. And finally, to all these qualities must be added strength of character, firm adherence to convictions drawn from clear deep insight.

Thus arises the ideal image of the leader towering above the mass, representing a higher form of mankind. His is true nobility and iron energy joined with superior intelligence, manly dignity, and supple power. The soul of the hero is "boldness under control of the spirit," the task of the captain "to reach heroic decisions on the grounds of reason."[35] One senses in every line that this is not a theoretical construction but a view gained from living experience—from reverence of great historic heroes but also from practical life, from close personal intercourse with such minds as Gneisenau and Scharnhorst, from fighting against Napoleon.[36] The book breathes the spirit of classic German idealism, when men were still innocent of expert specialization, mechanization, and narrowed interest. It was essential to this grand concept of the universal man that the inspired general must transcend the purely military sphere and grow into that of grand policy. "To achieve glorious victory in war or in a major campaign requires deep insight into the higher affairs of state. Leadership in the field and diplomacy here coincide and the general becomes at once a statesman."

Nevertheless, he must not cease to be a general. "On the one hand he envisages all the affairs of state; on the other he is fully aware of what he can accomplish with the means at his disposal." This calls for a rare breadth of intellectual perspective. In Clausewitz's view, even such major historical figures as Charles XII of Sweden and Henry IV of France failed to reach this stage of military-*cum*-political genius. "The necessary powers of the mind demand a unity of judgment enhanced to the level of vision. Scanned and discarded are a thousand half-formed notions which a lesser mind would laboriously examine one by one, to the point of exhaustion." Clausewitz was thinking only of the most dazzling figures of history, epitomizing mankind at its best, minds that embrace everything at a single sweep.

It is in the light of this concept of the universal mind that Clausewitz's views on the essential unity of statesmanship and war must be viewed—those famous formulations that have so often been misinterpreted: "War is the continuation of politics by other means." It is "not a mere political act but rather a political instrument proper, a continuation of political intercourse, carried out by other means. What remains peculiar to war relates only to the peculiar nature of its means" (Book 1, I, 24). "War is only a part of political intercourse, hence not at all something autonomous. . . . It is no more than a continuation of political intercourse with the intervention of other means" (Book 8, IIIb).

Why did Clausewitz repeat these phrases so often, so intently, in ever new circumlocutions? The primary reason is his profound concern to wrest discussion of the problem of war from the hands of the military experts, the lightning calculators of strategic theory, the parade-ground drillmasters, the tacticians of traditional combat doctrine. The bitterest experience of his life had been to watch the miserable failure, in the face of the realities of war on the grand scale, of this narrowly specialized academic knowledge, totally lacking in the over-all view of the political situation.[37] He was utterly convinced that the Prussian army needed no new and up-to-date strategic doctrine and tactical rules. What mattered was to cling to the new spirit in politics and war which the great revolt had unleashed—to clarify it, deepen it, and pass it on.

He must hammer away at the Prussian officer, insisting that conscientious observance of regulations in the style of the *ancien régime* was not nearly enough; that academic knowledge, let alone the rigmarole of mathematics, was bound to fail before the reality of war—for the essence of war is risk, chance, everlasting uncertainty. Boldness, strength of character, assured military vision, decisive action at the lower echelons coupled with breadth of intellectual grasp at the top—these were the crucial elements, and they never got mired in technical detail but kept the totality of war with all its political backgrounds always in view. Politicians must be made to understand that they shared the essential responsibility for the success or failure of war, that they could not delegate it to their military experts. War was part and parcel of the political process.

Yet even this characterizes but one aspect of the matter. The sweep of Clausewitz's thought carries much farther. Considering the radical single-mindedness with which, in his youthful notes and letters, he stressed the militant character of politics and called for total commitment of all resources in the liberation struggle, one might expect his *chef d'oeuvre* to show the same bias. Essentially this would mean the kind of unity between politics and war that is widely taken for granted in our own generation—politics as nothing more than a constant struggle for power, war as its intensification through the intervention of force, both sharing the aim of overcoming hostile power. Accordingly the task of government in wartime would be influenced by purely military considerations—making available every material and psychological resource for the purpose of annihilating the enemy.

This expectation, however, is doomed to disappointment. Reading Clausewitz's exposition as a whole rather than taking sentences out of context, it is impossible to doubt that the interpretation just given represents an unwarranted updating of the man's thought. It is true, of course, that he viewed diplomacy primarily as a struggle for power rather than as a system of peace, for he does describe war as the direct continuation of "political intercourse," a phrase that sounds almost cynical. Yet he says very plainly that the aims of international politics are by no means identical with those of war—or at least not invariably so. And instead of assigning to politics a mere subservient role in war he emphatically asserts its primacy: "It is politics that begets war. Politics represents the intelligence, war merely its instrument, not vice versa. The only possible course is the subordination of the military viewpoint to the political" (Book 8, VIb). Clausewitz consistently saw politics as a moderating rather than an aggravating element.

This can be understood only from the total context of his book. Neither polemic nor manual, it is deliberately a thoroughgoing philosophical treatise. Written between 1816 and 1830, it was no longer a product of the revolt and the war period, but of the halcyon years of peace and reconstruction when the German spirit, at the end of the great struggle, was able to ponder its inner meaning and historical roots. Clausewitz too was swept up in this pursuit of historical insight and perspective. It reinforced his innate propensity for taking a realistic view of political realities, for forming a world view of his own rather than by rote.[38]

He strove for a concept of war that was to be universal and comprehensive rather than dogmatic, suited only to a single era of history. As a militant patriot he had been ruthlessly singleminded in emphasizing the military role of politics and the educational mission of war in political life. But as a philosopher of war he saw that political and military aims by no means always coincided and that reasons of state could rank higher than military needs. He had always been quite free of Gneisenau's kind of passionate militarism that warped political vision.

His starting point is a conceptual definition of war which seems at first blush to exclude all political intervention in the military sphere.[39] "War is no more than an expanded duel. . . . It is an act of force to compel the enemy to do our bidding. . . . Violence—that is to say brute force—is the means; to force our will upon the enemy is the end. To attain this end with certainty we must render the enemy defenseless and this is the true meaning and goal of warlike action" (Book 1, II, 2). These simple sentences are fundamental; all else derives from them, and they embody indeed a crucial discovery. If the political purpose of war is to force our will on the enemy and this purpose can be achieved only by rendering him defenseless, then the concept of war proper necessarily includes the concept of a war of annihilation. Warfare never realizes its ultimate goal until it has actually destroyed the enemy forces, and strictly speaking the only purpose of military operations must be to render the enemy defenseless.

In principle at least this concept superseded the entire strategy of maneuver of the preceding age, which was by no means always intent on destruction but rather on weakening and exhausting the enemy. The most important lessons of the Napoleonic period for all subsequent war doctrine were that partial success never brought decisive results;[40] that a general must not fritter away his forces on subsidiary missions; that the all-important thing was to deliver swift, vigorous, and decisive blows with concentrated force and to follow these up with ruthless pursuit until the enemy's will to resist was totally crushed; and that a defensive strategy of procrastination made sense only when time was on one's side and one anticipated eventually turning to the offensive.

The major virtue of Clausewitz's book lies in its having drawn the consequences for the entire field of strategy and tactics from these simple principles —not in the systematic style of a textbook but in the form of a series of loosely concatenated reflections. These reflections deal with such subjects as the nature of war; the character of military genius; danger and physical exertion in the field; internal frictions in the war machine; the limitations of war theory and of what can be taught systematically; the moral and material resources of strategy; the husbanding of forces; positional and moving warfare; the relation of attack and defense; and the meaning of the fire-fight as the central method of warfare that is alone decisive.

All this is presented with a wealth of examples from the history of war, largely from Clausewitz's own experience; and he often moves on to consider elements from political history. He develops his problems logically but never becomes dogmatic; and he has something stimulating to say on almost every page. In their profusion his ideas sometimes overlap, admirably reflecting the realities of history but tending to confuse the novice.[41] What had the deepest effect on the teachings of the Prussian General Staff was his doctrine of the "bloody vigor of war" which winds through all his reflections. Yet he subjected even this doctrine to severe limitations, much to the consternation of later military readers.

While Clausewitz appreciated that the concept of absolute war (Ludendorff, echoing Fichte, was later to term it "veritable war") necessarily meant rendering the enemy defenseless by destroying his forces, he was assailed by doubts as to whether this theoretical notion of "absoluteness" accorded with historical reality. What we encounter here is the distinction between "idea" and "reality" peculiar to all idealist thinking. Ideally one might say that war is always absolute. In reality it is never so. In terms of the idea war involves the whole life of nations, for force invariably elicits counterforce. Whoever uses force ruthlessly, without regard to bloodshed, is bound to achieve preponderance unless the enemy resorts to the same policy. "Thereby he lays down the rule for the other and both sides escalate to the limit"—i.e., to complete mutual annihilation. "The principle of moderation cannot be carried into the philosophy of war proper without committing an absurdity."

But can this ultimate theoretical consistency of the militant principle ever seriously become the goal of political action? Do war aims always justify exertion to the very limit? Manifestly not. "In many instances this would mean a needless expenditure of resources, to be necessarily counterbalanced by other principles of the art of government. An effort of will would be required out of proportion to the ostensible goal." For war is never an isolated act. It is directly associated with the preceding life of the state. Nor is war a phenomenon complete in itself. "The political situation that will follow it reacts on it by calculation" (Book 1, I, 6).

The political situation that is to follow war is manifestly the enduring peace that is the ultimate goal of diplomacy. One sees how the idea of universality from which Clausewitz proceeds here gains enormous importance for his entire thinking. He expected nothing less of political leadership in war than that it should even in wartime take heed of the peace to come. He sharply and expressly rejected the view of war as an isolated phenomenon, "as though from the moment politics engenders it, it were quite independent of politics, displacing politics and following only its own laws—like a discharging landmine that is beyond control and can fire only in the way it has been originally set" (Book 1, I, 23).

Actually war is not simply a single discharge but a sustained "pulsation of violence, of greater or lesser vehemence," depending upon the changing strength and direction of its political motives. It remains ever subject to the will of a guiding political intelligence that envisages political as well as military contingencies. "For it is political intention that sets the end to which war is but a means, and it is impossible to conceive a means without an end. . . . There is a direct relation between the grandeur and strength of war motives, the way in which they sweep up the whole life of nations, the vehemence of the tension preceding it on the one hand and on the other the degree to which it approaches abstract [absolute] form and turns upon crushing the foe. When the prerequisites are present, military and political ends coincide and war seems to become more and more military, less and less political."

Conversely, when motives and tensions are weak, political purposes and abstract war aims diverge more and more, and war tends to become "politicalized." But if politics is taken to mean "a kind of cautious, crafty, and dishonest skill opposed to the use of force" and also the "personified intelligence of the state" (which may of course itself have a militant character), then both types of warfare may properly be termed "political instruments." Even a war of annihilation, absolute in character, is a mere instrument of politics—but of a more daring and radical kind, not content with partial success (Book 1, 24-26).

We see that the definition of war as a continuation of politics with the intervention of other means has a special methodological meaning for Clausewitz. It is to enable him to find a common denominator for every conceivable form of warfare, from the absolute war of subjection to the almost sportive campaigns of the Rococo age, representing only a "slightly more pointed form of diplomacy. . . . Only such an approach makes it possible to avoid coming into collision with the whole history of war" (Book 1, I, 27).

Clausewitz had no intention of offering an abstract conceptual framework. He wished to remain as close as possible to the diversity of historical events. History on its part showed "that there are many roads leading to the goal in war, that not every case is tied to the enemy's complete submission." There were other means for vanquishing the enemy's will besides the destruction of his forces—the conquest or occupation of his territory, invasion, passively awaiting his blows, or simply exhausting him with the smallest expenditure of forces. "Since war is not an act of blind passion but is rather dominated by political ends, the value of those ends must determine the degree of sacrifice we are prepared to make to attain them."

In many instances the war leadership will avail itself of political and diplomatic means rather than military. There will be diplomatic threats through the pressure of new alliances, the undermining of hostile coalitions, the incitement of enemy nationals, and personal connections of every kind. The possible political motives setting off a war may be very large in number, but so are the means for waging it; and it would be shortsighted to underrate and regard as a rare exception every war not aiming at total victory and annihilation. Especially when there is no prospect of such an issue or when the price for attaining it is unconscionably high, war leaders may simply find themselves compelled to employ less radical means or to conclude a peace in time. "If one were justified in discarding any one of these stages in theory, one might just as well discard them all, which would mean completely losing sight of the real world."[42]

But is it not true that such reflections throw overboard the very insight that we have just represented as the book's most important achievement and the most important lesson from the Napoleonic Wars, namely that half-measures are worthless in war, that expert war leaders can aim only at total destruction of the enemy forces? From many passages in the book it would almost seem as though Clausewitz placed the older "strategy of attrition" beside the newer "strategy of subjection" as a fully autonomous, alternate form of warfare.[43] Such an interpretation, however, does as little justice to his real purpose as does the interpretation by the later school of Moltke. Clausewitz's historical position is manifestly that of a link between the old age and the new. This intermediate role which makes many of his passages ambiguous is responsible for many misunderstandings and obscurities on the part of students of Clausewitz.

Many other passages, however, make it amply clear that despite everything, he clung to the view that the strategy of subjection was the better, more in keeping with the true nature of war—the normal form, so to speak. "Among all the goals that can be pursued in war, the destruction of the enemy's forces always appears as the commanding one" (Book 1, II).[44] When the enemy insists on a decisive passage at arms, this recourse can never be denied him; and no matter what degree of moderation of the abstract principle of annihilation circumstances may compel, this never delivers us from "the necessity for discharging the crisis in blood, for striving for the destruction of the enemy forces, as the firstborn son of war." This is "always the superior and more effective means to which others must give way" (p. 29)—but that is not to say that it is to be sought by blind recklessness, without careful skill.

At bottom Clausewitz regarded the various forms of the strategy of attrition as stemming commonly from human inadequacy, mass inertia, reluctance to face great effort, and a desire to put off great decisions as long as possible.[45] The feeble decisions, especially, that were customary in coalition warfare and that had but recently wrought such horrifying effects in the wars against the Revolution were "half-measures and anomalies; for in the last reckoning, war and peace are concepts incapable of gradation." It was true, however, that such measures were "deeply rooted in man's natural limitations and weaknesses."[46]

In theory both forms of strategy are indispensable; but a great distinction must be made in their application. What is necessary is that "the former [strategy of subjection] always form the basic concept, while the latter [the strategy of partial successes] be used only as a modification justified by circumstances. . . . Theory is obliged to give priority to the absolute form of war and to use it as a general guideline, so that whoever seeks to learn from theory will grow accustomed to never losing sight of it, regarding it as the basic standard for all his hopes and apprehensions and approximating it whenever he must or can."[47]

Clausewitz clearly wished that a distinction be made between his theoretical philosophy of war and its practical application. If he acknowledges a form of strategy with limited goals beside the absolute form, this carries theoretical and historical rather than practical significance. Time and again he gives emphatic descriptions[48] of how the system of revolutionary popular levies and of Bonapartism once for all overcame the older form of "half-war," how for the first time warfare approximated the character of "absolute perfection," and how fateful it was for the ancient powers of Europe that they could not muster the strength and resolution to meet this deployment of force at once with efforts on the same order. Clausewitz also knew that his own theory was made possible only because of this model. "But for the warning example of the destructive power of the unleashed elements it would vainly have shouted itself hoarse."

Odd as it may sound, his true originality does not lie in the doctrine that today comes at once to mind—the phrase about the higher unity of politics and war. In essence he took this over from the technical military literature of his time (see Chapter 7). His real discovery is the concept of absolute war—even though he did not mean to characterize it as absolute. It is because of this discovery that he has been so much read and celebrated by posterity and that he attained such high repute with the Prussian General Staff, above all others. The question arises whether the system of modern war and its relation to politics that he envisaged truly represents the concept of the war of annihilation—war among fully politicized and militarized modern nations with its built-in resistless dynamics and its imperious claims to the subservience of politics.

One notes at once that Clausewitz was by no means certain whether the tremendous crises of the Napoleonic age marked the birth of a new era of history or should be regarded as no more than an episode without lasting effect. The Restoration of 1815 had meanwhile brought the old monarchial cabinets back to power, forced the people to knuckle under once again to sovereigns "by the grace of God," returned foreign policy to the principle of legitimacy, created a new, peaceful, and enduring order in Europe with a careful balance of the great powers which were joined in a formal "Concert" under a precisely calculated pecking order and fixed rules of the diplomatic game. It might well be expected that under such an order the old system of limited warfare would come back into vogue. Clausewitz thought it unlikely that barriers once torn down could ever be built up again artificially. Yet he reflected that wars of limited aim and expenditure had been a fact of history in all ages, ever since the days of Alexander the Great—with the single exception of Bonaparte. Might not the very next decade restore them to their traditional scope? "It is hard to decide whether all future wars in Europe will be waged with the full weight of nations behind them, over issues of great moment, for interests close to the people, or whether eventually governments will again tend to hold themselves aloof from the people. . . . It is as unlikely that all wars will henceforth take on such a grandiose character as it is that the wide scope that has been opened up for that type of war can ever again be altogether narrowed."[49]

The future, in any event, remained obscure. Nor must we immediately assume that what Clausewitz envisaged as the style of war peculiar to the Napoleonic era was equivalent to present-day concepts of mass wars of annihilation. This becomes particularly clear in those passages where he speaks of the "general war plan." Whoever seeks to embark on war, he says, must first consider whether or not the political situation requires it to be waged in the style of "absolute" war. One's own forces and their relation to the political end to be attained must be weighed as carefully as those of the enemy. This, however, is likely to be less a matter of precise calculation than of a certain political "tact," an intuitive insight that is the test of true statesmanship. The "war instigator" must cling to the principle of "using only such force and pursuing only such goals in war as are just sufficient to attain his political objective. To render that principle feasible, he must renounce all absolute necessity of success, must leave remote possibilities out of his calculations." Otherwise "considerations of the dimensions of the political requirements will be lost; the means will lose all relation to the end; and in most cases the purpose of extreme effort will fetch up on the counterbalance of one's own internal situation."[50]

The reference is here quite plainly to the kind of political calculation that was current among eighteenth-century cabinet governments—whether the goal was worth a war at all and what degree of effort might at best be warranted. War once kindled, no matter what the occasion, is not in every case a bolt of lightning that instantly ignites and mobilizes all the dormant forces of a nation, heedless of whether so formidable a deployment of destructive energy bears a reasonable ratio to the war aims. It is not an immediate life-and-death struggle, seemingly recognizing no goals other than humbling the enemy and rendering him defenseless, irrevocably establishing one's own supremacy. Nor does it mean whipping up popular passions without regard to the peace to follow. In a technical sense mobilization does not at once become a precision machine catching in its cogs all private life, even the smallest enterprise, every last pair of hands down to women, children, and the aged, setting everything in motion for its own ends without possibility of any internal resistance or friction arising.

We have already seen[51] that Clausewitz expressly rejected the demand that every single war called for the utmost exertion, that he refused even more emphatically to acknowledge that war, from the very moment the initiative is taken to light the fuse, is possessed of certain natural laws of its own with respect to politics. "Whoever maintains, as is so often done, that politics must not intervene in the conduct of war," he pointedly wrote in a memorial of 1830, "has not learned the ABC of war in the grand manner."[52] War to him was neither a single explosion nor an "act of blind passion."[53] The sustained "pulsation of violence" that is its essence must be subject to continuous control. The effort to be applied must be doled out carefully, according to the judgment of a leading political mind, i.e., by detached political wisdom. And he kept reiterating such formulations as that "the political intent is the end, war but the means, and one can never think of the means without an end." War, in other words, must never be considered an end in itself. He was quite unable to regard as meaningful a war that is allowed to rage without a political aim, that stakes out such an aim only after victory is won, so to speak. "War has its own grammar but not its own logic."[54]

What Clausewitz failed to see or at least to acknowledge is that war, once set off, may very well develop a logic of its own because the war events themselves may react on and alter the guiding will; that it may roll on like an avalanche, burying all the initial aims, all the aspirations and apprehensions of statesmen, as happened in the two world wars; that it may get out of control, raging on to the ruination not only of millions of human lives but of any enduring peace for generations to come.

For it is a fact that Clausewitz did not yet comprehend such a thing as "total" war. When he speaks of the means of war, the modern reader misses any mention of the vast war potential inherent in a country's economic and technological development.[55] Neither does he, despite the experiences with revolutionary France, mention anything about propaganda to whip up sentiment for war among the masses; and indeed in monarchist Prussia such propaganda, despite all the war sermons by its clergymen and professors, despite all semiofficial efforts, played a relatively modest role.

What Clausewitz envisaged was a popular rising that was yet strictly disciplined and controlled from above, the subordination of a mass movement to direction by monarchist authority, much in the style of nineteenth-century constitutional monarchy. This is probably the reason why Clausewitz's doctrine of the nature of war enjoyed such dogmatic prestige down to 1914. In this respect too, by the way, one senses that his book was written only during the Restoration rather than in the actual time of trouble. How else explain his total neglect of the question of psychological leadership in wartime—and this by the author of the great *Protestation* of 1812, the literary associate of Scharnhorst? [56]

Despite those experiences Clausewitz evidently had no idea of the power of public opinion in a politically educated nation,[57] of the degree to which political passions could become inflamed in wartime, and of the reaction of such passions on the political leadership. In a word, Clausewitz was still unfamiliar with modern mass war conducted by thoroughly politicalized and militarized nations organized for war in economic respects as well. All he knew was the war of professional armies reinforced by mass levies and still willing to submit unquestioningly to direction by monarchial cabinets.

He does occasionally speak of how war reacts on politics. "The political end must not exert despotic control, but adapt itself to the nature of the means, and it may become quite changed in the process." But what he means is merely the self-evident necessity for government not to ask anything of its generals that flies in the face of the "peculiar nature" of war.[58] This does not change the principle that the goal and general trend of war as well as its duration and conduct must be governed by political rather than "purely military" considerations. "When the statesmen correctly assess the course of the war [as is to be expected of them] it is up to them and to them alone to decide what kind of policy and action accords with the war aims. . . . From this perspective it is wrong and even harmful to allow 'purely military' evaluation of any great war action or plan. Indeed it is self-defeating to consult experts, to ask them to give 'purely military' opinions on the kind of planning for war that cabinets should engage in. Even more pernicious is the demand of certain theoreticians that all available war resources be given over into the hands of the generals so that they may plan their wars and campaigns by purely military criteria."[59]

One can scarcely speak any more plainly than that. The entire distinction between military and political jurisdiction insisted on later in the nineteenth century is here totally rejected. The supremacy of political over military leadership in war is unequivocally acknowledged. To put it another way, the war plan as a politico-military totality is sharply distinguished from the campaign plan which is considered to be the result of mere technical considerations on the part of the military executive.

Now at last we can fully comprehend the dual position Clausewitz intended to take up with his formulation that war is a continuation of political intercourse through other means. He was on the one hand rejecting the artificial isolation of war and armed forces from the totality of political life, an isolation peculiar to the professional armies of the eighteenth century, nurtured by the professional jealousy of the officer caste as well as the needs of absolute monarchy, two interest groups that sought to conduct war not as a "popular cause" but as a "business of government."[60] In marking this type of rejection, however, we must not gloss over the other kind, equally dear to Clausewitz as a philosopher of war. In the face of the vast destruction the Napoleonic Wars had brought upon Europe, he pondered again and again the question of the proper relation of end and means in war, concluding that they must be in accord with each other, that the furies of war can be tamed, fighting rendered meaningful only when a clear-cut "political intelligence" firmly holds the reins.

His thinking was idealistic through and through; and as a true idealist he was filled with a triumphant faith in the power of reason, in this respect showing himself to be the heir of eighteenth-century rationalism. The superiority of "political intelligence" was to him self-evident—it was bound in the the end to reconcile the conflicting interests. Believing in ultimate unity of rational insight, Clausewitz really acknowledged no existential conflict between war and politics.

This issue alone may serve as a starting point for a fruitful critique of Clausewitz's basic thesis. He was able to envisage a harmful influence of politics on the conduct of war, leading to a conflict between the two, only in terms of a purely fortuitous and irrelevant impairment of the political reasoning power. "A quarrel between political and military interests," he assures us expressly, "cannot even at worst be relevant, and when it occurs it must be considered a flaw of insight." Such a conflict can arise only when statesmen are insufficiently familiar with the military instrumentalities they seek to employ and make impossible demands upon them. A danger of this kind is not too difficult to meet—all it requires is expert enlightenment.

This does not mean appointing generals to ministerial responsibility. That often leads to very untoward consequences, as Clausewitz seeks to illustrate by historical instances. For expert knowledge is less important than general qualities of leadership. It is sufficient to convey to the political leaders "a certain insight into the rudiments of warfare. . . . When there is no one person who is both soldier and statesman, only one appropriate expedient remains—to appoint the generalissimo a member of the cabinet, enabling it to share in the crucial elements of his decisions."[61] At the same time the seat of government should be moved close to the theater of war, so that it may more immediately follow the unfolding events. This was proved to be eminently useful in the case of Austrian headquarters in 1809 and Allied headquarters from 1813 to 1815.

For Clausewitz the much-discussed potential trouble source between politics and war was thus clearly reduced to a relatively unimportant technical difficulty that could easily be remedied. He seems to have been utterly oblivious to the fact that never was the conflict between generals and statesmen more severe than precisely in Allied headquarters from 1813 to 1815; he mentions only that it functioned well. Was there ever more cursing of diplomatic penpushing that ruined everything won in the field than among Blücher's staff, with which Clausewitz himself entertained the closest relations? Did his subsequent idealizing reflections blur his judgment?

On no account! It must be stated first of all that Clausewitz by no means always shared the *political* opposition of Blücher and Gneisenau during the years of the great struggle. He found their attitude toward vanquished France ignoble and politically unwise. Indeed, true to his principles he disapproved generally of the intervention in matters of grand policy of "purely military" considerations.[62] On the other hand he vigorously approved of the *military* opposition of his two friends to the feeble generalship of Schwarzenberg's headquarters in the winter campaign of 1813-1814, and he did so even in historical retrospect.[63] This, however, he did not view as a conflict between war and politics but rather as one between good strategy and poor.

For the rest, he thought it wrong to blame misguided political intervention for the inadequacies of the older style of warfare, especially as conducted against revolutionary France. The fault lay not in the fact that there had been excessive political meddling with operations but rather in that the policies themselves of the *ancien régime* were defective in their failure to assess correctly the dynamics of the revolutionary movement.[64] Reform, therefore, must start in the political sphere rather than in technical military matters.

While these views reveal profound insight, they do not dispose of the fact that the history of war has always been marked by conflict between political and military generalship and that this conflict has not only not abated with the rise of the new "absolute" style of war but has instead, if anything, gained in vehemence. Can this really be explained purely in terms of ignorance on the part of statesmen regarding the technical scope of military action? Even if this were so, is there any assurance that better and more objective communication among generals and statesmen would remedy the situation? Does not war, taxing all the resources of the state, carry the danger that political as well as military passions will override all the efforts of calm reason? Will not the ambitious pursuit of power, together with inflamed national hatred, obscure and blot out the reasonable assessment of possibilities, sometimes in the political sphere, at other times in the military? And will not these dangers grow ever greater and more sinister as war more and more assumes popular and mass character, with governments regarding themselves as no more than executors of the national will, and as the immeasurable intensification of weapons and war technology multiplies the destructive potential of war, sweeping up ever-larger segments of the population into the maelstrom?

Looking at the record of the nineteenth and twentieth centuries, one can scarcely doubt the answer. Clausewitz's theory of war predicates statesmen whose characters are utterly pervaded by impulses of grandeur, heroism, honor, national power, and freedom, men who are motivated by calm political reason far above petty intrigue or advantage rather than by blind hatred. He further presupposes soldiers accustomed to regard themselves as loyal servants of their supreme commander, never in danger of being ruled by political ambitions or jealousies, military men to whom the thought does not even occur that they might oppose their sovereign warlord or exploit popular support for their own purposes. Not in a single line does Clausewitz even so much as hint that the situation might be very different.

Even now we have not really reached the core of our problem. What about the argument that war theory deals only with the rational shape of things, hence must ignore all fortuitous circumstance that impairs the true idea of war in history? And can the kind of "political intelligence" that according to Clausewitz should dominate the total war picture always be so sure of itself? Do the ideas of true war and of equally true and reasonable policy that supposedly guide it in fact constitute a unified whole? What does Clausewitz really mean by "politics" which he so bluntly opposes to "war"—more specifically the direction of armed forces in war?

To my knowledge he expressed himself on this point in only one passage (Book 8, VIb). He says there that in planning for war it is inappropriate to bring two or more viewpoints to bear—of the military man, the administrator, the politican, etc.—since this detracts from unity of conception. The guiding principle must be "politics"alone. "It is taken for granted that politics combines and harmonizes all the interest of internal administration as well as those of humanity and whatever else philosophical reason may put forward, *for politics has no independent existence, being merely the steward of all these interests as against other states.* That politics may be misdirected or primarily serve private interests or the vanity of the governing class is not our concern here, for in no event can the art of war ever be considered its preceptor and we *can regard politics here only as the representative of society as a whole.*"

If this means anything it is that Clausewitz first of all saw the mission of diplomacy as the external representation of the common interests of a nation-state. His youthful writings have already taught us that his interest in foreign policy was one-sided. This one-sided view is confirmed by many of his later utterances.[65] In most cases safeguarding national interest internationally amounted to a diplomatic or military struggle for power.

Thus for Clausewitz the militant aspects of diplomacy were decidedly to the fore, and this explains why he found no trouble at all in subordinating the military element to the political. Yet he saw, in the second place, that the essence of politics is not completely absorbed in international representation; for was it not to "combine and harmonize all the interests of internal administration as well as those of humanity and whatever else political reason may put forward"? Politics "has no independent existence"—what else can that mean but that the struggle for power has no independent existence? It takes place only to preserve and secure a society whose way of life is likewise subject to political regulation.

True, Clausewitz's manner of saying this remains obscure and he was almost certainly deliberately evasive. But taking into account that throughout the book "politics" appears as the "moderating principle" in the struggle for power—not only because it embodies the "inertia of the masses" but because even while waging war it must be mindful of an enduring peace to follow[66]—one thing at least is plain: Even without profound reflection Clausewitz was well aware of the mission of politics in creating peace and order. He demanded that both goals be "combined and harmonized" in politics, the military stance and the principle of constructive peace.

This combining and harmonizing, however, constitutes the nub of the problem we have been discussing here. It is here that we find that irrational antinomy, capable of being resolved only in practice, from which all the deeper conflicts between war and politics have historically sprung. Not even Clausewitz's astute mind was able to strip bare and dispose of this antinomy. What he did do was to state with a reasonable measure of clarity the conditions under which alone it might be resolved. The only trouble is that what he, the idealist, seems to premise as the normal case is in fact the rare ideal case—that the thinking of the general should rise to the lofty level of great statesmanship while the mind of the statesman should combine a sense of social law and order, calm and lucid political wisdom, with the heroic cast of the dedicated soldier.

4

Popular Revolt and Cabinet Policy – Gneisenau and Metternich in the Wars of Liberation

T
HE CLASSIC human ideal Clausewitz envisaged was, as we have seen, the universal man of culture, not yet spoiled by mechanization and specialization. It was from this living tradition that he constructed his ideal image of the general in whose mind military and political leadership were to fuse into a higher unity. If there ever was a Prussian general who met these criteria, it was his much-admired friend Neithard von Gneisenau, beyond doubt the most inspired personality among all the generals who ever pitted themselves against Napoleon in combat. A quartermaster general without proper expert training, as he himself knew and frankly admitted, he possessed the qualities of character and the intellectual faculties of the born military leader. The sweep and grandeur of his mind exert their effect even on posterity, by the impact of his eloquence, the creative imagery of his style. He was a soldier who remained sensitive to the great political ideas of his time, apprehending foreign and domestic affairs with equal enthusiasm, ever pursuing the supreme goals of national policy far beyond petty day-to-day affairs.[1]

Yet it was precisely in the life of this man, who seems to have limited himself in such small measure to the purely military sphere, that the unceasing conflict between political and military thinking erupted with greater frequency and vehemence than in all but very few instances. His case shows with particular clarity that the problem was not one of jurisdiction or expertise but went far deeper. It turned on the dual nature of politics, as concentrated power on the one hand and the guardian of enduring peace on the other.

Gneisenau the soldier was in the end exclusively concerned with the concentration of military power in the service of high ideals. He witnessed the spectacle of the French Revolution as a supreme example of such concentration. Neither a dogmatic partisan nor a conservative opponent of its libertarian principles, he simply admired its stupendous political momentum. In 1808 he wrote:

> The Revolution aroused the full spectrum of energy and assigned each force to its proper sphere. This resulted in heroes being put at the head of the armies, statesmen being placed in charge of the leading administrative posts, and ultimately the greatest man of a great people reaching the top. . . . The Revolution set the full vigor of the French nation in motion. By giving equality to the several estates and by equitable taxation of property it transformed the living energy of man and the dead energy of goods into a proliferating pool of capital, upsetting the erstwhile relationships among states and the balance that rested on them. If the other states wish to restore that balance, they must mobilize and utilize the same resources.

For Gneisenau all demands for political reform flowed with marvelously simple and consistent logic from these general premises. He found it inconceivable that a nation could dedicate itself completely to the attainment of national liberty in exchange for domestic tyranny. "The people are beyond doubt the ruler's strongest support." Within the people slumber the forces the state requires to maintain national liberty. "What immense power lies dormant and unexploited in the bosom of a nation! In the breasts of thousands upon thousands of men dwells the spirit of greatness, its pinions shackled by their plight. The realm may languish in shame and weakness while some Caesar follows the plow in its humblest village, some Epaminondas ekes out a bare subsistence by the labor of his hands." The power of a militia is inexhaustible whereas the old-time hired armies destroy the people's militancy, divide the interests of the ruler from those of the people, and burden the people intolerably. The mercenary cares not whom he serves nor what cause he espouses, "but the citizen who knows his fatherland, who esteems just government under tolerant law, who appreciates progress in every sphere of domestic affairs, who puts his hopes in the future—such a one will eagerly dedicate himself to the attainment of these greatest of all goods, if not for himself then for those who shall enjoy their native soil after him."

These are the sensitive tones of the age of the Rights of Man. But we perceive at once that "just government under tolerant law" is not only a supreme desideratum on its own but a means for enhancing the power of the state. "The goal is to have a constitution other nations will envy. At the same time a state must muster the resources to stand fully armed in the hour of decision, to enable it to survive other states. Thither lead welfare, enlightenment, law-abidingness, and civil liberties. A slavish nation, poor, ignorant, and crude, is no match for one rich in knowledge and resources."

Abolition of serfdom, encouraging respect for every citizen's dignity, replacement of the brutal army discipline of yore, fostering the spirit of militancy among the people by national education—these are the prerequisites for the creation of a popular army whose virtues rest on a sense of honor and patriotism rather than on slavish obedience. "Give them [the inhabitants of the different provinces] a single fatherland, a single constitution they are to hold dear. Create a moral principle that will fuse the masses into one and set them in motion. . . . It is both fair and prudent in the interest of the state to give the people a fatherland if they are expected to defend that fatherland manfully."

It was only from this aspect of enhancing political striking-power that the reform laws of Freiherr vom Stein seemed necessary and useful to Gneisenau. Indeed, he did not think they went far enough and wanted the great reformer to have much more sweeping powers to carry out his task than Stein himself sought. Leaping ahead, he publicized Stein's administrative reforms as a "realization of the representative system," adding that "enlightened and law-abiding men of every estate shall have the right to vote."

When Napoleon demanded a shameful system of tribute after the defeat of 1808, Gneisenau advocated "boldly rifling the armory of revolution" and beating France with its own weapons. He counseled the king instantly to summon a representative assembly that would help him resist Napoleon's importunities and provide means for waging war. It was his general view that Prussia, to discharge its national mission, urgently needed a free constitution as an indispensable aid for enhancing its power and military strength.

When he was brilliantly vindicated in the Wars of Liberation, Gneisenau was vocal in proclaiming Prussia's claim to play the leading role in Germany. During the quarrels that arose at the Congress of Vienna between Metternich and Hardenberg, Gneisenau planned with Boyen and Grolman to assert this claim by force of arms. But to conquer Germany with the moral support of a free constitution seemed to him even more important and certain. "Only the triple supremacy of arms, constitution and learning will enable us to survive among powerful neighbors." A free domestic constitution and support for science seemed to Gneisenau direct aids to a country's fighting stance.

Small wonder that such radical determination to throw all political tradition overboard in the struggle for power appeared downright revolutionary to the supporters of the old order in the Prussian monarchy, the king himself in the lead. What concern was the hallowed three-estate order of old Prussia to this soldier of southern family, a kind of adventurer with a checkered past who had been cast up by chance with the Prussian army? What in particular did the privileges of the East Elbian Junker class mean to him? His reform proposals were totally unmindful of such rights.

More than that, no sooner had the French troops suffered their first serious defeats in Spain, opening up the prospect of a change in the over-all situation, than Gneisenau wanted the royal authorities to unleash a people's war of a ferocity that would have set at nought all traditional concepts of martial and international law, of order and discipline. Every male above the age of seventeen was to be armed. Local officials of dubious loyalty were to be instantly suspended, their conduct to be supervised by the clergy. Officers and noncoms were to be elected by the rebels themselves. Royal commissioners were to be installed in the provinces; they were to be superior to all the local authorities, with the power of life and death, able to commandeer public and private property, and not to be held accountable for the war measures they took. All peasants serving in the war were to be liberated from serfdom. The property of cowards and traitors was to be confiscated and distributed to the victims of war. All areas invaded by the enemy were to be laid waste. Women and children were to flee to the wilderness. The exhausted enemy was to be attacked by night. His flanks and lines of communications were to be subjected to ceaseless harrying and sniping. All German princes siding with France were to be deposed and worthier successors elected by their subjects. All their ministers were to be declared outlaws unless they shared in the war effort. Titles of nobility were to lapse unless merited anew by distinguished war service!

All this Gneisenau, supported by Scharnhorst and Stein, had the audacity to propose to the king in 1808 in memorials clearly drawing on the struggles of the Spaniards and on those of the Jacobin terrorists with their mortal loyalist enemies, the Chouans and Vendéer. These documents represented the ultimate potentiation of radical militancy, the strongest conceivable denial of all the principles underlying an enduring peaceful order. The radiant and triumphant confidence with which Gneisenau the soldier put forward these plans, staking his head for their success, demonstrates that he was untroubled by the kind of bourgeois restraint that can plainly be seen to lurk behind the gloomy if not desperate resolution of Stein the minister.[2] Gneisenau the soldier did not conceive of his plan as hazardous. To him it was no more than the logical result of weighing the options. "Let us stride ahead firmly and valiantly," he wrote, "along the path prescribed to us by *prudence and necessity.*"

Frederic William III rejected this plan for rebellion—not only because he was a timid man, uncertain of himself, who unquestionably lacked the intellectual stature that would have been commensurate with his historic role; his rejection was also the inexorable consequence of a clash in political principles. Militancy and peaceableness were pitted, one against the other—the one embodied in a revolutionary activist, the other in a conservative legitimist. We encounter here for the first time a situation that was to recur often during the nineteenth century: the case for militancy represented by the professional soldier, the case for order by the political leadership, giving the dialogue the character of a clash between generals and politicians. True, even the attitude of Stein, the responsible minister of state who was on Gneisenau's side, shows that the clash is only imperfectly described in terms of military versus civilian thinking. Yet it is only natural that the soldier should always think first (and often one-sidedly) of the requirements of combat, while the responsible statesman bears the additional burden of concern for an enduring peace beyond the battle. The whole complex of problems falls all too easily into the pattern of soldiers versus civilians.

It is in the nature of the soldier that he should be more concerned with what is necessary than with what is possible. And it is in the nature, although not an adequate definition, of politics that it is ultimately the art of the possible. To make the "impossible" possible is always the soldier's supreme ambition. This lies at the very heart of the "front spirit" that leads to supreme effort in life-and-death struggles among nations. For the statesman who never dares risk the life of his country with the ruthlessness that becomes the military leader in respect of the lives of his troops, such an approach is not only dangerous—it may become downright criminal in borderline cases, when political temerity may rise to the level of recklessness.

In any event political leadership calls for cool calculation and prudent forecasting, even more urgently than does its military counterpart. To be sure both (to speak with Clausewitz) move within a sphere of uncertainty, of chance. But amid the abnormally enhanced intensity of events peculiar to war, there is not always time for mature reflection. Indeed when there is no other way to clarify the situation and point toward success, venturesome risks must and may legitimately be taken in war. In politics this is never justifiable. The responsible statesman is compelled to play for great stakes, indeed for all-or-nothing, and he must have very long odds on his side.

He must understand the art of waiting as thoroughly as the virtues of action, although the former is much harder to learn and often carries intolerable mental pressures. The statesman is entitled to challenge fate only when there is no other practicable way out. The art of true statesmanship implies a never-ending weighing of the advantages of action or delay, resolute will power as against caution. Moderation is as much part of it as is daring. Yet how very rarely does history show us that ideal combination of audacity and prudence, of passion and calm, that distinguishes the true statesman not only from the blind plunger but from the timid nondescript incompetent as well!

In many of the wars since the Great Revolution mass passions, opinions, prejudices, and anxieties have unfortunately had a direct bearing on matters of grand policy; and whenever that happens the two aspects tend to fly apart. Heroism and prudence come to be at loggerheads, each bitterly inveighing against the other in such terms as "blind recklessness" and "cowardly appease-ment." The great antinomy of political life which we persistently seek to elucidate here is stubbornly characterized by the paradox that great achieve-ment requires staking everything, while on the other hand that very virtue may turn to fateful blunder, indeed become the crucial obstacle to success.

Beyond peradventure of doubt Frederic William III would never have mustered the resolution for the liberation struggle but for the militant urgings of such men as Scharnhorst, Gneisenau, and their friends. Even after the Russian disaster of 1812 he was very hard to persuade and the proper moment was almost missed. Yet it was not personal weakness and inadequacy alone that held him back for so long, but also a genuine belief in his moral duty as a ruler—an ethic he nevertheless embraced with neither flair nor grandeur.

In any event, there can be no question that Gneisenau's most famous politico-military memorials, those of 1808 and 1811 dealing with the general levy *(Landsturm),* contained demands that far transcended the limits of what was tactically and ethically feasible, reaching out into the realm of fantasy. They were the products of a revolutionary imagination comparable in grandeur only to the furious vengeful lays of Heinrich von Kleist; and while they fill us with admiration for Gneisenau's heroic sentiments, they do leave doubts as to his political vision, indeed even the soundness of his military judgment.

The peaceable denizens of the ancient Prussian provinces had been inured of old to the most abject submissiveness by their latifundian proprietors and town fathers; and to expect them to become suddenly transformed by fiat into conspiratorial bands along the lines of the Spanish juntas was surely the acme of utopianism! It did not happen even in the great patriotic ferment of 1813. True, patriotic zeal then managed to wrest the desired Landsturm edict from the hands of the king; but the edict was never successfully implemented, for it would have turned everything topsy-turvy. The measure never got beyond extremely modest beginnings; and the unrelenting intemperance with which Gneisenau at the time persecuted even patriotically minded opponents of the edict only put him further in the wrong.[3]

All the same, it is seldom possible to point so clearly to the natural limits beyond which activist militancy must reasonably give way to the vital needs of enduring peaceful order. In most cases reflection after the fact is no more able than the actors at the time to weigh with any degree of certainty the chances as between a policy bent on conflict and one that seeks to avoid it. The more the historian seeks to untangle the welter of argument and conjecture, hope and apprehension, that commonly precedes any great political decision, the more he realizes that rational certainty and a clear perspective of the true state of affairs are seldom vouchsafed its participants. He learns to appreciate that in many situations the proponents of militancy are able to put forward arguments carrying as much force as those asserted by the advocates of peace and that it is usually the basic character orientation that sways the balance rather than rational consideration of the best course.

It thus behooves us to practice a seemly restraint in passing historical judgments. For who can subsequently say with assurance whether, taking into account the character of the participants, there was any real alternative to a decision later shown to have led to disaster? In the end every participant fixes on the course of action most in accord with his nature; and as for the observer of history, will not his judgment also incline toward the side to which his own nature or situation draws him?

We tend today to view the brash plans of Gneisenau and the other patriots of 1808 as premature and misguided in conception, but the question arises whether a successful issue by force of arms might not have been realistically possible by 1811 at the latest, before the start of the Russian campaign. Scharnhorst, Gneisenau, Clausewitz, and their kind felt sure, on the basis of the total military and political situation, that the odds on their side were heavy enough for victory; but the king disregarded their counsel. He decided soon afterward on Prussia's accession to the Rhenish League whose member states were obliged to give the hated Corsican military support against Russia.

It was the nadir of humiliation in the history of Prussia, also marking the pinnacle of discord between military and political thinking. "Our fate," Gneisenau wrote to Stein, "will overtake us as we deserve. We shall go down in shame. For let us make no mistake, a nation is no better than its rulership." It seemed at times as though the Prussian monarchy would lose all the hopeful talent that had turned toward it from all over Germany in the preceding decades.

It was to justify his own entry and that of many of his fellow officers into Russian services that Clausewitz wrote the *Protestation* with which we are already familiar.[4] It upholds the ethic of military honor and dedication with supreme defiance of political prudence. Frederic William III on his part had no grand political design that foresaw the coming upheaval and that would have enabled him to claim superiority over his impatient officers. He simply followed his natural inclination. His straightforward instinct for self-preservation persuaded him to bow before the storm. For the time being his thoughts were directed solely toward safeguarding his dynasty and its heritage for a "better future."

In consequence he very nearly became an object of contempt for his bravest and most superior officers. "The King," added Gneisenau's letter, "still stands beside the throne he has never truly occupied, no more than an umpire of those who stand on its steps. His character is bound to foil any adviser who seeks to set grand policy in the sense of higher statesmanship. In military as in foreign affairs he still maintains his immense authority, all but emasculating those who seek to give sound counsel."

The disaster that ensued in Russia soon afterward, together with Hardenberg's political skill, did manage, sooner than might have been hoped or expected, to bridge the gulf between monarch and patriot party, at least to the extent of making common cause possible in the work of German redemption. Yet serious tension continued throughout the liberation struggle between the zealous military leaders, especially at Blücher's headquarters, and the Prussian diplomats with their political caution. This tension deepened greatly after Austria joined the anti-French coalition, for from that time onward the spotlight focused more and more on the man who was the embodiment of the opposition to the militant revolutionary spirit of the times—Prince Metternich. He was the incarnation, so to speak, of the idea of an enduring European peace. His whole "system," derived from the ideological world of the eighteenth century as lately detailed to us with such eloquence,[5] represents the most forceful and successful attempt ever undertaken to control the demoniac forces of the power struggle, by restoring and securing legitimate authority within the states and a balance among the great powers.

This and this alone was Metternich's orientation in the struggle against Napoleon. He was completely insensitive to the moral upheavals, the sense of violated national honor, and the thirst for vengeance that agitated the Prussian military. From the outset he endeavored to reduce military action and the danger of war to a minimum, in the interests of his long-suffering country. His chief aim was to return to a state of peace as soon as possible, primarily through a process of diplomatic give-and-take that would preclude a hegemony by either France or Russia. It was an attempt to oppose the world conqueror by military procrastination in the style of the eighteenth century, to contain but not destroy him. Small wonder it met with strenuous opposition on the part of the Prussian patriots in the field. Thus both sides represented their opposite principles of political action with dogged persistence; and the liberation struggle—especially the winter campaign of 1813-1814—became a classic example of the irreconcilable conflict between a policy intent on destroying the enemy and one seeking only reconciliation.

We need not pursue the emergence of this conflict in detail nor its exacerbation by personal animosities. These were inevitable in view of the deep gulf between the personalities—patriotic passion and moral pathos on the one side, cold-hearted urbanity and moral frivolity on the other. It will be sufficient to indicate the characteristic traits of this kind of conflict which recur as well in the subsequent wars of the nineteenth century.

There was first of all the controversy over continuing the war into France. At Prussian headquarters the lesson taught by Napoleon had hit home. The proper goal of war was not so much territorial gain as destruction of the hostile fighting forces to the point of utter paralysis. The character of the great adversary was known, the restless dynamism of his power politics understood, and it was fully realized that peace with this demoniac force was not possible in the long run.

The Prussian officers were quite clear on the point that the devastating blow administered to Napoleon's armies at Leipzig could be fully exploited only by ceaseless hot pursuit. Deprived of even a moment's rest, the enemy would be quite unable to rally any forces of consequence. Every consideration, military and political, argued for swift continuation of the war to the final triumph.

Great was the indignation among the soldiers when the political leadership interposed itself and allowed seven precious weeks to elapse before it mustered the resolution to carry operations further. Blücher raged at the diplomats. "They are rogues who deserve the gallows," he said, "and you know what they can do to me." And Gneisenau remarked: "If the generals do not sweep them along they will do the worst mischief. To get to Paris and there dictate the kind of peace we must have seems to them the height of recklessness."[6]

Yet the long delay did not really stem from pusillanimity but primarily from a covert conflict of interests among the Allies. Unlike Russia, Metternich did not desire Napoleon's complete rout, foreseeing infinite trouble in rebuilding France after his fall and wishing to maintain a strong power in France in the interest of the balance of Europe. France was to remain the great counterpoise to Russia in the east, although effectively enjoined from eventually teaming up with czarism against the Hapsburg power.

Nor did Metternich wish to countenance great military triumphs or conquests—they would only give the Czar a moral claim to large-scale territorial aggrandizement in the east. Russia might demand all of Poland, proposing that Austria indemnify itself along the Rhine—in Alsatia, say, or Belgium—thus perpetuating the feud with France.

We see that Metternich, the believer in clandestine diplomacy, based his position far less on immediate military needs than on considerations of what was to follow the war, what shape an enduring order in Europe might take. Only this explains why he kept on trying to tempt Napoleon to make peace at once, by offering him favorable terms—first the line of the Rhine and the Alps, later on at least the frontiers of 1792.

It is doubtful whether Metternich himself ever seriously believed in the success of these efforts. There is no doubt, however, that his public declarations to the French people were actually aimed at committing the Allied powers to moderate peace goals and at persuading the French to desert Napoleon unless he accepted Metternich's terms. For Metternich was well aware of French war-weariness and sought to avoid reversing this mood by any direct threat to French soil. The issue was one of attaining peace by political rather than military weapons.

This peace policy of the "diplomats," to which Metternich with his superior shrewdness managed to convert even the representative of England, was unalterably opposed by the zeal of men like Gneisenau and Blücher who thirsted for action, vengeance, and victory. There was no scope left here for mediation between statesmen and generals. King Frederic William III, ever the skeptic, lacking style and flair, and his clever though vacillating adviser Hardenberg nevertheless tried to strike a compromise, only to be resistlessly torn between Metternich's diplomacy, their own generals, and the Czar, who was being incited by all Napoleon's mortal enemies.

Even when the Rhine had at last been crossed the tensions were not lessened.

Quite the contrary, they were aggravated to the pinnacle of bitterness. In his efforts to keep the hopes for victory and the territorial claims of his Allies within limits and prevent great decisive blows from being struck, Metternich kept on meddling with the strategy of Schwarzenberg, the Austrian generalissimo, which even so was timid, hesitant, and old-fashioned.[7] This brought on the most fateful consequences for the situation of the so-called Army of Silesia which alone was still on the offensive. At Blücher's headquarters it was regarded as tantamount to treason.

So pointed grew the quarrel that the Czar threatened to abandon the Austrians and advance with Prussia alone, while Metternich announced that Austria would conclude a separate peace with Napoleon. Matters reached the stage where the winter campaign—which Schwarzenberg's main force, had it moved with any dash at all, probably could have concluded with a single major battle—at times turned into something very nearly like a general retreat.

All this accomplished was to strengthen anew the confidence of Napoleon who, under the overwhelming impact of Blücher's early successes on the battlefield, had been close to counting his cause lost and conceding everything that was asked. And he personally wrecked the peace negotiations at Châtillon by the intemperateness of his demands. From intercepted secret dispatches, even Metternich finally had to acknowledge that no really enduring peace was possible with an enemy who explicitly described any peace as no more than a truce, a stage along the way of reconquering his great empire. At the same time the fresh initiative on the part of the Prussian generals effectively refuted the Austrian commander's apprehensions concerning the hazards of offensive action. Their bold push toward Paris far in the rear of the main enemy force marked the final turn in Napoleon's fortunes.

Thus in the end the aggressive will to destroy the enemy was proved right, against the political and military cautions of the Austrian command. There can be little doubt that but for the vigorous determination of the Prussian generals the great task of liberating Europe would have faltered halfway to the goal and might even have failed ignominiously. Metternich's diplomatic shrewdness deserted him completely at the crucial point, in his estimate of Napoleon. He was without the slightest understanding of the Corsican's demoniac militant power drive, looking on him with the eyes of the true cabinet politician, as a cool and calculating antagonist, the representative of pure *raison d'état*.

The limits of Metternich's political genius come into clear focus here. The essential element of his great skill was at once his great weakness—the passionate rationalism of his thinking. He never allowed moral stirrings to interfere with his calculations, and this enabled him to recognize what was politically feasible, beyond the confused agitation and contradictory aspirations of the patriots, who were often blind to reality.[8] Even amid the life-and-death struggle of war he kept his eyes unswervingly on his goal of an enduring European peace, and he pursued this goal with sovereign diplomatic mastery.

Yet there was something abstract and almost unreal about the political wisdom of this diplomat, who was a European even more than an Austrian. Unlike Bismarck later on, Metternich was not linked by close ties of heritage to the history and power interests of the country he served; and since the Hapsburg monarchy ruled over many divergent ethnic strains, he was even less identified with purely German vital interests. Thus he remained immune to the powerful impulses that were then erupting from the irrational depths of the German people and convulsing the world. The sole aim of his policy was to set the world at rest again as soon as possible and to keep it at rest as long as possible, no matter how much vital and creative impulse had to be thwarted.

How very different were the Prussian patriots and standard-bearers of German unity, then foregathered in Blücher's staff and in the "Central Administrative Council" for the conquered German territories, headed by Stein! They had on their side a whole great circle of propagandists, "fanatical volunteers, littérateurs and poets of every stripe" as Metternich contemptuously dubbed these "German Jacobins." It was here among men like Gneisenau, Grolman, Clausewitz, Stein, Arndt, Görres, and Jahn that the true spirit of the rebellion was rife, a spirit of militant idealism that had so profound an effect on German political ideology into the twentieth century, a spirit in which all the moral, religious, and political impulses of national identity that ran rampant at the time were indiscriminately mingled.

Pride in the great creations of German culture in the age of Weimar was blended with spontaneous and instinctive hatred of foreign rule. The protest of a newly awakened religious awareness, shared by Protestants and Catholics alike, against cold and dry French rationalism, was mingled with the spirit of Frederic the Great. Romantic glorification of the German past coupled with a deeper understanding of the age-old German destiny was merged with modern libertarianism and unitarianism coupled with sneering contempt for the traditional princes now truckling to the foreign ruler. Admiration for the militant power of the French Revolution dwelt side by side with irredentist hostility to its destructive principles. The urge to be free coexisted with the sense of legitimacy and conservative justice.

Most astonishing and momentous for the subsequent growth of ideas was the manner in which religious and political motivations were joined into a new morality of political militancy. The struggle for national liberation became virtually a holy war, a crusade against Satan in the name of God, or at least in the name of justice and virtue arrayed against evil. If public opinion needed such an indirect approach to become aware of the justice of the people's political claims, their urge for power and freedom, it was because of Germany's age-old dismemberment into many impotent principalities. The derelict and dispirited German dynasties, encumbered with their obsolete political heritage, would never have been able to muster any enthusiasm for their restoration on their own.

But beyond these meager and unimpressive political realities the Germans were inspired by the shining ideal of a united and powerful national state such as had once been theirs in the middle ages. Still an inchoate and naive dream, it was nevertheless backed by an enduring awareness of a common German cultural and geographic heritage transcending internal divisions, an awareness that now, in the struggle against the foreign oppressor, revived in undreamed-of strength, took on the character of an almost religious fervor.

Volk und Vaterland was what Fichte had been preaching about, as the "outward form and medium of everlasting values in the world," as the "token and warrant of eternity on earth." The supreme moral duty was to fight to preserve and even expand this German dream and its cultural mission in Europe; and to that end Fichte was prepared to countenance even Machiavellian means. Freiherr vom Stein declared that he knew no higher goal than to "lift the nation's moral, religious and patriotic spirits, to restore its valor, self-confidence and willingness to make any sacrifice for national honor and independence from foreign rule."

The most significant element in all this was the unthinking juxtaposition of religious, moral, and patriotic values. In the writings of Arndt—his *Catechism for Soldiers,* for example—politics and religion are completely blended into one. Indeed one of the most noteworthy phenomena of the period was the endeavor to activate religious sentiments as direct adjuncts to the political struggle. The new morality of militant nationalism which we saw developing in the notes of young Clausewitz was by way of impressing all higher intellectual life into its service.[9]

The immediate consequence was that political thought grew highly charged with emotion, in contrast to the cool rationalism of Metternich's *raison d'état.* The impatient military group centering around Blücher inveighed with deep moral indignation not only against the tyrant Napoleon himself, the "enemy of mankind," but against his compatriot tools, the French, that "impure, insolent and indecent race filled with repulsive greed," as Stein put it.

Nor were these patriots merely concerned with restoring the balance of the great powers. What they were mainly after was the freedom of the people from despotism. Above all they wanted vengeance. "Providence has led us hither," Gneisenau wrote to Stein late in January of 1814. "Let us seek retribution for the great sufferings that have overtaken the people, for the depths of insolence, that we may prove that *discite justitiam moniti non temnere divos.* Unless we do so we are wretches who deserve no better than to be roused from our torpor every other year and threatened with the scourge of slavery."[10]

Right after the crossing of the Rhine he dreamed of "revenging the people" against the hated French nation by means of a triumphal entry into Paris: "We must repay their visits to our capitals. Until such a time our vengeance and triumph will be incomplete. Should the Army of Silesia be the first to reach Paris I shall at once have the bridges of Austerlitz and Jena blown up, together with the victory monument."[11]

One senses how a savage hatred, kept in check over many years only with great difficulty, seeks expression here. Such sentiments were part and parcel of the German fighting will, the emotional goad to the great uprising. They evidence the novel element in the liberation struggle, as a true people's war, in contrast to all the earlier wars waged by monarchial cabinets. Yet if the ultimate goal of the struggle was to be a new and enduring peace in Europe rather than the perpetuation of hatreds among nations, would it not have been necessary to keep such sentiments under control? Gneisenau here entered upon an internal conflict. On the one hand he wanted to take vengeance on the Parisians for Napoleon's deeds of violence. On the other hand he favored inciting those same Parisians to defect from their overlord.

It was the monarchs, the most qualified representatives of Old Europe, who intervened on this occasion. Even Czar Alexander, hitherto the strongest supporter of the patriot faction at supreme headquarters, would have nothing to do with unnecessarily antagonizing the vanquished French nation. Before Paris and in the city itself, at the end of a campaign that exacted an enormous toll in combat and effort, the leaders of the victorious Army of Silesia were consigned to no more than a subordinate role, which they understandably accepted only with bitter resentment.

Nor were they permitted to take part in the peace negotiations—the shrewd Metternich had laid down the basic terms in treaties among the Allies before the campaign was concluded. Gneisenau's private correspondence reveals the kind of peace he would have desired. He wanted France's internal unity destroyed for the greater security of Germany and especially Prussia. As the main power in the liberation struggle, Prussia was now to move up to actual preponderance among the German principalities. If the other powers were to oppose this too strongly and openly—as was indeed the case at the Congress of Vienna in the course of the controversy over Saxony—even the boldest methods should not be eschewed, in Gneisenau's view. Napoleon should be recalled from Elba and supported against the Bourbons, thus "inoculating France with civil war and rendering it external-ly inactive." Bavaria would be destroyed in league with Württemberg and Baden, Austria attacked shoulder to shoulder with the Russians. The Italians were to be incited against the Vienna government, from which Italy, Galicia, and Moravia would be wrested in "a few campaigns." Bamberg, Würzburg, Ansbach, and Bayreuth would be acquired for Prussia; the remaining booty, including Old Bavaria, distributed between Baden and Württemberg; and civil war kept alive in France. "Who knows, with some luck, it might be possible to establish two regimes in France, one under the Bourbons, the other under Napoleon, both locked in perpetual battle. That really would be the limit."

A new revolution, in other words, and warfare without end! When they were communicated to him, even Clausewitz found these plans "rather too parochial for anyone but the king of Prussia himself."[12] Clausewitz the fighting man was, however, scarcely destined to be a peacemaker. Even his well-known efforts to obtain the cession of Alsace-Lorraine for Germany were primarily based on military necessities. It was to secure the left flank of the German fortification system along the Rhine—but also to serve as an indemnification for North German princes whose territory Prussia could then acquire! [13] There was scarcely any mention of the traditional German ties of the Alsatians. On the other hand, the notion of securing a newly won frontier by a further military buffer zone was to be put forward again and again by the military in the later wars of the nineteenth and twentieth centuries. At the Paris peace conference and the subsequent Congress of Vienna such proposals did not yet meet with success. There the cabinets, Austria and England in the lead, still prevailed with their endeavor to reduce areas of friction among the powers as much as possible and thus secure an enduring peace.

But before that was to succeed, all the war gains and peace terms were to be jeopardized once again by Napoleon's return from Elba. The campaign of 1815, which again saw Blücher and Gneisenau at the head of a Prussian invading force, at once rekindled the previous year's tensions among generals and diplomats, indeed deepened them to some extent. Yet this time they did bear a different character. Politics did not again intervene in the course of military operations—at least no longer in the great battlefield decisions. The headlong advance of the Prussians from Waterloo to Paris was not delayed a single day.

On this occasion, however, Blücher and Gneisenau did everything within their power to anticipate the diplomats and take the main decisions about concluding peace as much as possible in advance by military decree, before the allied monarchs were even able to reach headquarters. Hence their ceaseless drive to overwhelm and occupy the enemy capital regardless of the truce bids by French generals, deputies, and ministers. Hence the speed of their advance even when the real danger in the field was long over.

From the first day of the campaign Blücher's headquarters was convinced that the diplomats, given a free hand, would again "forfeit everything the soldiers had won by their blood."[14] This time the soldiers hoped to foil the diplomats by engaging in grand policy on their own. Blücher instantly responded to the first truce offer after Napoleon had been deposed with demands that in large measure anticipated the peace negotiations to come. Napoleon was to be executed or handed over; all fortresses along the Sambre, Meuse, Moselle, and Saar were to be surrendered; and all French provinces to the Marne were to be evacuated. Soon afterward a peace delegation in Laon received even stiffer terms. The cities of Paris, Laon, Soissons, and Lafère were also to be surrendered together with all the art treasures pillaged from the various countries.[15]

Blücher, in one of his letters, left no doubt of his intentions: "By the time they [Allied headquarters] place the bit in my mouth I hope to have the most important matters settled. I expect to strike while the iron is hot.... There are still quite a few things to be put right."[16] The generals wanted to make up for what they deemed to be deficiencies in the Peace of 1814. The anti-Prussian attitude of Bourbon diplomacy at the Congress of Vienna had meanwhile greatly deepened their hatred of France, even under monarchial rule. They were convinced that only large territorial cessions along the northern and eastern borders of France could secure central Europe against future attack.

Gneisenau thought Germany's traditional enemy should be reduced to the territorial limits under Louis XIII, forfeiting all conquests since Louis XIV. The groundwork was to be laid even in the truce agreement. He regarded any thought of a later reconciliation with the vanquished foe as utter folly. Any effort in that direction would only be interpreted as weakness.[17] Added to these politico-military considerations was the insatiable thirst for vengeance of the patriots who were unwilling to let a "vain and treacherous people who had broken their pledged word" go unpunished. Gneisenau thought of himself virtually as the "instrument of providence" elected to mete out "justice everlasting." He wished to see Napoleon handed over and shot on the very spot where the Duc d'Enghien had once fallen victim to the Corsican's judicial murder.[18]

In Gneisenau's view the "honor of the army" required that French national pride be deeply humbled by a formal entry into Paris, and he succeeded in achieving this against the wishes of his British allies. The Pont de Jéna was ordered blown up and a tribute of one hundred million francs imposed on the city of Paris together with the obligation to re-equip one hundred thousand troops, including horses, to provide an "offering of honor" in the form of two months' pay for the army and to give special uniform allowances for the officers. Further contributions were imposed on the provinces. Prefects and bankers who refused to cooperate in raising the funds, invoking the orders of their Bourbon authorities, were taken into custody, some of them being incarcerated in German fortresses as hostages.

All this made sense only from a militant viewpoint that simply sought to taste its triumph to the full, without much regard to the work of peaceful reconstruction to come. Controversy on this point with the "diplomats" was inevitable. During the ensuing months Blücher's headquarters added further demands. Ignoring the incipient peace negotiations, it aimed at giving even greater military preponderance to the victors. Blücher wanted to see even strong points that had meanwhile given allegiance to the Bourbons carried by assault. The Prussian main forces were not to leave the country until the French had complied to the letter with all the peace terms, especially the surrender of all fortified places, in direct contravention of the provisions of the peace conference

Clashes with the political leadership over these terms kept increasing in intensity. Blücher bitterly resented the suspension of the contributions he had arbitrarily imposed. To him these funds together with the re-equipment of his ragged troops were a "matter of honor." Since the French exchequer proved to be completely exhausted, the king of Prussia offered him a preliminary indemnification from his own which Blücher indignantly rejected. Since he refused to be appeased in any other way, Blücher did in the end succeed in having greater pressure exerted on the French minister of finance.

The quarrel over the fortifications and the term of occupation grew all the bitterer. In the end it culminated in direct political rebellion on the general's part. The victor of Belle-Alliance and conqueror of Paris was well aware—or thought he was—that the cheers of the public were meant for him rather than his monarch, who had taken little personal part in the final campaigns.

We see this quite plainly in his brusquely worded resignation submitted to Hardenberg on July 26: "I shall publicly place my conduct before the king, the army, the whole nation and the German fatherland for judgment."[19] The incident created a great stir, threatened to lay bare the discord in the Allied camp in the most embarrassing fashion, and was settled only with much difficulty through the intercession of Hardenberg and Gneisenau.

Fanned into flame against the *deplomatiquer* by his chief of staff Grolman, Blücher's pride soon transcended all limits. His memorials addressed to the king are at times defiantly boastful, at times almost openly condescending. He had Grolman request Boyen, the minister of war, to delay royal decrees until he, Blücher, found time to capture the controversial fortresses, thus sabotaging the decisions of the diplomats' conference! He refused to acknowledge orders issued to his subordinates from royal headquarters.

In the end it was all in vain. The peace conference passed over the wishes of the Prussian generals. On October 3, the supreme army command was expressly placed under the chancellor of state in all political questions. Blücher had to evacuate France; the remaining occupation troops were placed under separate command. Hardenberg, sharply emphasizing his sole claim to political leadership, put an end to the old fire-eater's delaying tactics.

But Blücher, deeply resentful, was yet to strike his final blow. In a memorial to the king he sought to undermine the minister's position by throwing suspicion on him as a dangerous climber. On November 20, 1815, he wrote:

How sad and harmful to be dependent on prime ministers, how destructive to the army if this influence continued and *Yr. Majesty did not maintain direct control of the army!* Indeed it is high time to put an end to the curious assemblage that has hitherto ruled Europe under the guise of ministers plenipotentiary of the allied courts and to consign to their former station men who, while only subjects, nevertheless in this role have lorded it over their monarchs and actually made the laws. This is all the more necessary since their wretched handiwork has set them back in the opinion of the whole world, while Prussia and Germany, despite all their efforts, stand before that same world as betrayed over and over again.[20]

Hardenberg was able to parry this blow immediately. In a personal report he drew the king's attention to the danger that threatened his authority, once the army began to be a *corps délibératif* acting on its own judgment.[21] Frederic William, who had never supported the patriot zealots, shared this view and thus no immediate practical consequences followed Blücher's step.[22] In the context of our subject, it is nevertheless significant as a first attempt by Prussian generals to emancipate themselves from the political leadership by invoking the will of the army and the nation and to exploit their own direct access to the monarch against the "civilian" government. It was to be repeated less vigorously during the army controvery of 1860-1862 and the Bohemian campaign of 1866 and much more vigorously during the First World War.

What underlay this sharp clash? Was it a real conflict between military and political interests that could not be resolved by reason or bridged by compromise? Its objective significance seems to me much smaller than might be judged from the heat of Blücher's fury directed at the *Dispotie der Deplomatiquer.* At bottom the demands from which he would not budge were questions of distinctly second rank. Both the occupation of the strong points and the matter of tribute could be settled only in the larger context of the peace negotiations, i.e., in concert with all the victorious powers.

Evidently this was soon realized by Gneisenau,[23] whom Hardenberg this time shrewdly included in the diplomatic negotiations as the representative of the army. In view of France's extreme war-weariness Blücher and Grolman seem to have exaggerated the importance of occupying the forts, as shown by subsequent developments. The faster peace was concluded, the easier it was to forego such occupation. The tattered army's need for new gear and bonuses was undeniable, but this question too was not of fundamental importance. The tribute to be paid by the French depended in the end more on what could still be squeezed out of the vanquished and exhausted country than on the basic policy decisions that had now to be taken. The first question was whether beaten France was to be treated only as a vanquished enemy or also as a culpable "enemy of mankind." The second question was whether any future dangers threatening from France could be better averted by weakening the country permanently or by concluding durable counteralliances.

The former of these two questions already carries a hint of a recurrent difference of opinion of fundamental importance—the purely agonistic versus the moral approach to political struggle. The agonistic approach presents itself as the most consistent elaboration of power politics along strictly Machiavellian lines. Once it is appreciated that all political activity in the end amounts to hostile forces forever pitting themselves against one another—in other words, to a rival struggle for power, even though often camouflaged by various ideologies —one is tempted to look on these struggles as a kind of wargame, a kind of *agon,* and to do so with intellectual curiosity rather than emotionalism or moralism.

In matters of grand policy the issue is seldom a clear-cut one between right and wrong but quite often one of right against right. To put it more precisely, the vital interests and power drives of one nation conflict with those of another, and the question of who is right is hard to decide, if it can be decided at all.

Even in the heat of battle this insight is unlikely to desert men who are thoroughly imbued with it. It may at times become eclipsed by the passion that motivated the will to victory, but it will resume its hold once the decision has fallen, for magnanimity becomes the victor—the acknowledgment that the enemy too was justified in pursuing his own vital claims. In this way is born an attitude toward war that does not subsist on moral indignation but on the grim determination to stake every effort on the task of achieving a victory deemed to be objectively necessary. It becomes simply a matter of clearing away obstacles in the path of one's own party's vital interests and drive for self-assertion.

No deep insight into the nature of *Realpolitik* is needed to engender such resolution. There is indeed a natural agonistic stance to professional soldiering. This is the ethic of "chivalry," derived from the athletic contests of the early European nobility and handed down to modern standing armies with their officers' corps recruited from the aristocracy. When the professional soldier moves into combat he is merely obeying the command of his liege or warlord. It is not for him to inquire whether the war is just or unjust. He simply offers up his life, ". . . as commanded by law." Others bear the moral and political responsibility. The soldier is merely the instrument, politically blind, so to speak, indeed inwardly neutral, as in the time of the mercenaries. Moving to the front means to evade political discussion with all its torments. No further political decisions need be made. Henceforth all the decisions are military.

Opposed to this professional warrior outlook, its morality objectified so to speak, was the new idea of the politicalized people's host in the time of the uprising. As against the endeavor to isolate the act of fighting from the over-all pattern of life with its loves and hates came now the appeal to honor, patriotism, and love of liberty, coupled with the incitement of deep-seated, instinctive national hatred of the foreign invader. This appeal to the people's pride and covetousness was further deepened, as we have already seen, by efforts to glorify the power struggle by means of moral and religious ideas of many kinds. From the viewpoint of a people's war the old professional armies—including even those of Frederic the Great—were no more than a soulless power machine, and it was precisely their mechanical reflex servility that had to be supplanted by passion and sublime emotional impulses. Soldiers who believe they are fighting for the good cause against absolute evil are likely to regard themselves as instruments of a higher power, called upon to execute the verdict of an absolute justice. Their own thirst for vengeance appears to them as a moral sentiment, and to humble the enemy is no more than an act of just retribution.

Yet this outlook on war was very far from universal even in the Prussian army, which was not at all a "people's army" in the patriot sense but merely a popular levy attached to the hard core of a professional army in the tradition of Frederic the Great. We shall yet hear of the great political and ideological disputes that stemmed from this dual character after the war. We know all too well, after all, that the purely agonistic orientation among professional soldiers has not died out even into our own days.

It could have been no different in the Wars of Liberation. One can sense the code of chivalry of the professional warrior in the order of the day with which General Yorck took leave of his troops on July 4, 1814: "Amid the horrors of a bitterly waged national war, its every step marked by barbarism and devastation, you have proved that the true soldier need not be a stranger to humanity. The testimony of foreign generals and authorities bears eloquent witness to the spirit that prevails among you, guiding your steps toward both glory and humanity."

General von Bülow's protest against the demolition of the Pont de Jéna—which incidentally failed only because of a technical blunder by the engineer officer—breathes the same spirit. It was an act of petty vengeance, he said, out of keeping with the historic grandeur of events.[24] Of the same cast was General von Müffling, Gneisenau's quartermaster general in the campaign of 1814, the very exemplar of a modern general staff officer, splendidly trained in the science of war, living by the highest ideals of objectivity and self-discipline. In the matter of the treatment to be accorded Napoleon he was inwardly altogether on Wellington's side. Appointed governor of Paris at Wellington's request, he ran an administration the fairness and restraint of which were second only to its firmness.[25]

Of even greater interest is the criticism which Clausewitz expressed regarding the attitude of Gneisenau, whom he otherwise so greatly admired. We find more here than merely the professional officer's instinctive demand for strict objectivity and chivalry in war. Confirmed here is the clear and detached insight into the nature of politics as a power struggle which we already know from Clausewitz's writing. It was insight that did not at all weaken the passion of fighting.[26]

Clausewitz flatly posed the question of what political ends were served by the ostentatiously brusque bearing of the Prussians in Paris. Any durable peace, he said, must after all be the end of the war. Blücher was still fighting tooth and nail against surrendering his military authority and in the end almost had to be forced to leave supervision of the business of peace to the diplomats; but Clausewitz wrote as early as July: "My dearest wish is that this epilogue may soon end. For any posture that keeps one's foot on the neck of another runs counter to my sentiments, as does the unending conflict of interests and factions to my reason."

How else, indeed, was peace to be achieved but by recognizing Louis XVIII, getting him to disarm the country and thus "wresting weapons and spirit from the hands of the French nation"? In the light of the experiences at the Congress of Vienna the distaste of Prussian headquarters for the Bourbon court was all too understandable. Yet if its restoration was to be resisted, why allow Louis to return to Paris unopposed? Why above all deeply antagonize the French, the majority of whom also opposed the Bourbons, by pressing for the execution of Napoleon, blowing up his victory monuments, arbitrarily imposing tribute, exacting requisitions, engaging in looting (which was halted only belatedly)? And if there were no practical alternative to restoring the Bourbons, why weaken their authority from the very outset, draw their hostility by acts of violence and provocations of every kind? Were not the soldiers here on the point of committing political blunders no diplomacy could undo? Indeed, had they any clear political goal at all? "The worst of it," Clausewitz wrote his wife, "is that we have sat down between two chairs—we get in bad with the French Government and at one and the same time with the French people. We really don't know what we want." The unsuccessful mining of the Pont de Jéna completed his disaffection: "I think our behavior lacks the nobility that particularly behooves the victor. Indeed in the context of these curious crosscurrents it seems downright clumsy and ridiculous."

Perhaps such sharp self-criticism was exaggerated. As the most active among the victorious powers, Prussia obviously would have had to count on the hostility of France in any event. Yet what we see quite clearly here is the professional soldier's warrior chivalry blended with sober considerations of power politics. It was this particular blend that aroused Clausewitz's admiration for the Duke of Wellington's bearing.[27] What he—far from the center of political decision—overlooked was how sharply England's political interests which determined its generous policy toward France ran counter to the interests of Prussia.

Unlike Prussia, England had not suffered a period of profound humiliation and impotence. Quite the contrary, it was only during the protracted continental wars that England really completed its unprecedented ascent to world power. Small wonder that across the Channel the voice of political wisdom was never drowned out by the kind of elemental hatred that prevailed among the Prussian patriots. All the same, when Wellington opposed the execution of Napoleon, Gneisenau yielded, reluctantly but without much delay. "If they want to exercise histrionic magnanimity," he wrote in some irritation, "I shall not object. I do this from respect for the Duke—and from weakness."[28] Knowing Gneisenau's proud diction, one can scarcely doubt that this lame formulation concealed an admission that he himself was not altogether immune from that warrior chivalry Wellington had invoked. In any event, an open conflict on whether the war was to be ended by victor's fiat or penal justice was thus happily avoided. All the more serious was the controversy over the second problem: how the peace was to be secured.

In this respect Wellington from the outset built all his plans on the return of the Bourbons. The English aristocracy knew very well that its rule was based on the status quo and all in all regarded the legitimate authority of an *ancien régime* in France as the best available warranty of peace, even though this authority had to be artificially restored and would be weak for some time. Hence the English generals had unobtrusively seen to it that the court of Louis XVIII would return to Paris, thus actually anticipating the most important of all political decisions, even before the official diplomatic representatives arrived in Paris.

Yet if the Restoration was to succeed, everything must be done to make the Bourbon return appear to the French in a highly benevolent light. Hence the English clung strictly to their avowed policy that their war was directed against Napoleon and not the French nation. From the moment they set foot on French soil they treated all Frenchmen with Bourbon sympathies as their allies. Their strict discipline and the slower advance of their mercenary army facilitated the careful implementation of this policy, while the Prussian levies, uprooted twice within the year from their own soil, knew only that they were in enemy country, where their savage demeanor soon gave rise to much complaint.

This discrepancy at once affected the peace negotiations. The English felt they were adequately safeguarded against the French danger with the installation of the Kingdom of the Netherlands and the Prussian hold on the Rhineland. They did not wish to see the Bourbon power unnecessarily weakened. Louis XVIII was not to embark on his reign with large cessions of territory. They received support from the Russian czar, who now took on the role of France's protector, hoping thus to gain that country's friendship and secure his rear while carrying out his plans for liberating the Balkans.

Austrian policy was bound to seek to foil these hopes by undertaking its own rapprochement with France. Hence Metternich was no more inclined than he had been the year before to support any demands for Alsace-Lorraine, even though he did now consider certain strategic rectifications of the German and Belgian frontiers necessary. Once again the hopes of the Prussian patriots were bitterly disappointed. Everywhere among the great powers they encountered resistance to their demands that France must cede a deep buffer zone from the French Alps to the English Channel.

The bitter diplomatic struggle lasted for many months. At times Gneisenau actually considered resumption of the war with a turn toward England. Yet all this cannot really be called a renewal of the conflict between politicians and soldiers. For on this central question of the peace treaty, the leading Prussian statesmen, Hardenberg as well as Humboldt, stood shoulder to shoulder with Gneisenau as the representative of the army. So great was the solidarity that Gneisenau urgently advised against Blücher's resignation, since it would weaken Hardenberg's foreign policy position.

Gneisenau inveighed during these months against the diplomats with their "envy, selfishness and weakness," but he expressly exempted Chancellor Hardenberg and Wilhelm von Humboldt.[29] Prussian diplomacy, so often disappointed, had now, it would seem, itself appropriated the militant principles of the patriot party. Or at least it preferred a united front with them, even going so far as to summon Freiherr vom Stein to Paris to lend support, thus directly implicating the patriots in the responsibility for the issue of the diplomatic struggle. Once the czar had refused his aid, that issue could not be in doubt. Stein himself was constrained to offer compromise proposals which, further watered down in France's favor, were embodied in the second Peace of Paris. Germany, the Netherlands, Switzerland, and Savoy got modest border adjustments, but the Congress sought to secure peace in Europe by means of an all-embracing system of alliances among the conservative powers rather than by mutilating the territory of France.

The defects of this four-power system with its monarchial restoration are echoed familiarly in the plaints of a whole century. As Gneisenau foresaw, it survived no longer than half a generation in France: and in the rest of Europe too the makeshift settlement ultimately set off a whole chain of revolutions. It is nevertheless true that on the whole the peace structure created in 1814-1815 was the most durable the West had seen since the peak of the middle ages. Despite the powerful internal tensions that pervaded the countries of Europe, the nineteenth century appears to be by far the most peaceful in recent history and at once the century in which the civilization of Europe underwent its swiftest expansion. It is impossible to doubt that this stemmed from the settlement among the great powers negotiated in Vienna.

5

From Boyen to Roon –
People's Army or Royal Guard?

RESTORATION of legitimist authority, preserving continuity with the social and political situation that prevailed before the Revolution, these were the methods by which monarchs and statesmen of the age of Metternich hoped to protect themselves against new assaults, to secure lasting peace in Europe. This policy at once inevitably reacted on the armed forces. In Austria and most German states conscript armies, essentially resembling the professional armies of the eighteenth century, were instituted. Given a new lease on life, monarchism thought itself safe only behind an army of mercenaries enlisted for long terms, in the style of traditional cabinet politics.

Only in Prussia did it prove possible to salvage something of the spirit of the great popular uprising in the basic outlines of the defense system, as expressed in Boyen's famous Defense Act of 1814. In addition to a standing army this provided for an independently organized territorial force, the *Landwehr,* and it foreclosed the privilege of the propertied classes to buy their way out of serving. Here was the first major effort to bridge the problems inherent in the concept of a modern people's army. From the outset it never proved fully satisfactory, and the more attempts were made to secure improvement the plainer it became that the chasms were very deep indeed.

The struggle to free the soil of the fatherland from foreign tyranny had set in motion undreamed-of forces within the German people. Kindled by preachers of Fichte's and Schleiermacher's stripe, moral and religious sentiment had been injected into the political arena, helping to engender a brand of patriotic faith that seemed to surmount the discrepancy between bourgeois and military ethics. But could this synthesis endure? The great patriotic rising had turned peaceful citizens into pugnacious soldiers, had made the aristocratic career officers forget their arrogant contempt of "commoners" and "riffraff"; but would the impetus survive the humdrum realities of peacetime?

As late as the middle ages peasant and burgher had borne arms as a matter of course, but for centuries absolutism had suppressed this natural militancy, preferring to see wars fought by hired thralls led by professionals. This sharp class segregation of army from people was to revenge itself. No more than the peaceful, nonpolitical attitude of the submissive subject could it be abolished at a single stroke. The reformers had tried to awaken a sense of citizenship and genuine patriotism even in the common man.[1] But could this awareness stay alive when as soon as had peace been concluded, the old class distinctions were again emphasized, reform slowed down, the surviving privileges of the aristocracy zealously preserved?

In point of fact the conflict between citizen and soldier was not a mere accident of history. Stemming from the total incompatibility of two spheres of life, it was as old as time and went to the heart of human nature. The centuries that followed the middle ages had served only to sharpen the discrepancy.

What could be overcome was the burgher's contempt for the lansquenet, the officer's for the philistine—that mutual arrogance of status that had once ruled out all social intercourse, even at the tavern table. What could not be canceled out was the natural difference between the professional ethics of burgher and soldier. Indeed, within a people's army composed of citizen soldiers under professional officers it was bound to come more strongly to the fore.

So long as military and civic responsibilites were neatly divided between different professional groups their incompatibility never leaped to the eye. But this is precisely what it did now that the citizen could be suddenly summoned to the soldier's trade from his peaceful pursuits. Men who are drafted into a modern mass army rather than entering it as professional soldiers have to recast their whole personality, so to speak, must adapt themselves to an utterly different world—different not only in its customs but in its morality.

This is not to say, of course, that the virtues cultivated in the army have no application to peacetime life. On the contrary, punctuality, camaraderie, solidarity, selfless dedication to lofty goals, austere physical self-discipline, a calm and resolute bearing, singlemindedness, pluck, and audacity—all these are manly duties that retain their validity in all circumstances; and scarcely anywhere but in the army can they be cultivated on such a mass scale. The debt modern nations owe this educational process is incalculable. Nevertheless bourgeois and military virtue are so fundamentally different that they give rise to a complex of problems involving the modern mass army to which our forefathers were particularly susceptible. In the first half of the nineteenth century, especially, these problems precipitated a continual series of political struggles.

What is the gist of the difference between citizen and soldier? When the citizen dons the uniform he joins a fighting body pure and simple, wholly dominated by a single limited purpose, to destroy the enemy's will. The army acknowledges the generally accepted laws of morality only to the extent that they do not impede that purpose. As for virtue in general and accomplishment in creative or intellectual fields, these are tolerated only if they actively promote the army cause. Individuality, a man's unique mentality, is esteemed only if compatible with the soldier's calling or subservient to it in some way.

Whatever runs counter to these ends is opposed and suppressed by all possible means, not excluding public humiliation; for the military brotherhood can attain the goal of success in the field only when all its members function as a unit; and since it must insure such singleminded action in all circumstances, it can tolerate individualism in its ranks to but a very limited degree. Even when it allows scope for individual decision, it must make certain that all action will be along uniform lines.[2]

True, the common soldier in the mass army was no longer addressed as "serf" or "bully" or "rapscallion," as the hireling once was in the ranks of Frederic the Great. He was a defender of the land, a patriot in arms for whom the designation "soldier" was to be a title of honor. Yet no army can do without a certain measure of "leveling down" which, while it mainly concerns the outward forms of action, the soldier's "bearing," does not leave the core of the personality quite untouched.

In the lower ranks the individual has no claim to private honor. For him honor means the honor of the group to which he is pledged. Obedience, blind and unquestioning, becomes the soldier's highest virtue, while the rich unfolding of individuality, the basis for all intellectual achievement in civil life, is a trivial and often even irksome matter. What the soldier is called on to do is to carry out his orders without troubling himself about the whys and wherefores, especially in the lowest ranks. Nor is he to ponder the political background, as is the duty of the politically aware citizen. Here such reflection is admissible only if it enhances the fighting spirit.

As we have already seen, the thoroughly trained professional soldier does not really need political enthusiasm in order to do his fighting duty with complete dedication. What he is primarily concerned with is success in the field—political ends preoccupy him, if at all, only as a citizen, not as a soldier. His glory is victory—and more even than victory *virtù,* valor, his skill as a warrior in the test of battle.

Of course courage is not an exclusively military virtue; but it does serve to make plain the peculiarities of the soldier's moral code. The glory of the brave soldier is his contempt of physical danger; and this is a cast of mind that may stem from the noblest resolve of truly highminded men of sovereign spirit. On the other hand, it may also stem from mental and physical qualities that dwell beyond the moral sphere—from thoughtless frivolity to mere dullness of mind and physical insensitivity all the way to insensate fury, vengefulness, and bestiality.

This may serve to explain the curious phenomenon seen particularly after the First World War. Many tested and even heroic front-line veterans displayed a deplorable lack of what Bismarck called "civil courage," something a step beyond mere bravery and "manly bearing," a kind of moral steadfastness of character under pressure, a sense of being borne up by forces that ultimately flow from ethical and religious depths. As one of the leaders in the liberation struggle, Rühle von Lilienstern, put it: "Courage is the soul's clear and ever-present disposition toward freedom in all her forms."

Of course the soldier's valor may stem from such sources as well; and it certainly receives its highest consecration, its deepest roots thence.[3] Yet this does not at all determine its character; for it is in the violent nature of all military action that it involves all of man's resources with little distinction of their kind and origin. In a life-and-death struggle even base instincts of hate and vengeance have a certain military value—even mere pugnacity, trigger-happiness, the primitive greed for booty.[4] The more passionate the combat, the greater the share of such ignoble motivations, the more dubious—from the point of view of bourgeois morality—the educational effect of war on the armed masses which militarists are so fond of stressing.

For if war does indeed awaken man's loftiest virtues it certainly also arouses his crudest instincts. This is the very heart of war's ambivalence, a mere enhancement of the demoniac quality that already resides in all power politics. If we are content to call war a "moral test of nations," with Hegel and Ranke,[5] we must be nonetheless aware that military success as such need not by a long span be proof of moral superiority—else all vanquished nations would have to be accounted morally inferior. All too often pure physical force and superiority tip the balance.

It is true that the patriots viewed the Wars of Liberation as a great national school, war as such as a moral ordeal by fire; but unlike the later orators and publicists of academic nationalism such as Treitschke, they were far too seasoned to ignore the fact that the hour of truth is also the hour of temptation. The people's moral education for peace is tested precisely by the way in which they resist such temptations, the way in which—to speak once again with Rühle von Lilienstern—the savage urges that take shape in war may be curbed.[6]

It is necessary to our purpose that we see all this very clearly, for throughout the nineteenth century the developing relation between war and politics was closely meshed with the problem of the natural discrepancy between civil and military thinking, between the spirit of peace and the spirit of war—the kind of discrepancy that must be bridged in modern mass armies. The tension made itself most strongly felt in the upper strata of the population, especially the educated academic class which had led all others in patriotic zeal during the resurgence.

In the spring of 1813 Ernst Moritz Arndt praised *Landsturm* and *Landwehr* as a renewal of the ancient Germanic concept of a nation in arms. With his friend Steffens he reveled in the anticipation that a true people's war would now be ignited, consigning the standing armies and mercenary hordes of princely despotism to oblivion—"for the good of the world."[7] We see that warlike enthusiasm was quite able to dwell cheek by jowl with bitter hatred of the military "caste spirit"!

Opposition to the old military system was less deeply rooted in the lower population strata who were traditionally liable to serve. Hence most of the Continental governments evaded the whole problem by enabling the propertied classes to buy their way out of serving. Any prosperous young man could get some poor devil to take his place by paying him an indemnity. Of course this was no real solution at all—indeed it amounted to barefaced social injustice; but then, the belief that all classes should be fully equal in the eyes of the law was very far from universal. The educated and propertied middle class still took its privileges as much for granted as the aristocracy once had.

Today, with more than a century of popular military education behind us, it is hard to recapture the distaste with which the hitherto exempted classes contemplated the prospect of having to learn close-order drill in the barrack yard even when war was not imminent. But the mood speaks eloquently from the countless petitions for exemption emanating from the Rhineland as well as the older Prussian provinces.[8] It is also heard in many printed utterances in which the note of selfishness and sloth often sounds insistently in the background.

The most vocal protest came from the extreme southwest of the old Empire, from the idyllic backwater of Breisgau which for centuries had been but rarely presumed on for imperial purposes by the distant government in Vienna. In 1816 the Freiburg professor and pamphleteer Karl von Rotteck published a review under the title of *Standing Armies and National Militias* which mirrors the full gamut of grievances the educated bourgeoisie entertained against the former, those "instruments of despotism" and "breeding-places of venal servility." It accurately reflects French liberal ideas in the age of the Restoration.

Unlike their bourgeois predecessors of the last century, these liberals no longer stood in abject fear of the hired troops of absolute monarchy—their specter was the grenadiers of Napoleon, raised by universal conscription. Written in February, 1815, Rotteck's pamphlet was full of boundless admiration for the achievements of the Prussian Landwehr and the Spanish militia which he compared with the Athenian and Roman host and the *Heerbann* (levies) of the ancient Teutons.

In Rotteck's view deeds of glory throughout history always grew from mass levies of free and militant nations, while hired professional armies were always bent on destruction, conquest, and power for their own sake, without historical staying-power. Recent events had clearly demonstrated to him that modern states "required mighty fighting forces, equal to even the greatest struggle and ready for instant action"; and he took for granted that "every citizen able to bear arms is naturally liable to military service."[9]

But Rotteck also plainly perceived the central problem that would dog the new mass armies in the nineteenth century—was the army to be "civilianized" or the nation militarized? "Shall we turn the very nation into an army or shall we make citizens of our soldiers?"[10] The prospect opened up by Napoleon's policies terrified him—that "all young men growing up shall be called up into the standing army by conscription . . . receiving an education appropriate to that end"; that the whole nation must be militant, "permeated by the sentiments of the hireling, the blind combatant"; that all citizens must "absolve the school of military obedience to the overlords and of military arrogance toward the people . . . [so that] the spirit and principles of military subordination shall enter . . . all branches of the administration." Then shall "the people be controlled and directed like a machine, the state itself coming to resemble an armed camp or a military school. . . . All free and independent life would be extinguished. . . . In the end there would be no government proper, only a system of rule. . . . In such a state war would be the rule . . . war of conquest and oppression, dominated by personal passion, arrogance, and illicit gain. Such are the aims the nation would now serve." Indeed it would soon be infected by its tyrant's predilection for violence, sharing responsibility for his undertakings and becoming an object of hate and loathing abroad. "A single such state—we have seen it by the example of France—can bury a whole continent under corpses and rubble." When other states follow, taking recourse to mass conscription, "the cup of misery runneth over" and the war of all against all is resumed as in the dawn of history, only with a far greater and more terrible mustering of forces than ever before. War with its voracious claims would overshadow all economic and cultural life.

In other words, total mobilization of national life as a consequence of total militarization is already anticipated here,[11] although the liberal country pamphleteer, with no firsthand knowledge of large-scale armies and affairs of state, pictured the consequences with a certain naive pathos, purely from theory. He found the thought fearful that all citizens without distinction should be thrust among the "hirelings" of a standing army. He prophesied the decline of all commerce, art, and science, a "death of the spirit, a hopeless stupor on the Chinese model."

On top of that would come the ruin of family life, children alienated from their parents, army-trained youth in mortal peril of their souls. Averse to settled work, a crude seducer, coarse in manner, a dangerous asocial ruffian, the young man would return from the bullies' camp. Long forgotten are the concepts of civil honor—"the freeman's lofty sense of justice, his love of virtue and avoidance of all evil."[12]

The soldier's honor he has substituted knows nothing but crude courage readily compatible with "immorality, uncouthness, antisocial sentiments, servility and many other hateful qualities." In place of the freeman's dedication to the people's cause he has embraced abject obedience to despotic warlords. In place of the law he worships men. In sum, Rotteck viewed militarism and its standing armies as threatening everything the citizen cherishes, all "his notions of civil society, property, culture, happiness, humanity . . . honor, loyalty, and law-abidingness." In the same breath and with the same hyperbole he praised the ennobling influence of a "national militia."

Only in an army of the people do the soldierly virtues of discipline, honor, and loyalty receive that touch of grandeur and "free idealism." The catchwords with which the radical liberalism to come was to indict the "barrack-room spirit" of professional soldiering are all presaged here. "It is morale that grants the masses victory rather than physical force," a spirit purer, stronger, and fairer than what prevails in the ranks of the "hirelings," the spirit of freedom and selfless love of country rather than of fear and slavish obedience.

These moral impulses count for infinitely more than the "mechanical dexterity" engendered in standing armies. The hireling can be exploited for any purpose, even the most immoral; but unless the people have been "misled by scheming and impassioned demagogues" or oppressed by power-drunk rulers and covetous classes they can seldom be won to any cause but that of justice and especially the defense of their native soil. Never will they go to war to suppress popular freedom. Hired armies are instruments of tyranny while armies of the people are a warrant of freedom.

All this sounds as though the opposition of the Prussian army reformers to the professional forces of the eighteenth century were simply being continued against a South German background and with a distinctly liberalist tinge. Actually such ominous terms as "hireling" and "ruffian" were used to denigrate standing armies of any kind, even the popular levies enlisted for longer terms on the basis of universal service. The pamphlet's propaganda effect, felt into the revolution of 'forty-eight and even into the sixties, rested precisely on this failure to identify the opposition clearly. Anything and everything connected with the military system that bourgeois liberalism found irksome or suspicious could be attacked with such arguments.

Rotteck with almost prophetic vision sensed that total national militarization might some day carry the danger of destroying all the ideals of bourgeois liberal freedom and individualism. Yet how could he dispense with a "standing" army if he was in earnest with his vocal acknowledgment (p. 83) that only a fully armed nation could survive while an unarmed one was bound to be impotent and cowardly?

Well, even Rotteck preferred not to be without a small professional cadre as protection "against suddenly occurring emergencies" and as a nursery for military leaders; and if he was content to have the "municipal authorities" select the mass of militia officers from among "suitable" persons in civilian life, he still wished to see the command positions "preferably" filled with graduates of the military academies. He thus recognized that professionally trained forces were indispensable to a modern mass army. Was it then not a mere technical question how large those forces had to be to match the armies of other great powers?

Even in this earliest reform program we can sense the inherent impotence of the liberal opposition to come, in the face of the technical exigencies of modern armies. There is a floundering effort to camouflage the professional army as a "permanent national defense force," to keep its numbers as low as possible in proportion to the territorial forces. There is no clear picture of the practical needs of the situation. There is the dogmatic statement that the citizen is obligated only to "temporary war service in emergencies, not to permanent soldier's status" (p. 112)—as though there could be any military action to speak of without thorough, continuing training in peacetime! There is apprehension lest the "national militia" as such become a reserve force for the standing army to which it might then lose "the flower of its youth," besides being regarded with suspicion and treated as second-best by the government. Finally there is the fear of the professional soldier's exercise of his civil rights.[13]

In the end Rotteck concluded that a liberal ("republican") constitution was the best protection against the threat of militarization of public life and the coarsening of foreign policy—if only it were possible to organize armaments and wage war on a legal basis, i.e., with the participation of regular representatives of the people.[14] "When a war, in its objectives and origins, is not the nation's cause, then the nation that wages it denies its own meaning. If it does wage such a war, under the ruler's lash, it is no longer a nation but a horde of serfs" (pp. 108-109).

Rotteck's proposal for a militia represents one of the two theoretically possible radical solutions to the problem of organizing a modern mass army: the one in which the greatest possible civilian influence prevails. The alternative, the greatest possible militarization of civilian life, was to be seriously tackled only in the authoritarian mass states of the twentieth century.

Between these two extremes lies the Prussian army system of the nineteenth century, a major effort to reconcile civil and military thinking, people and army—which only in the "total war" of the twentieth century was to fuse into a single unit, at least theoretically. Within this Prussian effort there was to be a major evolutionary phase on its own, from Boyen's popular Landwehr system to the army reform of King William I. This chapter was to alter crucially the whole mutual relation of civil and military thinking, of politics and war.

Rühle von Lilienstern, whom we have already quoted, said that the highest goal of reform patriots of Boyen's stripe was the "fusion of public and private life," a "patriotic union" in which the dead mechanical elements of the power structure would be melted down to give way to a "whole and living nation."[15]

The army reform of 1808-1809 had already taken the first step on this road. It had humanized military service, abolished corporal punishment, encouraged the soldier's self-respect, removed the aristocracy's monopoly of the officers' corps, at least in theory, rooted out ancient administrative abuses—all to the end of changing army service from hated and humiliating servitude into an honorable privilege of free citizens.[16] The defense laws of 1813-1814 with their introduction of universal service and creation of the Landwehr brought the next step. They were meant to solidify the new patriotic spirit of the Wars of Liberation with its loyalty that went beyond the monarch.

Boyen's main concern was to avoid forfeiting this spirit in the drudgery of drill and everyday service. Hence he took care to place his Landwehr as an autonomous formation beside the standing army with its professional officers and its strong core of long-term noncoms, three-year ranks, and re-enlistees. The Landwehr was not meant to be a "national militia" in Rotteck's (and the senior Scharnhorst's) sense but to consist essentially of reservists of the line, i.e., ranks who had served several years and been expertly drilled. It was, in other words, not to be a volunteer army in the style of the Wars of Liberation, but a veteran second phalanx on the Roman model.

Nor was it, on the other hand, intended to be a mere pool of the line reserve, for the purpose of filling up and supplementing the cadres of the standing army in case of need, a mere adjunct of the line and dominated by the line. Instead, the Landwehr, in war as in peace, was to assemble in units of its own, while the line was to take its war reinforcements from the so-called "war reserve," veterans within the first two years after mustering-out, when they were not yet eligible for the Landwehr.

Landwehr battalions were to be trained in less formal fashion, limited to the immediate, practical needs of field service, under their own officers. The annual training period was to be brief, only four weeks for the first levy, a single week for the second, together with voluntary drill on Sunday afternoons. Only a small number of staff officers of the line were assigned to the Landwehr units, with a small cadre of professional noncoms. Almost all the lower-echelon posts of authority fell to elected Landwehr officers, men from civilian life. Boyen was intent upon preventing too many officers and noncoms of the line taking part in line training—indeed he wished to exclude even the Landwehr's own officers as a regular thing.

What seemed all-important to Boyen was to keep the free and easy patriotic spirit that had animated the rising of 1813 from being stifled by the aristocratic caste system and the kind of empty military routine that seemed to survive among the officers despite the work of reform. Among the Landwehr officers patriot zeal, social prestige, and maturity of character were to substitute for whatever was lacking in expert training and experience. All the nation's resources in political idealism, dedication, militancy, and pride in the craft of arms were to be harnessed to its military potential. Yet the claims of the military were not to go beyond reason. The quiet course of civilian life was not to be seriously interfered with, nor was the citizen—especially the educated man—to be pressed overforcefully into the professional soldier's mold.

It was unthinkable for Boyen that educated citizens of repute should be submitted to drill by ignorant and uneducated noncoms or placed under the command of young and immature professional officers. The Landwehr Act of 1815 therefore provided that even completely untrained men could be designated Landwehr officers if only they were locally domiciled and had a respectable income—estate owners, for example. The normal procedure for a young man of good family, however, was to volunteer for one year, the so-called *einjährig-freiwillige Dienst,* which carried many advantages, including preferment in promotion and discharge with an officer's qualifying certificate, which was normally followed by election to Landwehr command.

As we know, this institution survived all the subsequent army reforms, remaining essentially intact into the First World War. In the course of time, however, the one-year service privilege was opened up to broader groups and the training it entailed, handled with great laxity during the early decades, was taken much more seriously. This form of service embodies with particular clarity the propensity for strong civilian influence that is peculiar to Boyen and his army system.

Of course there can be no doubt that the Prussian Defense Act of 1814-1815, while in every detail eminently suited to the needs of its time, would in the long run appear as little more than a half-measure. In the event of a bloody, protracted war the standing army could not possibly manage on two years' reserves to fill up the gaps. The juxtaposition of line and Landwehr was bound to invite wartime integration, which would have to be carefully prepared for in peacetime.

From the outset the weak point in the entire system was the poor military training of the Landwehr and its officers; but these difficulties were aggravated to intolerable proportions by the extreme parsimony Frederic William III's bureaucratic absolutism was obliged to practice, for fear of the competing claims of the estates. Since only a fraction of the pool of young men of arms-bearing age were called up for line service at one time, the Landwehr was largely recruited from nonservice ranks, the so-called Landwehr recruits, who now no longer received military training of any kind. To arm such men and place them under officers who were able to exert little real authority because they themselves were inadequately trained meant to incur real danger in times of political crisis.

All these manifest defects were emphasized time and again by the opponents of the Landwehr system in arguments that lasted over the decades; and there could be no doubt that in the long run it could not possibly meet the technical requirements of modern war. Yet we shall have to guard against overestimating the importance of purely technical matters, at least during the long peaceful pre-1848 period. There was then no real question of progress in weaponry and tactical training, at least in the everyday service of the line.

Indeed, the tenacity with which the army clung to outdated combat forms and parade-ground drill is astonishing. In some instances elite troops were newly created on obsolete Russian models. None of this would have been of the slightest use in a real emergency. Yet every improvement and simplification had to be fought for tooth and nail. [17] On the other hand as long as there were still veterans of 1813-1815 in the ranks the achievements of the Landwehr on occasion drew high praise and recognition even from higher commanders. One thing at least is certain: From the outset political considerations played an important part in the fight against the Landwehr, over and above technical criticisms.

The institution of the Landwehr was one of the reforms deliberately opposed to the absolutist spirit of Frederic the Great and the triple-estate system. The more popular variant of absolutism that developed during the Wars of Liberation had to come to terms with it because it was unable to dispense with the army reinforcements offered by the Landwehr and the one-year volunteers. But with the return of peace these at once drew the distrust of those court circles that sought only to return to the prerevolutionary status as quickly as possible.

The views of the leaders of the reactionary party at the court in Berlin were clear—men like Duke Charles of Mecklenburg, commander of the Guards Corps, and Prince Wittgenstein, minister of police: "To arm a nation means to organize and facilitate rebellion and sedition." They were afraid the new bourgeois liberal spirit within the Landwehr might infect the old royal army of professionals. In peacetime garrison service the aristocratic officer snobs once again looked down on their commoner colleagues who, in their view, were totally lacking in *point d'honneur* and *esprit de corps*. Bad business, having half the army under the command of that lot! And was not the Landwehr the ideal instrument to achieve the political emancipation of the middle class?

There was an all the more intensive and successful effort to reserve the cadet schools exclusively for scions of aristocratic families where officer service was a tradition. The old code of unquestioning loyalty to the king was to be cultivated there, the caste spirit secured by special officers' courts of honor. A further goal was to expand the number of line officers in the Landwehr as much as possible and to keep them under the command of the line army.

A few reactionary hotheads went even further in their wishful thinking. Only two years after the Paris peace treaties, Finance Minister von Bülow offered a plan that would in essence have restored the old army system of Frederic the Great, eliminating only foreign recruitment. Duke Charles of Mecklenburg, the king's brother-in-law and commander of the Guards Corps, backed a similar proposal with the curious argument that the large number of Prussian Landwehr regiments was causing *ombrage* even abroad.

More effectively voiced were his suspicions that a demagogic Jacobin spirit, somehow connected with the young people's patriotic gymnastic movement *(Turnbewegung)*, threatened to prevail in the Landwehr; and that efforts were under way to wrest control over arming the people from the monarch's hands. These reactionary military projects met with no immediate success; but they did help lay the groundwork for the defeat by the reactionary party in the 1819 campaign of major constitutional reforms, when Boyen fell and was replaced by an old-style military bureaucrat. The reactionary tale-bearing about the alleged sins of the Landwehr had deepened the king's already profound distrust.

These suspicions went back a long time to the experiences of the Napoleonic Wars. As early as May, 1806, the patriot party tried to prod the hesitant monarch into accepting their bold and sometimes even reckless policies. And in that same year it had been the fervent petitions of patriotic ministers, princes, and generals that had pushed the king against his better judgment into the daredevil venture of an isolated struggle against Napoleon.

Again, in 1808 and 1811, the heads of the reform circle had urged a repetition of the venture on the king at a time when the situation was far more hopeless, this time with the proposed use of far more dubious and even revolutionary methods. The king never forgot how his official policy of reconciliation had been seriously compromised in 1809 when Major Schill, a member of the Berlin patriot circle and the conspiracy it was hatching, allowed a whole regiment to desert the royal standard and jump the gun in striking out against the French.

He had been wounded even more deeply in 1812 by the many resignations of Prussian officers who declined to support the alliance with France against Russia. And had not the uprising of 1813 begun with the defection from official Prussian policy of that strict monarchist, General Yorck von Wartenburg? Placing arms in the hands of all the people, in the form of an undisciplined Landsturm, had been proposed as early as 1811, only to be rejected by the king as the impractical fancy of addled heads; but during the troubles in the spring of 1813 the political zealots did talk him into such a plan.

He was to rue the concession soon enough. Even during the armistice in July he modified the Landsturm edict in such a way that little was left of the arming of the people except a harmless kind of auxiliary police. The outward occasion was the king's apprehension over the nocturnal rifle salutes fired by the Landsturm men of Charlottenburg to celebrate their beloved sovereign's return to the capital.

Even then the reactionaries at court had been intent on feeding fuel to the king's fear of the Jacobin menace. Berlin professors like Savigny and Eichhorn, later to be ministers under Frederic William IV, were suspected of dangerously seditious views because they were members of the official Landsturm commission. There were countless similar cases. The king's refusal to follow his ablest advisers—with their inspired plans, their moral and political zeal, their thirst for bold action, their limitless faith in the patriotic sentiments of the governed—was dictated sometimes by his fear of revolution, sometimes by his innate common sense.

Considering the sum total of more or less open criticism, some of it quite severe, that poured over this conscientious monarch's head for so many years, his self-control becomes admirable. Some of the carping must have stuck in his throat, but he swallowed it all, for he knew he would need these critical advisers when the showdown came. Indeed, to bind them to his service he was unsparing with gifts and other signs of the royal favor.

Yet the lack of common ground always comes to the surface in the end. When speaking off the record, the king often displayed considerable irritation with Gneisenau. To a British military plenipotentiary he is supposed to have described his general as "a wicked and insolent chap who needs constant watching."[18] We can well believe that much resentment and dislike accumulated on both sides.

The king's antipathy to generals who meddled in politics undoubtedly deepened in the campaigns of 1814 and 1815, which saw such serious clashes between the command of the allied monarchs and the headquarters of the Army of Silesia, to say nothing of the vainglory of Blücher and his staff and the old hussar's crude intervention in matters of high policy. Even Hardenberg well remembered this opposition with a pang and resolved never again to countenance any political meddling by the military. He would never rest, he wrote Gneisenau in March, 1816, "until order, subordination, and obedience are restored within the state."

Beyond question this was a praiseworthy aim. Unfortunately it was instantly exploited by the political reactionaries for their own purposes. Even in 1815 there had been reactionaries at the king's field court who exploited the aged marshal's bluff demeanor to sow the seeds of distrust of the new patriotic spirit. No Prussian officer could conceivably have behaved like that under Frederic the Great! Did not the new patriotic spirit clearly threaten monarchist discipline?

Such worries readily fitted in with the distaste the professional officers, themselves more technically than politically minded, felt for the entry of politics into army affairs. The influential adjutant general, von der Knesebeck, a close friend of Muffling,[19] in October, 1815, expressed this sentiment to the Russian State Councilor Pozzo di Borgo.[20]

The king himself, wrote Knesebeck, was disturbed by the influence wielded in the cabinet by Gneisenau, Grolman, and their sympathizers. He was now determined to smash this faction. The echo from the Russian side consisted of repeated warnings by Czar Alexander to Frederic William to be on his guard against the secret Jacobins among his generals and high officials. Their zealous defense of Prussian territorial claims at the Paris peace negotiations had long been a thorn in the side of Russian policy.

"Gentlemen," the czar is supposed to have said to several of his assembled generals in Paris on one occasion, "it is entirely possible that some day we may have to help the king of Prussia against his own army."[21] As a matter of fact there was a good deal of talk about the Prussian king among the foreign diplomats in Paris. Since both the king and Hardenberg were fond of invoking the temper of their army and nation in their fight against disgorging any of the fruits of victory, gossips insisted the king no longer had firm control over the army.[22] Such voices found a ready echo in Berlin. The notorious denunciation of Professor Schmalz took place even before the second Peace of Paris was concluded, marking the start of a concerted bureaucratically inspired reactionary police campaign against the *Tugenbündler* (members of the clandestine "League of Virtue") and other patriotic societies and alleged Jacobin conspiracies dating from the war.

It is not our concern here to trace the gradual emergence of these tendencies in domestic Prussian politics during the ensuing years of peace—State Chancellor Hardenberg's vacillating and sometimes openly ambiguous stand between moderate reform and absolutist reaction; the influence of the two great powers, Austria and Russia; the sharp shift to the reactionary side after the Congress of Aachen and the Carlsbad conferences. What is important to us is to appreciate the close connection from the outset between the fight against Boyen's Landwehr system and the endeavors of the archconservatives to turn the Prussian army back into a totally nonpolitical instrumentality of the crown, in the sense of the professional army of Frederic the Great.

The reformers themselves sensed this plainly. Even those among them like Clausewitz who remained inwardly cool and critical toward the liberal ideology watched with indignation or dull resignation as the great idealist sweep of the rebellion was being stifled by a whole platoon of petty nonentities, skulking incompetents, and selfish climbers.[23]

The fateful year in which things went against all the political and constitutional plans of the reformers was, as we have seen, the year 1819. There can be little doubt that the stronger dynamics, the greater faith in Prussia's future, lay on the side of Humboldt, Boyen, Grolman, Gneisenau, Stein, and their sympathizers; but what prevailed was the group around Wittgenstein, Schuckmann, Kircheisen, Kamptz, Ancillon, and Duke Charles of Mecklenburg. It was no accident that this group included the same men who in the years of Napoleonic rule had always counseled in favor of pusillanimity.

One result of their triumph was that within the Prussian aristocracy too the living traditional forces of Prussian self-assertion and German nationalism, as represented for example by Marwitz, lost out. Instead, a cautious kind of legitimism gained ground, an archconservative adherence to the still very respectable remnants of latifundian authority in the countryside, the aristocratic privileges of officers, a provincial family tree, the corporative social order of yore—traditions all that conflicted with universal military service. At home and abroad Prussia was pushed into a state of suspended animation and stagnation which had a disastrous effect on military organization as well. A pinch-pocket policy paralyzed all technical advance, while failure to utilize the draft fully only served to deepen the Landwehr's deficiencies.

Most important of all, the Landwehr lost its original purpose. It was meant as the defense organization of a people who were to participate in the work of public administration and legislation by means of constitutional bodies at the local, regional, and national level, as provided by the famous Constitutional Pledge of May 22, 1815. These organs of self-government were to educate the people to patriotic dedication and voluntary service for the public good, which were to be the moral foundation of the Landwehr as well, the ultimate ideal of its educational work.

The free citizen's political awareness was to be matched by the military zeal of the Landwehr volunteer. That was the reason why the various Landwehr battalions were organized to coincide with provincial districts, while its veterans enjoyed preference for certain posts in the local administration. Every village had its public notice-board identifying not only the township and county to which it belonged but also the Landwehr regiment and battalion, right down to the local company.

There are, of course, always great difficulties in the way of constitutional reform. It would be better if such reforms were the result of reason and insight on the part of enlightened statesmen rather than pressure of public opinion and insistent demand by the people. As it was, the initiators of the reform had to strike a mean between traditional corporate and modern liberal ideas. And when the reform efforts came to nought and the old bureaucratic absolutism with its sharp contrasts between subjects and rulers re-emerged, the institution of the Landwehr appeared increasingly as a curious foreign object within the body politic, a mere relic of the past.[24] The libertarian sentiments that had given it birth, intending it to play a constructive part in the life of the country, were shunted aside into a fruitless policy of opposition. Steadily deepening, especially during the forties, this opposition engendered more and more political doubt as to the arming of a poorly disciplined popular levy in the style of the Landwehr.

This vicious circle could have been broken only by military and constitutional reform. On the one hand, such reforms would have turned the whole army into an integrated, disciplined, and technically competent instrumentality of the crown; and on the other hand the reforms would have set worthy new goals enabling Prussian policy to revive and exploit for national ends the great moral resources that had first been tapped in the Wars of Liberation. These forces needed to be harnessed rather than forever suppressed. That meant newer and freer constitutional instrumentalities to make possible a rapprochement between government and people and turn the old bureaucratic dictatorial state into a modern mass state at every level of administration.

This is a long road to travel, seldom traversed without the impelling force of severe upheavals. Bismarck, for example, did manage in his own way to tackle and solve the problems of German foreign policy. Yet even he was never quite able to bridge the chasm between government and people that had opened up in the years before 1848 and again in the wave of reaction during the fifties. The Reich that he created was far more the work of monarchial government than of the people, even though it was so designed that a total national German entity swiftly grew from the many component parts. And the army by means of which this way was cleared departed in its whole structure from the ideals of the patriots of 1813. It had meanwhile again become much more a royal than a people's army, depending to a far greater extent on technical training and discipline than on patriotic fervor—though such sentiments were still destined to play a clear-cut and strictly disciplined part. The creator of this royal mass army was King William I.

Even in Prince William's earliest military writings the major issue is the maintenance of the three-year term of service for all foot soldiers, and certainly this was uppermost in their author's mind. For decades, in countless meetings, memorials, petitions, and edicts, both as prince and king, he pressed this point again and again with the greatest determination, often against all the military experts concerned, heedless of financial difficulties and of the important objection repeatedly made that a long term of service reduced the number of trained reserves while a short term increased them.

We know that Roon, and even Bismarck himself, were not prepared to offer serious technical objections to a term of two or even two-and-a-half years, such as had been in force from 1834 to 1856 and was to be reintroduced in 1893. Such a concession might well have avoided the great army and constitutional crisis of the sixties. But the king's stubborn opposition made that impossible. He said he would rather abdicate than make the slightest concession on this point.[25]

What was the reason for this inflexible, not to say unreasonable attitude? It was rooted in a very particular concept of the soldier's status dating back to the traditions of Frederic the Great and quite foreign to the spirit of the great rising. What mattered most to the prince and king was to remove the recruit as far as possible from his wonted civilian life, to make him a soldier body and soul, so to speak. He was not merely to be well-drilled and thoroughly trained—a few months were enough for that. He was to absorb the spirit of professional soldiering for life. The business of being a soldier was not to be regarded as merely a passing thing, to be finished as soon as possible. No, the peculiar "soldier's estate" was to be looked on as something that endured throughout life. The soldier was to become so deeply immersed in active service that he would be reluctant to tear himself away from it and prefer to re-enlist.

William had come to think of himself entirely as a professional soldier, and he wanted every man who was called up to feel the same way. He had acquired his military knowledge conscientiously, but also slowly; and he concluded that his men would also need much time to adjust themselves. In his view any shortening of the three-year term, even if only by a matter of months, would only help drive out of the army the true military spirit, the "essence of soldiering in its totality." There would then be "not soldiers, only drilled peasants."

The prince was quite unmoved when experienced and practical military men objected that overlong garrison service in peacetime blunted rather than fostered morale, that third-year men were not necessarily always the best soldiers, and that those who re-enlisted were commonly men who were unable to get on in civilian life, often coarse and disreputable types who were anything but models for the new recruits. William thought he could inculcate his own enthusiasm for things military in all soldiers by thorough training. He stubbornly insisted that candidates for noncoms could be expected in sufficient number and quality only if the term of service were kept long. He was even less impressed by the arguments of senior generals like Boyen and Grolman who still lived in the traditions of the Wars of Liberation and who expected much more from the patriotic fervor kindled by a great war than from long military habituation in peacetime. Boyen's notions about the Landwehr had begun to baffle him long before the unhappy experiences of 1848-1849.

"The Landwehr must drill," he wrote in 1841. "It must learn to use its weapons and move in the field like the line army from which it has learned such skills. What this means above all is obedience, discipline, and subordination. We must stick to these *cardinal virtues of the soldier.* Every patriot must know this by rote. To encourage the idea among the Landwehr that its members are to be treated differently under arms from the soldiers of the line marks the first step toward a revolutionary force."[26]

The contrast between Prince William and Boyen is sharp. It is primarily the difference between a professional soldier thinking in purely military terms and a political idealist who put patriotism above drill, voluntary commitment above conditioned reflexes. Boyen was evidently unable to envisage any kind of military morale stemming from coercion. He expressly rejected a purely technical approach to military questions: "They cannot be settled by tactical or so-called service considerations which on the contrary must be entirely subservient to higher considerations. Not even strategy is the sole authority—it must enter into a close and equitable association with politics and diplomacy and with them seek out the best possible result in a given situation."

This was especially true in the matter of integrating the Landwehr with the army of the line. The need for such integration "would have to be demonstrated by considerations of military and civil law and of political life rather than by abrupt demands put forward on the drill-ground in peacetime."[27] Such reasoning must have remained totally incomprehensible to a military man of Prince William's character.

It would be wrong, however, to dwell too one-sidedly on the purely military aspects of his thinking, which early displayed political motives as well. As early as 1832 he supported the need for a three-year term with the argument that only an army indoctrinated with the proper soldierly spirit could protect the throne against "the tendencies of the revolutionary or liberal party in Europe. . . . Discipline, blind obedience, come into being and endure only by long habituation and require a longer term of service so that the monarch can count on his troops in the hour of danger. It is precisely this blind obedience that the revolutionaries find most troublesome." That was why parliaments everywhere were seeking to curtail military budgets and terms of service.

To these political views too William clung tenaciously and without change. Traditional monarchism was under constant threat from revolutionary mass movements. A dependable and thoroughly disciplined Praetorian guard enlisted for long terms, locking ruler and people in a kind of latent state of war, constituted the monarchist answer to the new liberal radicalism with its dualistic concept of the state. Toward the end of the Restoration rulers had become uncertain of the loyalty of the masses, and monarchism itself was rapidly fading in popularity among the ruled.

The aftermath on German soil of the July revolution in Paris did its part to extinguish the spirit of the time of the rebellion. Prince William's political sentiments were profoundly molded by these events, the first major experience of his maturity, and his attitude was quite different from that of the reactionaries who had prevailed in the crisis of 1819. It never occurred to William to go back to the time before the Defense Act of 1814, i.e., to limit universal military service. On the contrary, he wanted to see it fully realized. Nor did he wish to restore the professional army of the *ancien régime* or have the army's striking power reduced by petty economies.

Indeed William was inspired far more than the archconservative bureaucrats at his father's court had been by ambition appropriate to a great power, by pride in the great traditions of Frederic the Great. He did not share the romantic legitimism of his brother the Crown Prince, subsequently King Frederic William IV, and the aristocrats in league with him. Despite his obvious fondness for the Prussian military aristocracy he would never have supported the selfish interests of the aristocratic class as such.

Yet he was far more out of sympathy with the liberal ideas of his time. At the heart of his political convictions was his sense of duty as a Prussian Guards officer who knew himself to be destined to defend the crown's traditional rights and prerogatives against all enemies, within and without, and who at bottom viewed parliamentary life as a source of disorder and upheaval, or at least as a factor that limited the crown's freedom of action.[28]

The only thing that changed under the impact of the bitter experiences of 1848 was that Prince William adopted a strictly legalistic approach and decided to accept the altered constitutional situation. This put him at odds with the reactionary trend of his brother and his brother's romantic friends. But while he thus slid into a kind of political opposition, further enhanced by his wife, a member of the Saxe-Weimar dynasty, and even became the hope of the liberals in 1858, his views on defense policy not only were not softened by the experiences of 1848 but actually stiffened, in the sense of the old absolutist traditions.

The revolutionary years after 1848 were epoch-making for the development of the German army system and coincidentally for the relation of military and political thought. They saw the climax and at once the failure of the many efforts by the older German liberalism to fuse army and people into one, to civilianize or replace with militias the traditionalist and monarchist troops of the German courts.[29]

None of the efforts in this direction succeeded. Having the troops swear allegiance to the constitution, first introduced in the Electorate of Hesse in 1831, merely led to painful conflicts of conscience among the officers when there were disputes between crown and parliament. Above all it tended to create military and even political disorder, for the execution of military orders was made dependent on prior scrutiny of their legality by totally unqualified people, the local troop commanders. An intangible element, written constitutional law, was interposed between the government and its executive organs. To arm the German people as a whole, as decreed by the Frankfurt parliament, organ of the great revolutionary movement of 1848, was a project beyond realization against the will of the various petty monarchist governments.

Similarly, having the troops of the several states swear allegiance to the provisional Imperial Vicar *(Reichsverweser)*, Archduke Johann, failed. The archduke remained in effect without power, as did the Frankfurt national assembly and the popular movement behind it, once the monarchist governments had put aside their vague fear of revolution. The citizens' militias that came into being everywhere failed to acquit themselves effectively, either against revolutionary uprisings in the street or against the regular troops of the monarchist-absolutist reaction. Indeed in many places they served as caricatures of what a modern force should be like.

An even unhappier fate awaited the efforts to substitute looser semiparliamentary forms of military organization for blind obedience: election of officers, soldiers' councils, relaxation of compulsory saluting, political education, exercise of civil rights, etc. This brought on profound demoralization, most acutely in Baden where there was a second and completely chaotic revolution by mutinying soldiers.

The great and hopeful uprising, welcomed with loud cheers by the best minds of Germany, ended in resignation and despair. This was also the fate of the idea of a true people's army, a force that was to be something more than a politically deaf-and-dumb bulwark for special dynastic interests, a national militia in which the spirit of the Wars of Liberation was to be reincarnated. Had it not now been clearly demonstrated that political libertarianism was worthless as a basis for military organization; that everything depended on the strict discipline, subordination, and technical skill of the troops; indeed that the domination of a modern army by political and civilian influences meant its virtual dissolution?

Such at any rate was the interpretation placed on his own experiences by Prince William, who had had to lead Prussian troops to Baden to put down the disorders there. He merely found confirmation of the defense policies he had always supported. The inglorious Baden campaign brought to light a number of deficiencies in the Prussian army—defects in leadership as well as organization. The inadequacies of Prussian army organization were even more glaringly highlighted during the mobilization of 1850, which ended with the diplomatic defeat at the conference of Olmütz.

Of all the things in need of improvement the most important to Prince William was to extend the term of service and to integrate the Landwehr completely with the standing army. It was the Landwehr's unfortunate organization and defective training that in his view bore the principal blame for the Prussian army's weakness in the crucial year 1850. True, as a fighting force it had by and large carried itself surprisingly well in putting down revolutionary riots. Despite the widespread political upheavals it had proved possible to call up and commit the Landwehr as reinforcements for the household brigades. The very militiamen who had but recently taken part in street demonstrations and disorders by the liberal democrats could be actually mobilized to put down insurrection, could be sent to fight a civil war under their own civilian officers. These were certainly extraordinary facts, and thoughtful officers pondered them.[30]

It became clear for the first time that in a modern army based on universal military service the attitude of the leaders is far more important than the political sentiments of the ranks. Up to a certain point iron military discipline could forge even reluctant elements into a useful instrument of war, so long as the loyalty—or at least the docility—of the ranks was not in question, which has always been true hitherto in Germany.

This realization, running counter to the ideas of the patriots of 1813, must have taken many liberals by surprise. It seemed to be a fact that Landwehr officers simply did not look on themselves as "officers of the people." As one of them later admitted in the Prussian diet, they "accounted it an honor to be officers of His Majesty the King."[31] They sought to emulate their colleagues of the line.

Even in 1848, therefore, the Prussian Landwehr never turned into a citizens', let alone a people's, militia. Yet its mobilization was not always unexceptionable. On occasion there was insubordination and disorder, and some Landwehr depots were even plundered.[32] In the Baden campaign of 1849 some Landwehr battalions turned tail under fire or were reluctant to march.

In the end such instances decided the issue. If the Landwehr were to be as reliable an instrument as the line army, its complete fusion with the standing army was essential. The reform efforts of the fifties never having gone beyond mere patchwork, this fusion became a key element in the great army reforms with which William I began his reign as prince regent and king.

The concept of the soldier's place, on which these reforms subsisted and which drew so much liberal distrust from the outset, goes back to the firm traditions of the Prussian officers' corps of Frederic the Great's time. Its essential outlines are found in Rudloff, whose handbook points back to still earlier predecessors.[33]

The army is here represented as a separate "military institution," the military profession as a special estate, entered by virtue of the oath of loyalty which at the same time surrenders certain civil rights. The entire inner workings of the army depend on unconditional subordination. All independent judgment by lower echelons on the morality, efficiency, and legality of orders is excluded, except for certain unusual and borderline cases affecting only higher officers.[34] Absolute loyalty to the king and absolute obedience to his orders, whether issued directly or through others, are the heart of the soldier's duties. He continues to belong to civil life only through a part of his private affairs, and none of his civil commitments may serve as a barrier to his absolute military loyalty and obedience.

Even the soldier's own honor is expressly subordinated to these duties. Indeed his personal honor is nothing more than the moral need to acquire the respect of others, especially his superiors, through the punctual fulfillment of his duties. It no longer bears any resemblance to the patriotic national pride of the freedom fighter, as idealistically portrayed by Ernst Moritz Arndt. It is more a matter of sharing in the honor of the unit which is proud of its brave soldiers whom it virtually owns.

Nevertheless, in contrast to the time of Frederic the Great there was now such a thing as the honor of a simple soldier, not merely of an officer, for soldiering had become an "honorable profession." There was even mention of the "duty to love one's country," placed immediately beside loyalty and obedience to the king. Yet like "love of honor" and "awareness of religious duty" it appears as no more than a desirable adjunct to the cultivation of military zeal, carefully nurtured by the army. It is not among the special characteristics of the soldier's estate, nor does it entitle the individual to any special respect.

Clearly the civil rights of political criticism and free expression of opinion do not apply to the soldier. It is part and parcel of military discipline that everything is kept away that might possibly "interfere with sentiments of true allegiance to king and fatherland."

This sharp separation of the "military institution" and the "soldier's estate" from the general bonds of society accorded precisely with the strict royalist sentiments of the officers' corps, still drawn preponderantly from the aristocracy.[35] The army was to represent the power of order within a bourgeois society threatened with disorder. In consequence it had to remain free of civilian ties and considerations and of political tendencies. Citizen officers could not be expected to have this freedom, only officers of the king—thus ran the argument of those who defended the old Prussian service regulations in print against the liberal trends of the times.

The "high morale" of an army, we read as early as 1831, is not at all dependent on its conviction that it is fighting for a good cause but solely on the state of its discipline. "Otherwise the army would have to resolve whether the fight be just, needful, and inescapable, in truth an absurd demand."[36] The gulf that separates this view from that of the reformers of 1808-1813 could scarcely be thrown into bolder relief. In the view of the liberals this sundering of the army from the people destroyed all the resources of militant patriotism which the rising of 1813 had mobilized within the people, replacing them once again with the "soulless machine" of the old power structure of Frederic the Great.

But the experiences of 1848 could not be glossed over. They turned into the strongest support for the traditional Prussian military view. The liberal campaign against the army's isolation as a "state within the state" was as fruitless as was the opposition to the "aristocracy of the sword" with its caste spirit and the support for a policy of imbuing the army with constitutional sympathies. The danger of·army demoralization through the spread of liberal ideas had become all too plain and even liberal-minded officers found themselves unable to outline a feasible policy by means of which discipline and libertarianism might have been reconciled within the army.

It is against this background that we come to understand Roon's stand in his famous reform memorial of July 21, 1858, with which he gained King William's confidence for life.[37] True, there is talk in this document of the "militant spirit of the people" which Prussia's monarchs had wisely used to gain for their state "seat and voice in the Areopagus of great powers that judges the destiny of nations, being ordained to shape and guide the growth and evolution of man's moral life under God's law."

Prussia's claim to be a great power is here artlessly equated with "man's moral life," with "mankind's highest and noblest interests"; but we listen in vain for any true note of nationalist enthusiasm. To this professional officer the notion of a people's army à la 1813 was a mere snare and delusion. "The Landwehr was no more than a stopgap. Its practical achievements in the field were for the most part grossly overestimated. Yet this overestimate left its mark, as did the after-dinner speeches and the phrasemongering of journalists in that spirited and overstimulated time. They spread the wrong idea that a nation in arms was irresistible, and thus what was a makeshift became the cornerstone of a whole system."

Among the reasons advanced for discontinuing that system, political arguments are now given pride of place. "The institution of the Landwehr is politically unwise, for it fails to impress other countries and is of doubtful significance to foreign as to domestic affairs." It contributes toward the government not being master in its own house since it must take account of the mood of the armed people at every step. "Its very existence ties the government's hands in some measure, makes it weak where the country's interests require that it be strong, hesitant where it should be prompt and resolute."

These militias of doubtful docility make the government dependent on the shifting winds of public opinion, while Prussia in its ever-exposed position needed the greatest freedom of action for its leadership. Particularly in a constitutional state where every Landwehr man was also a voter, "encouraged and entitled to use not only his arm but his tongue as well," the Landwehr represented a constant danger. The corporative Landwehr constitution threatened the principle that "the armed forces do not think, they merely act." The Landwehr man lacked the "firm and proper spirit of a soldier. . . . He feels himself to be a citizen, the head of a family. He is acquisitive on his own behalf and that of his family. His mind and his ambitions are all turned toward civilian goals." His military status is merely an irksome interruption; even in uniform he asserts his civil rights and interests as far as possible. "For the Landwehr man is not really a soldier. True, he has learned the military trade to some degree, but he pines for his fields, his tools, his lasts—his home rather than the flag of his country."

When military discipline failed one could of course appeal "to good will and patriotic sentiments—which in some instances were purely theoretical. . . . But the impotence of these moral factors is subject to the kind of doubt spotlighted by the experience of 1849." To imagine that in time of danger patriotic fervor could make up for the deficiencies of the armed forces shown up during the dreary revolutionary troubles of 1849 was the most dangerous kind of delusion. "Apart from the very special mood and situation during the Wars of Liberation" there was no real indication whatever that the Landwehr "would give a good account of itself in the hour of decision." Of course patriotic fervor could have a very useful effect; but it would be foolish to try to erect a military system on such a basis. "A sound and proper organization must always be capable of being inspired by patriotism, to whatever degree, but it cannot be based on such enhancement." Moral factors of that description develop as a matter of course in great armies—like those of Frederic the Great and Napoleon. "Solidarity and honor, loyalty and dedication to the leader's person all act in that direction, but they are effects caused not by the wording of the mobilization order but rather by common deeds, dangers and sufferings, mutual esteem, confidence earned and returned." The one indispensable foundation for all greatness in war was discipline.

The goal of this entire exposition can be summed up in a single phrase— complete "decivilianization" of the army. It became one of the main goals if not the main goal of William I's great army reform—in addition to modernized and tightened organization, large line cadres with more officers and noncoms provided, better utilization of universal services and accelerated mobilization. We know today that its basic elements—which then took the public by surprise, often to the extent of alarm—had been ripening for a decade. Although there was still much controversy over details, the essential thoughts were shared by the leading men in the Prussian army.[38]

Still, there were a few generals by 1859—men like Bonin, Steinmetz, and Prince Radziwill—who entertained reservations concerning the radical elimination of the Landwehr, whether for political considerations or because they clung to a venerable tradition; but there was general agreement that the Landwehr stood in need of reform and would have to lose its character as a militia. A new generation of officers had grown up in the long peaceful decades. More objective than the reformers of 1813, strangers to the political idealism of that age, they were much more narrowly specialized in their training. They knew thoroughly what they were supposed to know and did their work with punctilio. They were well trained in practical troop leadership, and their monarchist sentiments seemed to increase in the degree that liberalism attacked the "military caste system" and the "spirit of servitude."

Fully half of the officer replacements had come from the military academies (where Roon himself had been educated). More than nine of every ten general officers came from the nobility. Beside this replenishment from families of officers, especially the rural nobility with its military tradition, the sons of upper middle-class families scarcely figured in most of the regiments. All this resulted in an officers' corps of great homogeneity and firm traditions.[39] The political ideology to which these officers adhered was sharply at odds with the bourgeois thinking of the liberal age. It was precisely this isolation from civil life, this sharply marked military caste spirit, that was materially enhanced by the reform law of 1860.

One of its main effects was to reorganize the younger Landwehr classes as a mere war reserve for the line army, thus all but eliminating the influence of the civilian Landwehr officers. The large increase in scheduled officers and noncoms in the standing army moved in the same direction. This gave the professional soldiers far greater weight, lending new glamour to a profession that had long suffered from slow promotion. As a natural consequence more cadet schools and advanced military academies were established. Roon's memorial of 1858 therefore advocated restoring the cadet corps in its original sense—as a privilege for the sons of indigent officers and the impoverished nobility. This would have expressly defeated all the earlier reform efforts, initiated as early as Boyen's time, which aimed at undermining aristocratic privilege and the caste spirit of the cadet corps and putting in their place a claim to universal education by the middle class, in the sense of the reformers of 1813.

Roon's argument was that his plan would relieve the economic straits of many officer families. But was the inevitably resulting debarment of the middle class from supplying officer candidates really in the proper interest of the officer class? Was it wise, further, to deepen the gulf that separated officers from the social and intellectual life of the nation rather than to seek to bridge it in time? In the face of the inner estrangement between popular democracy and aristocratic caste spirit, presaged as early as the restoration era, some German military writers had long since recommended establishing a common ground for officers and bourgeoisie by encouraging the former to take a greater interest in the nation's cultural heritage. This, they argued, might well be useful in holding the new industrial proletariat in check.[40]

But these ideas made little impression. Indeed, in the face of the anti-intellectualism of many of the young officers—and some of the older generals as well—the Prussian military authorities were hard put to maintain an acceptable academic level at the military schools. In the literary remains of Prussian generals from the age of the creation of the Reich, little is left of that spirit of universal humanist culture that speaks to us from the letters and writings of men like Gneisenau, Boyen, and Clausewitz.

It is true of course that the semibarbaric swashbuckler's spirit that endured from the time of Frederic the Great into that of Blücher also virtually disappeared. The Prussian army, moreover, was always graced by a few general officers of high intellectual stature, men who dabbled in science and literature as well. In literary sophistication Moltke, Griesheim, and Roon rose high above the average.[41] Over-all the average level of education had indeed probably risen a good deal from the early years of the century, owing to the comprehensive military school system.

But this education had grown more highly specialized. It was more sharply oriented along technical lines. Expert training had begun to supplant the mere intuition of great minds. The spirit of the age of positivism was noticeable in the army too, especially since there had been a steep rise in the challenge to military skill and technical knowledge, in the intensity of troop field training. When the liberal opposition argued that the cadet schools encouraged narrow specialization, Roon replied that it was this very element rather than generalized training that provided the élan that was necessarily the goal of professional military education.[42]

This was the kind of reply to be expected of a modern realist concerned above all with the exercise of power. As a professional group the officers were far too inbred to worry about any gaps in their education. Nor were they impressed by the bourgeois worship of culture. Far from showing any inclination to absorb any of that culture, the army regarded itself as the nation's schoolmaster. For a man like Roon the goal of the officers' corps was not to win the respect of other classes by the level of its own culture but rather to drive home the lessons of the army to a misguided nation. What mattered now was to turn raw and uncouth recruits into clean and tidy soldiers of fine bearing, above all to inculcate in them unswerving loyalty to the king, to counteract the "deviations" of the age of liberalism.[43]

Commenting on Roon's memorial of 1858, Bonin, the war minister, argued that such reforms would only serve to alienate the army altogether from the people who would again become indifferent, as they had been prior to 1806. Roon probably did not even understand what Bonin meant. The army he and King William sought to create was not to be a professional army at all, as the Prussian army had been before 1806. It was to be a true people's army, an army based on consistently enforced universal service. Far from being alienated from the people, this army was to be a great national school in which the officer would be an educator in the grand style, a shaper of the people's mind. In response to the liberal argument that the new army without the Landwehr would not be a truly popular force, Roon could point to the unswerving monarchist loyalty of the rural population, which was his main reliance as it was Bismarck's, after the experience of 1848.

It is true that this army spirit was basically detested by bourgeois culture; but the tiny educated class no longer played a decisive role in realistic power politics. The reformers of 1813 had still viewed the educated as the proper exponents of the new political spirit, of the great national regeneration, and had sought to base their new state on the voluntary dedication of the intellectuals; but ideas had changed since the events of 1830 and 1848. What had been particularly clear since that time was that the educated class was practically powerless, both against revolution from the bottom and reaction from the top; and since that time the institution of the Landwehr too, with its softened terms of service, seemed to have become largely irrelevant.

Indeed, universal military service was now so completely accepted that the "iron screws" of war discipline (as Roon put it) could be confidently tightened a few turns without causing too much popular outcry. After all, the institution of one-year voluntary service for educated youths was preserved! Thus the hazard could be risked of blending the Landwehr into a royal mass army which was no longer (or at least to a far smaller degree) tailored to civilian needs while it regarded itself at the same time as an instrument of national education—even in political respects!

In the total context of our theme all this heralds a new era, indeed an almost complete reversal of the relation between military and political command. If the Landwehr of 1814 had meant a partial civilianization of the army, the royal mass army of 1860 already displayed a marked inclination toward militarization of the whole nation. Once upon a time the generals had taken pains to adapt the army organization to civilian thinking. Now they not only defied "bourgeois prejudice"—they went about the task of extirpating it by methodical military indoctrination of the people.

This was not accomplished without a bitter struggle. It led to the gravest domestic political crisis in the entire history of Prussia. The conflict went much deeper than might be judged from the parliamentary controversy that occupied the limelight. Indeed, the basic conflict was between bourgeois politics and the military approach. What was at issue was the very nature of the Prussian state—whether it was to be a state of soldiers and war or one of citizens and law. The constitutional crisis that lasted from 1862 to 1866 was in essence Prussia's second great conflict between war and politics.

6

The Army Controversy
of 1860-1862 and Its
Historical Consequences

THERE CAN be no doubt whatever that the liberal opposition to King William's army reform stemmed somehow from bourgeois instincts. Yet it becomes difficult to fathom its ultimate motives with any degree of precision. Almost from the beginning the objective discussion of problems of military organization was affected by partisan (i.e., power) politics which soon swallowed up everything else. Furthermore, the attitude of the Prussian liberals in these military questions was inherently ambivalent, uncertain, and often obscure. Nearly all their leaders had passed through the school of the Prussian army themselves. Except for the dogmatic revolutionaries of 1848, they were all in some measure influenced by the hard facts that dictated a rejection of the ideals of the old Landwehr, the pure people's army. Since they favored Prussian hegemony over Germany—although they differed on the way this was to be achieved—they scarcely had any choice but to approve any enhancement of Prussian—that is to say royal Prussian—armed might, so long as this was even reasonably compatible with their libertarian ideals. Above all, since every effort at liberal army organization, at civilianizing the royal army, had utterly failed in 1848-1849, they had no positive alternatives left with which to oppose the government bill with any real hope of success. It is indeed far easier to say what they were against than to define whatever ideal army system they may have favored.

This is particularly true of the so-called Old Liberals, the moderate center party which had been rescued from its opposition role by William's change of course in October, 1858, when he became prince regent. Henceforth they were to make every effort to demonstrate their fitness as a government party by loyal support of the so-called "New Era" cabinet. The Old Liberals, under the leadership of Georg von Vincke, were the group that initially set the tone in the chamber of deputies. Only with the sharpening controversies after 1861 did the radicals, the democrats of 1848, again find an echo. Their running opposition speeches (by such men as Waldeck or Schultze-Delitzsch) do not offer anything of more than passing historical interest regarding criticism of the army reform. In essence all they did was to reiterate the old suspicions of the standing army, with which we are familiar from Rotteck and which had erupted everywhere in the 1848 revolution.

The conservatives and reactionaries used the trick of lumping both liberal wings together into an undifferentiated whole,[1] and in this way they succeeded in encouraging the prince regent's suspicions of the Old Liberals. Actually the differences between the two wings extended far beyond the tactical sphere. They were rooted in essential principles, in the whole concept of the state. Any unprejudiced study of Old Liberal speeches in the diet, of letters and confidential utterances, will make that plain. There can be no question here of basic hostility to the military as such, of distrust of a standing army in general. But since opposition to Roon's army bill did originally issue from the Old Liberal side, with the practical effect of utterly destroying their political chances as a government party, the question of the inherent nature of their opposition becomes all the more pertinent.

To answer it we shall have to turn principally to the earliest expressions of objective criticism of a political and military character, elicited after 1859 by William's efforts at reform, before later political resentments and disappointments muddied the waters. It becomes quite plain that the principal concern was for the preservation of the popular institution of the Landwehr as an autonomous army formation. We first hear of this in April, 1859, when the constitutional hopes of the Old Liberals were still in their prime. Freiherr Karl von Vincke-Oblendorf,[2] reporting for the committee on the army budget, moved that this budget be approved uncut and without debate. He praised the government for its wisdom and prudence in having increased military expenditures from 1850 to 1859 by only 4 percent (from 42 to 46.6) of the total government budget. The committee was also prepared to pass the 409 additional company and squadron commanders for the Landwehr which the government wanted, with the proviso, however, that "no further change in the Landwehr system would be effected without legislative authorization."

Georg von Vincke, parliamentary leader of the Old Liberals, regarded this as an uncalled-for expression of no confidence. So far there had been only rumors about government intentions to change the character of the Landwehr, to turn it into a mere army reserve and more or less merge it with the army of the line. Of course, should these rumors be proved true, it would mean the destruction of cherished historical memories, of the "shield of Prussian liberty." Only experts were qualified to judge the military merits of the Landwehr; but surely technical training was not everything; what also mattered was "the spirit that dwells in the masses that are to be set in motion against the enemy." This spirit had had no mean part in the victory of 1813. Should reorganization of the Landwehr become necessary, the government would be confidently expected to carry it out "only upon the most careful and mature consideration, taking particular account of the living spirit of the Landwehr"; and if legislation were indeed required, the chamber would of course have to play its part.

These declarations had been preceded by statements from unnamed deputies in the committee, expressing deep concern. Apparently, it was said, the promotion of Landwehr officers was to be even further paralyzed in favor of the line army. Even now command of Landwehr companies and squadrons was going almost without exception to officers of the line, demoralizing the Landwehr officers. The higher officers of the line who had to judge the qualifications of their Landwehr colleagues were all in league against the latter. It was wrong to nibble away at the Landwehr in this fashion. If it were no longer wanted, this should be stated openly. In that eventuality the question would arise whether universal military service without paid substitutes should be left intact.[3]

This points to a deep-seated jealousy of the regular officers' corps on the part of the educated bourgeoisie as represented by the Old Liberals. The propertied middle class was simply asserting its social and political claims here. Bonin's answer in the plenary session shows plainly how insecure this semiliberal war minister felt in the face of this assault, how inwardly aloof he stood from the spirit of the reforms William I planned. He hastened to assure the chamber that the government too regarded the Landwehr system of 1815 as the law of the land, to be altered only by legal means. Rumors of an impending comprehensive army reorganization were made of thin air. In any event, "nothing will be changed in the basic principles and forms on which the Landwehr system rests, nor in the basic ideas of our entire army system, for line and Landwehr alike."

This is an astonishing declaration in view of the fact that from July, 1857, plans for completely recasting the Landwehr as a line reserve were being worked out in the war ministry and that the great new organizational plan by Roon, the minister to come, had been in Bonin's hands since January 8, bearing the strong endorsement of the prince regent![4] But the liberals were successfully misled. The prince regent on his part was indignant,[5] and in the Prussian diet the conservative leader, von Blanckenburg, Roon's nephew and political crony, at once publicly nailed the minister's slip. The Landwehr act of 1815 was by no means the law of the land but merely a royal edict, already violated by the supreme commander himself on numerous occasions and badly in need of reform. It would be presumptuous of the chamber to restrict in any way the royal prerogative to appoint Landwehr officers at will.

As in a prelude we see here outlined the basic party positions from which the subsequent army conflict was to grow—the Old Liberals' zealous championship of the standing and autonomy of the Landwehr (which was somehow felt to represent the civilian point of view) and at the same time their anxiety not to forfeit their position as a "government party" by too outspoken opposition. One senses also the conservatives' eagerness to drive a wedge between the prince regent and his liberal advisers and ministers, while commending themselves as the champions of unlimited crown privilege in the military sphere.

The liberal position was not fully developed in extended debate until 1860, during consideration by the military committee of the government bill sponsored by the new war minister, Roon.[6] The demand for a shorter term of military service in general was now injected into the Landwehr question. In the further discussions this moved more and more to the fore, as even the liberals, or at least their leaders, began to realize the impossibility of salvaging any vital part of the old Landwehr system.

Of great significance was the attempt by the committee in 1860 to find a compromise solution. Led by General Stavenhagen, it tried to do justice to both sides—the more exacting military requirements of the time and the political need and desire to keep alive the spirit of 1813 with its penchant for a people's army. The committee report mentions this great tradition in rather impressive terms. Men like Boyen and Grolman, it says, had by no means looked on the Landwehr as a mere makeshift. They saw it as the perfect means for mobilizing for war all the manpower resources of the relatively small Prussian state, without exhausting it even in peacetime. What Prussia lacked in material means had to be compensated for in moral effort; but such an effort could find its base only "in the ardent love of king and country, pervading the people with memories of their great past and with an awareness of their loyalty and dedication. . . . Prussia would be altogether unable to wage a great and decisive war without the participation of the people, for such a war demands sacrifices of such severity as would never be forthcoming unless the people were heart and soul in it." To maintain and cultivate such sentiments and qualities was the proper task of Prussian statesmen; and it was precisely to this task that Boyen's Landwehr system did proper justice.

True, expert military criticism of it had begun soon after 1815. The report gives a highly knowledgeable historical review of it; but the technical deficiencies of the Landwehr had always been grossly exaggerated, from political motives. The best method of eliminating them would be to maintain a sufficient cadre of trained officers and noncoms in the line army even in peacetime. Thus the committee expressly stated that it was prepared to recommend a sizable increase in scheduled officer personnel in the standing army.[7]

There was agreement, further, on the need for rejuvenating the army and for distributing the military burden by more intensive recruitment. There was "undivided acknowledgment" of the principle that if possible all men fit for service were to be called to the colors.[8] This would mean an immediate increase of twenty thousand men a year, doubling the current quota. Indeed some members of the committee were unwilling to accept any limitation upon fixed annual quotas but favored drafting all who were able to bear arms.

One government representative, presumably Roon, had on one occasion casually remarked that a two-year term of service would probably mean that Prussia too would have to introduce a system of substitutes if it wanted the kind of noncoms it needed. (Under such a system civilians who had the necessary means could pay professionals to serve their terms.) The committee emphatically rejected this, going so far as to declare that it would sooner favor a four-year term of service than assent to such an "un-Prussian" system.[9] In other words, the standing army was to receive such a greatly strengthened reserve that it would become unnecessary in future to mobilize larger Landwehr elements in emergencies, as had been done heretofore. The government bill would have included the younger Landwehr classes in the army reserve while excluding the older ones altogether from the mobile field force, using them in general only as a home guard.

The committee proposal provided for a sharp reduction of the Landwehr share in mobilization. It was to be reduced from one half to one third of the total forces.[10] But this remnant, at least, the committee wished to preserve. Under the government bill only eight annual classes would have been placed at the disposal of the mobile army (three active, five reserve), but the commission provided for twelve classes, six of them for the line army (two active, four reserve) and the other six for the Landwehr. These would be the age brackets from twenty-six to thirty-two, veteran soldiers in the prime of life, under trained officers, an elite rather than a second-rank force.

Was this still the Landwehr in Boyen's sense? Led for the most part by professional officers on active duty, these Landwehr men were indeed to be organized into their own battalions; but these were always to fight conjoined to the same line regiment and under the same commander to whom they were already assigned during peacetime maneuvers. We see plainly that under such a plan the Landwehr would in effect have become a line reserve. It meant a complete surrender of Boyen's principle that the Landwehr was to be kept strictly separate from the line, rendered completely immune to the dominance of the regular officers' corps.

It was a rather empty gesture that under the committee proposal two classes appearing in the government bill as "reserve" were still designated as "Landwehr." In formal terms the committee extended liability to frontline service by four annual classes more than the government plan. But since the government reserved the right to draw on further parts of the Landwehr for field service or replacement battalions in case of need, while the committee was convinced that the eight classes in the government bill would never suffice to cover real war needs, the practical effect would probably have been that either way just about the same classes would see field service. The only difference was that under the committee proposal the venerable institution of the Landwehr would not have been formally degraded to the status of a mere garrison force and abolished as a field force—that was how liberal public opinion saw it. It would have been acknowledged as a fighting force of equal standing. It would at least formally have retained its identity, even though not as a truly autonomous component of the army.

Viewed in this light the difference between the two plans seems rather insignificant, almost entirely a matter of prestige. The Landwehr—most of the liberal leaders almost certainly held officers' commissions in it—resented having to take second place to the line, becoming a mere garrison and occupation force. Its ambition was to be led against the foe from the first day of war, to share in the laurels of victory.[11] The government representative on the committee actually expressed surprise that the opposition seemed to aim at an even closer merger of Landwehr and line than did the government, that it wanted to send more classes into the field; and in the intimate circle of the onetime "camarilla" there was not a little astonishment that the Old Liberal ministers had offered virtually no resistance to the "abolition" of the Landwehr.[12]

We see indeed how the Landwehr question soon vanished as an issue of concern to the Old Liberals. During the ensuing years it was to play a role only as a propaganda theme for the radicals, whenever it was a matter of pillorying the antidemocratic sentiments of the "reactionaries" and their army organization. The democrat Waldeck, for example, praised a popular Landwehr as the best insurance against unnecessary wars, indeed as "one of the firmest bulwarks of our constitution and society."[13]

Another dogmatist in this matter was the great jurist Gneist, who could see the militant ideals of popular liberty realized only in terms of a citizen army, independent of the professional army right to the top, i.e., its general officers, and even directly represented in the crown council.[14] Such utopian ideas had long been abandoned by the Old Liberals; and as Georg von Vincke himself admitted in 1862, the committee proposal of 1860 with its adherence to some aspects of the Landwehr system found no response from the people. On the contrary, the country was glad at the easing of Landwehr obligations brought on by Roon's army reforms. Most of the Landwehr officers themselves were anything but enthusiastic over the committee plan, under which they would be incorporated into line regiments and placed under the direct command of regular army officers. Vincke's parliamentary party expressly dropped this point from Stavenhagen's 1860 draft.[15]

In the great military debate that immediately preceded the constitutional crisis all the luminaries of rightist liberalism—Heinrich von Sybel, both the Vinckes, Count Schwerin-Putzar, even the moderate progressive Twesten—expressly declared their agreement with the basic outlines of Roon's reorganization plan, except for the three-year term of service. Indeed they openly greeted the transformation of the Landwehr as a form of "relief." Vincke-Olbendorf described the standing army based on universal military service as a "grand warrant of liberty" rather than a threat. Count Schwerin went so far as to deny that there was any difference between a royal army based on universal service and a "people's army." Twesten remarked that the political significance of the Landwehr had been grossly exaggerated by the democratic opposition. It "had neither played any part in bringing about the constitutional state of 1848 nor served to insure the rights and liberties of the people since 1848." The recent limitations on it were a natural and inevitable consequence of increased recruitment for the standing army; and from the viewpoint of practical politics there was little difference whether a reservist was mustered into the cadres of the standing army or whether he went into a special Landwehr battalion if there was a uniform command system for both. Only a militia on the Swiss model could really be regarded as a "people's army"; and none would seriously regard its introduction in Prussia as possible or desirable.[16]

It will be seen quite plainly that faith in the Landwehr of 1813 no longer had any living force in the liberal party grouping that dominated the Prussian diet of 1859-1860. Not without reason these Old Liberals regarded themselves as the legitimate spiritual heirs of the great resurgence and its circle of reformers,[17] bearers of an emphatically German brand of liberalism, opposed to the French ideals of liberty, and hence basically antidemocratic. As up-to-date realists, themselves coming for the most part from higher military circles or at least remaining in close touch with such circles, they grew rather quickly convinced that the Landwehr system of 1815 was hopelessly obsolete. Thus the ideal of a people's army was not really revived in their ranks. When the Landwehr issue was reopened in 1863, at the height of the conflict, the initiative came from the radical progressives rather than from the Old Liberals who no longer played the leading role within the combined opposition.

In view of this background we can see that it was certainly not the Landwehr issue that brought the differences with the government to the level of a constitutional crisis. Of far greater importance was the controversy over whether the term of military service was to be two years or three. We already know why the liberal chamber majority after 1860 demanded reintroduction of the two-year term. They owed their parliamentary power in large measure to the election boycott by the democrats of 1848. This made it all the more necessary for them to consider the mood of their constituents.

Should the liberals launch their regime on a tremendous increase in the military budget, coupled with a rise in taxes by one quarter, without offering any commensurate relief for the individual? They cited the economic necessity for making up the loss of twenty thousand additional workers through the draft by reducing the term of service. They offered numerous declarations, old and new, by respected generals who clearly favored the two-year term.[18] They insisted that this faster turnover would result in the same number of trained reserves at much lower cost and with fewer scheduled peacetime officers.[19] It was hoped to save no less than 2,500,000 thalers in the regular annual budget, not including military construction.

Knowing the history of the army bill of 1860—the desperate fight waged first by the undersecretary of war and ultimately by the whole war ministry against its high cost, and especially against the regent's stubborn insistence on the three-year term which even Roon had been prepared to drop—we can judge the full dimensions of Roon's dilemma in having to make an impressive and convincing case for his monarch on precisely this point. The strongest argument he advanced time and again was the need for the greatest possible number of line cadres and veteran soldiers on active service in peacetime in order to facilitate mobilization and the firm integration of reservists into the standing army.

Yet it was precisely this argument that provoked the sharpest opposition from liberal public opinion. People saw the country in danger of being smothered in countless new barrack buildings, a vast increase in professional officers and noncoms trained at military and cadet schools—the growth, in other words, of a machine staffed with men known to oppose the liberal spirit of the time and resolved upon fighting that spirit by every possible means, including nationwide military indoctrination.

The other arguments the minister put forward on behalf of the three-year term of service amounted in the main to the well-known notion Prince William had entertained ever since 1833: The conscripts not only had to be taught certain technical skills, they had to be imbued with a "proper military spirit." Against this the liberals cited highly persuasive utterances by the former chief of the General Staff, General Krauseneck: To separate the individual soldier from the rest of society and indoctrinate him with a military caste spirit flew in the face of the idea of a Prussian people's army. This was possible only in armies with the terms of service running into many years. In a military sense, moreover, this long habituation of veteran troopers was by no means of undisputed value.

"Let the officers and noncoms preserve their caste spirit," concluded the committee; "but to extend it to the common soldier serving his obligatory term is neither the will of the nation nor in the nature of things; and it is illusory to believe this could be better done in three years than in two. For the great majority military service is an onerous duty, accepted under the law and from an understanding of the country's needs. Only exceptionally will a fondness for the profession of arms be displayed, which does not preclude everyone readily flocking to the colors when king and country call. Discipline is adequately learned even in two years, and the recruit will submit to it all the more readily when he sees that he is not being kept away from his domestic environment any longer than necessary. It is for that reason that the largest number of disciplinary actions is incurred by ranks serving in the third year, for the men believe that a needless burden is being imposed on them and that they already know what they are supposed to be taught." As for the noncoms, to bring them up to the mark would require increased expenditures, which were necessary in any event, and not merely a third year of service.

These are memorable words. The spirit of the people's army was here putting up a last-ditch defense against the king's professional army. The bourgeoisie was fighting a rearguard action against the idea of its total militarization. The debate moved within a precarious border region between technical military and purely political considerations; and in the ensuing years Roon evaded it as much as possible, especially before the full house.[20] His hands were indeed virtually tied by his sovereign's unshakable resolve.

The unfavorable impression the defense bill made on the liberals was greatly deepened by a series of demands that seemed to stem less from genuine defense needs than from a snobbish fondness of parade-ground troops—a sharp increase in guards regiments, an excessive effective strength for the guards battalions in peacetime, great new expenditures for the cavalry, and the like. Even zealous proponents of the three-year term like Theodor von Bernhardi took umbrage at these "frills," and Roon's intimate, the archconservative Moritz von Blancken-burg-Zimmerhausen, gagged at them;[21] but even more important was liberal distrust of the men behind the whole reorganization scheme. Among those in the know the story went round that only the Junker party, represented pre-eminently by the influential adjutant general, Edwin von Manteuffel, had raised the military demands to such a high level, "partly for the purpose of creating an army of professional soldiers whose officers would belong to the Junker estate and party—an army that party could use for its own purposes, with which it could 'keep down the revolution,' i.e., maintain its own rule— partly in the hope of using the occasion to topple the liberal government if the bill did not pass, and of disrupting the intractable chamber of deputies," subsequently forcing a conservative election with official propaganda backing.[22]

There were reports, moreover, of vain efforts already made by the government to reduce the monetary burdens, widely deemed to be intolerable.[23] There was apprehension that inordinate additional burdens would arise when the reorganization was put into effect and that Prussia, despite its current fiscal soundness, might find its general defense policies paralyzed—in respect of fortifications and naval expansion, for example—and its cultural growth impeded as well.

These apprehensions, however, assumed their proper weight only by virtue of the political mood that has already been indicated, notably the unpopularity of the royal officers' corps among the liberal bourgeoisie, stemming from jealousy, distrust, and bitter experience with political generals after the "camarilla" of 1848. Did not the whole reorganization in the end amount to a strengthening of antiliberal elements, the creation of a kind of conservative partisan army?

Such fears were bound to rise even further when General von Prittwitz, in the very first plenary session that discussed the army reforms, praised the government bill as being calculated to protect "the army, the oldest and stanchest pillar of ancient Prussian tradition and institutions, a hitherto still untouched bulwark against all the leveling trends of the new age" from the intrusion of democratic principles, preserving its "spirit of pure soldiership."[24]

There was a hail of complaints in the committee sessions about the preferment of members of the nobility as officer candidates and the discrimination against bourgeois elements, especially those from liberal circles; about the snobbishness of the officers' corps; about its alienation from the life of the people. The government kept pointing to existing regulations that outlawed such discrimination, to the fact that all professions were called up on an equal basis, to the need for cultivating a certain *esprit de corps* among the officers. Alas, the realities, especially in the guards and cavalry regiments, showed only too clearly that snobbery continued to be deeply rooted; and it was this that outraged bourgeois sensibilities.[25]

Despite these resentments an understanding between government and chamber of deputies seemed by no means beyond reach by the spring of 1860. The two Vinckes in particular continued to pursue this goal. Both in the chamber and in the press extremist argument was deliberately avoided. There is general agreement that had the government given way in the matter of the three-year term and accepted certain economies, agreement on the remaining questions could have been reached without too much trouble. But that would have meant a willingness to compromise—on the part of the prince regent as well; and that was missing.

William regarded the great reform scheme as his own personal work, closest to his heart, the most important achievement of his sixty years. From the very outset the three-year term of service was at the heart of his thinking. The prince, moreover, had difficulty in prevailing over the demands and reservations of his ministers. And now, here were all these deputies who thought they knew all the answers! Indeed they had the effrontery to counter with a complete draft law of their own!

"Those gentlemen of the military committee are all running round in circles—the retired generals are the worst of all; well, I shall soon poke a stick into that hornets' nest!" It was with such words that the ruler apostrophized the Old Liberal mediator, Freiherr Vincke-Olbendorf, in front of witnesses at a court musical. As early as February, 1860, soon after the parliamentary deliberations had begun, the prince was in such a state of ire that Vincke no longer dared convey his utterances to the deputies. Unless the bill passed without change, he was heard to say, he would either have to send the chamber packing (i.e., prorogue the diet), or abdicate in favor of his son.[26] It was a threat he repeated many times—until he summoned Bismarck to the helm—in order to keep his ministers "in line." Not even on minor points was he to be swerved in any way.[27]

The liberals themselves later realized their utter and unprecedented folly in not foregoing their opposition without a quibble in the face of the existing situation. Like their government they should have accepted the defense bill "lock, stock, and barrel," without cutting a comma, if only to maintain their position as a party of the government—such was the subsequent conclusion. The military writer Theodor von Bernhardi, a shrewd observer who sympathized with the liberals, gave them this advice repeatedly and was horrified by their truculence. Other middlemen at court, like the historian Max Duncker, inclined to the same view.

The liberal historians in general, with their pronounced interest in questions of foreign policy, favored army reform because their main concern was to enhance the power of Prussia. Ever since the decay of the Russian and Austrian alliance the old defensive system of 1814 had seemed to them no longer adequate.[28] And thus they gave smaller weight to financial considerations.

Party politics, however, is always primarily concerned with the question of power. Being a "party of the government" became rather meaningless if it meant blind assent to every government proposal, no matter how unpopular, without gaining the slightest influence on the course of foreign and domestic policy. To Sybel's complaint that the Old Liberals were abandoning their own government Vincke replied: "The ministers have told us often enough they comprise the sovereign's cabinet, not that of any parliamentary party."[29] In the eyes of William I that was undoubtedly true. He expected and demanded unquestioning personal loyalty of his ministers and would not have hesitated to dismiss them, had they showed any signs of wanting to play the part of a liberal party ministry in earnest or of invoking the desires of the liberal parties.

They were thus under the necessity of practicing extreme caution, and this constant tactical maneuvering earned their already vacillating policies a reputation for abject pusillanimity. In the foreign policy field the "New Era" scored nothing but failures. What hurt the work of reorganization more than anything else was the doubt and distrust it aroused in liberal circles. They suspected that the government would not really know what to do with an enlarged army; that national union in particular would not be brought a step nearer; that the whole thing would amount to little more than a huge military machine intended largely for parades and show.

There was already at the time—spring of 1860—a great deal of frustration in domestic affairs. The staff of the civil service still dated from the period of reaction, and in practice little or nothing had changed. The first timid reform efforts by liberal ministers—the civil marriage bill and the property tax equalization bill, which would have hit the large landowners among the nobility—had twice failed because of the opposition of the upper chamber. Any reform of that chamber seemed out of the question for the time being.

In these circumstances there was a natural groundswell of voices that declared any further pulling of punches to spare the prince regent and his archconservative military advisers to be treason to "liberal principles," little short of party suicide. In a sense the liberal party leaders were caught between Scylla and Charybdis. If they turned thumbs down on the government bill—even if they only insisted on their amendments—they ran the risk that the regent might turn his back altogether on any liberal policy, picking more amenable supporters, such as the loyalist Junker party, which was only waiting for the chance.[30] In any event, the notion then much discussed among the liberals was surely an illusion: that the monarch might be forced to adopt a more clear-cut liberal course by having difficulties put in his way, by the use of the parliamentary power of the purse to foil his pet project. Bernhardi and his friends saw this quite clearly.

On the other hand, was the opposite course any less illusory? Could the liberal party be certain of gaining William's favor permanently by surrendering its legitimate goals in the military sphere, its following among radical sympathizers, indeed its popularity as a whole? Once the army reform had been pushed through, was there not the chance that the regent might feel he could still do without the liberals? Might not some other pretext serve to bring the deeper policy differences out into the open?

Judging by all we know today about William's basic political orientation and the political intrigues of his military advisers, there is a strong temptation to answer these questions as did those critics of 1860 who said that the stiff-necked Georg von Vincke lacked even "a single shred of statesmanship."[31] What must crucially affect the verdict of history is that the controversy over the army reforms involved much more than increased or decreased appropriations and terms of service. It was not a question of details on which one might compromise or simply yield. It was a basic issue, the role of the army in a constitutional state.

Just how much authority was intended by "supreme command of the armed forces," which Article 46 of the constitution gave the king? Did it include complete discretion over general army organization and over liability of citizens to military service? Did the diet as a second legislative power have a voice that meant anything? Was the army merely one instrumentality of the state among others, incorporated like all of them into the monarchial-constitutional system, dependent in its widest legal foundations on both of the sources of state power? Or was it, at home and abroad, exclusively at the disposal of the crown, supporting only the sovereign's power and authority? All these doubtful questions, stemming from the dual character of the new state constitution, had been left unclarified in 1848-1850. There was never any thought that there could be basic agreement between William I and liberalism in answering them. For that very reason, from the vantage-point of history, the policies of the "New Era" seem mere illusion.

They could continue only while neither partner was as yet aware that the fundamental and essential conflict between them could not be bridged by compromise. As things stood, neither crown nor parliament was initially certain about ultimate goals, about the core of the constitutional question. We hear nothing about Prince William opposing submission of the defense bill to the diet from the very beginning.[32] Conversely, even after the first clashes in the military committee Vincke was at pains to protest in the name of his party that there was no thought of restricting the prerogatives of the supreme commander. All that was sought was control over military appropriations.[33]

Yet by and by the constitutional problem—really one of political power—came more and more to the fore. As early as 1860 the government (presumably in the person of Roon) hinted before the military committee that "it was entirely at the government's discretion whether or not the Landwehr was to be organized into separate formations." Why then had the government presented its defense bill? came the response.[34]

The government seemed to regret that action soon enough. Its reply to the committee's detailed counterproposal was to withdraw the bill and ask for the famous "stopgap." For the time being the chamber was requested merely to authorize a blanket appropriation of 9,000,000 thalers until July 1, 1861, to carry out the reorganization, leaving detailed disposition of the funds to the government. True, the liberal minister of finance, von Patow, was at pains to explain that this measure was purely provisional. The appropriation would merely provide the funds to finance an increased state of preparedness for one year. At a later date the chamber would have complete freedom to decide on the definitive organization.

Actually the prince regent never for a moment considered the possibility that the kind of reorganization for which he requested funds in this fashion should ever be revoked or altered. To rub this in unmistakably, the new line regiments were created and their commanders appointed even before the blanket appropriation passed. Roon, the minister of war, showed himself quite irritated when Vincke cautiously dared to criticize this government action as "ill-considered."[35]

The liberals, all the same, breathed a sigh of relief at the new turn. They thought that for the time being they had escaped the fateful quandary of choosing between opposition and self-immolation.[36] Vincke in his optimism went so far as to boast of a parliamentary victory! Now that the decision had once again been postponed, both he and his friends nourished the illusion that the government might prove more tractable at a later date. The opposite was true. Once called to awareness, the real conflict hardened and deepened day by day until it became utterly irreconcilable.

The chief blame falls on the immediate military entourage of William I–Adjutant General Gustav von Alvensleben, Chief of the Military Cabinet Edwin von Manteuffel, and War Minister Albrecht von Roon, new in his post. Only Manteuffel among them had any military record, as a member of the military "camarilla" of Frederic William IV. Alvensleben and Roon had come into closer contact with the prince only during his years in the Rhineland, as part of the broader circle of the semiliberal *Wochenblattspartei*. All these men were nevertheless absolutist at heart, "thoroughly out of sympathy with the whole constitutional muddle." Roon, like his friend Alvensleben, had no real party ties, nor did he suffer from class prejudice. He looked on himself as a soldier, pure and simple, the shield and right bower of a strong monarchy.

The essence of the monarchial-constitutional system is that all political decisions are basically worked out by agreement and compromise between crown and parliament. That approach was thoroughly at odds with Roon's pugnacious character.[37] If we can properly describe the liberal approach as a political offensive, then it certainly ran head-on into a carefully prepared counteroffensive.

Manteuffel was fond of confirming a story about himself, to the effect that during the early years of William's regency he avoided discussing anything except military questions with the prince.[38] Naturally enough, for he knew the prince's profound suspicion of his brother's reactionary entourage. Yet it was precisely by these tactics that Manteuffel gained not only William's confidence, but great political influence over him as well. As far as can be seen, the main interest of this ambitious man during the "New Era" lay in expanding the power of his official position as chief of the military cabinet, reconstituted in 1858. In this capacity, as we shall hear, he endeavored to remove any ministerial limitations over the sovereign's command power, to create a state of complete military absolutism. This spirit may even explain his initial distaste for the defense bill of which Gerlach tells us.[39] He may have wished to see the army reorganization effected by fiat of the military cabinet rather than by general cabinet deliberation. It is certain that the archconservative group to which he belonged begrudged the liberal government of 1858 the triumph of bringing about reforms greater than any the reactionaries had produced when they held exclusive power.[40]

The fall of Bonin, war minister of the "New Era," and his succession by Roon may well have been the common work of Alvensleben and Manteuffel. Roon himself declared he was taking office as a nonpolitical expert, solely to carry out the army reorganization. Actually he began to drive political wedges into the liberal cabinet from the day of his appointment. Roon's self-announced main goal was to combat the "treasonable" view that the prince regent was a kind of Frankish figurehead king, with the war minister as his proper major-domo and the real power.[41] In other words, like Manteuffel, he was out to restore complete absolutism to the crown in the military sphere.

Every step forward in realizing such a program was bound to drive Roon into deeper conflict with his liberal ministerial colleagues. The diet had scarcely passed the blanket appropriation when Roon went to work on the definitive reorganization of the army, urged on by Manteuffel with almost feverish zeal. If it were only tentative, he wrote, "the army would look to the rostrum rather than the commander-in-chief. There would be a clear-cut demonstration that it is not up to the sovereign to form new regiments, that he has no power to safeguard the careers of his officers, that all this is entirely dependent on resolutions passed in the chamber. . . . In place of a royal army we would have one under the thumb of parliament. In my view, unless the regiments are established here and now on a permanent basis the morale and integrity of the army will be jeopardized and the prince regent's position compromised."[42]

Roon yielded, and he did so with his eyes wide open, knowing full well that he was "burning his ships behind him." There would be open battle in the next diet session. The first trooping of the colors for the new regiments was held on January 18, 1861, and Roon himself regarded the ceremony as putting the "final seal" on the new organization.[43] All the same, before the military committee of the 1861 diet he did not yet dare come out in the open with his absolutist views of the "supreme war lord's" prerogatives. He still had to consider his liberal cabinet colleagues. All he did was to speak rather ambiguously of the need for creating new organizational forms "as though they were permanent." He left the question open whether any further legislation were required to assign two more Landwehr classes to the line army. He did hold out the prospect of an amendment to Boyen's defense act for the following year, or at least an authentic interpretation of its disputed paragraph 15.[44] The minister had to be guarded in his speech, but the conservatives in the diet proclaimed all the more triumphantly what he could not say.

In the plenary session of May 27, 1861, the editor of the *Kreuzzeitung,* Hermann Wagener, delivered a speech, every phrase of which was meant for the ears of the former prince regent, now king in his own right. Unlike the liberals, he said, the conservatives would not seek to create a new stopgap by adding the increased military appropriations to the supplementary budget. Let the liberal minister of finance argue with his friends over new provisional measures—for the conservatives the new regiments and squadrons were an accomplished fact that no legislative act would ever overturn!

This matter, he went on, was bound to be settled in a way the liberals had evidently never dreamed of. It had long since become a political question, that is a question of power. Let there be no illusions—the army reorganization had come about, not on the basis of any law passed the previous year, but "on the basis of the supreme authority of our commander-in-chief, expressly acknowledged in our constitution." The authority of the chamber extended exclusively to fiscal matters. Let it beware of abusing the constitution for political purposes! If it overreached itself, the only consequence could be a coup d'état! And if it came to that extremity, there would certainly be another General Yorck, this time in mufti, who would see to it that the necessary appropriations were forthcoming. What the liberals were now trying to do was merely to postpone the inevitable conflict that would break out some day. Well, the conservatives were ready! They would fight on the side of the king! A sovereign might abdicate, but he could never be compelled to make concessions that "would destroy for all time the source and support of his power."[45]

Agitated counterattacks on the part of the liberals forced the conservative leader von Blanckenburg to soften the provocation and expressly acknowledge that modification and reductions in army strength might very well follow from the chamber's power of the purse. At the same time he fed fuel to the flames by denying that the chamber had any right to use its fiscal powers for "political purposes," indeed by characterizing any such effort as an "attempted coup d'état."

The liberal minister of finance Patow tried to speak in favor of peaceable compromise on defense matters between the two legislative powers; but Blanckenburg threw down the gage of battle. The conservatives could not imagine that any royal government would settle for the kind of half-measure the liberal majority now proposed—shifting the army appropriation to the supplementary budget in order to emphasize that the army reorganization, actually long since an accomplished fact, did not yet enjoy legislative sanction. That would mean knuckling under to a wholly unwarranted power play on the part of the chamber to which end no conservative would lift a finger. If the government allowed itself to be pushed in that direction, it would have to bear the responsibility alone. Was there really no minister of finance to be found with the courage to renounce a supplementary budget altogether, in the circumstances, and accept responsibility before the house for exceeding the regular budget? "A man, a man! A kingdom for a man!"[46]

There is no way of establishing whether and in what measure these tactics by the small conservative opposition had been agreed upon in detail between Roon and his nephew Blanckenburg.[47] There can be no doubt, however, that both were pulling in the same direction. As for the goal they envisaged, this was hinted at soon afterward by Roon to his friend Perthes: "Prussia might emerge with renewed strength from the mudbath of another revolution, but it will inexorably rot in the cesspool of dogmatic liberalism."[48] Dogmatic liberalism was the term used to describe the approach at which the whole monarchial-constitutional system of the nineteenth century was aimed—the constant endeavor to harmonize differences between the various power factors, to achieve agreement among them without heat. In military matters this process was now to be ended. The exclusive command power of the crown in matters of army organization was to be asserted without regard to the inevitable exacerbation of the political struggle that would result.

The session was the last one of the diet elected in 1858. Ever since 1860 liberal frustration over the course of domestic and foreign policy had steadily deepened. Both parties, the conservatives and their opponents, were preparing for the impending election campaign. Hence the whole tone of debate was much more pointed on this occasion than during the preceding year. There were sharp sallies by the radical left which had broken away from Vincke's leadership. The catchword about the Landwehr being a true people's army was dusted off again. Countless minutiae of army organization, especially the cadet schools and the methods of officer recruitment, were sharply criticized. The rising distrust of the Old Liberals had been demonstrated as early as April when Karl Twesten, in an attack that quickly gained wide notoriety, had criticized Edwin von Manteuffel and the military cabinet system within the government.[49]

Last year the stopgap measure had been passed almost unanimously, but now Vincke had the greatest difficulty in pushing through his compromise. In the end the appropriation for the enlarged army did get through, severely cut back and only as part of a supplementary budget and with the proviso that the reorganization must gain legislative approval *ex post facto.* It was precisely the kind of "dilatory compromise" Wagener had pilloried as a mere evasion of the issue, while Blanckenburg had spoken of "knuckling under." All the same, Roon, as a member of the government, thought it wise to go along.

It was to be the last time he did so. The war minister had long since begun systematically to undermine the king's confidence in his liberal ministers. Of Roon's confidential discussions with the king we know, of course, only those that somehow got recorded. In the context of our theme, however, these are of great interest, because they show that the authoritarian principle, sharply emphasized within the army, automatically tended to reach beyond that sphere, turning the army into a political factor of the first order.

In March, 1861, the king, already under strong conservative influence, had only reluctantly approved certain bills, chiefly because of a cabinet crisis.[50] They concerned county reorganization, ministerial responsibility, and budgetary control by the auditor's office. Liberal opinion had been pressing for this long-promised "implementation of the constitution." The letter Roon wrote the king on March 1, advising him to stiffen his resistance, provides memorable testimony of the old Prussian feudal spirit, a curious blend of reverence and arrogance toward the throne. It is even more significant in its confident assertion of the soldier's claim to be the chief buttress of the monarchy.

The constitution was viewed as a gift conferred by royal grace and favor.[51] That did not mean that its mandatory power was denied—that would have been contrary to William's nature. He remained true to his attitudes during the period of reaction. But the fulfillment of the prospects held out in the constitution was left to the monarch's free discretion. A government that would oppose the king was inconceivable in Prussia, for he was sovereign in the fullest sense. A minister who could not or would not follow him had no choice but to submit his resignation.

As for the reform bills before the king, whether they were meant in earnest by the ministers or constituted no more than a political gesture in the election campaign, they would have a most serious effect on the loyalist sectors of the population, "especially those parts of the nation that bear Your Majesty's arms and which Your Majesty has always found your throne's firmest support. Those who mean well with Your Majesty are reluctant to consider the possibility that this *rocher de bronze* should ever be undermined."

Couched in servile terms, we have here an unmistakable threat—of army and officer disaffection, if not indeed disloyalty. "That I shall not survive!" William noted in the margin with consternation. He assured the ministers of his "sincere and everlasting gratitude" and withdrew his assent to the liberal reform bills.[52]

This was by no means the only time Roon invoked the army as a political power factor in settling controversial questions of domestic policy, one of Manteuffel's favorite tactical devices. As long ago as 1848 Roon, in despair over the chaos that followed the month of March, had clung to the hope that the authority of the throne might be restored with the help of a politically activated army. "The army," he wrote at the time, "feels itself to be part and parcel of the fatherland in a most honorable sense and not in the least as representing a separate class. . . . They are by no means a homeless horde of hirelings, bereft of rights and forever subject to the sovereign will of Philistines and proletarians."

On the contrary, because of its achievements—especially the work of the officers in indoctrinating the people—the army had a far greater right to share in the country's regeneration than those "idle literati" who, by their seditious activities, had helped to bring the present chaos about. Yet the army was not asking for the franchise or the right to stand for office.[53]

Since that time Roon had come to realize that even a royal army, if it had the character of a mass army, was subject to the demoralizing influence of these same "idle literati," once the door was opened to politics. Even a three-year term of service was not actually long enough to separate the recruit completely from his home environment and imbue him with the spirit that animated the aristocratic royalist officers' corps. Hence Roon would hear no more of the franchise for military personnel and suppressed it soon after the constitutional crisis erupted, mainly, it would seem, on Manteuffel's instigation.[54] When it came to the army as a political factor, only the officers henceforth really counted for Roon.

These, however, he did quite naturally conceive of as a solid political unit, with himself as its speaker before the throne. If he stayed in office in the face of countless vexations—so he wrote his friend Perthes late in 1861—it was solely to preserve the army's political pride. "The army, hitherto the sole reliable anchor and pillar of our future, must not be swerved in its confidence and its convictions—or chaos will burst upon us." In a similar vein he said half a year later: "The army must not be hurt in its feelings, for with the ruin of army morale Prussia would turn red and the crown roll in the dust. I am afraid morale would suffer even if the surrender were limited to the appropriations question."[55]

Such utterances inject still another dimension into the conflict that continues to preoccupy us in this book, the conflict between royal and mass army. What the war minister was saying was that his main political mission was not to mediate between crown and parliament in military matters but to protect "army morale" from the liberal spirit of the time. "Army morale"—that meant the *esprit de corps* of the professional soldier, especially the officers' corps in which, as before, the military cabinet and the military training establishments carefully perpetuated the dominance of the aristocratic element. These officers did not regard themselves as soldiers of the nation, members of a single political community, as once had been the case with the leaders in the Wars of Liberation. They looked on themselves solely as paladins of the Hohenzollern throne, loyal followers of the monarch to whom they had sworn personal fealty; and they expected that he in turn would be loyal to his followers, i.e., protect their privileges against the onslaughts of the liberal spirit. Considering themselves indispensable, the only trustworthy pillar of the throne, they demanded not only that the king see to their military wishes and needs but that he oppose all the efforts on the part of the liberal bourgeoisie to expand its political power and influence on affairs of state; for to keep down that influence as much as possible seemed to them in the common interest of crown and military establishment.

What a change since the days of the Wars of Liberation! Even then Prussian generals had at times addressed political demands to the throne; but they did so not as spokesmen for an army that looked on itself as a separate class—"pillar of the throne"; they spoke in the name of the nation itself which stood behind them in the form of a people's army and whose passionate militancy they represented. It was in the name of national liberty that Gneisenau had asked the king to sanction the resurgence. It was in the name of the people that Blücher demanded greater security for the western borders of Germany.

Between those events and the sixties, of course, had fallen the revolution of 1848 with its deep estrangement of the army from the people, the unforgotten humiliation of the Prussian crown, the chaos that had destroyed the traditions of Old Prussia and absolutist authority; and ever since, the Prussian officer nobility had caught an ugly whiff of revolution in every popular movement—even the movement for German national unity. They felt it to be their mission, these officers, to form a protective wall between crown and people, to stand shoulder to shoulder with their monarch against the new spirit.

Actually, the spirit of the popular army of 1813, of the nation in arms, was lost beyond recall,[56] no matter how often Roon's speeches before the diet emphasized that an army based on universal service was always a "people's army." There was no real communication between Roon and his opponents. As the gulf widened between royalty and bourgeois public opinion, the officers' corps hardened more and more into a kind of Praetorian Guard, which in turn served only to enhance the resentment and radicalism of the liberal opposition.

The exceptionally close ties between King William and his military following were based not only on current political events but on the purely military outlook they shared. Freedom is not nearly as important a need in armies as authority and discipline. This is indeed part and parcel of soldiering. Soldiers are accustomed to obey, to follow; and they are inclined to view every social grouping in coercive terms, looking for a clear-cut chain of command. This is the soldier's strength, dangerous because it is so limited in outlook.

King William, a soldier pure and simple, had not the slightest affinity with the intellectual world of liberalism. For this reason alone the policies of the "New Era" were illusory from beginning to end. This was made clear again and again in every one of the ministerial conflicts that arose. Whenever a minister did hand in his resignation, finding himself unable to accept the political responsibility expected of him, the king regarded this as disloyalty or insubordination or even desertion. He would refuse to accept the resignation and demand, under threat of his own abdication, a brand of obedience that placed the minister in an impossible crossfire. Indeed, the king's stubbornness and inner insecurity, in the face of a world utterly strange to him, often caused him to consider retiring from the throne.

The soldier king's military advisers fared no differently. It seems very likely that in his heart of hearts Roon too never really understood the political mission of liberalism. What in liberal eyes seemed an upright and valiant attitude toward those in power was no better than insolence to the Prussian general—undisciplined arrogance with revolutionary overtones. To him the liberal demand that the governed should have a share in their governance savored of anarchy.

For centuries, the officer class had been inured to uncritical and unconditional obedience to the "warlord," the possessor of sovereign power within the state. Since the days of Frederic the Great it had become a tradition that an officer had to do what he was told, that his was not to argue or reason why. Indeed, this pattern has colored the political views of officers into our own day. In the case of Roon this was a frequent source of troublesome inner conflict, between his parliamentary responsibility as minister of war on the one hand and his commitment to obedience as a general on the other. His insight as a statesman was pitted against his instinct as a royalist soldier.[57]

No such inhibitions stemming from their official positions seem to have troubled the two adjutants general, Alvensleben and Manteuffel, convinced royalists who were willing foils for William's purely military approach. Indeed their military discipline seems at times to have risen to the level of sycophantic servility. As advisers behind the scenes they had no need to mince words.

As early as August, 1860, Gustav von Alvensleben was convinced beyond a doubt that the only reason for the liberal opposition to the three-year term of service was a deliberate plan to undermine army discipline, sweep aside this support of the monarchy, and open the way to complete parliamentary rule and revolution. He regarded even liberal criticism of the army and of the upper chamber as a "breach of law" that allowed the monarch to ignore the constitution. Every concession by the cabinet represented a kind of coup d'état against the monarchy, since it made the chamber of deputies supreme commander of the army![58]

Such utterances are echoed in Edwin von Manteuffel's confidential discussions with the king. In a secret note dated April 1, 1862, he had this to say about another abdication threat by William: "I replied to the king that I had told him four years ago that we were living in a period of revolution. The question was whether he wanted to follow Charles I and Louis XVI in allowing power to be wrested from his hands even before open battle had been joined. He still had the power and the army today. If he yielded at the expense of the army, solely to influence the election outcome in his favor, he would miss that goal. All he would achieve would be to undermine the army's faith in his steadfastness."[59]

We see again the old mixture of warnings and threats, to "harden" the sovereign on the army's side. In time Edwin von Manteuffel built up a kind of orthodox order of military royalists who addressed a flood of memorials to the sovereign, couched in the most elaborate rhetoric. Manteuffel had originally treated Roon with condescension, but when his fellow protagonist became minister, an element of jealousy crept in. Nevertheless Manteuffel had the effrontery to practice a kind of continuing political thought control over Roon—always on the pretext of speaking with the voice of the "all-highest."

There was scarcely any need for such a thing. Since the spring of 1861 at the latest, Roon had been determined to get rid of his Old Liberal cabinet colleagues as soon as possible. Since we are not here concerned with a complete documentation of the army controversy, only with pinpointing the political motives that underlay it, we need not follow in detail Roon's efforts to trip up his colleagues through confidential remonstrances with the king. His campaign confirms a law of political struggle—he had to wheel out heavier and heavier artillery.

By April, 1861, Roon was already mounting massive attacks against the liberal ministers. They were "shackled by their party," he told the king, and would thus necessarily paralyze the king's free will, bringing "the fatherland to the brink of the abyss." Nothing was further from Roon's mind than to favor any of the other parties, the party of the *Kreuzzeitung,* for example.[60] (Roon knew William's deep concern to avoid identification with the "camarilla" he had opposed so sharply during his time in Coblenz.)

Nevertheless Roon consulted constantly with Blanckenburg, of whose exhortations, addressed to the king during the military debate in the diet, we have already heard. When the diet had adjourned, the onslaught began afresh. This time the pretext was the question of whether the provincial estates were to go through the traditional ceremony of paying homage to the new king. After vain efforts to secure the appointment of Bismarck, Roon settled for the liberal compromise, which provided for solemn coronation in place of the homage ceremony. His friend Blanckenburg felt that this was almost tantamount to treason to the cause.[61]

The king was not won over to an open change of policy quite so quickly. The domestic influences brought to bear on him in favor of the Old Liberals were still formidable.[62] In the fall of 1861, just before the election, Roon openly defended the "moderate conservatives" in a long memorial, rejecting the charge that they were plotting reaction and breaches of the constitution.[63] This too brought no practical results for the time being.

The election brought a sharp radicalization of the chamber of deputies and formation of the semidemocratic Progressive Party as a determined opposition group. The situation was now so acute that the Old Liberal cabinet simply could no longer carry on. By December Roon was convinced that its disruption was only a question of time, and he did all in his power to accentuate the tensions.[64]

During the winter months a mood akin to civil war began to develop. The military party at court, including Roon, was convinced that no government was possible with the newly elected diet, while its prorogation would lead to riots. A virtual counterrevolution was therefore worked out in secret, providing for the dispatch of massive military forces to Berlin. Great hopes were staked on a concomitant coup d'état that would suspend the constitution.[65]

When the new diet convened on January 14, 1862, and failed altogether to behave in a "revolutionary" fashion, the hotheads in the military cabinet felt something akin to disappointment.[66] By March, nevertheless, the joint efforts of Roon, Bernstorff, and von der Heydt managed to disrupt not only the diet, but the Old Liberal government itself, over a technical issue between the chamber and the liberal finance minister Patow.[67] The end of the "New Era" was at hand.

But the only thing that was actually destroyed was, as we have long since recognized, a mere illusion—the illusion that the Prussian military state could ever change its character without the harshest kind of external coercion. This kingdom of barracks and drill grounds was simply not minded to allow its citizens to meddle with its command power in earnest. Also destroyed was the illusion of the citizens' army of 1813.

But could there be a simple return to the conditions of William I's youth, the situation before 1848, which he felt to be so ideal? Would a parliamentary façade be good enough, coupled with nothing more than a limited degree of publicity on the government budget? Could Prussia keep out of the great liberal and nationalist movement that was sweeping through all of Europe?

In Italy it had led to the establishment of a new nationalist state. In Russia it had called forth the greatest political and social upheaval of the century. In Poland it had touched off a revolution. England was witnessing the classic completion of its political and economic system. In France the first relaxation of Caesarism had been exacted, with a profound effect on foreign policy. In Sweden, Denmark, and Belgium the whole state structure had been modernized. In Austria-Hungary absolutism had failed. Indeed, a Pan-German nationalist reform movement had come into being, causing the reactionary system of the fifties to collapse in most German principalities.

Since 1859 there had been the German National Union *(Nationalverein)* which proposed to prepare public opinion for German unification under Prussian leadership. Its work, however, was severely hampered by the army controversy. True, its membership consisted of the liberal bourgeoisie, chiefly of radical persuasion, and the Prussian king therefore execrated the Union. In the diet of 1861 the conservative Wagener went so far as to vilify it as a mere tool of Napoleon.[68]

Austria under Schmerling's leadership, however, was taking advantage of the current low fortunes of the movement for Prussian leadership (the so-called "Little German" approach) by seeking to fill the sails of the Hapsburg ship of state with the wind of a renewed campaign for the "Great German" approach—German unification under the Austrian hegemony. Hard-headed policy considerations should certainly have dictated a counteraction on the part of Prussia, yet such a thing was scarcely feasible so long as the Prussian monarchy was earning only widespread unpopularity throughout Germany.

The adherents and prophets of Prussian leadership, at home and abroad, were driven to the brink of despair during the ensuing period. King William and his military advisers were obsessed by what to them seemed the revolutionary element in the great nationalist movement. When Schultze-Delitzsch, at a great German shooting fair in Frankfurt in July, 1862, offered a toast in which he spoke of the host of German marksmen and athletes as the backbone of the movement for freedom and unity, William took this as conclusive proof that the democrats intended to smash the standing royalist army.[69]

But was such a stiff-necked negativism in nationalist questions still good enough now? Even the conservative von der Heydt-Roon-Bernstorff cabinet that succeeded the Old Liberals had to walk in their footsteps. To protect Prussia's prestige in Germany as the "guardian of law and order," they once again had to intervene vigorously in Hesse-Cassel, on the side of the diet, against despotic interference.

At home even Blanckenburg warned emphatically against yielding to the temptation to alter the electoral laws by fiat or engaging in other reactionary experiments. Such steps would result only in shaking the people's faith in the government's sincerity, he said, and in increasing the adverse vote. It would be far better to woo popularity by means of tax reductions.[70]

This is precisely what was done. Almost the first step of the new government was to drop the 25 percent defense surtax and reduce the military budget substantially. Even the three-year term of service was cut in spirit if not in name, through the device of winter furloughs; and the very kind of budgetary specification over which the chamber had only just been dissolved was now carried into effect. All this was done in a deliberate effort to win over public opinion to the government side in the impending elections.

Alas, it was all in vain! —the agitation by the conservative People's Union *(Volksverein)*, newly founded in 1861; the election slogans meant to simplify the issues, such as "royal rule by the grace of God, yes—parliamentary rule, no"; the official propaganda and "information." The conservatives suffered another severe defeat. Not a single minister was re-elected. The radical opposition registered further growth. Roon had hoped that the government's clear-cut conservative appeals would bring a turn in the country's mood, allowing traditional royalism and above all the rural voters to come to the fore.[71] But the only real result seemed to be a further dangerous radicalization of the opposition.

Any objective discussion of military needs in the chamber of deputies had now become vastly more difficult than in 1860; every argument put forward by the government provoked the deepest suspicion and was likely to run counter to intrenched democratic prejudices. Yet the flood of criticism advanced by the progressive party before the military committee represented a rather amateurish jumble.

Many of the reservations now voiced seemed largely based on agitational considerations. Any increase in army strength, it was contended, would endanger the constitutional liberties of citizens, for it would mean that the military authorities had supervision and jurisdiction over more and more men, even while they were on leave. The Landwehr was cheaper and at least as effective as the standing army! So long as the Landwehr was required to be mobilized in case of war, there would be war only *in extremis,* while under the army reorganization it would be much easier to pick a fight for trivial reasons. Prussia did not really need any increase in its armed forces since the international situation was favorable at the moment. Once German unification had been achieved—by the liberal method of "moral conquest," of course, on the Italian model—the military burden on Prussia would be lightened of its own accord.

As was to be expected, the spirit of snobbery among the officers drew even greater fire now. There were even demands that cadet schools be totally abolished. The right of regimental commanders to accept or reject officer candidates was to be modified, to enable noncoms to climb the ladder. Discrimination on account of social background was to be outlawed. This would have meant a truly democratic revolution of the traditions of Old Prussia.

Selfish bourgeois philistinism, hostile to the interests of the state, now had the courage to come out into the open. Objections were voiced against withdrawing sons from the private sphere for such a long period to serve the country. The use of available tax revenues for welfare and cultural purposes was favored. The effect on the economy of calling up so many young men was deplored.

The major issue, however, was still the power of the purse of the people's representatives, unhampered by considerations of national defense which the moderate liberals had still been willing to take into account. There were to be no more stopgap measures. In the military committee only a minority were content to make solely those budgetary cuts as would force a reduction in the term of service. The majority were determined, come what may, to cut back all the way to the level of 1859—until such a time as a new defense bill was offered and approved.[72]

Predictably enough, no agreement on the budget proved possible under these circumstances. An open constitutional crisis had become inevitable, a prospect that caused deep consternation on both sides. As we know, the moderate progressive Twesten, in company with General Stavenhagen and the historian Sybel, undertook an effort at mediation. What they proposed was another blanket appropriation as a stopgap, this time, however, contingent on government agreement to introduce a new defense bill providing a two-year term during this same winter session.

The debate over this compromise proposal on the floor of the diet's plenary session took up seven days in September, 1862. Sybel, the two Vinckes, Count Schwerin, and Twesten fought for it with the utmost vigor and with every ounce of eloquence at their command; but the situation was already all but hopeless, and they were at first able to marshal not more than a fifth of the vote.

They found words of warm praise for the objective virtues of the reorganization of 1859-1860 and expressly forewent restoration of the old Landwehr.[73] Since they also sharply rejected the demands of the democratic opposition, there seemed to be no substantial difference between them and Roon, except in the matter of the two-year term of service; but they could sense the political conflict behind this issue—the conservative government's reluctance to grant the diet any voice in the matters of army organization.

Here Heinrich von Sybel above all others moved to the attack, with deliberate acerbity. There had been a glaring breach of formal law, he insisted, by the permanent appointments of 1860 when only a temporary budget had been authorized. On the very day of its birth the new organization had "received the stamp of illegality," not to be extinguished until the government admitted it had done wrong and formally made amends.

As we can see today, Sybel correctly spotted the point at which the military cabinet and its royalist hotheads had crucially altered the course of negotiations. But unlike the leftist opposition, Sybel did not concentrate solely on legalistic questions, such as the contention that the reorganization violated the defense law of 1814.[74] On the other side, neither did the government stubbornly cling to its plenipotentiary power to effect the army reorganization without benefit of legislation.

In January, 1862, the Old Liberal cabinet had submitted to the upper chamber a new conscription bill on the grounds that it would "eliminate for good all doubts, even those that might seem baseless" of the coverage of the Act of 1814 and thus prevent any further debate—although there was no absolute need for such a measure.[75] The bill was passed by the upper chamber unanimously and without debate, but it had failed to be submitted to the lower chamber following its dissolution and reconstitution.

Even the conservative von der Heydt-Roon government, however, shrank from the ultimate step of formalizing the reorganization by royal edict rather than legislative act. On the contrary, at the very outset of the plenary debate it promised in no uncertain terms to introduce a bill on military service at the coming winter session. It expressly acknowledged, moreover, "that the present army organization, insofar as it requires a permanent budget increase or a new legal settlement of universal military service, cannot be regarded as definitive, until the constitutional assent of the diet has been granted."[76]

In the circumstances it was at least conceivable that the promised defense bill might be regarded as the kind of amends Sybel had insisted on; and indeed it seemed for a moment as though the issue of political power might after all be settled peaceably. Despite everything that had happened Sybel and his friends still were hopeful of carrying the house, if only the government were to show a conciliatory attitude[77] on the single point on which, in Sybel's view, popular opinion was irrevocably clear—the question of a two-year term of service.[78] It was on this very point that the war minister now expressed himself most ambiguously, displaying evasiveness, however, rather than rejection.

We do not have nearly enough insight into Roon's thinking during these critical weeks. It seems certain, however, that even with von der Heydt and Bernstorff by his side he did not feel that his political experience and skill were equal to mastering a great constitutional crisis without the help and leadership of a much stronger political personality, that is to say Bismarck. Apparently his tactics once again aimed at warding off the ultimate collision by conciliatory gestures of one kind or another until such a time as the king could be persuaded to summon Bismarck as minister president.

These dilatory tactics may serve to explain the concessions of the preceding spring—dropping the surtax and agreeing to budget specification. The new budget cuts and winter furloughs probably served the same end, as did the evasive response to the question of the service term and the confidential talks with Vincke and Twesten (indirectly also with the progressive, Forckenbeck) to explore possibilities of further delay and compromise.[79]

The military cabinet was of course at once disturbed by this seemingly conciliatory attitude. Manteuffel urgently warned against yielding too readily. "Any further reduction would endanger army strength, not only in terms of effectives but of morale as well. Once the king, in the eyes of both the army and the nation, ceases to be the supreme arbiter the very foundations of the army will be shaken. Here lies the dividing line. What is more important to the state and its future—a temporary disagreement with the chamber or the undermining of the army?"[80]

This intervention merely served to anger Roon severely. He was not deterred from continuing work in his ministry on a new organization plan, probably begun as early as September, that would enable him to put off the chamber with the prospect of a shortened term of service, while throwing the liberal bourgeoisie the sop of many exemptions from military service. Actually, Roon's plan would have pushed the idea of a people's army even farther into the background. He sought to do only just enough to end the irksome bickering with the diet over army questions once for all.

There never has been a satisfactory explanation for the curious incident of September 17, in which Roon created a sensation by suddenly showing himself in a conciliatory light. The two-year term, he hinted, might after all be a suitable topic for discussion, provided there were a *quid pro quo*. This astonishing surrender at the very peak of the crisis seemed to Roon's admirers greatly to tarnish his image of exemplary steadfastness, especially when only two days later the king exacted a retraction, demonstrating that the conciliatory gesture was ill-conceived and enjoyed no backing.

The impression this vacillation made on the other camp may be imagined. It was viewed as either a symptom of internal discord on the government side or a deliberate ruse. Even the Old Liberal Bernhardi was indignant when he read about the affair in the newspapers, concluding that such wavering might destroy both the army and the king's prestige.[81] Later critics have suggested that Roon simply lost his nerve, or that his skill as a politician left something to be desired. In a letter to his friend Perthes he encouraged this view. Left in the lurch by his king before the chamber, he chivalrously accepted the full blame himself, speaking of a "feeble attempt at conciliation" on the part of the cabinet, with himself, unfortunately, cast in the leading role.[82]

In fact there was nothing feeble or inconsistent about Roon's role on September 17. Unless we are mistaken, his conduct was part of a grandiose plan that was to give a new turn to the whole army controversy. As it happened, the plan was submitted to the king in written form only on October 10, three weeks after Bismarck was appointed. Yet there is good reason for believing that in its basic outlines it had long since been concerted between Roon and his assistant, Colonel Bose; and that the war minister had envisaged it as an expedient during the crisis in September—perhaps as no more than a means for once again postponing the consitutional crisis proper.[83]

Under this plan, the new military service bill announced for the winter of 1862-1863 was to include revolutionary innovations. To offset the concession of a two-year term, a quota of re-enlistees was to be demanded sufficient to make up one third of the infantry battalions. In practice this would have meant that there was no need for the third class of draftees.

Increased costs were to be met by "stand-in payments" *(Einstandsgelder)* on the part of those wholly or partly exempted from military service. Whoever was not drafted for active service (whether because of some handicap or simply a lottery) would have had to pay his stand-in money as a kind of defense tax. In addition there were to be equivalency payments by affluent young men who did not wish to serve the obligatory year with the infantry, foot artillery, or pioneer units. No such ransom was to be available for other types of units.

Whoever was unable or unwilling to pay his stand-in money would be retained in service for the third year, if necessary; for it was anticipated that despite the financial incentives not enough veterans would re-enlist for at least two years, so that the third recruit class could not be dispensed with altogether. There was another important innovation. Peacetime army strength was to be fixed by law at 1-1.2 percent of the population—in other words to grow automatically with the population. Military expenditures too were to be fixed permanently in form of an amount per capita of army strength. All these measures would immediately expand the legislature's participation in army matters, although at a later date that participation would be virtually eliminated.

By present-day social standards these provisions seem highly questionable. True, the French ransom and substitute system was only skirted, for it was up to the draft boards to determine whether a man was to be called up or exempted against payment of stand-in money. Yet there was always the plausible suspicion that military budget considerations played a part in such determinations. Nor was it made clear whether payment of a defense tax was intended to free a man from having to risk his life in wartime.

As for the question of the third service year, instead of being settled it was thrown into even greater confusion. Whether or not it was served would depend in part on chance—whether a soldier was assigned to horse or foot—in part simply on his purse. There would henceforth have been men who had to stay in for their third year for lack of money, while others, equally poor, would be discharged at the end of their second year because the regiment in question had a sufficient number of re-enlistees; and men who re-enlisted for four years might find themselves serving that same third year at higher pay, side by side with poor devils who had to do so at the ordinary rate.

Criticism of the plan was not slow in coming, and Roon defended the military establishment by asserting that "the affluent, educated, and propertied are called on for greater sacrifices in serving in person than the day laborer, artisan, or farm hand. . . . The justice of the old one-year service plan is now, under rather different social circumstances, made available to broader circles, among whom education and possessions make the three-year term of service appear irksome and superfluous [*sic*]."

In effect, however, the plan provided for a privilege that could be purchased with money rather than education. One critic, probably Manteuffel himself, objected quite rightly that "the whole relationship of army service would be altered. It would no longer be an honorable duty, to be absolved by every able-bodied man alike. It would receive the stamp of a burden the poor man has to bear in its full weight, while the rich man could evade it at least in part." An actual difference in the term of service as between different types of units was one thing: to leave it up to the affluent whether they wished to serve two years or three was quite another.

No doubt about it, there was little social thinking in this reform plan. Its object was not to strike a mean between royalist and populist army, between the ideals of authoritarianism and democracy. In essence it sought to create a Praetorian Guard after all, one in which the barrack-room spirit of the veteran soldier was to prevail. It denied the ideals of the resurgence even more clearly than before.

Even as a makeshift, as a way out of a difficult political situation, the plan bespeaks the spirit of its authors. It is the product of a purely military professionalism to which the notion of a nation in arms had become completely foreign. It appealed to the basest selfish instincts of the liberal bourgeoisie rather than to patriotism. It was plainly modeled on the army of Napoleon III whose performance in the Italian campaign of 1859 had deeply impressed the Prussian generals and whose long-term troopers Roon had held up to the chamber in 1860 as exemplifying the virtues of extended enlistment.[84]

Did Roon seriously believe that he could win over the liberal opposition to such a plan? We recall the indignation with which the military committee in that year had rejected the idea of the French system of substitute service, introduced into the debate by the war ministry at the time.[85] What reason was there to assume that this attitude had suddenly changed? Surely such a thing was scarcely plausible.

Still, the Old Liberals themselves had offered certain compromise proposals in which a reduced term of service would have been offset by an increased quota of re-enlistees—eighty men per battalion—and by permanent training camps on the French model, for the purpose of raising military efficiency. In making these proposals to the minister, Max Duncker flattered himself with the hope that the liberal deputies, fearful of a constitutional crisis, would "grab them with both hands."[86]

It is hard to judge whether he was right. Bernhardi entertained serious reservations. The "fine and chivalrous character of the army," he thought, would be shifted in the direction of a mercenary army by too many re-enlistments.[87] Vincke-Olbendorf, on the other hand, actually considered the possibility that men who were not called up for service should pay an indemnity to help defray the added expense of re-enlistments. Liberal idealism had indeed begun to pale into sheer opportunism![88] Here was the beginning of an evolutionary process which Bismarck's government was to foster with growing success through the decades.

Much more fruitful and promising was the notion of fixing once for all, by means of legislation, the level of the draft and of military expenditures generally. This too took its point of departure from a liberal suggestion. Roon had publicly voiced the proposal for the first time on September 12, in response to a speech by Gneist urgently warning the government against treating army reorganization, on the British model, as a purely budgetary question, to be submitted year after year anew to the whims of changing majorities.[89]

The minister probably counted on winning the approval of at least the moderate liberals for his bill, for he well knew, from his confidential discussions, how greatly they feared an open constitutional crisis. At the very least he may have hoped to postpone the crisis once again. The house certainly responded to his first conciliatory hints with the greatest alertness and attention. If he succeeded meanwhile in persuading the king to summon Bismarck, the new minister president might find a way of resolving the intolerable tensions by means of the kind of vigorous foreign policy all the liberals longed for.

In the end Roon succeeded only with the second part of this program; the first part fetched up against the king's stubborn opposition to the new army plan. He was not against the system of re-enlistment and professionalism as such—indeed he probably welcomed that aspect because it promised him the kind of Praetorian Guard that would be eminently suited to protecting the throne from internal upheaval.[90] He did find fault with the arbitrary choice of men who had to serve three years, side by side with those who had to do only two—to say nothing of those called up only as replacement reserves. This, he felt, might harm morale and create disaffection.

But for the king the crucial element was the shortened term of service, disregarding for the moment some technical points like the reduction in recruit cadres. He had identified himself so closely with the three-year term as the fulcrum of his program that to budge from this stand even in the slightest seemed to him a failure to keep faith with himself.[91] He objected equally to the "irksome limitation" of the right of the crown to set the strength of the army—to his mind the diet had no business in that sphere.[92]

Behind these objections one can clearly hear the exhortations of his courtiers and military advisers. Manteuffel happened to be away on leave, but as Alvensleben explained to the crown prince: "To yield would mean setting up the chamber of deputies as commander-in-chief in place of the king—in other words, it would amount to a breach of the constitution initiated by the king."[93]

The entreaties of Roon, von der Heydt, and Bernstorff were in vain—their warnings that the king would be violating the constitution, the repeated resolutions of the cabinet. Incited by his adjutants general, the king had decided once for all to leave "the path of concession and compromise," which they insisted he had followed so far. He had long since adopted the conservative theory of the "constitutional gap," according to which the government could proceed in an emergency without budgetary legislation,[94] and he was indignant that the council of ministers hesitated to adopt this view. Turbulent council sessions would end with him solemnly proclaiming his decision to lay down the crown since "his ministers had abandoned him." This of course, was the very act Roon had long feared, the main reason why he had shrunk from an open conflict.[95]

Once again the ministers, and especially the general, had no alternative but obedience. Only von der Heydt and Bernstorff, who bore the heaviest responsibility (for the treasury and foreign affairs), departed. A so-called crisis cabinet took form, headed—after more wrestling for the king's conscience—by Bismarck, who pledged himself to see to it that the monarch's will prevailed. The chamber had already rejected the budget for 1862. What had been an army controversy now developed into open constitutional crisis.

Its further progress in detail is irrelevant within the context of our theme, for no new aspects emerged in the dispute over royalist versus populist army. The sides were clearly drawn. The issue before the house was now the maintenance of its basic constitutional rights. For the king, on the other hand, it was a question of turning back an outright challenge to the crown—quite along the lines of the slogan formulated in the *Kreuzzeitung* at New Year's of 1862— "royal rule by the grace of God, yes! Parliamentary rule, no! "

As bitterness deepened on both sides of the power struggle, all thought of any understanding on army matters went out the window. What is important to see is that Bismarck, despite his avowal of unconditional loyalty, never for one moment envisaged adopting the king's uncompromising stand on the question of the length of army service. In a technical sense, he was completely indifferent to whether it should be two years or three; and we know today that his assurances to Twesten and other liberals in the fall of 1862—to the effect that, with Roon, he still hoped to win over the king to the two-year term—were quite sincere and by no means a deliberate ruse.

If only to confuse and divide the opposition, Bismarck would have liked to see a new defense law along the lines of Roon's mediation draft of October 10. He actually succeeded in having the council of ministers accept a version embodying this draft in outline—especially the imposition of legal limits to the level of conscription; but there he met stiff opposition on the part of the military cabinet. Manteuffel insisted that any legal limit on peacetime army strength imposed by the diet meant a capitulation by the crown. The army would "gain the impression that the law rather than the king was its master." Yet the "king's personal rule" was an indissoluble part of the Prussian military state, to be defended against the power greed of the progressives. To submit meant "destruction of the state."[96]

King William postponed his decision on Roon's compromise proposal until his adjutant general had returned from his leave and then decided in the latter's favor. He characterized the draft as a "death sentence for the army" and rejected it. After a bitter struggle in which Bismarck and Roon vainly tried to salvage the fixed draft quota and some kind of indemnity payment by those not drafted in peacetime, the service bill of 1863 was presented in the form the military cabinet wanted. The accompanying message insisted expressly that army organization was among the constitutional executive powers of the crown, impinging on the sphere of the legislature solely regarding the power of the purse. The government persisted steadfastly in this stand until 1865. Again and again it submitted a service bill providing for a three-year term for all branches. Draft quotas, peacetime strength, integration of line and Landwehr—these were aspects on which it claimed complete discretionary power, with no need for legislative approval.

The reaction from the diet was not long in coming. To let the military set peacetime army strength at its pleasure meant that the diet would be completely hamstrung. The generals could simply raise it higher and higher, leaving the chamber only the privilege of approving the appropriations *ex post facto*. Despair and indignation were greatest in the Old Liberal camp as not only liberal hopes went aglimmering but the whole "Little German" nationalist dream as well—or so they thought.

In the 1863 diet Heinrich von Sybel with fiery words excoriated the war minister—in his eyes the main culprit—for having mutilated the work of the preceding year as the henchman of a party of reaction, serving the "narrow-minded professionalism" that had infected the military establishment ever since the fateful turn in 1819. He reserved his strongest words for the traditional liberal demand for limiting the king's arbitrary power in the military sphere by means of clear-cut legislation. His own draft bill, offered as an alternative to the government's, actually showed the influence of the radical left. The only policy now left to the Old Liberals was to appear as the allies of the progressives.

But the aims of the liberal-democratic majority now went much farther. The more the crown insisted on its military monopoly, the more the chamber wished to extend its own jurisdiction. An elaborate bill introduced in the spring of 1863 went so far as to regulate every detail of army organization, recruitment, and service. The struggle now actually revolved around the issue the conservatives had long stressed in their election slogans—"royalist versus parliamentary army." It had long passed beyond the original issue of reaching a basic understanding on army reorganization. The liberals now wanted the army largely civilianized,[97] the extreme radicals like Waldeck and Schulze-Delitzsch a return to the Landwehr of 1814.

The king on his part forbade his ministers to allow a draft quota to be set by legislation in any manner or form. Both before and after the Danish war he foiled every effort by Bismarck and Roon to split the opposition by reaching an understanding with its moderate wing or to settle the unhappy controversy in some other way.[98] He was absolutely convinced that parliamentary intervention in organizational matters meant the dissolution of the army and thus a step toward immediate revolution.[99]

On the conservative side Kleist-Retzow in the upper chamber had given out potent slogans as early as 1862: The survival of the Prussian monarchy was at stake—the democrats wished to humble it as they had in 1848 and "remove it from the constitution"; the army was to be demoralized and even replaced, by popular sports and rifle clubs; the old Prussian monarchy was to be bent to the foreign power of a Pan-German democratic parliament. The royalist army must be maintained as the rock on which all efforts at revolution would founder. Any compromise with the chamber of deputies meant a slide toward parliamentary government; for if any agreement were reached, it would be the parliament rather than the king who would have reorganized the army![100]

The propaganda of the conservative Prussian People's Union *(Preussischer Volksverein)* was pitched in a similar key. This group actually tried to proselytize inside the army,[101] which was scarcely necessary for there could be no doubt how the officers felt. Care was taken that liberal ideas would have no opportunity to infiltrate these circles—or at least that they would make no headway there.

The whole conflict put the final touch on turning the Prussian army into a bodyguard for the old monarchy. Let us not forget, however, that the resemblance of monarchial authority to the Führer principle of later authoritarian states is quite superficial. Hence it is an oversimplification to compare the quarrel over army reform in 1860 with the latter-day struggles between militant and pacifist mass sentiment. Not even the radical democratic wing of the Prussian bourgeoisie was pacifist-minded or internationalist in the modern sense during the 1860's—this was true only of the social-democratic proletariat of later decades; and not the least reason why these masses became so deeply alienated from the traditionally "militant" thinking of old Prussia lay precisely in the course and issue of the army conflict of 1860-1866.

For the true substance of the quarrel was not rearmament versus disarmament but autocracy versus democracy. It is true that hostility to high taxes, reluctance to face the burdens of military service, and a measure of stubborn individualism all played a part in the opposition to Roon's reforms, but this applied almost exclusively to the extreme left wing which acquired political weight only after 1861; and essentially it was only a reaction to the attitude of the king and his military advisers.

The Old Liberal leadership on the other hand was by no means lacking in promilitarist spirit, and initially it played a crucial role. Indeed, if it had been vouchsafed even partial success—which Roon and after him Bismarck were quite willing to grant it—it might well have prevailed in the critical phase of 1862. What the Old Liberals opposed was not monarchial authority as such but royal absolutism. In more precise terms, they rejected the reactionary approach of the archconservatives and the high nobility, a system closely identified with memories of Prussia's darkest hours, with a period of dreary stagnation at home and ineffectiveness in foreign affairs.

In the unanimous judgment of the shrewdest observers—and even of Bismarck—the reason the aristocrat officers were so profoundly suspicious of the whole army reform and its instigators lay precisely in the narrow-minded Prussian particularism that lived on in the royal army. Nothing at all was to be found there approaching the nationalist fervor that inspired the liberals; and this was seen to be the source of the curse of utter political sterility that afflicted the royalist government.

Until the entry of Bismarck upon the scene, the initiative in the field of foreign policy lay far more on the liberal than on the conservative side—and of course none could have foreseen that this supposedly ultrareactionary Junker would one day stand revealed as an inspired statesman of international stature. Judging William's reign from the vantage point of Bismarck's later successes, one is likely to ignore the fact that the king not only threw away an uncommonly favorable domestic constellation by inciting the constitutional crisis instead of seizing political leadership, but that he thereby came perilously close to ruining forever the great opportunities in foreign policy afforded Prussia by an exceptionally favorable European constellation.

Prussian historians have heaped praises on William for the "heroic fortitude" with which he maintained the Prussian "soldier state" against all liberal efforts to undermine it and soften it up. He himself doubtless believed he was only doing his duty as a soldier and as the heir of his forerunners by clinging so tenaciously to his "command power" and to what he viewed as military necessity. But does mere adherence to absolutist traditions really strengthen royal authority? If the reign of Frederic the Great appears to posterity to shine with such a splendid light, is this because of the absolutism of his rule or because of the immense dynamics of a vigorous policy in the pursuit of power?

It was precisely the deep chasm that separated ruler and people that the reformers of the resurgence deplored so passionately as standing in the way of the enhancement of Prussian power; and the interests of Prussian power politics were certainly ill-served when the constitutional crisis reopened this gulf and the liberal parliamentarians once again referred to the "militarist state" as the enemy of the "democratic state." Real political authority is gained only in performance, not by rigid adherence to hereditary powers.

After the experiences of 1848, the masses no longer believed in the self-evident, historic, and divine right of kings with a faith so profound that they thought Prussia permanently immune to domestic upheaval. To be accepted as a true leader, the king could not in the long run dispense with popular government. It was only Bismarck's policy of national unification that rid the Prussian monarchy of the hazard of being regarded as a venerable relic of the past, completely out of touch with the people and the times and maintaining its position in a vastly changed world only with difficulty. By investing the crown with new glamour, Bismarck at once elevated the Prussian army above the role of a royal bodyguard with mainly police functions, a mere "pillar of the throne."

The army that won the victories of Düppel and Alsen, of Königgrätz, Metz, and Sedan was nothing like a mass army in the present-day sense. It was a highly disciplined royal army led by officers who were largely aristocrats, held together by a strong *esprit de corps*. Military service was by no stretch of the imagination truly universal, nor was there any such thing as total mobilization—even less so than in the Wars of Liberation. No, the army that took the field during the campaigns associated with German unification consisted of no more than a well-trained selection among the country's able-bodied young men, supplemented in the war of 1870-1871 by a vanishingly small number of volunteers.[102] All the calculations were centered on the fastest possible mobilization, on swift and vigorous offensive that would quickly decide the issue.

When the French, in the winter of 1870-1871, began to establish mass armies in the true sense and Paris defended itself tenaciously, Roon's mobilization scheme was seriously embarrassed.[103] These difficulties were overcome only through the technical superiority of German generalship, supported by troops who were then still better than what the enemy could field. It was this royal army that not only won the highest glory in battle for its overlord, but that also raised the Prussian monarchy to a position of supremacy in Germany. The proclamation of the German Reich on January 18, 1871, was a purely military spectacle.

The splendor of that spectacle drew a mantle of oblivion over the harsh and bitter struggle that had raged only a few years before on the issue of royal versus parliamentary or people's army. The main credit again belongs to Bismarck who, at the conclusion of the victorious Austrian war, persuaded the king to end the constitutional crisis. The king fought every step of the way, but in the end the settlement went a long way toward meeting liberal views of constitutional law.[104] The indemnity bill Bismarck introduced in the diet in the late summer of 1866 was no feeble half-measure, no "dilatory compromise formula" papering over rather than clarifying the legal dispute. It openly acknowledged the legislature's power of the purse, though without curtailing the crown's constitutional privileges and the king's supreme command power.

The diet was persuaded to give *ex post facto* approval for the government expenditures made without budgetary authority—in other words, to acknowledge that they had been objectively necessary. In the matter of the extent and limits of the king's powers of military command, no concessions were made, contrary to the desires of the liberals.[105] On the other hand, neither was any obstacle placed in the way of some future settlement. The whole question was simply passed over in silence. No doubt was thus left that the Prussian army reorganization, as already put into effect, was indeed legal; and for the future the whole question of army organization was shifted from Prussian to national constitutional ground. In the constituent North German Reichstag Bismarck unhesitatingly proceeded, by struggle and compromise, to provide the federal armies with a firm legal basis anchored in the constitution. He could never have pushed this through in a purely Prussian setting against the will of the king.[106]

The ultimate aim of Bismarckian policy was thus not to perpetuate the dispute but, for the time being at least, to achieve a true compromise, as Count Eulenburg in 1866 expressly assured the Prussian diet. This was clearly recognized to be an inescapable political necessity. It might have been possible in the wake of military victory to institute an absolutist regime by the crown which would have ignored the parliamentary power of the purse and suppressed liberal opposition; but as Bismarck himself persuasively argues in his memoirs,[107] this would have hamstrung Prussia's policy of German nationalism.

"Absolutism," Bismarck was quick to add, "is a form of government ill-suited for success in Germany in the long run. . . . Absolutism by the crown is no more durable than absolutism by parliamentary majority. The requirement that both must approve any change in the legal status quo is equitable, and we had no need to make any substantial changes in the Prussian constitution. One can govern under it, and the very foundations of German politics would have been buried, had we changed it in 1866."

As we shall yet see Bismarck, with the help of the federal constitution, did put into effect a kind of absolutist crown power in the military sphere; but the point is that he did so through constitutional provisions, through agreed and settled legal standards; for Bismarck entirely shared the liberal view that arbitrary sovereign power should be limited by fixed ordinance. He had no sympathy whatever with the coup d'état plans of the military cabinet and reactionary hotheads, not even while the conflict was on, though he himself at the high point was capable of flouting the law with callous brutality.

The concept of a government of law and order by a consensus between the two elements of power within the monarchial-constitutional system was part and parcel of Bismarck's consititutional approach. Yet his own constitution falls far short of meeting the exacting standards of modern constitutional lawyers for clear-cut delimitation of sovereignty and strict and rigid conceptual clarity in general. Irrational in all its parts, it stemmed more from practical political needs and historical circumstance than from theoretical considerations. It viewed representative participation in public power as a beneficent limitation rather than a dangerous diminution of royal authority.

Durable understanding reached in struggle with the opposition, such then was the goal of Bismarck's policy, at home and abroad. It was distinctly not a policy of perpetuating struggle as such. To concentrate military power around the crown was not to be an end in itself. Not pugnacity, not mutual distrust between the governors and the governed, but the settlement of conflicting interests under secure royal authority was to be the normal stance.

This was the very goal seen as already within easy reach by the Old Liberals of 1860 who, following the indemnity act of 1866, called themselves "National Liberals" in the North German Reichstag. They now hoped that a process of fusion would unite at a higher level the conflicting concepts of the state as arbitrary military power and as civilian rule based on law and order. The ideal envisaged by the reformers of the resurgence had been that of a militant democratic society, joined in free dedication under monarchial leadership, and this ideal seemed now at last to be realized within the larger framework of a new national entity.

This was the reason for the deep satisfaction felt by the best minds among the German bourgeoisie during the years when the German Reich was actually being established; and it was also the reason they streamed into Bismarck's camp apace. Yet the degree to which these hopes were fulfilled turned out to be extremely modest. Bismarck's foreign policy after 1871 was clearly pointed at securing an enduring balance of interests among the European powers, at the maintenance of a lasting peace. Of this we shall hear more. But his domestic policy was plagued by constant, bitter, and enervating struggle.

There were many reasons for these controversies, but in the final reckoning they were all associated with the fact that Bismarck's Reich was launched under autocratic rather than democratic auspices, as the product of the Prussian monarchy and its royal army. The chasm that gaped open in the years from 1860 to 1866 could never be entirely closed. The long mutual distrust had its baleful aftereffects. Despite the military splendor that accompanied the founding of the Reich, the Bismarckian state never cast a spell over the nation's spiritual life to compare with the Wars of Liberation or the rising of 1848.

The Reich's progenitor probably planned it that way. His thinking on the content and limitations of politics was coldly objective. The Reich never lost its character as a creation by monarchial cabinets, and thus the political education of the German people never got beyond the midway point. The conservative nobility retained possession of many of its traditional bastions—the courts, the army, the civil service, the upper chamber of the Prussian diet—without gaining the kind of political realism and popularity that made the British nobility almost into our own times a perpetuator of political traditions and a genuine buttress of the throne.

The conservative party Bismarck founded turned more and more into an agrarian party—mainly the party of the large landed proprietor class—although it also attracted elements of big capitalism from industry and banking. The effect of Bismarck's regime on the liberal bourgeoisie was ambivalent. Part of it, in following the chancellor, lost its political and spiritual independence, and with that its popularity as well, turning into a purely opportunist party of the propertied bourgeoisie and sacrificing its ideals of liberty to its faith in power. This, by the way, is a process readily traced in the biographies of most of the liberal leaders.

Another liberal group never found its way out of the blind opposition of the years of crisis and hardened into dogmatic nihilism, into a kind of individualism hostile to the state as such. The masses of Catholic churchgoers had great difficulty in feeling at home in Bismarck's Reich—more and more so after the *Kulturkampf;* and as for the new classes of industrial workers and employees, they too never overcame their hostility.

Amid such deep inner conflicts the Prussian army—and on its model those of the other German federal states—endeavored to train the German people in monarchist sentiment and patriotic dedication. The strict monarchist allegiance of its officers never wavered, and this *esprit de corps* exerted its effect deeply among the sons of the educated bourgeoisie who served the army as reserve officers. The patriotism that came into being in such fashion looked backward rather than forward, subsisted on hoary tradition rather than promising new ideas. As often as not, the bourgeois would simply ape the customs and even the snobbery of the nobility.

This only served to accentuate German class differences, already well developed for various reasons. At the same time German life under the Reich sustained a distinct militarist tinge that repelled Western European sensibilities. That kind of ostentatious militarism had been quite foreign to the student volunteers and Landwehr officers of 1813; and we are probably entitled to regard it as a consequence of the retrogression from people's army to royal army which has already preoccupied us for some time. The end of the army controversy had frozen that militarism into place.

What is far more important, the army's unique role within the monarchial-constitutional state was also frozen into place. It was an instrument of monarchial power beyond party strife; and after the experiences during the crisis no parliament again had the stomach to meddle with it in earnest. The relation between statesmen and generals in Prussia-Germany was thus fixed in a very particular way, quite different from the countries of Western Europe under parliamentary government. An essential element in this development was the supreme Prussian military agency to which we shall now turn our attention: the growth of monarchial command power within the military cabinet and the General Staff.

7

Army and Constitution – Military Cabinet and General Staff

W
AS THE ARMY a state institution like any other, or did it occupy a special position as an arm of the crown rather than of the constitutional state as a whole? We have seen this question lurk in the background of the struggle over army organization dating from 1860.[1] Frederic the Great, the *roi connétable,* personally led his army in the field. His officers were his immediate lieges. No state agency was interposed between him and them. From his day onward this pattern was envisaged by every single Hohenzollern ruler, unchanged down to the end of the monarchy, despite the vast growth and rising complexity of the military machine, despite the expansion of Prussian to Reich army, despite the inclusion of large non-Prussian contingents.

This goal was reflected in the organization of the highest military echelons. An essential element in that organization was the desire to vouchsafe the monarch the largest possible sphere of military command power, free of any influence from the side of the legislature. The resulting political, organizational, and constitutional problems lay at the heart of all the difficulties of the Prussian and German constitutional states, from 1848 into the First World War; for if any internal defect aided the enemies of the Second Reich in overwhelming it, it was the lack of coherence in military leadership, the sharpening conflict between the military and political spheres. These issues in turn were part and parcel of the special position occupied within the Bismarckian state by the army as a monarchial household force rather than an instrumentality of the state. It is only here that we clearly begin to see the fateful significance of the questions about which our inquiry revolves.

An army system that fails to stand up in war is worthless. To a greater or lesser degree all the inheritors of Frederic's throne clung to the model of the *roi connétable* without meeting the all-important requirement of genius in both statesmanship and generalship, a rare combination indeed. Its absence finally sealed the doom of the Hohenzollern dynasty; but long before that day, even under the earlier successors of Frederic the Great, it wrought its baleful effects on the state.

Frederic had been his own war minister and chief of staff. To be sure, he availed himself of military assistants. There was a "Minister of War," as chief of the military department within the directory general. There were inspectors general of the various service branches and a "military suite" consisting of aides, adjutants special and general, and a small quartermaster general staff. One of the adjutants general, Wilhelm von Anhalt, who greatly distinguished himself in the Seven-Years' War, was actually appointed quartermaster general in 1765. When it came to major strategic decisions, the king would on occasion consult one or the other of his troop commanders. None of these aides and advisers, however, had the right of independent initiative.

The jurisdiction of the quartermaster staff was quite modest. It was limited in the main to the construction of fortified camps and field bridges, the selection of positions *(Castametrie),* and reconnaissance. No formal agency or fixed corps of general staff officers ever came of it. Indeed the whole military department was concerned almost exclusively with supply and logistics. The main business of the adjutants general seems to have been supervision of army personnel matters, and they worked without regularly fixed jurisdiction. Civilian cabinet secretaries dealt without distinction with military and nonmilitary orders in council. None of these officials was entitled to offer proposals of any kind. Their sole function was to receive orders and see to their execution.

Such a system required the monarch to possess a knowledge of minutiae so intimate that none of Frederic's successors could come even near it. Even while the old king was still alive, by the way, there was a great deal of complaint that his orders were capricious and lacking in detailed knowledge. Hence a "Superior War College" was created under Frederic William II, originally conceived as a kind of central authority for all branches of the military. Only in wartime was operational control to revert to the king or his commanding generals.

In practice this agency turned out to be limited solely to administrative tasks, failing to gain any influence on war plans. It was soon, moreover, watered down and paralyzed by other newly created agencies.[2] Among these was a quartermaster general staff (shortened to general staff), organized as a separate body with a distinctive uniform; but it too attained no real stature. In the judgment of Boyen, Clausewitz, and Müffling it remained a collection of impractical paper strategists without inner coherence and above all without any real contact with tactical leadership. It had access to the sovereign only by way of the adjutant general who gradually emerged from the role of a mere royal military secretary and handyman to become a central figure in the whole military sphere. From

1787 on his functions were organized into a regular office, marking the beginning of the Prussian military cabinet, which was to draw so much fire in later years. Together with the regular cabinet, its purpose was to serve as a buffer that would protect the king from direct pressure by the highest military and civilian echelons.

Every ruler, republican or monarchial, requires a chancellery of his own, a "privy cabinet" to cope with his daily correspondence and his many private affairs. It is matter of foremost public concern that the principal of such a secretariat should not become a political power in his own right, an adviser of commanding influence whose counsel the head of state seeks in place of listening only to the advice of the officials in charge of the various branches of the executive.

Frederic the Great had accepted no advice whatever from his officers and councilors, regarding them all as "servants of the king," mere instruments without claim to a will of their own. He received the heads of his departments collectively but once a year, for the so-called "Ministers' Review." Individual ministers gained an audience with him only on very rare occasions. Virtually his entire contact with them was in writing, through ministerial submissions with which he dealt by means of marginal notes or orders in council.

The example of this mode of rulership "from the cabinet" was a temptation for lesser successors to maintain the proud pose of the autocrat outwardly, while hiding their own inner insecurity. They would avoid oral exchanges with the full complement of their ministers, and even with individual ministers likely to irritate them by their superior expertise. Everything would be settled in the secrecy of the "cabinet," where their sole advisers were unctuous courtiers, cabinet councilors, or adjutants general of pleasing manner, adapting themselves to their ruler's every whim and foible, nonentities one and all, without public responsibility of their own.

In the case of Frederic William II, a man of weak character incapable of sustained effort, the pattern of inconsistency was enhanced by the added influence of favorites of every kind. The result for the army was a complete absence of coherent leadership. The poorly organized and slow-moving military agencies were incompetent to prepare war plans while the loathsome clique of favorites and adjutants general paralyzed the authority and initiative of the generals commanding in the field.

One talented general staff officer, Major Christian von Massenbach, came forward with proposals for a remedy soon after the end of the inglorious crusade against France. The most remarkable element in this organizational plan, presented to the Duke of Brunswick in November, 1795, was the notion that closer coordination between politics and war be sought by means of organizational measures that would end the confusion of multiple authorities and produce realistic war plans of a higher order.

Massenbach envisaged close collaboration among the ministers of foreign affairs, war, and commerce. All three were to be heard in the crown council, to consult on political aims and military and economic capabilities in the event of war and to harmonize these among themselves. The general staff would then draft operational plans in detail, following these considerations. A novel demand was that the chiefs of the general staff must have direct access to the sovereign. It was not made clear what was to be the staff chief's relation to the war minister who appears in Massenbach's crown council as the sole representative of the army. Perhaps he envisaged that the office of war minister in the modern sense should be combined in the same person with those of the chief of staff and the commander-in-chief.

Many details in this memorial are impractical, if not bizarre. Massenbach was a man of literary bent, highly imaginative but undisciplined, enormously industrious, and ambitious. For more than a decade he inundated the court with countless prolix memorials, couched in the flowery style of the period. They deal not only with military but also with political and economic matters, and to this day they are the terror of the library researcher.

Personally, Massenbach failed miserably as a troop leader before, during, and after the battle of Jena; and his military writings mark him as a true paper strategist in the style of the Rococo. It is widely acknowledged, nevertheless, that he deserves some credit for improvements in the Prussian general staff; and that organization itself attributed some principles of its modern organization to proposals originally made by Massenbach, the ingenious Swabian graduate of the *Hohe Karlsschule* in Stuttgart.[3]

His memorial of 1795 is thus not without profound historical interest. The notions developed in it stem from a proper insight into the higher unity of war and politics—collaboration among statesmen and generals on war plans and regular training trips abroad by Prussian general staff officers who were to serve stretches in foreign armies and share in the diplomatic service after the later fashion of military attachés. Massenbach himself declared that he owed this idea to his Württemberg teacher Colonel Nicolai, and it soon became a kind of truism within the Prussian general staff, echoed at times by Scharnhorst and Boyen.[4] It was formulated with particular emphasis by the aforementioned Rühle von Lilienstern, the later chief of the general staff, who actually credited Massenbach.[5] The passages in Scharnhorst and Rühle so strongly prefigure Clausewitz that we realize plainly that the famous basic axiom of that military theoretician's theory of war must be viewed as a legacy from the eighteenth century.

What Massenbach proposed in 1795 was an attempt to restore in some measure by reorganization at the top government level the unity of state and army command which the Prussian monarchy had forfeited after the death of Frederic the Great. He met with no practical success—although government by favorite did come to an end under Frederic William III. Considering the situation that had prevailed it was a distinct step forward. Government organization was tightened up through an improved civilian cabinet staffed with men of insight. The issuance of military orders was centralized in a strengthened adjutant general's office.

The internal structure of the general staff too was improved shortly before the war of 1806, in accord with Massenbach's proposals; but like all the reforms prior to Jena, these in the military sphere were totally inadequate, not least because the key posts were filled with men who were mediocre, if not incompetent. The campaign of 1806 offered the dreary spectacle Clausewitz and Boyen have described to us so graphically. Instead of centralized leadership there was an endless confusion of consultations among commanders, general staff officers, and adjutants general from which no firm views could crystallize and in which even so talented a head as Scharnhorst could no longer prevail. Instead of strengthening unified leadership, the king's presence in the field served only to disperse it still further. The authority of the commander-in-chief, the duke of Brunswick, was weakened and casual opinions voiced by royal adjutants general acquired an altogether disproportionate weight.

Immediately after the defeat at Jena the reformers rose up in force against the power of the cabinet. Hardenberg and Freiherr vom Stein fought the "cabinet council behind its veil," while the military reformers led by Scharnhorst fought the interposition of the adjutant general. The aim in both spheres was to tie the monarch's will more closely than before to the proposals of his responsible advisers. The system of royal absolutism was to be transformed into one of bureaucratic absolutism.

It became quite clear that such changes would be far more difficult in the military than in the civilian sphere. For the monarch to appear in the role of commander-in-chief of his army was the Prussian royal tradition. An army, moreover, cannot be run by majority vote. For this reason alone Stein's endeavor to tie the king in all his decisions to the vote of his ministers, including the minister of war, was foredoomed.

The system of direct access to the monarch by all the ministers, which Hardenberg and Altenstein considered for a while, was also bound to encounter much difficulty. This was owing not only to the peculiarly shy and insecure nature of the monarch and the very limited oratorical gifts of Prussian bureaucrats,[6] but above all to the need for at last bringing to the conduct of government business the coherence and planning that had been lacking. The most efficient remedy in the circumstances was to institute a prime minister or state chancellor who would guide all branches of the administration. He would, so to speak, step into the gap that had opened up since the death of Frederic the Great, insuring the integrity of the government.

During the Prussian state's period of real crisis, it was this system that prevailed, first under Stein and then under Hardenberg, in very different fashion; and it is to the great credit of Frederic William III that he was sufficiently shrewd and selfless, despite a thousand inward qualms, to give these two men freedom of action. For a while—though only after a bitter struggle—the "cabinet council behind its veil" was forced back into the role of a clerical staff.

What about the relation of statesmen and generals during this period? Clearly, true unity could be insured only if the army too was in some manner under the jurisdiction of the chief minister. This is indeed what happened under Stein and Hardenberg. Stein, to be sure, limited his immediate sphere to home and civilian affairs, strictly respecting the formal autonomy of foreign and military matters. The foreign minister von der Goltz and the representative of the commission on military organization—initially Count Lottum, later Scharnhorst—had the right of direct access to the king. But they were under instruction to appear only in the company of the premier; the latter formally presided at conferences of the foreign department and was entitled to participate in the sessions of the military commission whenever they dealt with "political matters, the financial situation, and questions of state policy."

During his brief term of office Stein actually exerted a crucial influence on Prussian foreign policy and worked on military reforms in closest touch with Scharnhorst—although we do not know the full details of his intervention. So little sign of conflict was there then between the military and civilian spheres that the army reformers themselves urgently pleaded for Stein's cooperation. When Stein was away from Königsberg, he on his part requested that Scharnhorst regularly participate in all cabinet appearances before the king.[7]

How far removed Stein was from regarding the Prussian army as a separate military estate, the monarch's household force and "pillar of the throne," is seen from his protest against swearing it in on the "supreme warlord." Commenting on Gneisenau's draft for articles of war, he said: "The notion of a warlord is the counterpart of that of a mercenary. When war service is seen to flow from the citizen's relation to the state, the king appears as head of the state rather than as warlord, and it is to the head of state and to his country that the soldier swears fealty. . . . I would omit the term warlord from the oath and replace it with king and country, etc."[8]

To Stein military service on the part of citizens was part of the general process of popular political education, just as army reform was part of general government reform. In both cases it was a matter of concentrating, simplifying, and rationalizing the official machinery. He was in complete agreement with the military reformers; in his great draft for government reorganization of November 23, 1807, he simply took over Scharnhorst's proposals for military reorganization. By the board went the cumbersome multiplicity of superior war college, military department, provincial supply departments in Silesia and Prussia, intendancy general, army inspectorate, and adjutant general's office. All these agencies were replaced by a single one, the war department *(Kriegs-departement)*, which under the original reform plan was to form a single authority under a war minister and as such a special section of the council of state. The war minister was to report to the sovereign in person, entirely supplanting the adjutant general. The army was placed on the same footing as all other branches of the government.

To this the king took exception. Much against the will of the generals concerned, especially Count Lottum, his adjutant general, but oddly enough with Stein's support,[9] he insisted that the two main divisions of the war department be given completely equal status—the one, under Scharnhorst, concerned with general army administration and command; the other, under Lottum, concerned with supply and logistics. The two divisional chiefs were to report to the king directly. Evidently he wanted to see the conservative Lottum regularly, in addition to Scharnhorst, leader of the reform party which so often kicked over the traces.

Scharnhorst, of course, carried by far the greater weight. In addition to attending to matters of command, personnel, and general organization, he was also in charge of general staff affairs, for he was also "first officer" of the general staff, which alone was kept out of the war department. Scharnhorst was in effect war minister and at once chief of staff, though he did not bear these titles. We already know, from the 1808 plans for the rebellion (see Chapter 4), that he used his power to intervene vigorously in foreign affairs; but since this was done in closest unity with Stein, the chief minister of state, we can scarcely speak of any conflict between the military and political spheres. The two men were bound together by a spirit of passionate militancy. It was left to the king to play almost the only moderating role, to pursue a policy of maintaining peace, as against his leading advisers.

During Hardenberg's chancellorship the subordination of the military to the leading state authority came even more plainly to the fore. As early as September, 1807, in their great Riga reform memorials, Hardenberg and his assistant Altenstein openly dealt with army organization as a political question. Unlike Stein, their proposals went into great technical detail. The concentration of all military agencies into the new war department, prepared for under Stein, was put into permanent effect by Altenstein's ministry (order in council of December 25, 1808, posted on February 18, 1809).

Hardenberg did not make any immediate changes; but as state chancellor he was superior to all the ministers, including those of the war department. They retained the formal right of access to the king,[10] but in practice it was Hardenberg who presented all the more important issues himself, unattended, for his charm and urbanity fascinated the king. He was entitled to be present when any minister was received and thus kept a tight rein on the affairs of state.

Even military matters passed through Hardenberg's office if they had any general political aspects or might have "an effect on the administration." The things the war department was expected to settle with the king without Hardenberg's participation were solely those of a "purely military" character, and even of these he received reports. All cabinet orders except those in this latter sphere were engrossed in the chancellor's office.

The chancellor, in other words, had virtually become chief of the royal cabinet. The limits had been reached of what could be done to maintain administrative unity under the old monarchial system. This unity of political leadership was in no way threatened by segregating a narrow area of "purely military" business, which was indeed perfectly feasible for reasons of efficiency. On the personal level too, relations between Hardenberg and the circle of military reformers were friendly and trustful.

Yet, as we saw in Chapter 4, serious differences of opinion and clashes were inevitable between the passionate militancy of the generals and the king's cautious hesitancy. The chancellor himself, intent on maintaining unified political leadership, was constantly torn between the extremes that constitute the antinomy of political life and that cannot be mastered by organizational measures. It is true that in 1811-1812 he was caught up in a highly complex and obscure situation, while in the actual Wars of Liberation he was chained to capricious allies; but the fact is that Hardenberg at times lacked the strength and stature that would have enabled him to master his internal conflict with a sure instinct for what was possible and necessary.

However that may have been, Hardenberg's leadership was never in danger from the military. There were not even any serious personal quarrels between him and members of the reform circle. Only Blücher, as we have seen, protested Hardenberg's political power, without being able to shake his position for even a moment. There never was the kind of virtual disintegration at the top that marked the First World War later on.

It may be asserted, therefore, that the new military system pioneered by Stein, Hardenberg, and Scharnhorst did indeed stand the test of battle against Napoleon.[11] The war years even saw an increasing tendency toward military centralization. After the first Peace of Paris Boyen was appointed minister of war, the first to carry the title. The partition of his ministry into two coeval main divisions (the general war department and the military economy department), each with direct access to the sovereign, was revoked and the general staff was incorporated into the ministry as a subdivision, the so-called second department, with Grolman as director.

The war minister now was at the head of the whole military establishment. Command, general staff, personnel, organization, administration, the whole lot were under him. This situation continued for only a few years, but it has long been regarded as ideal when contrasted with the subsequent dismemberment of the Prussian and German military establishment into a multiplicity of agencies and commands with direct access to the sovereign.[12] The ideal envisaged by modern observers is evidently the kind of organization Germany had in the years from 1934 to 1938—a single defense minister, responsible for the whole military establishment to the head of state, combining in his person command (as commander-in-chief of the forces) and administration (as head of the military bureaucracy).

This meant that the defense minister must be commander-in-chief of the army in wartime as well—a real field general, not a mere administrator.[13] Thus the constant clamor raised by the German general staff is entirely plausible; in modern war, with its lightning mobilization and its swift and complex technical deployment, deployment as well as operations in the field, they insisted, must lie in the same hand that prepared the whole plan in peacetime. If the war minister is also to be commander-in-chief of the army, he must be the responsible chief of the general staff in peacetime.

One could go further and say that the technical structure of modern warfare leaves strategic operations in such a state of dependence on thorough peacetime preparation in arms, equipment, training, mobilization, etc., that no command authority other than the general staff is equal to exercising the power of decision. This automatically moves the general staff into first place, and the administrative machinery of the war department appears as a mere adjunct in the service of the operational plans prepared by the general staff.[14] For in the end all military organization merely subserves action in the field. From that point of view it seems monstrous to incorporate the general staff into an administrative agency.

In Scharnhorst's and Boyen's day it was not seen in that light. The great importance of general staff work was only slowly beginning to be appreciated. It was Napoleon's style of war, with its massed forces advancing at unprecedented speed on only a few roads and with the bold sweep of its marches, that made the quartermaster general with his plans room, his carefully marked maps, his speed calculations, and march tables quite indispensable. Even Gneisenau, Blücher's chief of staff, was not a trained general staff officer but rather an inspired troop leader, imitating the methods of his great adversary with instinctive assurance.

His innate and intuitive generalship, coupled with the aggressive pluck of that old swashbuckler Blücher, earned the Prussian army its greatest successes. They cannot be credited to careful campaign plans worked out by staff officers, and even the technical support given by such highly intelligent map-table experts as Müffling and Grolman was secondary. Had Scharnhorst, the reorganizer of the Prussian army system, really possessed the major strategic talents with which his disciples and posterity credited him,[15] he would indeed have represented a unique blend of generalship and administrative skill. In any event, he did combine the posts of war minister and chief of the general staff, and he retained this joint tenure even in wartime, down to his untimely death.

His successor Boyen was already far more the organizer and administrator. He neither possessed nor claimed any influence on military operations, not even in the campaign of 1815, when his department head Grolman worked with

Blücher's staff (as quartermaster general to Gneisenau, however, rather than in a direct command capacity). Boyen himself remained with the king at royal headquarters, as remote from the scene of operations as the "supreme warlord." We do not even know whether he was active, during those troublesome months in Paris, along the lines by which Grolman wished him to champion his plans (see Chapter 4, above).

Indeed, this campaign offered the same spectacle as all the later ones to be waged by the Prussian army. The position of the war minister at the head of the entire military establishment proved to be a mere peacetime expedient that meant virtually nothing when the chips were down. The real leadership lay elsewhere, and the war minister did not even act as the army's spokesman in political questions (e.g., the peace negotiations). Even here the chief of the general staff and the commanding general whom he advised were the real driving force.

We should be careful, therefore, not to attribute too much practical importance to the formal organization of Boyen's war ministry. The main purpose of incorporating the general staff as a second department was to provide a firm place and internal structure in the bureaucracy for this organ which had become somewhat disorganized and dispersed during the preceding years.[16]

Only a few years later the whole arrangement was once again changed. The occasion was an entirely fortuitous anomaly. Lieutenant General von Müffling was to rejoin the general staff in 1821, and he happened to have seniority over Major General Rühle von Lilienstern who was then head of the second department in the war ministry which comprised the general staff. Accordingly the latter was made chief of the "grand" general staff which included the staff officers working at the Berlin center, and as such he remained directly under the war minister. Müffling, on the other hand, was made chief of the "army general staff" which in addition to the grand general staff embraced staff officers seconded to higher troop commanders. In that capacity too he was Rühle's superior.[17] In other words, after that time the army general staff was only in part a department of the war ministry. As a whole it was an autonomous agency.

Müffling, however, the new chief, set so little store by his formal autonomy that he wanted to see all affairs in any way touching the general staff combined in the second department of the ministry.[18] Four years later, in 1825, this reorganization was effected in the opposite direction. All the affairs of the second department including the plans room were transferred to the army general staff and the department itself was dissolved. We can thus scarcely speak of any jurisdictional jealousy on part of either side.

Rühle, by the way, remained with the ministry as liaison officer ("General Staff Officer for War Ministry Affairs"), while Müffling was instructed as early as 1821 to "retain a close connection" with the war minister. He was required "to submit his orders and proposals to the war minister before their execution and always to act in concert with the minister."[19] The war minister could thus continue to consider himself the superior authority, with the general staff his auxiliary. The chief of the general staff did not by any means as yet have the formal right of direct access to the sovereign. In the pre-1848 royal army everything was tailored to pure peacetime service.

Yet not even in peacetime could formal subordination of the highest military authorities to the war ministry insure uniform handling of all military affairs. The chief obstacle to such integration was the hoary fiction (surviving only in peacetime) that the Prussian king led his army in person and that its officers were his personal lieges. In practice this was expressed in the right of direct access to the king, possessed not only by the war minister but by the highest-echelon troop commanders. They looked on the minister as an official with jurisdiction over their own office *(Generalkommando)* only in certain administrative questions rather than as a military superior.

In peacetime there simply could be no second commander-in-chief of the Prussian army beside the king. It was amazing enough that Scharnhorst had succeeded at all in staffing his reorganization commission and his ministry with officers so lacking in seniority as Gneisenau and even Boyen. Again and again the old army dignitaries railed against this and we know how often their complaints reached the king's ears. This is especially true of the Guards Corps whose commanders under Frederic William III were the king's closest kinsmen, Duke Charles of Mecklenburg and Prince William. Their *Generalkommando* was the focal point for all the reactionary trends in the army fostered by the high nobility. Even so the right of direct access to the king by the commanding generals weakened the authority of the Prussian war minister right down to the end of the monarchy.

A second element was the exclusion from the over-all running of the military establishment of a certain direct "command power" wielded by the sovereign. This is no Prussian peculiarity but is found in all the German nineteenth-century principalities, an expression of the sovereign's need to assert his supreme command over his troops. Additionally it was to some extent a result of the natural difference between troop leadership proper (by "army order" or "command") and the general running of the army (by "army ordinance") in such areas as supply, replacements, military justice, etc.[20]

This royal "command power" leaned heavily on matters of army personnel in peacetime—the appointment, promotion, and retirement of officers; the awarding of decorations and favors of many kinds; grandiloquent orders of the day; matters of military ceremonial, uniforms, courts martial, etc., etc. A delimitation of the two spheres, one from the other, in legal terms, never took place, at least not in Prussia.

In the Scharnhorst-Boyen ministry the most important of these spheres, personnel matters, was dealt with by a special subsection of the first (general) war department, the so-called "first division," known from 1824 onward as the "section for personnel affairs" *(Abteilung für die persönlichen Angelegenheiten,* abbreviated to AfdpA). Its head occupied a special position in the high bureaucracy by the very fact that like the war minister himself he had regular access to the king.

His office was lent further distinction by the fact that he was entitled to present to the king not merely routine personnel affairs but matters of command *(Immediatsachen),* and that he took over and ran the former adjutant general's office which dealt with the so-called cabinet correspondence.[21] In other words, the head of the AfdpA was subordinate to the war minister in only part of his capacities. In another part he was successor to the one-time adjutant general and chief of the military cabinet, although that term was introduced only in 1817.

Even under Major von Boyen the position of this section head acquired great importance. After Scharnhorst's formal retirement it was Boyen who, from 1810 to 1812, as Scharnhorst's confidant, had to present all the major military and political aspects of army reform to the king. When Boyen himself became war minister, his successor, Major von Thile, painstakingly stuck to his narrow sphere of authority, feeling obliged to support his minister in every way. This was also true of Colonel von Witzleben who succeeded Thile late in 1816 and regained the title of adjutant general the following year. A man of stature in his own right, Witzleben followed in Boyen's footsteps by also becoming war minister, in 1834.

We perceive no cross-currents between military and general cabinet in these decades. Nevertheless these section heads, also serving as military cabinet secretaries, gradually acquired extraordinary status beyond the regular cabinet, for they saw the king virtually daily and in any event much more often than the war minister himself. Already combining command with personnel concerns, they also performed many indispensable services in the private sphere, in the capacity of adjutant. They escorted the king on field exercises and military inspection tours and had countless opportunities for commanding the sovereign's attention.

Long before he was appointed minister Witzleben was accounted Frederic William's military oracle. This monarch was so constituted that he simply needed additional private consultation outside the formal attendance of his war minister. For a long time after 1806, for example, he continued to require, at military consultations, the presence of his old adjutant general Köckeritz, who was then without official standing and a complete nonentity to boot.

What distinguished the new adjutant general's office from the old was the more careful demarcation of its authority, the fact that it could no longer bar the war minister's direct access to the sovereign, and the subordination of its head to the minister as a section head, even though he served as head of the military cabinet. This last factor, however, did not mean too much. Those closest to the sovereign always have an immense tactical advantage. Not a few war ministers were actually toppled by military cabinet chiefs, while the converse occurred on only one occasion (1841). In practice the subordinate position of the AfdpA became more and more an empty formula as the years went by, except for the years immediately following the revolution of 1848. In 1883 it was formally abolished.

Much legal acumen and library research has been spent on studying the history of the reconstituted military cabinet in detail. What has been documented with particular care is the danger to the war minister of unlimited power accruing to the military cabinet by virtue of overlapping jurisdiction and blurred distinctions between administration and command. There was often serious friction between ministry and cabinet, especially in the second half of the century, and these internal tensions have been given part of the blame for the disaster of 1918.

Yet it does not appear that in the course of the century the number of royal orders in council issued by the military cabinet grew very much beyond what were considered "command affairs" from the outset. It is quite true, however, that the exclusion of these and even more of personnel matters from the war minister's sphere of direct influence was harmful in many respects. It again dispersed responsible management instead of concentrating it, weakened the minister's authority within the army, turned the adjutant general into a much-wooed figure and thus carried the danger that court expediency rather than merit would govern choice and promotion of higher officers. Most of the heads of the reconstituted military cabinet are credited with making a sincere effort to pick men by strictly objective criteria from their qualifying reports; but that does not change the fact that after decades of living in a court atmosphere they were bound to be out of touch with the realities of field service and had lost the knowledge of character acquired only in that way.

The work of these military cabinet heads was meant to embody the king's direct and personal relationship with his officers by skipping ministerial intervention, so to speak—this was another hoary tradition handed down from the time of Frederic the Great. But as the Prussian and later the German army grew in size—in the end numbering in the millions—this relationship became mere fiction. The sovereign's face-to-face perspective did not and could not extend very far beyond the old guards regiments. War Minister Bronsart von Schellendorf was not very wide of the mark when he insisted in 1888 that there was no good reason for taking away command matters from his ministry, since the sovereign's command power could be preserved just as well through a responsible minister as through an adjutant general. Bronsart deplored the likelihood that resultant jurisdictional disputes would serve only to aggravate the already excessive friction within the military establishment.[22]

Yet the real danger that threatened from the military cabinet side did not lie in this kind of friction with the war minister, which never, so far as we know, transcended the limits of minor and often purely formal jurisdictional disputes. More serious was the prospect that the military cabinet might develop into a new intermediate instrumentality between the ruler and his ministers, as in the time before 1806. Here the war minister's right of direct access to the king, established between 1808 and 1814, stood in the way. There was no serious break in this privilege right down to the end of the monarchy, though in practice, as we shall yet see, it was allowed to lie idle to an alarming degree under William II.

There was another real danger. The military cabinet offered ambitious and unscrupulous men a chance to exert political pressure "behind the veil" without any let or hindrance—at least this was true when there was no powerful and resolute figure occupying the minister's seat, no one who might have made sure of the cohesion of the political line. It took real character and integrity on the ministerial side to get the better of the insidious daily influences exerted on the sovereign by his entourage.

These were precisely the qualities lacking under the aging state chancellor Hardenberg and even more so after his death in 1822. The office of state chancellor was left vacant, and thus was lost—for good, as it turned out—the supremacy of the prime over the war minister and his minions which Harden-berg had achieved. At the time the loss seems scarcely to have been noted, but in my opinion its repercussions on the subsequent relation of state and army are far more significant than the growing autonomy of various military agencies vis-à-vis the war ministry.

Indeed, after Hardenberg there was to be no Prussian government able any longer to confront the king as a solid political unit, in the manner envisaged by the reformers of 1808 to 1814, and to assert authority in military matters as well. There was only a loose aggregation of ministers functioning as bureau heads. In the army, in the meantime, there took place that quiet transition from the people's army of the Wars of Liberation to a royal guard which preoccupied us in Chapter 5.

For the rest, it was only now that the jurisdictional mania of specialized ministers who were bureaucrats rather than statesmen came into full flower—an obsession Bismarck was to curse on many occasions later on. Here lay the danger that government would again revert to the king's privy council. In place of the lapsed civilian cabinet system, one of the ministers would merely be instructed to report on general government matters, the function formerly performed by Hardenberg. The king's civilian cabinet council itself was limited to purely secretarial duties. Yet scope enough was left for a "premier behind the veil," none other than house minister Prince Wittgenstein, a dangerous and furtive plotter and a man after the heart of all the reactionary cliques. During the old king's declining years he actually managed to involve the adjutant general and chief of the military cabinet in his schemes.

The succession in 1840 put an end to these machinations. Up until the revolution of 1848 the military cabinet played no further political role. All the more important was to be its political importance in the new constitutional state. Only the creation of a representative assembly and a government answerable to it brought to full fruition the problem of integrating the army with the constitutional state, the problem originally introduced by Stein and Hardenberg.

Hardenberg's reforms had endeavored to replace sovereign absolutism with its bureaucratic counterpart, so to speak. Under such a system, political wisdom was embodied less in the sovereign than in the chancellor[23] who, in certain exigencies, might have to force his superior insight on the king, invoking public opinion. This meant primarily the higher bureaucracy, the progressively minded sections of the nobility, and the educated bourgeoisie—though all of this was without the element of public accountability anchored in the constitution.

It had not proved particularly difficult to fit the monarchial army into such a system of bureaucratically organized state rationale. The individual ministers were after all bureau heads, managers of specialized departments, rather than political figures. Over-all political direction was vested essentially in the chancellor, later on in the king, advised by his cabinet; and thus a conflict between the war minister's loyalties as a soldier and his political responsibilities was not likely to arise.[24]

But a war minister as a member of a government accountable to a representative assembly—that was an altogether different matter. If that accountability was taken seriously, it meant that the minister must be quite free of political commitments to anyone else. To put it another way, in a monarchial-constitutional state only a politician is qualified to be a minister. A soldier never is, for he cannot act as a completely free and independent adviser to his supreme commander whom he owes military obedience. As was shown by the example of Roon, that disciplinary relationship may well prove to be the stronger tie in case of conflict.

That is why the third French republic, in its later stages, did not hesitate to appoint civilian war ministers. In Prussia that would have been deemed intolerable, mainly because it would have meant interposing a civilian between the army and its commander-in-chief. In the Prussian view it ran counter to the nature of an army to receive direct orders from any but military leaders or to grant scope to any but military authority within its sphere. A bourgeois politican has only his authority as a politician, and that is forever exposed to partisan strife. Military authority on the other hand must prevail unconditionally, subject to no doubt whatever. It must be based on qualities of military rather than political leadership.

In England, for these reasons, at one time the expedient was adopted of entrusting command of the army in the narrower sense to a purely military commander-in-chief while placing by his side two purely political officials, both of them members of Parliament, one for matériel and the other for finances. The commander-in-chief was answerable to the sovereign rather than Parliament, but like the administrative chiefs was subject to the political control of the War Office, headed by the Secretary of State for War as a member of the Cabinet.[25]

This type of organization was by no means ideal, on the contrary led to serious friction, but it did try to do equal justice to the military desire to hold out a purely military sphere from party politics and to the political desire for political control of the army in a constitutional state. The reason this solution was not feasible in Prussia was that it would have taken direct command of the army out of the king's hand even in peacetime. The actual commander-in-chief, dependent on political control even though not on military orders from a party minister, was thus not under the full command of the king.

The English army system, in other words, could exist only under the English monarchy which had long since had to surrender all thought of ever again using the army as the sovereign's bodyguard against "internal enemies" and which had to rest content with the watered-down sovereignty of a constitutional monarchy—to the point where there was very little difference in the formal legal sense between the king of England and the president of a republic. This was precisely what the Prussian kings held out against; and in the army crisis of 1862 Manteuffel held up the Parliament-controlled British commander-in-chief as a bogy when exhorting King William not to yield an inch in the diet.[26]

Yet once the revolution of 1848 had swept away the absolutist constitution there was no alternative to instituting the strange hybrid of a monarchial-constitutional war minister vis-à-vis a popular assembly—an officer whom the deputies could never regard as one of their own, but only as a tool of the crown and a representative of his class. At the same time his authority within the army was greatly circumscribed, for three reasons: If war came, he was out of the running as commander-in-chief; even in peacetime his authority was weakened because so many of the commanding generals had direct access to the king; and finally because he had had to surrender personnel and command affairs to the adjutant general.

In the final years preceding the First World War the Prussian war minister was described in the Reichstag as the "whipping-boy" of the monarchial-constitutional system. This was the same role he had played before in the Prussian diet. During the years of crisis Roon had to withstand an unending flood of reproaches for acts of his sovereign, with which he had had nothing to do, but which he had to defend all the same. He had to countersign all the military orders in council forwarded to him for that purpose from the military cabinet, and all too often he had no chance to offer counterarguments.

The only thing that made this system tolerable was that the concept of parliamentary responsibility was never completely defined in law and amounted in practice to no more than a "question-and-answer game." The earliest war ministers of the constitutional era, nevertheless, squirmed under their responsibility to the diet. At first they struggled vehemently against playing the double-role Frederic William IV assigned to them: against the diet as tools of absolutism, and with the diet as servants of the constitution. As Ernst Ludwig von Gerlach's diaries reveal, there were unending quarrels with the king, sometimes of great severity—all of which may serve to explain the five different incumbents between April, 1848, and December, 1851.

In the years that followed, the diet turned out to be all-too-complaisant, and the matter of responsibility did not weigh too heavily. All the ministers resumed thinking of themselves as servants of the crown, state officials, mere bureau heads in the prerevolution style, rather than as politicians with a responsibility of their own. That only meant the disintegration of the government as a whole, as a political unit.

An attempt by Otto von Manteuffel to put teeth into his powers as minister president met with only partial success. He did, however, manage to extract the cabinet order of September 8, 1852, which almost forty years later, in 1890, hastened Bismarck's fall when the Iron Chancellor sought to refurbish it. Under that order all ministers were required to consult with the minister president on all important departmental matters before reaching decisions, to submit to him their reports to the king so that he could annotate them, and to notify him when they were to be received by the king so that he could be present.

Here was an effort to reassert, in slightly more limited scope, the right of political control of the government which Hardenberg had once exercised. This time, however, the regular personal reports to the sovereign by the war minister were expressly excluded. In other words, general political control over the army was not restored. On the contrary, military affairs were accounted a sphere in which civilians had no business. They continued to be the special domain of the king.

This privileged treatment of the war minister appeared as a form of preferment. He moved up to first place in the crown council, beside the minister president, a step closer to the throne than the other ministers, so to speak. This aloofness from the over-all policies of the government, however, also weakened his parliamentary accountability; and when the question of ministerial responsibility (to be embodied in a law) was deliberated within the Prussian government in the winter of 1861-1862, the king strove to secure special status for the war minister.

Roon himself expressly declared that as a general he was pledged to unconditional obedience to the king as commander-in-chief of the army.[27] From his special vantage-point as war minister and soldier, there was complete consistency to Roon's efforts to disrupt the liberal New Era government, which was determined to implement its parliamentary responsibility and maintain freedom of action vis-à-vis the king. What Roon wanted was a government pledged to unconditional loyalty to the crown.

Yet even a war minister who was a soldier himself, imbued with absolutist notions of duty, was not as pliable a tool of the crown as an adjutant general. He was still obliged to justify his actions before the public forum of the diet. From this point of view, the military cabinet gained added importance to the crown after the constitutional reforms of 1848. Our task is now to examine its development as a political agency.

Our point of departure is the crown's need for securing a sphere of unlimited command power as the core of its entire position. This need for an executive organ removed from all political control was all the more urgent from the absolutist viewpoint since the crown had no alternative to accommodating itself to the legislative intervention of a representative assembly, especially in matters of finance. To achieve really comprehensive success would probably have required an agency of substantial size, perhaps along the lines attempted by Prince Schwarzenberg in Austria in 1850 and to be repeated after 1866. There a formal army high command was created, combining personnel matters and organizational questions in the widest sense with general staff affairs and leaving the war ministry with nothing more than economic administration.

Such a development would have indeed meant extreme attenuation of parliamentary control over the army, and it could have been put into effect only if the legislature were completely paralyzed. As in Austria, it would have completely split the military establishment, presumably giving rise to endless friction between army high command and army administration; but at least it would have given concrete meaning, in peace as in war, to the crown's military leadership claims, replacing the traditional image of royal command power as based largely on privilege and ceremonial.

It is true that so consistent a view of the royal command power, dominated by the perspectives of war, would have imposed an intolerable burden on the sovereign, requiring the appointment of a professional soldier as his deputy and commander-in-chief. Such considerations alone explain why elaboration of the command power along these lines was never contemplated in Prussia, at least not in respect of the army.[28] Instead, resort was taken to the crown's old stand-by, the adjutant general's office, soon expanded into a formal agency, the military cabinet.

There was no dearth of obstacles along this road. The earliest war ministers after 1848 naturally tried to extend their authority over the entire military establishment, as in Boyen's time, while curtailing the influence of the adjutant general, who had no political responsibility. They wished to see the military cabinet formally abolished. These requests Frederic William IV rejected. Yet the term "military cabinet" did vanish from the state handbook, and this agency was retransformed into the war ministry's AfdpA (section for personnel affairs), and it was physically moved into the ministry.

Yet in principle the king clung to his prerogatives as commander-in-chief of the army. He had a Major von Schöler deal with personnel matters as head of the AfdpA in the war ministry but also retained his former cabinet chief, General von Neumann, as a liaison man between himself and the ministry. To maintain the integrity of the army as a "state within the state," he kept it from being sworn in on the constitution, denied the diet's right to use the power of the purse for intervening in army minutiae, and in his proclamations to his ministers sharply defended his claim to personal command of the army, under Article 46 of the constitution.

In his capacity as commander-in-chief the king issued orders on such matters as army organization, troop transfers and marches, assemblies and operations, appointments and changes in command; and he insisted that the chamber had absolutely nothing to do with all this.[29] At the same time he formally acknowledged that the constitution required that all his military orders, even when they dealt with "command matters," had to be countersigned by the war minister; and he had this done in many though not in all cases,[30] thus himself blurring the limits of his command power.

If this power was to be clarified, an unambiguous legal interpretation of Article 46 of the constitution—defining the limits of the royal command authority, free of parliamentary intervention—was an urgent necessity. But the government of this king with his romantic notions was scarcely calculated to shed legal light on anything, and the confusion it left behind was to have political consequences with which we are already familiar from our study of the great army controversy. In actual practice the scope of the king's command authority remained within much the same bounds as before 1848. Indeed, until 1856 the head of the AfdpA played a rather modest role beside the war minister and the unofficial chief privy councilors, shortly to be mentioned. It has not even been established with certainty how often he saw the king. What is certain is that Frederic William IV did not take the purely military aspects of his royal office very seriously. He was by nature quite unsoldierly.

The political influence which he conceded to his military entourage was all the more important; but this did not issue from his war minister or from the head of the AfdpA. It came instead from a second private military cabinet behind the scenes which the king kept to salve his conscience. Following General von Neumann, direction of this unofficial body was held first by Adjutant General Gustav von Rauch and after his death by Adjutant General Leopold von Gerlach. Around these men gathered a whole group of political officers and privy councilors. This was the notorious "camarilla" to whose work can be traced all important political decisions in Prussia during the decade after the revolution—relegation of the fear of revolution, appointment of the government of Count von Brandenburg, imposition and progressive revision of the constitution, the declining emphasis on Pan-Germanism, the surrender at Olmütz, the whole system of political and ecclesiastic reaction in the fifties, the policy of neutrality in the Crimean War.

These conservative, not to say feudal-minded, generals virtually constituted a clandestine government checking on the monarchist loyalty of the civilian cabinet, the authority of which their snoopers helped undermine with the aid of subsidiary agencies. They intervened directly or indirectly in various affairs of state and even had their own foreign liaison: the Prussian military plenipotentiary in St. Petersburg, a Prussian aide-de-camp who traditionally enjoyed a position of great trust at the court of the czar. Yet despite these formidable resources they achieved nothing, not even in their very own sphere, the military establishment. The king's command power was maintained in principle, but it was neither defined nor expanded over what it had traditionally been. Overdue army reforms never got beyond wishful thinking. Here as in most other fields the government of the romantic king was dogged by the curse of sterility.

By way of compensation the camarilla bequeathed to the next king its youngest member and the greatest firebreather among them. As head of the AfdpA, Edwin von Manteuffel wound up lending altogether new impetus to the military cabinet. Yet this romantic adherent of Prussian absolutism scarcely had any political ideas of his own. Despite his enthusiasm for the study of history, nourished in personal contact and correspondence with the great historian Ranke, Manteuffel stayed as far away from historical reality as possible.

In the foreign policy field he was obsessed by fears of Europe-wide revolution dating back to the Age of Restoration. At home he believed with mystical devotion in the infallibility of kingship "by the grace of God" and in the vassal's unconditional duty to secure obedience to the ruler's will. From his first day as chief of the personnel section—an office he assumed as deputy as early as 1856[31]—he endeavored to make up for what the camarilla had hitherto failed to do: to limit the jurisdiction of the responsible war minister in favor of expanding Manteuffel's own agency, answerable to no one under the constitution.

In Manteuffel's view this was the way to enhance crown absolutism. To the army, the king was once again to play the role of "our field marshal general," as in the days of Frederic William I. He soon persuaded the king that the army would regard as personal orders from "on high" only those issuing from the military cabinet without the war minister's countersignature; and that, in order to accord with Prussian tradition, even correspondence with commanding generals and army inspectors should run exclusively by way of the military cabinet, giving the war ministry a wide berth.

William I was indeed the first Prussian monarch since Frederic the Great who was in earnest about personally commanding his army in wartime, for he had grown up as a professional soldier. This design was to be reflected even in peacetime. "The commander-in-chief commands the army, not the war minister," he wrote in the margin when Bonin, in one of his reports, complained of inevitable confusion arising from the fact the *Generalkommandos* always went straight to the king and received their order directly from him, the ministry being bypassed altogether.

Under such a king Manteuffel soon regained all the powers the military cabinet had lost after 1848. More than that, Bonin strove in vain to keep even military administration centralized in his ministry. As early as the winter of 1857-1858 the military cabinet once again moved into premises of its own. In 1859 the old name was restored. Soon afterward began the first jurisdictional disputes with Bonin in which Manteuffel got the unswerving support of his master by promptly submitting his resignation. These quarrels ended with Bonin's fall. Roon, the new war minister, was heart and soul with Manteuffel in using the military cabinet to carve out a free sphere of military command power, untouched by parliamentary control.[32]

Roon was even prepared to countenance a certain curtailment of the powers of his own ministry, a situation of which Manteuffel took full advantage. The most important result of all these machinations was to encourage direct correspondence between king and *Generalkommandos*. Royal orders to the army in matters of personnel and command were published in their original wording rather than being recast into ministerial ordinances. Ministerial initiative was restricted to purely administrative matters; and as already noted, the war minister's countersignature on royal edicts to the army was also severely restricted.

To underline the king's freedom in such edicts, the countersignature was to appear only on orders touching on the budget in some way—and even on them it was not always to be made public. These regulations (embodied in an order of January 18, 1861) remained in force down to the end of the monarchy and caused many legal headaches. While they were undoubtedly motivated by a desire to have the king's command power appear as great as possible from the outside, they carefully kept within established constitutional law[33] so that not even the opposition in the diet objected—not even Twesten who at the time was vehemently attacking the military cabinet, describing its head rather precisely as a "baleful man in a baleful post."

Technically alone it was highly significant that the military cabinet under Manteuffel managed to regain a high degree of autonomy virtually on the same level as the war ministry rather than under it. All of its affairs, especially the running of officer personnel, were more and more withdrawn from war ministry control. The resulting complexity and atomization of army business—especially the minister's communications with the *Generalkommandos*—seem in the end to have severely irritated even Roon, and there was much disagreement and strife.

Yet the political significance of these jurisdictional disputes must not be overestimated. In the end it was not these quarrels that brought about Manteuffel's downfall, but his constant intervention in political affairs, threatening the very integrity of the government. We have heard in Chapter 6 about these troubles in which Manteuffel proved himself the worthy heir of the camarilla. His efforts at political tutelage of the war minister may have been irksome but remained within tolerable limits so long as military cabinet and war ministry were united in fighting the diet majority.[34] They began to threaten the security of the state the moment Bismarck's policies, following the Schleswig-Holstein war, veered from domestic issues to the Pan-German question, which meant locking horns with Austria.

The adjutant general's physical removal from the court became an urgent necessity when, at this fateful juncture, he took it upon himself to inundate his royal master with the most confused advice, in the style of Gerlach's romantic circle.[35] Bismarck's problems at home and abroad were difficult enough without these additional diversions. In June, 1865, Manteuffel was appointed governor of Schleswig, and later on he was kept away by a series of military and diplomatic missions; but this by no means terminated his activities as a political adviser to the king. His papers include an almost endless sequence of drafts for direct addresses, running on for decades, in which he emphatically made his political views heard as a confidant of the "All-Highest." He thus continued to play a major role in the game of politics, an irksome and often dangerous adversary whom Bismarck could hold in check only by exercising the greatest ingenuity and tenacity, for he served as the perfect foil for the aged sovereign's personal prejudices, buttressing the king's absolutist propensities.

In the years from 1873 to 1879 Manteuffel was again in a position to influence his master face-to-face, even though he held no permanent appointment. In the latter year he created an enormous amount of trouble for the chancellor who was trying to win the king over to a new policy of alliance. A seasoned courtier, Manteuffel was gifted with great eloquence and his chivalrous nature never failed to charm the king-emperor. Only the most honorific appointments—the last one as governor general of Alsace-Lorraine—could keep him away from Berlin for any length of time; but in the end this was accomplished time and again, at all the critical moments, and his written remonstrances could never equal the power of his presence. Edwin von Manteuffel was the embodiment of the kind of personal military absolutism that represented an essential and enduring element of Prussian tradition, and its effect must be borne in mind by anyone who wishes to comprehend the peculiar character of the Bismarckian system of government. Manteuffel and his ilk set certain limits to Bismarck's power.

One major change did take place. After Manteuffel the military cabinet was no longer permitted to play a political role. Beginning in 1865, it was headed by Major General von Tresckow, an officer of impeccable integrity and loyalty. The danger of a collison between the military and the politicians was thus greatly lessened. Roon himself, the minister of war, was among Bismarck's closer friends and fought shoulder to shoulder with him on the political front—although even Roon was not equal to the inspired flights of Bismarck's political ideas. In the matter of German unification particularly, Roon, as an old ingrained Prussian, was inclined to drag his feet; but as far as can be seen he always sided with Bismarck in military matters during the wars attending unification. This was all the more important since Bismarck had no legal handholds to enforce agreement among the generals and the politicians.

Nor was Bismarck in a position to block the war minister's right of direct access to the sovereign, if only for the reason that he owed his own appointment as head of the government largely to Roon's efforts. In appointing him, moreover, King William had expressly charged him with safeguarding his own plenipotentiary privileges as "supreme warlord" and the character of the army as essentially a royal guard, even within the constitutional state. The king had ignored his serious reservations in respect of Bismarck's appointment only when the chancellor solemnly pledged himself not to exercise his office as a constitutional minister in the usual sense, but rather to function as a chief of staff who would obey his commander even when this conflicted with his own convictions.[36] It is true that this promise did not keep Bismarck from having his own way in all important political questions, even against the king's will; he was not above threatening to resign when he thought that necessary; but he could never have touched the army's privileged position except at the risk of destroying forever the relationship of confidence that existed between himself and the king.

Even after Manteuffel's going, in other words, the door was open for the "voice of the army" to reach the throne directly, with the possibility of direct conflict arising between the military and the responsible political adviser. Yet this was no longer the voice of the military cabinet, which was after all a subordinate agency tailored to the needs of peacetime. It was the general staff that now took over, the "supreme army command" to come.

The general staff attained this role of central importance only gradually. As we have already noted, it did not originally have even the right of direct access to the throne. The revolution of 1848 actually did nothing to alter its formal dependence on the war minister, though the records support the view that this state of dependence was not narrowly interpreted, and in time a certain direct intercourse did develop.[37] We note that after 1857 the chief of the general staff was on more and more occasions asked by the war minister to give his expert opinion on operational questions of one kind or another.[38] The stormier the times, the oftener the government seemed to feel the need for the kind of technical-strategic consultation Moltke provided so brilliantly in his famous memorials.

Officially these consultations still went by way of the war ministry; but after 1861 there was no longer any real barrier to the general staff chief's direct access to the sovereign.[39] Still, it remains a noteworthy fact that the general staff was not consulted at any phase in the planning of the great army reorganization of 1860. This was exclusively the concern of the war minister, acting with the expert advice of a few troop leaders. Only in 1862 was the general staff chief casually asked about possibilities for effecting economies in the military budget. Even on the subject of the reorganization of the general staff itself and the required training for its officers, the war ministry, in talks held in 1861, failed to leave the initiative to the chief.[40]

So little recognized was the central position of the chief of the general staff in army matters that the guards corps, in 1861, was able to modify its mobilization plan by merely notifying the war ministry, without so much as a word to the grand general staff![41] Even at the start of the troubles with Denmark over Schleswig it was still taken for granted that the initiative in matters of war plans and preparations lay with the war ministry rather than the general staff; and since the Prussian invasion of Jutland was only a limited operation, involving no more than part of the army, with the king not actually in operational control, direction of the campaign was initially left to the troop staff. For months on end the chief of the general staff was reduced to the role of a spectator—and a poorly informed one at that.

Following the battle of Düppel, the king did travel to headquarters, but without taking along Moltke, who complained that he was not even apprised of the decisions made there. His position, in other words, was no better than that of his general staff officers posted to the troop commanders. They too complained that they were scarcely listened to even in strategic decisions of the greatest import, because of the long-standing habit, ingrained in the Prussian army over the peacetime decades, of holding technical military scholarship in low esteem as against sheer will power and practical skill in field service.[42]

In consequence, crude errors in strategy were committed, and the only saving graces were the aggressive valor of the Prussian troops and the material inferiority of their Danish enemies. Only when serious difficulties arose was the chief of the general staff dispatched to headquarters. From that time onward, step by step, he began to stake out a position of leadership. This, however, was achieved solely on the basis of the high quality of his military skill and the practical exigencies in the field.

The main factor in strengthening his position was the personal trust of the king which his successes gained him. After 1865 he was summoned at the request of the adjutant general whenever important matters affecting his jurisdiction were argued before the king; but it was not until June 2, 1866, that an order in council authorized him to communicate directly with troop commands, without the interposition of the war ministry, and that the orders he signed went out in the name of the king; but even after that date he had to contend with much stubborn jealousy on the part of high-born and other army generals. He countered this by direct written communications with the troop general staffs—he had, as a matter of fact, been building up this *Generalstabsdienstweg* (general staff service channels) ever since 1862.[43]

The more impressive Moltke's successes grew, the greater waxed his personal authority and the focal position of his office. For decades it had languished in a backwater, scarcely noted by the public. It had originally been little more than a specialized war ministry bureau for topographical surveys, historical documentation, and intelligence about foreign armies. It had little to do in peacetime, subsisting on modest resources and operating at a jog-trot. All the more remarkable is the achievement of its officers, who managed to maintain their spirit of tireless zeal through several generations, despite the small rewards their positions offered ambitious men.

Despite their lack of practical war experience, they refused to fall victim to the process of ossification often noted in Prussian troop leadership in the days before the revolution of 1848. This danger was deliberately avoided by frequent alternations of field and headquarters service, so that there would be no chance for a spirit of paper-shuffling to arise. A succession of competent chiefs—von Müffling, Krauseneck, von Reyher—each developing his own new sphere of activity, laid the groundwork for a firm body of tradition and managed to attract a staff of well-trained officers—the raw material from which the brilliant strategist Moltke was subsequently able to build up his famous general staff.

It behooves us to study the character of this man and the spirit that prevailed in his military entrourage before we turn to the great issue of politics versus war in the campaigns of German unification that must now command our attention.

8

Moltke and Bismarck –
Strategy and Policy

Part 1
The Personalities

OUR INQUIRY now reaches its climax. At no other point in German history does the problem engaging us present itself in such classic perfection as in the era of Bismarck and Moltke—the one the acknowledged master of a creative, constructive policy that was at once militant and responsible; the other, his great foil, embodying the best traditions of the Prusso-German soldier as in an ideal type. If we may find them anywhere, we may hope here to see the laws peculiar to political and military life and thought acted out in full clarity, undimmed by human inadequacies. Here we stand a chance of getting at the roots of the conflict between politics and war.

The first important fact we must establish, however, is that Moltke represented far more than the typical Prussian soldier. He might indeed be described as a kind of ideal of German manhood generally, more specifically North German. No Prussian officer was ever less confined within the limits of technical military expertise. In a certain sense, he must be considered the great exception, in any event an absolutely unique figure in the ranks of German generals, an astonishingly talented and versatile man, infinitely curious and open-minded.

When he was an old man Moltke once said it had been by the sheerest accident that he had been put in the Danish cadet corps and thus forced into a military career. Had he been able to follow his natural bent, he would have studied archeology or history and probably have become a professor in the latter discipline. The study of technical treatises in the military field actually took up very little of his career. As a young general staff officer he dabbled in languages, attended lectures on literature, read an amazing range of works in several tongues, displaying equal interest in fiction, science, and the humanities. He was a student of economics and in his plentiful leisure time translated

Gibbon's multi-volume *Decline and Fall of the Roman Empire.* His earliest writings were stories in the late romantic style. Later on he wrote pamphlets on historical and political subjects, such as the Belgian and Polish questions, basing his views on a very broad study of the original sources. He also composed technical treatises and newspaper articles on railway matters.

His interest in Frederic the Great and Napoleon, on the other hand, never seems to have gone much beyond what was officially required; and only one military work appears among the books he considered to have influenced him decisively—Clausewitz. Only two areas of military science did he pursue with more than ordinary ardor, far transcending official requirements—topography and historical geography. His consuming passion was travel, the careful observation of nature and man, the precise recording of the countryside with transit and level, the collection of historical, political, and cultural impressions, the study of foreign nations and their social and economic conditions; and good fortune enabled him soon to achieve mastery in these skills.

Escaping from actual field service while he was still a second lieutenant, Moltke had occasion to visit all the major countries of Europe, as a military instructor with the sultan of Turkey, as adjutant to Prince Henry in Rome, and later as traveling companion to the Prussian crown prince at the courts of England, Russia, and France. He became an expert connoisseur of Turkey in Asia Minor and won his first renown as a cartographer of Turkey and Rome, as well as a chronicler of the Turkish campaign, which he witnessed in person.

His travel reports, from Turkey and other lands, are among the most distinguished examples of German prose. His graphic descriptions, the poetic grace and power of his language, the wealth of his memorable imagery—often recorded with pen and brush as well—reveal a creative talent of rare force. They testify as well to his surprisingly broad and versatile political and historical knowledge. He was always able to enliven his descriptive narrative with incidents from history, and equally to give a clear, up-to-date, and authoritative account of social, political, and economic circumstances.

He was particularly knowledgeable in the economic field. His thoughts on opening up the Balkans and the Near East through German colonization in many ways echo the ideas of Friedrich List and of the subsequent neo-German imperialism of the 1900's. His technical knowledge of railway matters was astonishing; and his proposals for the German railways system were governed by economic rather than military considerations.

Nor did he stop with the academic discussion of economic problems. Moltke participated in the expansion of the German railways system as early as 1841, as a director and shareholder in the Hamburg-Berlin railway company. One of his life-long dreams, on the other hand, was to engage in large-scale farming, using the latest technical agricultural methods. The great benefaction of 1866 enabled him to realize this dream in part. Actually, in the wake of the frustrations of that stormy year, 1848, he seriously considered resigning his unsatisfactory post and trying his luck as a farmer in Australia. Indeed, he was by no means firmly attached to the military profession.

This breadth of intellectual and practical interest was not a matter of native endowment. Moltke had to work his way up step by step from modest circumstances. His education was acquired entirely by his own efforts and is explained neither by the school he attended nor by class tradition. One searches in vain through the memoirs, diaries, and correspondence of Moltke's colleagues and contemporaries for anything comparable. Reading the account of Moltke's closest circle in the war of 1870-1871 left by his most loyal disciple, Verdy du Vernois, one can scarcely avoid the impression that the universal spirit of their chief, held in awe by these estimable and expert department heads, one and all coming from the cadet corps, must have seemed like a manifestation from another world. In a word, Moltke was not at all a professional soldier in the narrower sense but essentially a humanist of the post-Goethe era—although a "humanist" of a very special brand.

Moltke, first of all, stood in marked contrast to the entire cultural style of Weimar and Jena which had dominated the great soldiers of the Wars of Liberation—Rühle von Lilienstern, among his predecessors in office, had been entirely under its spell. One has only to place a single line from the writings of the verbose and sensitive Rühle beside the splendidly spare and chiseled locutions of Moltke, or to compare the sweepingly poetic imagery of Gneisenau's letters with the younger man's austere objectivity, to comprehend the difference at a glance.

It is the difference between a world of ideas rooted primarily in the realms of esthetics and philosophy and a new approach pointed much more at grasping the realities of history and politics. Moltke too not only carried his copy of Goethe's *Faust* in his traveling bag but knew the play by heart. He too—especially in his letters to his bride—could revel in poetic images and moods that do not lack the magic of romanticism; and the devout enjoyment of good music was an indispensable element of his life; but Moltke never remained caught in mere sentiment. His style always presses on beyond rhetoric and effective phraseology to spare and austere objectivity. His understanding of the world moved from the brilliant play of ideas to prompt and practical conclusions.

One senses the change in the intellectual atmosphere even when comparing Clausewitz's strategic memorial, reprinted in the fourth volume of Moltke's military correspondence, with the latter's elaboration of the same theme. Everything has become much more taut, precise, lucid. It is not merely that the younger man was dealing with a finished body of thought which the elder had to strive painfully to achieve. One senses a harder, more disciplined will to come to grips with things. When it came to practical strategy, reflection for its own sake meant nothing to Moltke.

No doubt about it, Moltke was a man of lucid, sober, modern reality—the reality of the nineteenth century[1]—rather than of the wishful thinking of the sage of heroic romanticism. He was a man of practical insight rather than philosophic contemplation. Yet compared with the pure man of action who is the customary prototype of the field captain, Moltke himself appears as the "scholarly officer," the academic type among the generals, a man of foresight and calculation rather than a straightforward daredevil.

Moltke, to be sure, was in no sense lacking in boldness of decision. Never were more daring deployment plans devised nor more hazardous encirclement operations carried out than in the campaigns of 1866 and 1870. But the distinguishing element here is boldness in conception, a boldness that actually risks very little because it is clearly aware of the absolute superiority of its planning and the unswerving reliability of its executive organs. Thought and action are in complete harmony with each other.

Nor was Moltke lacking in personal ambition.[2] Great achievements never come about without ambition and a sense of self-assertion. What Moltke did lack altogether, however, was the thirst for fame, the vanity of wanting to shine, the need for projecting himself as a hero—and here lies a striking difference from other great historic captains. "What some day settles the value of a man's life," he wrote an admirer defensively in 1880,[3] "is not the glamour of success but purity of purpose, loyal adherence to duty. . . . For we ourselves never know how much is due to our own efforts, to others, or to the workings of a higher will. It is wise not to claim too much under the first heading."

He often expressed himself in a similar vein—"circumstance" merited a greater share than the will of the individual; anyone who took part in the grand drama of world history was in the end no more than a tool wielded by a higher hand. When he thought of his military triumphs, he was put in mind of the Bible saying that "God's strength is made perfect in weakness." That in turn led to the devout understanding of one's own achievement as mere "service," and on this point he was at one with his great opposite and fellow player Bismarck.

It is quite true, of course, that the sense of being called to great tasks by a higher power may breed arrogance and self-adulation as well as humility. It all depends on how sincere is the religious conviction—whether (in the Christian view) the "higher will" that supposedly determines events is taken in deep seriousness as the divine will, infinitely superior to the will of man, or whether it is merely viewed as confirming man's work, transfiguring it ideologically. Beyond any question Moltke, like Bismarck, still adhered to the Christian view of higher vocation; but there was one noteworthy difference. Bismarck needed his faith in a divine world governance that uses us as mere instruments, in order to bear the burden of responsibility that came to him as a statesman. His world concept, stemming from Lutheranism, implied an interpretation of his mission in life as an everlasting struggle against man's selfishness and malice, against the spitefulness of chance, that diabolical power beyond all reasonable calculation. *Fert unda nec regitur!*

It took faith in divine guidance—a faith equally beyond reason—not to lose the courage to make decisions in the dark, as it were, to grope ahead in the fog that is the proper ambience of the statesman's every action. "I wanted it one way," he said to one of his well-wishers, "but it happened quite another. Let me tell you something, I'm always glad when I can make out the direction in which the Lord is moving so that I can hobble after him."[4] And this is what he wrote a one-time party friend after his first great successes in 1864: "The longer I'm in politics, the less faith I have in human calculation." Soon afterward he wrote his wife: "In this business you get to learn that you can grow as wise as the wisest, yet the next minute grope about in the dark like a child."[5]

These doubts never for a moment kept him from making up his mind, and his fertile political imagination always came up with a wealth of expedients. In the exercise of common-sense reason he was the peer of Moltke who once described strategy as nothing but a "system of makeshifts." Moltke's strategy, however, was always based on a methodical plan of deployment to which he clung with such iron conviction that no mischance could make him falter. No frustration, no subaltern's failure could shake his calm confidence in victory.

As a matter of fact, Moltke the humanist possessed a much stronger faith in the power of human reason, in man's capacity to shape the world along rational lines, in the inexorable advance of culture and civilization. Since God's wisdom ruled the world, using us as its tools, it was merely a matter of everyone doing his job in "pure endeavor and loyal adherence to duty," as his vocation dictated. One could not then fail to master unreason and blind chance. The rational optimism and faith in progress rooted in the depths of Moltke's harmonious nature were moderated by the realistic insight of modern empiricism and therefore free of eighteenth-century illusions. Yet his world concept was also entirely free of tragic and gloomy overtones.

By contrast, Bismarck's life-long heroic struggle was superimposed on a deep sense of resignation in the face of what he viewed as the world's incorrigible irrationality and demoniac malice. He felt himself to be the last great steward of the old monarchial order, whose duty it was to "stand in the breach and be immolated aforethought." But Bismarck was a born fighter and leader who flung himself athwart the world's orbit, rightly trusting himself to best even the devil. His divine mission confronted him with the gravest responsibilities. He was ever mindful of the ethical goals of all true political collectives, of the state's function as a source of order. At the same time these ideals for him set an ultimate limit to human caprice and power struggles—a limit that, for one thing, ruled out pre-emptive war on principle.

Yet, born fighter that he was, this sense of responsibility never kept him from identifying himself completely with the cause for which he fought and thus pursuing power with consummate passion. True, his political career was to him merely a matter of "service," as was the military career to Moltke. A certain inner detachment kept Bismarck from indulging petty ambitions. His ultimate motive was neither outward glory nor high position, which he would have been prepared to exchange at a moment's notice for the life of a country gentleman, but a passionate dedication to the cause of the monarchial state he served. To separate himself and his personal power from that cause was quite beyond Bismarck's capacity. His naive genius spent itself in his lifework—*in serviendo consumor!* Bismarck's full-blooded nature was so completely absorbed in the struggles he waged that there could be no distinction between the man and the cause. He loved as he hated, and if he was prepared to accept the heavy burdens of power, he also claimed its exclusive enjoyment, unable to share it with anyone.

Moltke was very far removed from so naive a power drive, such resistless vitality. Militancy, self-assertion, the robust will to survive were foreign to his nature, and this is precisely what rendered him so unique among the great captains of history. In a youthful story, *Die beiden Freunde* (Two Friends), he subtly outlined the direction of his own ambitions, the limits he put to his character.[6] To the blithe and naive Count Warten, the man of action who takes all hearts by storm, he opposed the brilliant, introspective young officer Ernst von Holten, in complete control of himself—Moltke's ideal of manhood.

Holten knows his limitations. "Skepticism was rooted in his character . . . he never over-estimated his own merits." Modestly Holten gives way before the virtues of his friend, is even prepared to sacrifice his own happiness. He "never played pranks, nor ever pulled off a coup. He was the kind whose glass is always still full when the bottle passes a second time." Yet his secret ambition is to outdo the others—by means of his clear intellect and iron self-discipline which never fail him, even in the most difficult situations. He never allows himself to be led astray. When others lose their heads he always finds a way out on the instant. In short, he is the superior man.

Such a vision of superiority probably always implies a bit of deliberate self-discipline. Moltke worked particularly hard to achieve it. At times he deplored his "shyness" and "stupidity," a consequence, he thought, of his harsh and loveless boyhood training in the Danish cadet corps. He looked with something akin to envy on men who seemed born to the leader's self-assurance.

Moltke did indeed lack the immediacy of the man of action, the charisma of the true leader. It is no accident that after his stretch as a lieutenant he never again saw line service. Quite clearly he had no urgent desire to command troops. As early as 1855 he voiced doubts about his ability to command a brigade.

"Quite possibly I have already reached my full potential," he wrote to his brother, "and if I sense the slightest suggestion [of a brigade command], I shall withdraw my name."

The chiefs of the General Staff under whom he served also seem to have considered him less well suited to practical troop leadership. In 1836 Krause-neck slated him for a post as military attaché in Paris; von Reyher, in the early fifties, recorded a curiously critical note in Moltke's file: "Lastly, he lacks the force and vitality without which a troop commander cannot in the long run maintain his authority."[7]

There can be no doubt at all that Moltke was not a man of action and iron will along accepted military lines. It should be borne in mind that such men do base their self-assurance entirely on willpower. At moments of supreme danger they have no choice but to shut their eyes, so to speak, lest they falter. Moltke's, on the other hand, was the unshakable calm and assurance of the intellectual, a firmness that never failed to impress his associates on the battlefields of France and Bohemia. It sprang from an insight of incorruptible clarity rather than from iron self-discipline. In this uniquely individual identity of rational and ethical character traits, giving rise to an optimism that was reasoned and at once practical, Moltke showed himself, in one aspect of his personality, to be a true heir to the traditions of Frederic the Great.

Why then was Moltke as Chief of the General Staff himself at odds with the political high command during the wars of German unification? What were the true reasons for the bitterness between him and Bismarck during the winter of 1870-1871? The character traits we have just discussed lend added interest and urgency to the answers to these questions.

It was certainly not, as Bismarck thought, the narrow one-sidedness of a man who "has spent many years preoccupied with one field, and one field alone," hence was receptive only to the military viewpoint. Moltke is the last one to deserve a charge of ingrown thinking, to be guilty of a limited professional outlook. The broad range of his cultural interests extended very definitely to the political sphere, and especially to foreign affairs, which he probed with great energy, as we shall soon see.

By the same token, one cannot describe Moltke as being consumed by political ambition, of seeking power beyond his professional sphere. For one thing, Moltke, unlike his disciple and successor Waldersee, never made the slightest effort, even in peacetime, to misuse the confidence reposed in him by his sovereign for political purposes. He accepted the political leadership of the minister president (and later chancellor) with complete loyalty, even when he found himself in disagreement with his aims and methods.[8] More than that, he never even tried, in peacetime, to expand the military jurisdiction of his agency or to enhance its stature; nor did he make use of his right of direct access to the sovereign in peacetime unless he was summoned. As he put it: "His Majesty will send for me if my counsel is wanted."

It was only during wartime, while military operations were underway, that he asserted the exclusive right to advise the king. He jealously warded off every invasion by politicians into the purely military sphere, just as he objected in general to the intrusion of political considerations into military matters. This attitude was not dictated by his thirst for power—either as a soldier or as a man—though it is true that at the height of the conflict a certain personal irritability played a part.

Bismarck the diplomat and born political infighter sensed personal power drives whenever he encountered opposition, no matter how objective. He was certainly less than fair to the chivalrous nature of an adversary whose profile he described in occasional outbursts of anger as that of a bird of prey. "It gets more buzzardlike day by day," he said.[9]

Moltke's attitudes were never purely personal, but always governed by objective considerations; and there has scarcely ever been a general less influenced by passion, more given to ice-cold reason. It was precisely this unswerving objectivity that gave him such a lead over more willful and emotional men. We may indeed go so far as to say that he needed this kind of superiority in the precise degree that he lacked the born leader's titanic sweep and compelling power. Bismarck was repelled and chilled to the marrow by this aspect of Moltke's nature, so different from his own, even while he acknowledged and indeed admired his qualities.[10]

Moltke's lifelong goal was to prove himself by great and real achievement, whatever was the field, rather than to rise to power by struggle and victory. What drove him to resist political intervention could have been only the vital laws of war, as he understood them.

Part 2
Moltke's Military Theory on the Vital Law of Absolute War

MOLTKE REPEATEDLY voiced his views on the vital laws of war and the true nature of the relation between war and politics in theoretical terms. They are formulated with both precision and concision:

1. "Diplomacy avails itself of war to attain its ends, crucially influencing the beginning of a war and its end. It does the latter by reserving to itself the privilege of raising or lowering its demands in the course of the war. In the presence of such uncertainty, strategy has no choice but to strive for the highest goal attainable with the means given. The best way in which strategy can

cooperate with diplomacy is by working solely for political ends but doing so with *complete* independence of action."[1]

2. "The course of war is *predominantly* governed by military considerations, while the exploitation of military success or failure is in turn the province of diplomacy."[2]

3. In the conduct of military operations, "political elements merit consideration only to the extent that they do not make demands that are militarily improper or impossible."[3]

These formulations became basic to the view of the German General Staff in the second half of the nineteenth century. Despite the fact that they deliberately hark back to certain formulations by Carl von Clausewitz, they represent a clear departure from Clausewitz's basic views. The supremacy of political leadership is challenged even in wartime. The first sentence quoted is a mere truism—it concedes that the general aims of a war are dictated by political considerations,[4] which also exert a decisive influence on its beginning and its end; yet it stands in sharp contrast to certain of Clausewitz's contentions. Clausewitz had said it was nonsense to hold that war plans could be made by purely military considerations. Further, he declared it an utter fallacy to acknowledge that, from the moment "the mine was touched off," war could be waged under laws of its own. And, finally, he made it part of his "ABC of warfare" that even during actual military campaigns politics must maintain a continuing influence on the course of operations.[5]

According to Moltke, the war machine must maintain complete independence of action in regard to the political leadership, the uncertainty of whose waxing and waning claims left the military no alternative but to "strive for the highest goal attainable with the means given." The general, in other words, must fix his eyes solely on what Clausewitz would have called "the absolute configuration [*Gestalt*] of the war." It is not up to him to consider the political repercussions of his triumphs or failures. Political war objectives, moreover— even so urgent a one as the accelerated capture of Paris—could be taken into account only if they did not involve anything that was "militarily improper," the "propriety" being, of course, within the sole discretion of the military leadership.

Not even the General Staff failed to note that these formulations could not be reconciled with Clausewitz's theory of war. Yet the strategists never quite dared admit that this meant a complete break with Clausewitz's basic views, and many attempts to bridge the gap were made.[6] Actually there was nothing here that needed to be papered over. What had happened was simply that a new stage had been reached in "purely military thinking." Clausewitz had been willing to concede war a "grammar of its own" but not a logic;[7] but war had now attained its own inescapable objective logic.

Immediately this is seen to be no more than a consistent—albeit one-sided—elaboration of the idea of "absolute war" which we have already described as Clausewitz's original discovery (see p. 57). War as an expanded duel, war waged for the purpose of rendering the enemy utterly defenseless by physical force—such concepts, considered in isolation and thought through to the end, leave no room for the intervention of political elements.

Moltke's rational mind strove for a clean and logical demarcation of spheres. Once the political power has resolved upon war, the duel must be fought out under the proper rules of fencing—i.e., military technique and rationale—to the bitter and unequivocal end. Unless the strength of the combatants has drained away or unless concern for third parties compels a premature cessation, it is inconceivable, under the logic of war, that intervention in military operations from extraneous sources can do anything but mischief.

Even Clausewitz had noted that "moderation cannot be carried into the philosophy of war without committing an absurdity." Actually, Prussian-German military power had grown so strong since the great army reform of 1860, with its radical application of universal service—and even more so since the accession of the armed forces from South Germany—that it appeared to have achieved absolute superiority over all its neighbors, if properly applied. The nation's politicization, i.e., the awakening of its political self-awareness and the enhancement of its militancy, had not only not declined since the Wars of Liberation—it had actually accelerated. Clausewitz had been proved quite wrong in his expectation that an age of waning military and political vigor might supervene, an era of limited military goals in which resources were carefully husbanded and the stake was measured against the possible gain.

In practice, "absolute" war had become the only possible form in which modern nations could fight a duel; hence political meddling with its technical parameters was futile as well as harmful, as a general thing. The mischief was all the greater since in the meantime the challenge to the technical skills of general staffs had grown in the same proportion as had the spatial expansion of war and operational control; another consideration was its dependence on certain technical modalities in the age of rail and telegraph.

What possible considerations should keep the strategist from going after the ultimate attainable goal, rendering the enemy utterly defenseless? Did not its attainment create the best basis imaginable for political action? We must realize, writes General Colmar von der Goltz, quite in the spirit of Moltke, "that the complete defeat of the enemy always serves politics. Observance of this principle not only grants the greatest measure of freedom in the political sphere but also gives widest scope to the proper use of resources in war."[8]

The cogency of this argument is compelling, but only if three conditions are met: There should be no natural limit to the application of military resources beyond which even total military victory would be in effect meaningless; the enemy's complete subjugation should always represent a military objective that remains politically desirable; and it should be possible in the first place to effect a clean separation between political and military problems. Moltke obviously thought that these three conditions were indeed met, without further ado. We shall still have to ask ourselves whether he was right in any sense except one strictly limited in time.

Beyond question, the times had changed. Eighteenth-century governments had been limited, both in their war aims and their military resources, and always sought to keep the stake well below the greatest possible gain; and it is for those reasons that they did not insist on their enemies being rendered utterly defense-less. Clausewitz had still held such a limited war policy to be feasible—although he was inclined to tar it with the brush of human weakness and inadequacy (see p. 59). In any event, it seemed virtually out of the question in the age of modern national war.

This was again stated most clearly by Colmar von der Goltz, and again quite in the spirit of Moltke. It was not, he remarked, that war had escaped from the influence of politics—it was only that the political influence had become simplified. In Europe wars of coalition, in which every participant contributed a clearly delimited stake, were scarcely conceivable any longer.[9] Such limited campaigns as the Prusso-Danish war of 1864 could not be described as anything more than military exercises.

As for the basic laws of modern war, they found expression only in great national wars. "When two top-rank European powers are at loggerheads, their total organized defense forces will be committed as a matter of course to force the issue. All political considerations contingent on halfhearted allies are thus eliminated." Above all, modern mass armies made it impossible to start a war except in pursuit of truly important political interests. When the outward occasion for a declaration of war was trifling, it formed "but the pretext for long-smoldering political hatreds. In a sense we approach an original state of nature, when wars among neighboring peoples could be set off by mere hostility. There is this difference, however, that the enmity is now no longer purely instinctive. It stems from a clash of supposed interests among which power and prestige are particularly prominent."[10]

In any event, continued von der Goltz, modern warfare was impelled, not by cold calculations of political advantage, but rather by hatred among nations, and the resources committed became greater and greater. "In the face of the tremendous impact of war nowadays, politics recedes into the background even more than before, no sooner do the guns begin to speak. . . . Now everything is at stake as a matter of course, and destiny must decide how the die is to be cast."

Modern wars of nations, in other words, must no longer take lukewarm confederates into account; and thus there was need to acknowledge limitations neither in the aims nor in the means of war. Such wars are always a matter of life-and-death. Political considerations drop away—whether they are intended to protect one's own forces or those of the enemy, or whether they seek to shorten the war before complete victory has been won. The only type of political consideration of legitimate military interest would concern the attitude of third powers—since their intervention might indeed shift the balance of military power. As for factors dealing with peace, they are quite out of place in the power struggle until it has been unequivocally settled.

But just when does such an issue occur? To Moltke and his school the war of 1866 always represented the ideal case. The decisive battle in that war was fought within two weeks of its outbreak, and after its loss the Austrian government rapidly lost heart to continue the fight. Yet this did not mean that the resources of the Danubian countries were completely exhausted—indeed, Vienna had not even marshalled them! What happened was that the Austrians were neither able nor really determined to risk everything for the limited goal they had set themselves, the maintenance of their position in Germany. On the contrary, they hastened to make peace, in order to retain formal possession of their dominions.[11] Moltke himself rightly considered this "Brothers' War" of 1866 a mere cabinet war, in contrast to the life-and-death wars of modern nations.[12]

Can there really be "decisive battles" in such wars among the great powers? [13] In this respect the experience of the war of 1870-1871 already stood as a bitter disappointment to the German General Staff. Even after Sedan the fighting strength of the French nation was very far from being exhausted. Since then two world wars have added much evidence to the record. When the very existence of a whole nation is at stake—not merely that of its government, or form of government—there can be theoretically no "decision" that ends the war until the resistance of one of the two powers is utterly broken. This may happen quite swiftly if one of the contenders enjoys overwhelming material superiority.

But what happens when the adversaries are about evenly matched or when the weaker manages to secure powerful allies? The issue will then be protracted in proportion to the success on either side in mobilizing the nation's moral and economic resources for war, in convincing the people that sheer survival means holding out at any price, accepting even the heaviest casualties and most far-reaching destruction of resources. Alternatively, these sacrifices may be exacted by the use of organized terror.

The technical scope for such total war has grown tremendously since Moltke's days. Among the major powers of Europe there has been a boundless growth in war potential—the manpower that can be mobilized, techniques of militarization, arms output, the number and destructive effect of modern weapons systems. In consequence reserve power has accumulated at such a huge rate that even a single battle may go on for weeks and even months. Its loss, entailing the annihilation of whole armies, may no longer be sufficient to destroy the will to fight on at a single stroke. Once political considerations have been set aside on principle—such questions as the proportion between commitment and gain, and what is to happen after the dust settles—it may take years of titanic struggle, the attrition of a whole cultural heritage, to decide such a life-and-death war in purely military terms among nations running into the hundred million; for the dominant thought is that "destiny must decide how the die is to be cast." In such cases the "inherent laws of war," the momentum engendered by mechanization, mushroom completely out of human control. The relation of politics and war is reversed. From an instrument of politics, war turns into its dictator.

As drastically demonstrated in the First World War, such a development carries the very grave risk that reason may abdicate in favor of blind passion. There is no longer any question of whether any conceivable victory can justify the hecatombs exacted to win it, of whether the imposed peace that is always the natural goal of total war can possibly serve as the basis for a stable order. That, of course, can eventuate only if the vanquished nation can be persuaded to accept its military inferiority as its inexorable destiny—unalterable at least for several generations.

But can such an issue always be enforced? European experience since 1815—the cases of vanquished France and Germany in particular—clearly speak against such a conclusion. No victor nation in history has shown itself capable of holding down its defeated enemy in the long run. Powers—and even groups of powers—seem to lack the required internal cohesion.

If such be the case, it becomes a matter of grave doubt whether total subjugation of an enemy is always a desirable war aim. Bismarck for one did not believe it was. He always considered it his objective to achieve the swiftest possible reconciliation among former enemy nations and thus pave the way for an enduring peace.[14] He kept his eye fixed on this goal even in wartime, not only in the Austrian but also in the French campaign. As will be shown, this was by far the most important reason for his clashes with the chief of the General Staff.

That is also why he was against the idea of an imposed peace. He thought it completely utopian to want to "draw the fangs" of a nation of forty million once for all. Keenly aware of his responsibility as a statesman of European stature, he was never tempted to sanction crude violations of the vital needs of other nations. His conscience would never have allowed him to risk drawing the obloquy of the whole European continent, either on himself or on Germany.[15] It is not that Bismarck in any way overestimated the practical effects of European solidarity sentiments on the policy of the major powers. It is simply that he always remained steeped in the traditions of European diplomacy.[16]

Bismarck was quite capable of deriding a policy of impotence, of relying on "Europe" rather than on one's own resources at the critical moment, of using the continental cover to disguise selfish aims;[17] but he was always aware that Germany was the land of the middle, that it must not take a single step in foreign affairs without considering its possible effect on the total European situation. That is why he declared that from 1871 onward it should be the ideal goal of

German foreign policy to gain the trust of the great powers by the pursuit of peace, justice, and conciliation.

Once the goal of German unity had been achieved, Bismarck held that his country's central position virtually compelled him to adopt a peaceful policy; and his deepest concern after his resignation was that impatience, vanity, or national sensitivities might cause a departure from such a course. In his memoirs he admonished his successors that he himself had never embarked on a war without considering with the greatest care whether the immense sacrifices of modern mass war were indeed worth the prize. "I never applied the traditional private code of honor to international issues that could be settled only by mass war. My sole criterion was their relevance to the claims of the German people to a national life of political autonomy at a level of equality with the other great powers of Europe."[18]

Such sharp limitations on war aims left no room for arbitrary warfare under purely military guidance. "The object of an army command," Bismarck wrote, "is to destroy the enemy forces. The object of a war is to achieve peace under conditions that are in accord with the country's policies. Establishing and limiting the avowed war aims and counseling the sovereign in respect of those aims is always a political task, in wartime as during the preceding peace, and the manner in which this task is absolved cannot but exert an influence on the manner in which the war is waged. The ways and means of war will always be dependent on whether the ultimate result is more or less than what was originally envisaged, on whether territorial cessions are to be demanded or renounced, on whether hostages are to be seized and for how long."

An added element was constant reference to the attitude of third powers, the likelihood of their intervention, the position they might take at international conferences, the risk of setting off further wars. Lastly and most importantly, there was the difficult task of judging "when the right moment has come to initiate the transition from war to peace." These are all matters that must not be settled by one-sided military considerations but "require a knowledge of the European situation with which military men are not necessarily familiar, as well as information to which they may not have access."[19]

In other words, the clean separation between political and military problems which Moltke demanded is a practical impossibility. One sphere continually merges into the other, and instead of rigid segregation what is needed in counseling the sovereign is a constant "mutuality between diplomacy and strategy." The commanding general must know the political intentions of the supreme command, just as that command needs precise and running information on the military situation and the intentions of the strategic leadership. More than that, to decide what is politically desirable or necessary "requires a fully effective influence on the direction of the war, its nature and volume," as originally determined by the strategic leaders. Bismarck was fond of showing, by the hypothetical example of a victorious campaign against Russia, followed by a redistribution of Russian territory, that military desiderata can always form but a part of political considerations.

Thus the third of the three conditions which Moltke thought necessary to a proper relation between politics and war (see p. 197) is also proved untenable. Moltke himself actually knew this to be the case. In his writings he referred more than once to the inseparable unity of politics and strategy: "To separate politics from strategic considerations is quite impossible." In the last analysis the military sphere could not be distinguished from the political.[20] But Moltke was here writing in the context of wishing to justify his interweaving of purely political considerations into his own deployment plans, or into his agreements with the Austrian General Staff. It never occurred to him to draw the logical conclusion from such passages, i.e., that politics must be granted the right to intervene in the military sphere.

Moltke probably never realized this paradox in his attitude. For us it merely confirms what we already know. The doctrine of the "inherent laws of war" is a figment. It actually destroys natural links. At the very least it greatly exaggerates whatever natural conflicts may exist. Of course technical contingencies, in war as in every other sphere of life, impose certain dynamics of their own which none can ignore with impunity. This is a matter of particular urgency in war—and to that extent Moltke was amply justified—for a military misjudgment not only risks countless human lives but may have even graver consequences. War seldom offers a second chance, and a single blunder may cause a major operation to fail, possibly undermine the whole strategic enterprise, and even bring on ultimate defeat.

Political leaders with good sense take such contingencies into due account and necessarily give great weight to the judgment of military experts; but that does not at all mean that they are simply at the mercy of such judgment while military operations are on, nor that strategy must be allowed to operate "with complete independence of action" from politics, ever pursuing only the supreme goal of the enemy's total destruction, as Moltke thought.

True, there is a danger that political considerations may impede military success; but against this there is another danger, no less serious—that the responsible statesman becomes the slave of mechanized war, that technology outweighs man, that total military success becomes an end in itself. Yet the true art of statesmanship is always to maintain its sovereignty, however deeply it is enmeshed in technical contingencies. It must, of course, consider the exigencies of war, but it must never take its eye off the goal of a durable peace to come, and it must not allow itself to be pressured into approving measures that would block the way to that goal for good. This certainly does not mean ignoring the technical requirements of war; it may, however, mean transcending quarrels among military experts caught up in the purely technical aspects of their profession.

To maintain such a sovereign stand in practice is a task of the most immense difficulty. It did not take the First World War to teach us that lesson, which is already clearly exemplified in the story of Bismarck. That is precisely why his conflicts with Moltke are so instructive, for in them personal rivalry recedes almost entirely behind objective differences of opinion. Unlike similar conflicts both before and afterward, on this occasion the statesman was unquestionably the general's superior—in the impact of his personality, in passionate militancy, in ruthless vigor. One shudders to think of the disastrous consequences that might have arisen if the masterful Bismarck had been matched by a professional soldier of equally ruthless dynamism!

Even so, Bismarck was able to realize his own objectives in the way the war was conducted in 1870 and the peace was concluded in 1871 only imperfectly and in part, at least in respect of ending the war as quickly as possible and sparing the vanquished enemy as much as possible. His aim, of course, was to avoid handicapping the new German Reich with any deep-rooted French revanchist movement in the field of foreign affairs. Unfortunately the states-man's arguments in favor of a moderating political influence on the conduct of war are usually rooted in the uncertainties of political psychology. He deals in conjectures concerning the possible effects of certain political events abroad, where the soldier puts forward clear-cut facts and figures concerning tangible power. Bismarck's own bitter reaction was that the politician lapsed all too readily into the role of a Questenberg, in Schiller's play about Wallenstein; and within the Prussian General Staff, at least, there was a fixed tradition of long standing that diplomats, by a stroke of the pen, were always wont to give away what soldiers won by the sword.[21]

Moltke found this view confirmed by the disappointing experiences of Denmark in the war of 1864 and of France during the crucial weeks of August, 1870, when political authority meddled with strategy.[22] Evidently he never appreciated that these were instances of crude political dilettantism, that one had to distinguish—as Clausewitz had done earlier[23]—between good politics and bad, without at once generalizing the defects of the bad. Before Moltke's eyes there always loomed the specter of endless and pointless "councils of war," now as in earlier ages, which never reached any clear-cut decisions because no member bore the ultimate responsibility.

Moltke was, of course, quite right in stressing the need for an unambiguous chain of command in wartime when everything depended on swift and decisive action.[24] And surely the rapid and uniform exercise of such command could be severely compromised when the political high command had the right to intervene in military decisions at will—especially when this privilege was wielded by a responsible parliamentarian who had to consider irresponsible public opinion at every step. Again, it was surely one of the virtues of the Prussian state and army systems that supreme command was vested, not in a parliamentary minister of war, but in a sovereign who was not formally accountable—or rather, accountable only "to God and his conscience."

We see that Moltke too had weighty arguments on his side; and it is scarcely fair to join Bismarck in attributing Moltke's opposition to the chancellor's sharing in military presentations before the sovereign to professional jealousy and the mystery-mongering of the "demigods" at headquarters. We cannot jump to the conclusion that Moltke's apprehension of pointless debate with nonsoldiers on operational matters was totally without foundation.[25] As we shall yet see, Bismarck's hasty and unfair criticisms of Moltke's operational plans together with his evident misjudgments of military necessities often made objective discussion with the chief of the General Staff extremely difficult, if not impossible (see Part 3).

But that did not alter the objective need for the two men, statesman and general, to establish the basic campaign plans in concert—nor, indeed, did Bismarck ask for anything more than that. He did not wish to meddle with the details of operational decisions, but was content to ask to be present at consultations with the sovereign only when political issues were touched on—especially, of course, the major policy decisions. Beyond this demand, he merely wanted the privilege of military briefings whenever the political situation made that necessary.[26]

By opposing these demands, which Moltke's staff did even more stubbornly than he himself, the General Staff, far from insuring uniform direction in wartime, only created internal tensions that at times threatened to burgeon into a full-fledged dualism, a complete split between the military and political leadership. Bismarck's military criticisms, on the other hand, could scarcely have taken such unfair form, had he himself been better informed. The General Staff did not altogether overlook this hazard and occasionally even went so far as to acknowledge the justice of Bismarck's demands.[27] What the soldiers really feared was Bismarck's personal force, the sweep of his vigor, his enormous power drive, qualities that respected no jurisdictional demarcations and were calculated to prevail over the more chivalrous and reserved chief of staff when the two men reported to the sovereign together. In consequence, Moltke invoked his right of exclusive access to the king in military matters and in addition claimed full equality with the chancellor and minister president as political adviser to the crown.[28]

In the light of all these circumstances, we can see that the tensions between Bismarck and Moltke stemmed in part from their characters, in part from the peculiarities of the monarchial-constitutional system. We are already familiar with the special position the army occupied in royal Prussia. During the years of conflict this position had become further accentuated. Bismarck had assumed office on the express understanding that he would defend the unlimited royal right of command and the army's privilege of direct access to the throne. Thus he was never even close to thinking of himself as holding political authority superior to the army—in the way, say, that State Chancellor Hardenberg did after the reforms of 1808-1814 (see Chapter 7). In this respect the limits of his power were sharply drawn; and the subdued tone and much-revised form of the charges against the General Staff which he addressed directly to the king in the winter of 1870-1871 plainly show the extreme care he had to take to avoid arousing resentment on the part of the military against a mere civilian minister.[29]

Bismarck knew well that this would always be a touchy subject. Throughout the war he had to put up with a rival for the king's confidence—though his own relationship with the king was otherwise one of the profoundest trust. During the critical days and weeks of decision, moreover, this rival enjoyed unquestioned precedence over him and was intent on putting up an impenetrable smokescreen of confidential military consultations. Nothing so annoyed and irritated Bismarck. "If only once I had the power to say: This will be done, and this will not be done!" he sighed in the privacy of his intimate circle. "I have to worry about the whys and wherefores of the simplest matters, to submit evidence and humble petitions. That sort of thing went much better with men like Frederic the Great who were themselves soldiers, who knew something about administration and served as their own ministers. With Napoleon too! Here I have to be forever on my knees and talk myself hoarse!"[30]

Moltke, on the other hand, though without personal ambition, felt that his position constrained him to defend the interest of the army against "that civilian," to scrupulously perpetuate its privilege of direct access to the throne, to avoid any semblance of being subordinate to political authority; but if he was occasionally pedantic in these pursuits,[31] this was because he felt himself to be the guardian of Prussian military tradition, as understood in the army ever since 1848. In a sense, he had moved into the position, as army spokesman, occupied in 1860-1861 by men like Roon, Manteuffel, and Alvensleben.[32]

In sum, the fact that the existence of two coeval supreme advisers to the crown led to so profound a power struggle is seen to be an inevitable consequence of the Prussian state and army systems. Once again we find that the example of Frederic the Great gave rise to untoward repercussions. In theory the system guaranteed unity of command in wartime. The *roi connétable* was meant to combine both political and military leadership in his person, using his advisers merely as instruments in arriving at decisions that were in the end entirely his own, determined by a kind of infallible *raison d'état*.

But what happens when the ruler lacks the sovereign clarity, the military insight, the firm political will without which great decisions cannot be made? A dangerous power vacuum then arises at the crucial point, as the disastrous events of the First World War showed only too clearly. Top leadership then completely disintegrated. William I too was no Frederic the Great. Presented with two different courses of action, perhaps mutually exclusive, he was virtually incapable of reaching a decision without seeking recourse with a third adviser, such as his adjutant general.[33]

Yet he was at least scrupulous in considering every argument brought forward, motivated by a pure sense of justice and eager to reconcile conflicting viewpoints among his advisers; and though he stubbornly clung to certain pet notions, he was quite free of conceit, hence willing to follow the lead of a stronger mind; nor can there be any doubt as to which one of his two top advisers was the more dynamic. Unlike the circumstances of the First World War, political rather than military authority ultimately prevailed in all the great decisions under his reign. Unity of command was indeed preserved, though at times only after bitter controversy and long vacillation. In the long run the worst consequences of the friction between Bismarck and Moltke were avoided.

A major element in this fortunate outcome was the fact that despite many differences, the two men shared many viewpoints and attitudes. By heritage Bismarck was actually much more deeply rooted in the Prussian tradition than Moltke. He was thoroughly receptive to the military approach and more than willing to acknowledge military achievement.[34] He was fond of citing his innate military orthodoxy—shaken only by his experiences in 1870-1871. "I carry the heart of a Prussian officer in my breast," he once exclaimed extravagantly, "and that is the best part of me."

Moltke, on the other hand, in addition to his complete freedom from personal political ambitions, towered above the typical Prussian officer. He was a man of culture and intellectual stature, with a deep knowledge of history. Thus he could not but acknowledge his adversary's political genius, even when his own ideas moved along different lines. For the same reasons, he not only scrupulously observed the jurisdictional demarcations of the military sphere but went along wholeheartedly when success confirmed Bismarck's mastery and adapted his own political views to the new situation Bismarck had created.

Moltke was originally oriented in the "Great German" (i.e., Austrian) rather than the Prussian direction; yet in the 1866 clash he fully supported Bismarck's "Little German" (i.e., Prussian) solution to the unification problem; nor did he insist on waging a bitter-end struggle for his own ideas in the armistice and peace with France, though military interests were here directly affected. What is even more important, Moltke never tried to supplant the chancellor's peace policy with his own pre-emptive-strike policy, which was part and parcel of his political creed.

What we touch on here is a point of general rather than merely biographical significance; for the problem of preventive war is only one outward aspect of a deep schism that continues into our own time, a fundamental division in political outlook rooted in history. Moltke's views on this matter—indeed his whole approach—won wide allegiance in the German officers' corps. It is not too much to say that to a considerable degree it became a common substratum of the whole modern German culture. All this can be comprehended only in the context of historical and political ideas that have long been characteristic of German nationalism. The all-pervasive influence on political life of a philosophy of pure militancy—here is the fulcrum to any historical understanding of the changing relation of sword and scepter since the days of Bismarck and Moltke.

Part 3
Moltke's Political Attitude— War as Destiny

THE GERMAN intelligentsia was brought to an awareness of their nation's vital claims only by the upheaval that attended the disaster of Jena—the total loss of German freedom. The German nationalist movement began with a rebellion against foreign tyranny—the Wars of Liberation; and incipient German political philosophy from Herder and the early romanticists to Hegel developed in deliberate opposition to the political rationalism of West Europe. The most important upshot of this march from cosmopolitanism to nationalism was the emergence of the idea of the national state as an entity interposed between the individual and mankind. It was seen to encompass the lives of individuals, welding them into indissoluble bodies politic that are the real instruments of history.

In place of the cold abstraction of a "political contract" that was supposed to have effected the formation of states by inherent forces that were universal and unvarying, what was now envisaged was a multiplicity of political condensations, each determined by a unique national heritage (the so-called *Volksgeist*), as well as by historic destiny and outward circumstance. The ardor and enchantment of German romanticism in the face of this pluralistic world of infinite variety and vitality reverberatès even in the writings of Ranke when he speaks of the inexhaustible wealth of "tangible spiritual entities" *(realgeistige Wesenheiten),* "moral energies," and "creative forces" he sees unfolding in the power struggles of the great national states. Yet this philosophical approach at a very early date moved on from esthetic delight to radical political implementation.

German thinking, influenced for centuries far more by the ecclesiastic than the political community, had much difficulty in finding its way, by many arduous detours, into the world of political struggle for power and interests. Access to it was long barred to the docile Germans by the moral traditions of the church, secularized in the Age of the Enlightenment into cosmopolitan and humanitarian ideals of universal application; but once the break had been made, once the German intelligentsia, under the whiplash of the

Napoleonic empire, had come to understand what the loss of national independence and political power really meant, the change among the leading minds
took place with a single-mindedness that has ever since left our western
neighbors uneasy.

We have discussed this intellectual juncture on a previous occasion, in the
context of young Clausewitz's political development (Chapter 3). It was experienced at almost the same time by men of the most diverse character and
background. This was by no means purely a matter of emotional outbursts or
bellicose xenophobia, of the kind found in the super-heated and sometimes
intemperate battle songs and paeans of hate by such as Heinrich von Kleist and
Ernst Moritz Arndt. The national idea itself had simply taken a decided turn
toward militancy.

This is seen most clearly in Fichte and Hegel, the philosophers of the new
German idealism. As recently as 1800, in his curious design for a state based on
economic reason, the "closed mercantile state," Fichte had dreamed of a
guarantee of peace everlasting, once all the nations of Europe had attained their
"natural boundaries"; but that dream had gone aglimmering in the hapless year
of 1807. At about the same time as Clausewitz, the philosopher thought he had
discovered a profound political truth in the doctrines of Machiavelli, namely the
law of power: "He who waxes not, wanes while others wax." Armed to the
teeth, the politically organized nations were drawn up, watching one another,
ever ready to anticipate their neighbors in the exercises of force—such was his
view.

"It is not at all sufficient to defend your proper territory. You must keep
your eye unwaveringly on anything and everything that may affect your
position. You must not on any account allow anything within your sphere of
influence to be altered to your disadvantage; and you must not hesitate a
moment to take advantage of any opportunity to change things to your
advantage; for you may rest assured that the other will do the very same thing
whenever he can. If you miss your own chances, you will lag behind." This
paraphrase of Machiavellian principles already contains in embryo a philosophical *apologia* for pre-emptive war.

Like Clausewitz, Fichte maintained the need for constant military preparedness, lest men grow soft. Indeed, in his mouth the Machiavellian argument takes
on a sharp, imperialist tinge: "Every nation, moreover, is intent on spreading the
virtues peculiar to it as far as possible, indeed, if possible to incorporate all
mankind. This desire stems from a drive implanted by God, a drive on which
rests the community of nations, their friction, one against the other, and their
growth and development."[1]

These sentences, flung out with the vehemence characteristic of Fichte, by
no means encompass the whole of his political philosophy. That was in fact

completely devoted to the utopian goal of creating a state according to philosophical ideals. Indeed, his argument on power politics in 1807 seems almost
like a temporary drift along a bypath quite foreign to him. At heart Fichte
always remained the theologian, the preacher of a "subjective idealism" that
sought to purify the earthly world to the level of a higher moral sphere, to be
looked for beyond the limitations imposed by the senses, as a kind of panthe-
istic transfiguration of the secular power struggle into a spectacle of world
reason incarnate. Fichte was able to reach this point only by means of a certain
transcendent moral exaltation. Hegel, on the other hand, employing his brilliant
dialectical skill, succeeded far better, and his influence was far more sustained.

He too manifestly received a powerful impetus from the political events of
his time. His piece on a constitution for Germany was written (in 1802) under
the dismaying impact of the old Empire's impotence in the face of the forays by
France's revolutionary armies. "In order for a multitude to form a state, it is
necessary that it form a common defense and state power." This notion, basic to
Hegel's novel and exceedingly virile political philosophy, was derived not from
books or philosophical broodings, but from a living apprehension of political
realities.

This indeed was the Swabian thinker's unique contribution—combining the
most abstract concepts of his rigid system of philosophy with the realities of
political life, into which he had uncommon insight. Hegel's basic approach in his
philosophy of history and law, the culmination of centuries of effort on the
part of Western metaphysics to elucidate the order of the world along rational
lines, lay in his constant effort to reconcile reality and reason, to show that
the seemingly impenetrable jungle of history, with its myriad coincidences, was
in fact a tissue of reasonable interconnections, representing the unending albeit
dialectically fragmented progress of ideas, the self-realization of divine reason.

Within this system the state played a crucial role, as the most important
organ of world reason, carrier of all higher historical life. The state is the "reality
of the moral idea," the epitome of all higher societal concretion. Since objective
morality exists only in the collective, never in the isolated individual, man
"achieves objectivity, truth, and morality only insofar as he is a member of the
state"; and to thinking awareness the laws of the state constitute moral truth.

Hegelian philosophy, originally feeding in equal parts on Christian and pagan
tradition, achieved in its ultimate form the secular pinnacle of the Christian
world concept. Religion is explicitly stripped of its top rank in the "realization
of the moral idea" and assigned second place behind the state. In considerable
measure this represents a return to the political ideals of antiquity.[2] The state
"is the divine will, present as the spirit that develops the world's true form and
organization."[3]

This, of course, eliminates any possibility of judging acts of state by ordinary standards of law and morality. "The state knows no higher duty than to perpetuate itself," Hegel wrote as early as 1802. States face one another in sovereign autonomy as "individual subjects," each one a "moral totality," an ethical world on its own, beholden solely to the "right of its concrete existence," with no judge above it other than the world spirit itself whose judgment becomes apparent in the course of history. Enthroned high above individual joy and sorrow, guilt and virtue, history lends support only to that element in the self-realization of the idea that is needed at the moment. At any given time history recognizes but a single epoch-making nation, compared with which all others are absolutely in the wrong; and history avails itself of war as the indispensable means for its progress.

Hegel sees the moral justification of war in the fact that the power and autonomy of a state as the highest collective entity are historically inexorable, while the lives and property of individual citizens are trivial and purely adventitious. This fact alone necessarily imposes on the individual the unconditional duty to sacrifice life and fortune for the state. Hegel does assume, however, that the state will exact such sacrifices only in the event its autonomy is seriously threatened, while lesser disputes would be fought out among professional soldiers. He is prepared to leave it entirely to the state's discretion what particular occasion is to be regarded as a threat or an actual violation of the state's honor and privileges. The sense of political honor will be the more easily outraged, the stronger the state is, the greater its accumulated internal pressures, clamoring for an outlet. "The state, as a moral entity, cannot rest content with taking notice of an actual violation [of its rights]. It must consider conceivable violations as well, possible dangers threatening from other states, their waxing and waning probability. It must seek to read the intentions of those states, for all of these elements may become the cause of a dispute." Here too preventive war finds its philosophical *apologia.*[4]

Hegel, however, is very far from advocating a policy of unrestrained violence and war. He expressly clings to the view that war represents an emergency, a situation quite out of the ordinary; and he posits as a matter of course that states will continue to recognize each other even in wartime, "so that even in war, war itself shall be regarded as a passing phase," lest the possibility of peace be destroyed.[5] Yet his radical reversal of the relation between the individual and the state, with the state given absolute primacy,[6] does serve as an impediment to the pacifist argument. Hegel goes so far as to credit war with preserving the moral health of nations "as the motion of the winds keeps the sea from stagnation, to which it would succumb by constant stillness, just as would nations by an enduring peace, let alone peace everlasting." It is a thought that has since been reiterated in infinite variations.[7]

As in Fichte's Machiavelli essay, foreign policy has become the field for constant struggle, latent or manifest. There is virtually no echo in Hegel of the traditions of the medieval *res publica christiana*, of the idea of an Occidental family of nations, of a European confederation, of the *intérêt general* or the balance of Europe, of a culture of the West—indeed, no awareness at all that a political union on a moral basis might be formed at a level higher than the individual sovereign state.[8] Hegel's political philosophy represents the most explicit expression of the movement away from the old ideals of European universalism and toward ruthless individuation of the sovereign state, a movement that received tremendous impetus in the struggle against the universal empire of Napoleon.

Hegel himself took no part whatever in this struggle—because of the imperialist turn of his thinking, if nothing else. Fundamental to his philosophy was the "world nation" *(Weltvolk)*, the "epoch-making" state at a given juncture, beside which the claims to dominion by other nations paled into insignificance. At the height of his triumph Napoleon was almost bound to appear to Hegel as the epitome of the "world spirit." For Hegel, in the context of his historical analysis, did not view the world of states as consisting of units with equal rights, but rather as a succession of nations struggling for world dominion, their bids for power being interpreted in terms of a constant process of "ennobling the spirit."

This militant philosophy of politics and history won Hegel an astonishing number of converts. The pervasive influence of Hegelian ideas is discernible throughout nineteenth-century German historical and political literature. It was an influence that kept on spreading—but even as it spread it grew more and more shallow. The inner fiber of Hegel's idealist system was lost, his political philosophy reduced to the level of a political *Weltanschauung,* his philosophical ideas turned into popular catchwords.[9]

Sobered by the unsuccessful revolution of 1848, impressed by the practical success of Prussian power politics under Bismarck, the German nationalist movement itself turned more and more to "practical politics," and as it did so, the overemphasis on militancy came more and more to the fore. About mid-century, Konstantin Rössler, perhaps the most important journalist to herald the age of *Realpolitik,* pictured history in terms of a contest among the great powers, quite in the spirit of Hegel, his teacher. The struggle, according to Rössler, was for the crucial "strategic positions," and its outstanding feature was that "one powerful nation got hold of and held onto the important positions against the will and despite the combined efforts of the rest of the world."[10]

Rössler, in other words, viewed the multiplicity of states purely in terms of a permanent power struggle. "But for this multiplicity, but for the rivalry among states, the idea of the state as the epitome of power could not have evolved. As things are, state is state's worst enemy. To maintain itself, a state must emerge as the supreme power, i.e., live up to its concept; and to be truly strong, power must foster moral life, for morality alone confers true and enduring strength."[11]

The state's militant thirst for power is virtually the crucial impetus for giving moral form to public life. "Man begins with struggle and violence. . . . Strength, power constitute the earliest form of ideality, the first great impression man makes upon man. . . . Every nation has the right, nay the duty, to extend its power as far as its strength reaches—reaches in earnest and for good. Sentimental considerations do not figure in this, such as the argument that people of different disposition have a right to live and must be spared—indeed possess all manner of estimable qualities that should be preserved for now and for the future. . . . That every kind of national vermin must be preserved is no more than a nonsensical tradition handed down to us by the sentimental eighteenth and the doctrinaire nineteenth centuries. It is the duty and vocation of strong nations to divide the world among themselves."

Among nations the only fair gauge is power, physical or spiritual. "The only credential entitling a nation to rule is power, and this is gained only in war. The fortunes of war constitute the verdicts that settle the trials among nations; and these judgments are invariably fair, once every appeal has been exhausted." Mankind progresses only through war, hence war is "the most necessary of all, great and beneficent." There is such a thing as international law, based on humanitarian stirrings and simple common sense—"the feeling that no single nation, not even the most powerful, must be allowed to carry out a consistently negative policy toward all other nations." Yet the principle remains: "The power sphere of a nation is regulated only in open struggle."

Such views are by no means limited to mid-century journalism. They are found in even more pointed form in philosophical writings of rightist Hegelian tinge, notably those of Adolf Lasson.[12] "Every state," says Lasson, "is by nature coordinate with every other state. The reason is clear enough. By its very existence, each state provokes the others to put forward the greatest efforts to maintain themselves, to become more perfect in every way, to improve their citizens." Thus the power struggle brings immediately beneficent results in terms of public morals, while the pursuit of peace everlasting is downright immoral. War is "the sole praetor to pronounce judgment on states in terms of justice rather than by the law books. His is the only true judgment, for it is based on power—the powerful state is the better state, its people are the better people, its culture is the more valuable culture—such is the everlasting justice of history." Since unlimited sovereignty carries the right of pure selfishness, it follows that "among states any legal or moral association must be impossible. . . . The dream of a binding order above and among the states is wanton and paradoxical. It stems from cowardice and false sentiment." Any question of law among states becomes a question of power, and whoever has the greater power remains in the right.[13]

Formulations in this vein push to the extreme Hegel's teachings on the natural conflict of interests among sovereign states. Here the great powers are viewed as standing side by side in coy aloofness, without any "legal or moral association." Hegel saw war as the indispensable spur to progress in history, but here it no longer represents a special state of emergency. It is regarded rather as a higher form of political morality. Yet while this exaggerates Hegelian philosophy, it does not actually alter or expand it.

In another context later on we shall consider the evolution of Hegelianism under the influence of Darwin's theories of natural selection and the struggle for existence. At that stage the idealist justification of war as the realization of moral ideas was to be supplemented by a "biological" argument. It becomes understandable even now, however, why the Hegelian approach exercised such a profound fascination on educated professional soldiers.

Military thinking is always inclined to regard the state as a powerhouse, instituted to maintain a nation's place among the nations by struggle. "The main idea underlying the state," Clausewitz wrote Gneisenau in 1824, "is defense against the enemy without. All else may, strictly speaking, be viewed as *faux frais.*"[14] A highly illuminating remark! In practice this approach necessarily leads soldiers to the old motto of Frederic the Great—*toujours en vedette!* And this attitude of vigilant suspicion was invariably reflected in Germany's attitude toward France.

To assemble further evidence of the fundamental importance of the Franco-German power struggles between 1792 and 1815 to German political thinking into the days of Bismarck would mean carrying coals to Newcastle. The whole system of the Restoration was based on the notion that France was the real focus of revolutionary unrest in Europe. The whole ideology of the German nationalist movement subsisted on the quarrel with the "Gaulish archfoe," who was seen to threaten not only political freedom but spiritual autonomy.

Here is the very point where Moltke's political views come closest to the ideological world of neo-German nationalism. His inner relation to that movement is not so easy to define; and we must carefully distinguish between Moltke's utterances as a professional soldier and the political ideas that came to him from the great nationalist trend of his century.

We have an abundance of historical and political comment from Moltke's pen—literary studies, letters, and military memoranda in which, unlike his predecessors, he always bases his strategic plans on an evaluation, often extremely detailed, of the political situation. These notes bespeak not only a surprisingly broad historical background but a personal political orientation that underwent little change over six decades.[15]

In home affairs Moltke was a moderate monarchist with a decided predilection for enlightened popular reform imposed from above. In foreign affairs he tended toward the German rather than the Prussian view—he was certainly untouched by Prussian particularism. Yet he was also free of any resentment of Austria and never accepted the feudal relation with the house of Hohenzollern that marked the military aristocracy of Old Prussia. Moltke's nationalism was ethnic *(völkisch)* rather than political. His pan-Germanism was broad in scope. He was receptive to the idea that German culture had a colonizing mission throughout the world, while Austria had one of its own in Southeast Europe. He flirted romantically with the dream of a union of all the Germanic nations against the Slavs and Gauls, and he was convinced that Germany and England had a natural community of interests.

By and large these views did not lead to points of practical policy. Moltke's voice speaks to us not in the tones of a militant politician—nor even of a political theorist. He appears to us in the role of the cultured amateur historian, the shrewd observer with a perspective that is likely too broad rather than too narrow. We do not hear the ring of political passion but rather pronouncements that bespeak an interest in every sphere of culture. Only when the immediate interests of the army are at stake, notably in the stormy year of 1848, does a note of agitation creep into Moltke's voice.

Of all this, what interests us most is Moltke's position on war as a moral problem. Here the influence of nineteenth-century German military philosophy becomes almost palpable. At the age of forty, in his essay on Germany and Palestine, Moltke openly professed "the much-scorned ideal of universal European peace." Forty years later he declared: "Peace everlasting is a dream—a dream that is not even appealing—while war is a link in God's world order. Man's finest virtues unfold in war—courage and renunciation, obedience to duty, and readiness to give up one's own life. But for war, the world would be caught up in a morass of materialism."

The words might well have been written by any true-blue Hegelian. Even the modern biological pretext for war was not lacking: "Man's life, indeed the whole of nature is no more than a struggle of the new against the old, and the life of national entities is no different."[16] Yet a closer look shows that Moltke's views had not radically changed. Even in 1840 he was not contemplating general disarmament in any form; and as late as 1881 he made this noble pronouncement bespeaking true humanity: "Who would deny that any war, even the most triumphant, is a misfortune for one's people, for territorial gain and many millions in gold do not make up for the loss of life, for the grief of families."[17]

On the battlefied of Königgrätz Moltke sought to avert his eyes as he rode past the ghastly spectacle of Austrian batteries shot to pieces. Deep in his humanitarian nature he loathed the cruelty of war.[18] But Moltke was a soldier by profession, unswervingly loyal to duty, and he was helped over the rough spots by an optimistic rationalism that in the end reconciled all his diverse utterances on the problem of war. In 1840 he expressed the hope that the resistless advance of civilization would naturally cause wars to become more and more rare; for is not "the whole course of world history an approach to peace? " In place of the war of all against all (of medieval feuding), only a few great powers today could be expected to war among themselves, and as these conflicts grew more and more costly, disrupting and harming economic life and destroying resources, they would become even rarer. "Is it inconceivable that Europe might witness mutual disarmament in a matter of decades or centuries?"

True, such radical pacifist hopes dwindled later on. The lesson of history, we now hear, is that wars are inevitable as long as there are conflicts of interest among the great powers that are unwilling to submit to the judgment of any superior authority. The Hegelian notion that war is a moral "bath of steel" is now eagerly embraced—possibly through his late friendship with Heinrich von Treitschke—though it plays but a subsidiary role in the total context of his thinking.[19]

More important, and likewise conceived along Hegelian lines, is Moltke's moral justification of war as a historic necessity, as "destiny." War is not a crime—it is "the ultimate, wholly justified means for maintaining the existence, independence, and honor of a state." Still, Moltke continues to acknowledge that war is a "misfortune. . . . Yet who in this world is able to escape misfortune and necessity? Are not both, by God's unfathomable ways, conditions of our earthly life?"

The words have an almost Lutheran ring. They can indeed be understood only against the background of an indestructible humanitarian faith in progress. We are up against a mere compilation of the most heterogeneous thoughts for purposes of self-justification. Even now Moltke still dares hope that "this last resort will, with advancing culture, be ever more rarely used" and that warfare itself will grow progressively more humane. "The time of cabinet wars is past." He now looked for salvation to the wisdom of enlightened and responsible governments, reluctant to risk the destiny of whole nations for frivolous reasons. (Apparently he had Bismarck in mind.) Were not the savage customs of war of the seventeenth century long since outdated by the strict discipline of modern professional armies, by universal service which brought the noblest elements of the land to the colors, by the termination of campaigns in a matter of months through operations carried out with ruthlessness?

We see that the rational and cultural optimism of the nineteenth century lived on with undiminished force in the aged field marshal. Yet Moltke the soldier was always intent on keeping his freedom of military action untrammeled by considerations of international law. He would have nothing to do with treaties limiting the right to requisition, or with protective martial laws that would shield spontaneous, unorganized rebellion. "The greatest mercy in war is its swift end, and to this end every method that is not downright reprehensible should be available."

War, in Moltke's view, was by no means limited to the weakening of the enemy's armed forces. "No, all the resources of the hostile government must be put under pressure—its finances, railways, food supply, even its prestige." In other words, the right to turn the war into a total war was expressly reserved to the belligerent general. Moltke does not seem to have shared the fear that with the use of such methods warfare would again lapse into barbarism. He expected virtually nothing of international agreements, but all the more from the "slow progress of morality," the "better religious and moral training among peoples."[20] This, rather than codified martial law, was the basis on which he sought to build.

All this would have been well and good from the viewpoint of a convinced liberal or democrat who believed in the basically peaceful propensities of the masses. But it sounds very strange coming from the lips of an enlightened monarchist who expected only governments to exercise reason and insight, and viewed the politicized masses as the real menace of the new age,[21] and who scored the kind of mass war first experienced in the winter of 1870-1871 in France as a "relapse into barbarism."

Did Moltke have any inkling that all wars would henceforth necessarily be mass wars, as the masses were more and more militarized and warfare itself was made more and more totalitarian? And did he realize that this would mean a "relapse into barbarism" against which all the horrors of the war of 1870-1871 would pale into insignificance? In his last Reichstag speech, delivered when he was ninety, he pointed with alarm to the danger of nationalist and racialist war looming from neighboring nations. Such a war, he prophesied, might well last seven or even thirty years. Yet even in this speech there is no sign that his rational optimism had receded at all. A powerful German government and strong German armaments, these remained the safe buttresses of his hopes, even after the fall of Bismarck, which had occurred only a short time before. The danger that war might paralyze, indeed destroy all cultural progress still lay beyond his horizon. Standing on the very threshold of total war, he was still totally immersed in an era that felt able to trust its ability to master the demoniac dynamics of war by calm and statesmanlike reason.

It is this faith in reason, in the sense of responsibility on the part of governments, this distrust of passion and national ambitions that fundamentally distinguishes Moltke's nationalism from anything that may be termed national chauvinism. Moltke had nothing in common with the kind of xenophobia that is blind to the vital rights of other nations, let alone with any unrestrained drive for power and conquest. His sentiments were far too humanitarian, his sense of justice and chivalry too strong, his intellectual horizon too broad to reject the claims of other nations out of hand. He always supported a policy of consideration and conciliation toward Denmark and strongly favored the return to that country of the Danish-speaking sectors of North Schleswig as an act of plain justice.[22] In 1868, in the presence of the Danish and Swedish ambassadors, he remarked that in his view Prussia's wisest policy would be to gain the good will of the Scandinavian people by renouncing Alsen and Sundewitt. As late as 1875 he proposed to the Chancellor that the Danes be appeased by a new settlement of the northern borders of Schleswig, thus securing Germany's flank for the coming conflict with France.

Deep inside, Moltke was always opposed to the war with Austria. He viewed it as a fractricidal quarrel, bound to assume terrible proportions and exacting from Germany the price of surrendering provinces right and left to its neighbors.[23] At the crown council of May 29, 1865, when the question of war or peace with Austria was debated, he was grieved—by the testimony of a note in his own hand—that none was minded to take into account the justified claims of Austria for indemnification for its contribution to the Danish campaign.[24]

This was the reason, moreover, why he never thought of humiliating the Austrians by a triumphal entry into Vienna, but insisted instead on reaching a clean settlement with the vanquished foe as quickly as possible. He certainly would have liked to continue the victorious advance beyond the Danube, after Königgrätz, yet like Bismarck he had no thirst for vengeance and triumph. "We must look to our own advantage, not to vengeance" was the way he formulated the objectives of German diplomacy. His comments on the failure of the Austrian commander-in-chief Benedek were chivalrous in the extreme, and he even defended Benedek against his Austrian critics.[25]

All the more noteworthy is the brusque manner in which he always discussed the "archfoe" France and dealt with the defeated French. In this matter he unreservedly shared the views and prejudices the German nationalist movement had entertained ever since the Wars of Liberation. He too viewed France as Germany's most dangerous neighbor, ever restive, the French people as insatiable in their greed for German territory, capricious in their moods and passions; and he regarded Napoleon III as a dangerous adventurer, inscrutable in his ultimate aims, driven to grab at outward success to maintain his prestige.

The conviction that war over the Rhine border would inexorably come some day and that it would be the best and surest—perhaps the only—means of uniting Germany under Prussian hegemony can be traced in Moltke's letters from 1831. All of his military memoranda from 1859 to 1870, in particular, are built on this assumption, and his whole political attitude during this decade can be understood only when this is taken into account. As early as 1859 he vigorously favored taking advantage of the Italian diversion to strike out against France, regardless of whether that country planned an attack on the Rhine border—"not to fend off an immediate and inescapable threat but to prevent future danger in the interest of Germany, not for Austria but with it."[26]

Bismarck, of course, wished to exploit the same favorable juncture to strengthen Prussian power against Austria, while Moltke saw the "Germanic center of Europe" threatened on the marches of Lombardy as on the Rhine. He favored hostilities without the long wait for negotiating Prussian military leadership within a German alliance against France. He wanted action without ifs and buts, confident that the war emergency would compel even the petty German princes to yield to Prussian leadership, while a great victory in the field was bound to sweep Prussia to the top of the German heap in any event.

His hopes were curiously at odds with the experiences of 1814-1815, and they were shared not even by the Old Liberals, the most zealous advocates of national war. Yet Moltke, unswervingly held to this policy of the sword, meant to cut the Gordian knot of the national question in short order. He did so particularly brusquely in the negotiations on a Prusso-Austrian military agreement he had to conduct in 1860 as Prussian plenipotentiary—negotiations that repeatedly took a highly political turn, owing not least to Moltke's initiative. (In Old Liberal circles his possible appointment as foreign minister was actually discussed!)

In sharp contrast to the policies of the incumbent foreign minister, Schleinitz, Moltke at this time, exploiting his right of direct access to the king, worked for a military alliance that would have guaranteed Austria possession of Venetia against attack not only by France but by Sardinia as well, and this without any prior *quid pro quo* on Austria's part. The allies were to prepare a common war against France, regardless of the danger that these military preparations might themselves provoke such a war, which Moltke held to be inevitable in the long run anyhow. In a rather lopsided interpretation of military geography, he also regarded Venetia as an indispensable outpost of the Middle-European defense position; and as a soldier he wanted a clear and binding agreement in the event of war. What he apparently failed to see was the danger that open-ended pledges of alliance might only confirm Austrian policy in its military stubbornness and frivolity, while turning Prussia into Austria's willing liege.[27]

Moltke continued to be guided by his conviction of the inevitability of a Franco-German power struggle. That was why he found the fratricidal war of 1866 so unwelcome and sinister—and also why, after the unexpectedly swift and complete triumph of the Bohemian campaign, he was prepared to respond to Napoleon's intervention with instant hostilities, if necessary, though on this occasion he was quite aware of the serious situation that might arise. When war with France threatened in 1867 over the question of German occupation rights in Luxembourg, Moltke's advice was to strike before France had a chance to strengthen its armaments, whereas Bismarck would have been content to let Napoleon have Luxembourg, to appease him—provided a formula could be found that would avoid an impression of Prussian weakness and softness.

Moltke put obstacles in the way of this cautious policy of evasion in a written opinion that emphasized the value of the fortress of Luxembourg to a degree far greater than accorded with his known views on fortified positions in staging areas. He did this probably to sharpen the crisis and to win over the king to the idea of war.[28] When France increased its armaments in the ensuing years and the first threads of liaison between the Paris and Vienna courts became visible, the Prussian chief of staff saw this as confirmation of his view that war with the French archfoe was inevitable and that Germany could not be unified without it.[29] He worked out a basic mobilization plan to this end, providing for a German declaration of war the moment Austria began to rearm. "We must not be deterred by the fact that we may give the appearance of aggression."[30] Mentally Moltke was always ready for action and he greeted the crisis in July, 1870, with a positive sigh of relief, as dramatically reported by Bismarck. Moltke felt that the tensions that had weighed so heavily on him were at last released, that the dreams of a great German future he had nurtured since boyhood were near fulfillment.

Manifestly Moltke's attitude at this juncture can no longer be explained on purely military grounds. It was at least in part determined by deeply held political and historical convictions.[31] The strongest proof of this is perhaps that he clung to his policy of conciliating Denmark as late as 1875, at a time when Bismarck had long since concluded that the return of North Schleswig was not feasible. Of France, on the other hand, Moltke never expected anything but hostility, a desire for conquest and general revanchism.

Had Moltke been guided by purely military considerations, he could scarcely have advocated a policy in 1868 and 1875 that would have surrendered German border regions to Denmark, without regard to Bismarck's military reservations and the sentiments of the king, who would never have voluntarily relinquished Düppel and Alsen, the scene of Prussia's triumph. For Moltke Denmark, the home of his youth, was ethnically part and parcel of Germany which he saw locked in unending fateful conflict with the Romance world. France was the rallying point of these anti-German powers, and Germany could be unified only under the stress of war against this archfoe.

All through the 1860's Moltke viewed a Franco-German war as an inexorable fact of destiny, since France's ambition was insatiable, its hostility irreconcilable, while the French sense of prestige would not tolerate Germany's rise to the status of a great power. There was no question that war with France would ultimately come—the question was one of timing rather than politics. Under such circumstances it was best to start the war on one's own initiative, to pick the best moment and to over-run all the enemy's preparations at the first blow.

Moltke seems to have viewed the question of starting a war, of the initial spark, essentially as a matter of military expediency, closely linked to the technical problems of deployment, rather than as a matter of great political import. This, however, was the light in which it appeared to Bismarck, who thought that it would govern Germany's whole position in Europe—its credibility in foreign affairs, the attitude of the neutral powers and the federated governments in Germany, and not least the attitude of the German people themselves, their good conscience, the integration of inward and outward preparedness, faith in the justice of the German cause in a life-and-death struggle. "Bismarck's position is unassailable," Moltke remarked coolly in 1867, when told of the chancellor's reservations about a preventive war on the Luxembourg issue, "but in time his stand will cost us many lives." What he meant, of course, was that France's military power would grow more and more formidable.[32] He understood Bismarck's reservations, but he did not share them.

For Moltke war between Germany and France was not a question of moral responsibility but of inexorable destiny. He did not consider it an eventuality that would ultimately involve all the great powers, change their balance, and seriously upset the concert of Europe. He looked on it basically as a duel only between the two countries, the concern of no other. Such a duel had to be fought strictly by the rules, without the meddlesome intervention of political considerations, until the enemy was rendered utterly defenseless.

Hence the noteworthy and uncompromising harshness that marked all of Moltke's dealings with French negotiators during the war, a form of behavior quite at odds with his basically humane orientation. "In war I have an iron hand," he said on a later occasion, when efforts were made to persuade him to accept the office of prime minister of Prussia, "but in peace my hand is too gentle."[33] This harshness was not innate;[34] it stemmed from the way he understood his official duties. As chief of the General Staff he felt obliged to keep watch lest military advantage be sacrificed to the diplomats, lest the army be robbed of even a tittle of its triumphs. True, there are occasional hints of nationalist sentiments, of hatred of the enemy—how could it have been otherwise in the superheated atmosphere at headquarters? [35]—but these emotions did not really influence his decisions.

As early as the surrender negotiations at Sedan a first slight difference of opinion emerged between him and Bismarck. Bismarck considered making peace at once, with Napoleon III's help, and was thus intent on not weakening the captured emperor's authority unnecessarily; he hoped perhaps even to leave him in charge of his army, a hope soon dashed by Napoleon's own reluctance; while the chief of staff thought only of exploiting the military triumph to the fullest. He displayed the same attitude toward Bismarck's vain efforts, continued over many months, to use Marshal Bazaine, encircled in Metz, as a peace mediator. Bismarck wanted Bazaine to put him in touch with the ex-empress and regent Eugenie and would have freed Bazaine with all his troops, had Bazaine promised to support France's submission to the peace terms Bismarck demanded. The chief of staff would seem to have been but sketchily informed of these plans and negotiations, for his opposition to them was entirely predictable, as was that of Prince Frederic Charles, the besieger of Metz. To the extent, however, that

Moltke did know about this affair, he sharply opposed any attempt to detract from the triumph at Metz for the sake of an uncertain political gain.

Moltke's war plan aimed at total destruction of the enemy forces, rather than at piecemeal military operations that would be succeeded by diplomatic negotiation. Bismarck wanted the war to end as quickly as possible. He was interested in furthering the formation of a new government with which peace might be concluded; and such a peace was likely to be durable only in the measure that French national passions had not been whipped up in a long mass war, that French *amour propre* was humbled as little as possible. Moltke too, of course, did not desire or expect a long people's war. After the great and decisive battle of Sedan he indeed regarded the issue as settled, since the forces of imperial France had been destroyed. For that very reason he did not overly hurry to continue the war. Yet he was far removed from Bismarck's line of reasoning.

Bismarck considered halting any further advance into France, since complete occupation was not feasible in any event. Even the German army, moreover, was not of unlimited size and too great an extension of the front was at best a dubious thing. What Bismarck considered instead was to occupy Alsace-Lorraine and a few other territorial pawns behind a strong line of defense and then to wait until the political chaos in France subsided or a stable government was formed that would be prepared to respond to the German peace terms.

Obviously such a plan, which would have facilitated a rapid recovery in France, entailed certain risks. In style it plainly harked back to the eighteenth-century cabinet wars. Actually, Bismarck did not go far beyond its mere discussion and consideration, without lending the plan the dignity of an official act, and in mid-October he dropped it altogether. Yet when the war unexpectedly grew protracted and the German armies, scattered across the land, at times got into serious difficulties, he reverted to it, this time in official submissions.

Bismarck now criticized the whole basis of the campaign, the advance all the way to Paris, the encirclement of the capital with insufficient forces, the delayed siege, the continuation of the campaign into South and Northwest France. In objective terms, Moltke was quite right in reacting to this *ex post facto* reproach with indignation. Once Bismarck's peace endeavors with the Bonapartists had failed, the war certainly could not be won by remaining on the defensive, nor could the issue now be forced by mere dash. The storming of Paris was a bloody ordeal, to be ventured only after thorough preparation; and it would also take time to vanquish the French mass armies.

Bismarck would have been justified in criticizing the military only if he had been able to come up with an alternative that was politically and militarily feasible. What he advocated as late as December—concentrating the army on a smaller area of occupation[36]—meant foregoing the enemy's complete defeat and was clearly at odds with the stringent peace terms. If the general political situation was indeed so perilous and the danger of neutral intervention as great as the chancellor said it was, there would really have been but one way out: scaling down the peace terms—foregoing Lorraine and Metz, for example—in order to make the conclusion of a peace treaty more palatable to the French national government or the Bonapartists.

Yet this was precisely what the Chancellor was unable to agree to, for reasons yet to be discussed; and if he now, from pique, sought to blame the military, its stubbornness, its limited political outlook, even its alleged greed for conquest, for the bad way things had gone, this was simply a case of passing the buck. One can scarcely avoid the judgment that Bismarck was wrong in his criticism of Moltke's operations (not, however, in his criticism of the General Staff's mystery-mongering and its attempts to keep him away from important consultations). This is true even when it is admitted that in the Crown Prince's headquarters military stubbornness and mistaken notions on the available scope of attack unnecessarily delayed preparations for the bombardment of Paris.[37] Bismarck's manifest unfairness not only unnecessarily embittered the debate but rendered objective discussion between the leading men all but impossible, as shown by the unhappy outcome of the Crown Prince's efforts at mediation on January 13.

We gain indeed the general impression that the unexpected transformation of the war into a true people's war, running entirely contrary to the basic concepts of Bismarck's policy, made him increasingly nervous and at times even uncertain about the means to be chosen to force the swift conclusion of peace. His judgment of the effect political and military measures would have on "reasonable governments"[38] may have been excellent, but it applied far less predictably to masses whipped into a frenzy by political and patriotic sentiments. There is no other explanation for his official recommendation that the sufferings of the French civilian population and the terror on the battlefield be deliberately heightened, in the expectation that this would the sooner render the French war-weary and keep them from flocking to the *Garde Mobile* and guerilla bands.

Bismarck believed that it was the political terror exercised by the national government formed by Gambetta which kept the French masses fighting rather than true patriotism, and it was his plan to outbid this terror, so to speak—always within the limits of existing international law, to be sure, but straining those limits to the farthest point.[39] We know today that such calculations never come out even, if only for the reason that every increase in terror only seems to weld the people under pressure into ever greater national solidarity.

There is another reason. A population living under terror and martial law has, in fact, no opportunity to form a political opposition on any considerable scale and force its leaders to make peace, at least not until complete military collapse has rendered all the fighting words meaningless and public order has crumbled.

But the American general, Philip Sheridan, happened to be at German head-quarters and his advice apparently made a great impression on Bismarck. Sheridan advocated copying the totalitarian methods of the American Civil War and leaving the vanquished "only their eyes, to weep over the war."

In a political sense, this counsel was misguided, just as were the attempts in the Second World War to generate pacifist sentiment in Germany by stepping up aerial terror. In Bismarck's time, of course, this failure lay yet in the future and modern techniques of dictatorship were not nearly as refined as they were to become in the twentieth century. In hindsight, Bismarck's error thus becomes more comprehensible. It was the error of a militant, of a vehemently assertive man whose virtues did not include patience.

During the months of the greatest tension, Bismarck, angry and impatient, was often carried away into brutal-sounding utterances about the atrocities of snipers, the chauvinism of Frenchmen in general, the misdeeds of French troops from Africa in particular, and the necessity for imposing Draconian penalties. He made these remarks in private conversation, often over a glass of wine, solely as a matter of personal opinion. His official reports, by contrast, breathe a spirit of cold and sober political reason. It was a spirit not immune to miscalculation but quite free of unrestrained passion, hatred, and vengefulness.

The fact that he was indeed solely motivated by the desire to conclude peace as quickly as possible is demonstrated by the complete reversal in his attitude toward the French after the capitulation of Paris, when for the first time there appeared to be a practical possibility of coming to terms. Yet this very change gave rise to a new conflict with the General Staff in which the already existing tensions were to reach their peak.

Bismarck was firmly determined to use the fall of the fortified capital as the occasion for making peace at once, preferably with a Bonapartist government, which would have been entirely dependent on German good will and the support of the propertied classes, who craved peace. Yet Bismarck would also have been willing to recognize a republican government, provided it pursued a policy of peace. The all-important thing was that the surrender terms must not be so harsh that they would destroy the moral authority of those in control of Paris who might otherwise be prepared to accept them, or deter from further negotiations any government in Bordeaux in search of peace.

Bismarck was convinced that the French people were now ready for peace. It was simply a matter of lending them a hand in making the leap, and consider-ations of military triumph could not be permitted to supervene. Moltke, however, had rather different ideas. We have only recently come into possession of his draft for a surrender document, submitted to the king on January 14, the day after his ill-starred discussion with Bismarck.[40] It demanded that all French troops in Paris should be made prisoners of war, after the model of Sedan; that all other troops of the line and *Gardes Mobiles* be shipped to Germany; that the entire city of Paris with its fortifications and military equipment, arms, and colors be surrendered and occupied; an immediate payment of five hundred million francs as the city's war indemnity, together with defrayment of the current costs of the German occupation; and an advance on the ultimate war indemnity of four billion francs, from Paris resources.

It will be seen that these terms were expressly designed to drain the military triumph to the dregs. Military considerations were considered in an almost complete vacuum, no thought at all having been apparently given to the political consequences. Indeed, Moltke seems to have been blissfully unaware that his demands for indemnification touched on a political question par excellence—they would have rallied the propertied classes of Paris on whose war-weariness Bismarck counted unanimously against Germany. No Paris government subscribing to such terms could have stayed in office more than a few days and the result would have been chaos, with the Paris Commune taking power at once. The Germans would have had to subdue the city by force at great cost in blood. Peace with France would have become more remote than before.

But Moltke did not count on a negotiated peace. He was solely concerned with military advantage, with gaining control of Paris as a great transport center and staging area for continuing the war, which he wanted to carry deep into South France, to destroy even the enemy's last resources, render him utterly defenseless, and impose peace on his own terms.[41]

On that same day, January 14, 1871, Bismarck also submitted to the king a memorandum on a proposed armistice. It would appear that he was originally quite willing to leave the military aspects of the surrender negotiations to proposals to be made by the General Staff. His statement was expressly limited to the political aspects—with what agencies truce and peace had best be concluded and on what terms.[42]

It was not until Bismarck saw Moltke's memorandum—such is the inference—that he became convinced of the necessity of taking into his own hands the whole question of military surrender negotiations as well, leaving the military no more than a subsidiary role. What Bismarck wanted was peace, while Moltke—to use the word of the Crown Prince—wanted a "war of extermination."[43] The inherent conflict between army and state now gaped open to its full depth.

The clash that now ensued among the advisers to the crown was the most serious ever. Bismarck mustered all his strength to seize full power at this crucial juncture and neutralize his military counterpart. Bringing up his heaviest ammunition in this struggle for the king's decision, he let loose all the accumulated resentments against the General Staff. The bitterness on both sides transcended all bounds. "Never have I seen such bitterness turned against one man as is presently the case against Bismarck," so Albrecht von Stosch described the mood of the military during those days.

The Chancellor's ire, on the other side, was no less profound. Hitherto he had submitted to the military like a lamb, he said, but there was no question of that now. After the war the whole military system would have to be given a new character. It could no longer be allowed to dominate as before.[44]

And what about King William? Quite clearly the clash rent his very heart and soul. Basically the old gentlemen was a devotee of peace, inclined to accept Bismarck's views, which were strongly supported by the Crown Prince. Yet this inclination was at odds with his feelings as a soldier. Above all, he wanted to avoid a "second Olmütz," to preserve jealously the "honor of the army." To complicate matters, the final wording of the proclamation of the second German Reich also had to be settled during these days; and the king's inner conflict was undoubtedly one reason why his irritation increased to the point of tears, why he became extremely brusque with Bismarck. He was obviously not equal to the task of reconciling the inward clash between political and military considerations in these crucial hours.

In the end, however, he was ready on this occasion, as always, to be carried along by his Chancellor's clear insight and firm will. Two days after his proclamation as emperor, Bismarck had won the day, though the precise reasons are not too clear. When a French parliamentarian appeared in Versailles on the evening of January 20, the Emperor and the Crown Prince first discussed the event with Bismarck; and Bismarck conducted the crucial surrender negotiations with Jules Favre alone, the General Staff chief being called in only for subsequent consultations on whether the agreed terms were to be accepted or rejected.

There was still to be a long and searching debate within the inner crown council of "paladins"; but Bismarck was no longer in a mood to have power wrested from his hands. No more doubts seem to have been admissible that what was now contemplated was a genuine peace rather than a cease-fire. The chief of the General Staff was reminded of the limits of his jurisdiction and once again enjoined to keep the Chancellor loyally informed on military operations, through the medium of two cabinet decrees Moltke regarded as both unfair and ungracious.

His response took the form of the notorious bill of indictment of Bismarck of January 26, which, in the draft by department chief Bronsart von Schellendorff, sounded almost like an offer of resignation, suggesting that the king place direction of military operations in the Chancellor's hands as well. We know today that Moltke never seriously considered committing so flagrant an act of insubordination and that, unlike a parliamentary minister, he did not think himself entitled to put his resignation in terms of an ultimatum.[45]

But Moltke did, in unmistakable terms, demand that the chief of the General Staff be placed completely on a par with the Reich Chancellor, at least in wartime. It was all in vain. No written answer was ever given to his complaint, and only a marginal note by the adjutant general suggests that the king took care of the matter orally, with some words of praise and recognition to Moltke. Bismarck had his way all down the line. He even settled the cessation of the bombardment and other military details with Favre, without Moltke's participation.

The armistice was negotiated on very moderate terms, in the form of a "convention" rather than as a "capitulation." Paris was not to be occupied nor were prisoners, flags, and trophies to be surrendered. Even the indemnity and the entry of German troops were foregone for the time being. Every outward humiliation of vanquished France was avoided. Nor did Bismarck yield to Moltke's subsequent efforts to put sharper teeth into the armistice terms when individual clauses were negotiated and the question of an extension came up. On all these points he imperiously ignored the wishes of the General Staff and even the king. In particular, he never insisted that the French agree to the kind of arms limitations Moltke had favored even for the armistice terms. As for the entry into Paris of the victorious German troops, Moltke prevailed in this matter only when the actual peace treaty was signed and even then only under severe limitations of time and place.

The military were inclined to regard all this as mere weakness. Initially the armistice terms aroused a great deal of indignation among the higher staff officers, but this was quickly drowned out by the general rejoicing over the fall of the great city. Moltke himself appeared to the French negotiators in an unapproachable light, unrelenting in the severity of his military demands. More than ever he felt it to be his duty to guard the desires and claims of the army against the encroachments of diplomacy. The pen was not to sign away what the soldier's sword had won.

"I must be very certain of army discipline," he told Favre on January 27, "to dare offer our convention." Thus the manner in which he himself preserved this discipline becomes all the more admirable. Instead of feeding fuel to the flames and staging a political crisis, Moltke endeavored to calm down the generals. He sent a message to the Crown Prince of Saxony, explaining why the armistice terms could not go further. Favre's government would otherwise fall, he said, and at the moment German policy favored its preservation, since it was prepared to conclude peace.[46] In the end everything depended on such willingness to yield to reasons of state. In a splendid display of self-control, Moltke on January 26, the day after filing his bitter complaint, accepted Bismarck's summons to a preliminary discussion of the armistice terms, limited entirely to the two men. They reached agreement on essential matters, and Moltke thereafter managed to content himself with his role as a mere military expert and consultant to the statesman.

In return, Moltke later on had the satisfaction of seeing Bismarck display much understanding for military demands that were based on something more than vanity. This was especially true in the question of the cession of Lorraine and Metz in the peace treaty. The fact that military and geographic considerations here prevailed over all political reservations was of much greater historical importance and drew farther-reaching consequences than any of the armistice terms on which Moltke had had to yield.

We shall have to consider further on the changing arguments that ultimately persuaded Bismarck to insist on the retention of Lorraine and Metz as prizes of war, in addition to Alsace (see Part 4). He never doubted the necessity for tangible safeguards against French revanchism; he only questioned their extent. Was it really necessary to annex Lorraine with its alien population and its fortress of Metz? Would not possession of Strasbourg suffice, perhaps with Belfort, which was part of the *Departement* of Upper Alsace?

In such questions Bismarck was dependent on the judgment of his military experts. When they submitted that the torrents of blood shed to take Metz made it impossible to return the fortress, he rejected this argument just as he did the far more extravagant claims for territorial aggrandizement put forward by various generals.[47] Yet Moltke's statement that possession of Metz was equivalent to an army of at least 120,000, while Belfort was of lesser military value,[48] evidently played an important part in Bismarck's decision to retain the former and console the French negotiators, so to speak, with the return of the latter.[49]

Nothing could have been better calculated to relieve the tension between Bismarck and the General Staff than the outcome of the peace negotiations. Conversely, this tension would have been exacerbated in the extreme, had Bismarck let Metz go. This is seen from the resentment with which military headquarters received the news that Bismarck might be obliged to renounce Lorraine in order to conclude peace. "The return of Metz," Count Leonhard von Blumenthal wrote in his diary, "seems to me tantamount to a defeat and is likely to raise a terrible storm in Germany. I can scarcely believe that all that blood is to have been shed before Metz in vain! The sound military line we secured at such sacrifice would be relinquished, solely for the sake of getting a peace treaty. The army is not that war weary. On the contrary, it is champing at the bit." It was the Emperor and the Crown Prince, alas, who were war weary. Bismarck was "pursuing a policy that is too subtle, anticipating things that seem to me beside the mark. Sometimes it is the enemy who is not to be embittered beyond endurance, sometimes other powers, and the like. To the mind of a simple soldier all this seems quite absurd. The vanquished foe must be put in a place from which he cannot rise in a hundred years. He must be shackled in such a way that he cannot soon even dream of revenge."[50]

This was, in cruder terms, merely what Moltke was thinking himself. France was to be beaten in such a fashion that it could not rise again for a hundred years. Yet despite all the "military rectifications" to the western frontiers, the peace Bismarck concluded had no provisions that would have prevented the defeated nation from rearming as soon as possible. Thus the German side retained a keen distrust that the French would soon seek their revenge. The patriotic zeal with which they carried out their war obligations to get rid of foreign occupation before the agreed term, the vigor of their reconstruction work after the widespread destruction, the country's surprisingly swift economic recovery, all this awakened new concern. As early as the spring of 1872 Moltke anticipated that within the year the French army would have regained sufficient strength to engage in another war.

Moltke did not conceal these worries from foreign diplomats. In March, 1873, he frightened the British ambassador with the remark that war was bound to break out again sooner or later, and from the military viewpoint one had to say the sooner the better for Germany.[51] In fact, from 1872 onward Moltke seriously considered the possibility of a war of retribution, an eventuality for which he drafted a secret mobilization plan, on the premise that a purely defensive stance on the part of France was unlikely. In it he at least hinted at the possibility of a German pre-emptive strike[52] and described the German war aim in these terms: "At last to cap the volcano that has been shaking Europe for a century with its wars and revolutions."

Yet how was this to be accomplished? How did Moltke envisage a new imposed peace? The question was put to him in 1875 by the Belgian envoy Baron Nothomb, to whom Moltke had openly declared that Germany could not wait until France had completed its rearmament but must take pre-emptive action. By striking in time we could avoid the loss of a hundred thousand men. "And what will you do with vanquished France?" the envoy inquired. The answer had a ring of uncertainty: "I do not know. That decision will surely be a great embarrassment. Alas, war, war! When one has seen it close up, as I have, one can only be filled with a deep sense of revulsion. It is mankind's worst scourge, and surely one must do everything to avoid it."[53]

If the French report on this exchange is indeed correct, we are here brought face to face with the profound paradox in Moltke's character. Moltke the humanist recoiled from the horrors of war. As an advocate of detached political reason, he shrank from the unrestrained barbarism and internecine hatreds of modern mass war. Yet as an expert in annihilation he saw no alternative to striking ever new and devasting blows, "at last to cap the volcano," though without any prospect of escaping the ever-deepening hatred between the two nations that would give rise to new eruptions.

Practical experience had taught Moltke the general that in modern mass war there are no more battles of Cannae or even Königgrätz. In an age when whole nations went to war, the issue lay no longer between mobile armies in the field, but between the reserves, the economic and psychological war potential. Moltke's own campaign plans after 1871 amount to a kind of strategy of attrition—in the grand style of Frederic the Great, it is true. Hence one might well ask what was the value of a pre-emptive strike, since protracted warfare was certain in any event?

Yet Moltke saw no alternative to a strategy of anticipating the enemy and striking devastating blows. His thinking moved along preordained lines that form a sinister vicious circle,[54] once it is accepted that in the relations of the great powers among themselves no law applies but the law of constant power struggle and ambush, once the very possibility is excluded that nations might join hands at a higher level to form a firm body of international law under which their differences might be settled peacefully.

The exchange with Baron Nothomb was connected with the so-called "War-in-Sight Crisis," which Bismarck set in motion in April, 1875, when he countered the new French army act (the scope of which the German General Staff at first overestimated) by unleashing a storm in the press[55] and applying various forms of diplomatic pressure, apparently with the intention of intimidating the French and perhaps slowing the pace of their rearmament. Bismarck was probably not at all displeased at the time that Moltke should drop saber-rattling remarks in discussion with foreign diplomats.[56] Yet this did not keep him from disavowing the aged field marshal when it suited his convenience and even at times describing him as a political dilettante whose personal opinions were without significance. Bismarck himself never for a moment considered the possibility of preventive war at the time, any more than did Emperor William, who protested with the greatest vigor against any toying with such ideas.[57] Moltke offered no open opposition to this official policy of peace. He was by no stretch of the imagination a warmonger. He did, however, believe that the possibility of war within a matter of years had to be taken into account, even if such a conclusion was most unwelcome.[58]

A major argument along these lines, put forward on occasion by Bismarck himself, held that France might be unable to afford its inflated military budget in the long run, pushing it in the direction of a settlement by force of arms. Such prophecies remained unfulfilled. France's high military costs turned out to be contingent on reconstruction rather than maintenance; and in any event the country was under no financial strain. Besides, the insistence on peace by the French bourgeoisie was sufficiently strong to quell all thought of revenge for a long time to come. Even Moltke became convinced in the end that France would not dare strike without the support of strong allies. What this meant to him was that henceforth the Russian question would be of growing importance.

Unlike Bismarck, Moltke considered this question more from the ethnic point of view, for its as yet dormant potential, rather than in the light of dynastic relations and sober political reason. The vastness of the Russian land, the frighteningly rapid growth of the Russian nation, that "largest homogeneous mass of people in the world," the strong expansionist tendencies in Russian policy—all these elements had impressed themselves on Moltke at an early stage.

In his travel letters from Moscow in 1856 he predicted a great future for Russia.

Yet whenever Moltke saw a concentration of power, he was inclined to posit such dangers as bellicosity and irreconcilable interests. After 1859 the thought recurs in his military and political writings that Europe's Germanic center would some day necessarily have to defend itself against an alliance of "the Slavic East against the Romance West." As early as December, 1859, he had drafted a plan of deployment against Russia, on the then most unlikely premise that eastern and western neighbors might join in league against Prussia. By April, 1871, even before the Peace of Frankfurt was signed, Moltke's first mobilization plan against the eventuality of a two-front war against the new Reich was completed.

His foresight was remarkable. Moltke thought he saw even then, long before the conclusion of the Austro-German dual alliance, that Russia would some day look on Prussia-Germany as the main obstacle in its march toward Constantinople. There was, he remarked, "an unmistakable mutual aversion in faith and custom, a conflict in material interest" between the German and Russian people. Both of these differences would become aggravated by Germany's rise to the status of a great power, which was also bound to wear away the traditional sympathies of the Russian for the Prussian court. Conceivably the seizure of Danzig and Königsberg might be one of the Russian war aims.

These were views notably at odds with those of Bismarck, who was unwilling to acknowledge any vital difference of interest between Germany and Russia. But Moltke does not seem to have held his as firm convictions, derived from practical political experience. They were rather hypothetical, based on broad historical generalization, meant to envisage certain contingencies in an experimental way. Moltke seems simply to have imagined certain possible war situations, to which he then applied a process of military and technical calculation. If Russia ever did declare war on Germany, Austria would seem to be Germany's natural ally, just as France would be Russia's natural ally—that was the main direction in which Moltke's thinking went. All the rest remains doubtful—whether or not East Prussia was envisaged as a realistic Russian target, whether Russian ambitions were directed more toward Turkey or toward Galicia, indeed whether or not there was any true conflict of interest between Russia and Germany. On all these points Moltke made conflicting statements.[59]

Yet after 1876 the tension between Russia and Germany lost whatever hypothetical character it may have had and became more and more real. The quarrel among the eastern powers as to who would inherit Turkey's former hegemony in the Balkans deepened, and Bismarck's efforts at mediation met with ever greater difficulties. The dual alliance of 1879 involved Germany even more deeply in the haggling between Russia and Austria over Balkan issues. The pan-Slavic movement began to engage in its anti-German propaganda campaign. French rearmament began to be matched in Russia, which kept reinforcing its western border garrisons, feeding fuel to the suspicions of the German General Staff.

Thus opened the era of the arms race among the great powers, which Moltke had seen coming with alarm as early as 1872.[60] Decade by decade it was to inject an element of increasing tension into the European political scene. The specter of a two-front war rose up before Germany as a growing menace, even though it still loomed only in the distance. Moltke's strategic plans, conceived in order to banish it, gained more and more practical substance.

The central thought in his numerous memoranda after 1871 was always the same. In the face of such a dual threat, Germany's military resources were no longer equal to the kind of total victory achieved in 1866 and 1870-1871; nor were tempting targets for territorial aggrandizement in sight either in the west or the east.[61] All that was left to Germany was the strategic defensive—a defensive, however, that would resemble that of Frederic the Great in the Seven-Years' War. It would have to be coupled with a tactical offensive of the greatest possible impact until the enemy was paralyzed and exhausted to the point where diplomacy would have a chance to bring about a satisfactory settlement.

The crucial issue within such a system of active defense was whether the main weight of action was to be shifted to the east or the west. The plan of 1871 gives no clear answer to this question. A subsequent one, dating from Febuary, 1877, counted on only a Russian declaration of war, but anticipated with absolute certainty swift intervention by France, which it sought to anticipate by declaring war on France on the fifth day of mobilization "without regard to the position France might have taken by that time." Moltke hoped to win a "great decisive battle" with superior forces in the west as early as the third week of the war, freeing masses of troops to be thrown against the east, where Russia would need more time for deployment.

The whole thing has a strong foretaste of the events of 1914. In particular, one already sees here that sinister and inexorable sequence set in motion by precipitate declarations of war made for purely military reasons, without regard to their political effects; and one sees also the fateful pressure for a swift decision in the west, for which a two-front war would allow but a few short weeks. At the same time Moltke entertained no illusions that another Sedan was any longer possible in the changed circumstances—the threat from the east, fortification of the French border, the tremendous increase in France's armed forces. Even in the wake of a great triumph over France it "would have to be left to diplomacy to try to gain us relief from that side, even though only on the basis of the status quo."

It seems likely that the whole bias of the plan goes back to political desires voiced by Bismarck, with whom the chief of the General Staff was then working very closely. The Chancellor wished to avoid provoking Russia even in the slightest, for he held that a war with Germany's eastern neighbor would be a bootless undertaking of incalculable scope. He always clung to the conviction that even in the event of a two-front war Germany would have to seek to precipitate the decisive issue in the west.[62] He never seriously doubted that France would exploit the opportunity for revenge, no sooner was Germany involved in a conflict with the eastern powers. So convinced was he of this hazard that he was determined to force the issue openly if need be.

For once war was viewed as a necessity rather than a mere matter of conjecture, a philosophical proposition, even Bismarck did not shrink from the pre-emptive strike.[63] To forego it would have meant turning an unsecured back on a certain enemy, virtually inviting him to strike the mortal blow at the very moment when the German armed forces would be involved in vast struggle in the east. In theory he allowed for the possibility even then that France might keep Germany from the necessity of attacking by offering dependable peace guarantees—but he never truly believed in such a possibility.[64] In any event, he was totally opposed to risking a war with Russia until Germany's western borders were absolutely secure.

He was not swerved from this position even by the alliance with Austria concluded in 1879. Then as before he vigorously opposed any warlike involvement with Russia, and he was willing to come to the aid of the new ally only *in extremis,* and even then only if the western frontier were first secured. Bismarck never regarded a war with Russia—or indeed any two-front war—as preordained, as "automatic" in any sense, any more than he had the war with France. His whole complex system of alliances negotiated in the eighties was no more than a continual effort to escape from this "automatism."

Any commitment to campaign plans that meant an initial offensive in the east on the side of Austria harbored the danger of encouraging Austrian pugnacity; and Bismarck feared nothing so much as a frivolous Austrian expansionist policy in the Balkans, based on German military power, that would provoke Russia and place the entire burdens of war on Germany. Against such an eventuality, he actually considered (according to well-authenticated utterances[65]) as a last resort "to buy Russian neutrality at the last moment by dropping Austria [i.e., Austria's claims in the Balkans] and leaving the Orient to the mercy of Russia."

To Moltke's military thinking the situation presented an altogether different picture. He staked everything on swift and major initial success. Yet with the extension of the French fortification system along Meuse and Moselle, the enlargement and modernization of the French army and a corresponding acceleration of mobilization and deployment, such initial successes were no longer attainable, unless the enemy ventured far beyond his fortified belt in order to reoccupy Alsace-Lorraine. All the more favorable, however, seemed the prospect of quick victory in the east, particularly since the conclusion of the dual alliance. The unprotected border, the isolated situation of East Prussia, the Russo-Polish salient projecting deep into the west—all of these made an offensive strategy virtually inevitable. Above all, concerted action by German armies operating from East Prussia and Austrian armies operating from Galicia opened up major opportunities for large-scale encirclement; and the slow pace of any Russian deployment made rapid initial success even more likely.

For these reasons Moltke's own deployment plans had provided after December, 1878, that in the event of a two-front war the bulk of the German forces would instantly proceed to the offensive in the east, while lesser forces would take over the defense in the west, a task rendered all the easier by the relatively short border, the strong natural barriers of the Vosges ridges and the Rhine, and the powerful fortifications and great arms depots in Alsace-Lorraine and along the Rhine. Considerations involving Austria also played an important part in this strategy. Unless the Austrian army could be swept up into a grand offensive at the very outset, it was likely to fritter away what strength it had in feeble defensive action from a sense of numerical inferiority. It would never venture beyond the Carpathian mountain ranges, thus giving the Russians the many weeks they needed to deploy their full armed might.

It was on this very point that Moltke's military and Bismarck's political thinking were to come into sharp collision. If salvation really lay in a great impetuous Austro-German surprise offensive in the east, then everything clearly depended on the most careful military advance agreement between the two general staffs. Mobilization and deployment plans had to be integrated, the troops had to be massed, and the logistic support for them had to be set beforehand.

These needs were indeed repeatedly discussed by the two general staffs from 1882 on, mainly, it would seem, at the instance of Quartermaster General Count Waldersee, who at that time became the field marshal general's deputy, with broad autonomy of action. In his restless ambition, the younger man sought to activate the alliance with Austria in a military sense. He shared the Austrian staff chief's conviction that a Russian attack could be anticipated with certainty in the near future and that it must in turn be forestalled by aggressive action in the grand style.

When signs mounted in the fall of 1887, in connection with the Bulgarian crisis, that Russia was arming for war on Austria, Waldersee had a report compiled for the Chancellor which openly called for a pre-emptive strike on the side of Austria, to take the form of an immediate joint attack on Russia. Russian rearmament and the political temper in Moscow and St. Petersburg were painted in the gloomiest colors, in terms of direct war preparations, partial mobilization, and indeed deployment already underway. War would break out no later than spring and must be anticipated now. Waldersee succeeded in having Moltke sign this memorandum and the even shriller political cover document that accompanied it. During an audience with the Emperor late in November the aged field marshal, in the presence of the quartermaster general, emphasized with raised voice "that we must never leave Austria in the lurch."[66]

Bismarck did not allow these representations by the military to upset his composure. With the recently concluded reinsurance treaty with Russia in his pocket, he did not share their worries about impending war, and once again he emphatically rejected the idea of preventive war. What he did do, however, was to exploit the General Staff memorandum to goad the Austrian government into intensifying its defensive armaments. He had it transmitted to Vienna with the advice that the Austrians protect themselves against possible surprise attack by reinforcing their Galician garrisons.

This initiative, however, was foiled by military suasion exerted through other channels. The Austrian military attaché, Lieutenant Colonel Carl Freiherr von Steininger, reported from Berlin that Moltke favored an immediate strike against Russia; and the German military attaché, Major Johann Georg von Deines, in Vienna put similar pressure on the Austrian General Staff and Emperor Francis Joseph, to whom he held out the prospect of large-scale support from the German army, in accord with Moltke's deployment plans for a two-front war.

Von Deines was only implementing the intent of his superior, Quartermaster General von Waldersee, who during these years was maintaining extremely close contact with the German Foreign Office through Baron Friedrich von Holstein as an intermediary. Together with Holstein, Count von Berchem and Joseph Maria von Radowitz, Waldersee seems to have formed a kind of "war party." Bismarck's shrewd maneuvering between Austria and Russia was too cautious and complex for their taste. They considered his trust in the political wisdom of the czarist government, based on the growth of Russian nationalism, outdated, and they found fault with Bismarck's ruthless interference with Austro-Hungarian power politics in the Balkans. They were convinced that a new and more dynamic German policy was in prospect, tied to the succession of the youthful Prince William, whom they were already assiduously wooing. They entertained far fewer reservations than the old chancellor in yielding to the power drive of neo-German nationalism.[67]

The government at Vienna was not at all inclined to allow itself to be driven into a preventive war against Russia, nor was it in a hurry to reinforce the Galician border garrisons, as recommended by the chief of the General Staff, Count Friedrich von Beck-Rzikowsky. In addition to financial limitations, there were technical problems, to say nothing of a general political pusillanimity. Vienna soon noted that there were discrepancies between military and political views in Berlin; and Bismarck himself authoritatively briefed his ambassador in Vienna who had initially thought Bismarck had gone over to the advocates of preventive war. Von Deines was threatened with recall for having exceeded his authority as a military observer. With Count Waldersee Bismarck minced no words. He told the quartermaster general to mind his own business.[68] If there were any further intervention in government policy, Bismarck would complain to the Emperor, threatening his own resignation.

In Viennese diplomatic circles meanwhile great confusion had been caused by the conflicting reports emanating from Bismarck and the German General Staff. The Austrian General Staff hoped that since Bismarck himself now took so grave a view of the situation they might at last succeed in forcing their German ally to enter into firm commitments in the event of war. They made plans for a military convention that would above all fix the largest possible troop contingent as the German contribution to an eastern campaign. Other matters to be settled were a common date of mobilization, a common declaration of war, a common start of operations and offensive warfare. Lastly, all these obligations were to come into force even in the event of a pre-emptive strike against Austria.

Such was the sense of the draft treaty *(Punktationen)* the Austrian General Staff presented in Berlin in late December through its military plenipotentiary Freiherr von Steininger. Bismarck agreed that Moltke might discuss these questions with Steininger, but he made it abundantly clear that such a discussion would not be permitted to interfere with his basic policy and reserved any final decisions to himself.

It was at this time that Bismarck personally and confidentially informed Moltke of the content of the reinsurance treaty with Russia, rejecting outright any encouragement to an Austrian attack, regardless of how militarily advantageous it might appear. If Austria went ahead, it would have to look for support from Britain, Italy, Turkey, and Rumania. Germany would simply not agree to changing the defensive character of the alliance of 1879 by subsequent military provisos. He let the Austrian foreign minister know that he was deeply concerned "lest the right to provide political counsel to our sovereign might actually slip from our hands into those of the General Staff." Bismarck was determined that the rude soldier fist should under no circumstances tangle or tear his gossamer network of diplomatic alliances.

Once again the aged Moltke submitted to the sweep of Bismarck's will. Unresistingly and unreservedly he swung into line, so much so that Bismarck's son and state secretary saw him as "the calmest and most thoughtful among all our generals." The discussions with the Austrian military plenipotentiary were of course foredoomed to failure. The old field marshal did not dare yield on even a single military demand put forward by Germany's ally. In his response to the draft treaty he limited himself to meaningless generalities, maintaining a discreet silence on the question of the scope of German military assistance in the event of war with Russia.[69]

The military convention therefore fell through, yet in his last great operational plan of February, 1888—which, of course, was never revealed to the Austrians—Moltke provided for the commitment of more than one third of the German armed forces for immediate offensive purposes, completely ignoring Bismarck's contrary views. Moltke persisted in believing that war in the east would not long be delayed.

Waldersee and Holstein too maintained their covert opposition to Bismarck. Both counted on force of circumstances one day convincing Bismarck of the hopelessness of his peace policy. They hoped that a younger sovereign would muster the resolution for war of which the nonagenarian Emperor William was no longer capable. Waldersee's influence is echoed in the well-known letter to Bismarck of May 10, 1888, written by Crown Prince William, in which it was anticipated that a war against Russia would result in that country's complete and permanent policial paralysis, and in which the military considerations militating in favor of an eastern offensive were once again sharply emphasized.[70] This conflict between military and political views continued to play its part into the time of Bismarck's dismissal.

As long as Bismarck was at the helm, he prevailed over all the secret opposition of the officers and younger diplomats, maintaining complete unity of diplomatic planning and leadership. It is true, however, that the military problems attendant on a common deployment by the Central Powers in the east were unresolved and remained so until July, 1914, to the grave detriment of a common strategy; but the responsibility was not really Bismarck's. There were sound political reasons why he was able to forego careful technical preparations for an eastern campaign. At the time extended defensive operations still offered good prospects of success, for Bismarck counted on his ability to banish the specter of a life-and-death struggle even at the last moment by diplomatic means. It was for that very reason that he was so anxious to avoid an offensive stance on the part of his ally.

Bismarck's successors abandoned this policy line. They were far more willing to envisage simultaneous war with the two great Continental powers as preordained, and they ceased to interfere with the designs of their generals. Meanwhile, however, the German General Staff, acting on its own initiative and from purely military considerations, had discarded Moltke's deployment plan and staked everything on a great decisive battle in the west. So firmly fixed was this plan that the younger Moltke was greatly embarrassed when Conrad von Hötzendorf pressed him to set a definite date for the intervention of the German main force in the east.

Thus, in the end, the military experts had their way. Full freedom of action was theirs; but by that time the "necessities of war" before which diplomacy had capitulated had escaped from the control of the generals.[71]

"He thought through Bismarck's foreign policy on his own, usually agreeing with him, but in a few memorable instances clashing with him"—these are the words in which "one aspect of Moltke's strategic genius" has been characterized.[72] Our review of Moltke's military and political memoranda has shown that this actually applies in only a limited sense. It is true that Moltke developed his own views of history and politics in methodical form, and that his approach sometimes coincided with Bismarck's. He was no more a headlong swashbuckler than was Bismarck and thoroughly believed in looking before leaping. After 1871 Moltke, as the responsible strategist, was even more disillusioned than Bismarck by the "coalition nightmare."

Yet it is scarcely true that Moltke "thought through" foreign policy with Bismarck. The foundations of Bismarckian policy were very different, as will be shown in greater detail further on. It was above all far more flexible and diverse, less rigidly tied to militaristic premises, and thus richer in scope. Particularly characteristic of Moltke's cast of mind is one of his first lengthy memorials, *Prussia's Military and Political Situation,* dating from the spring of 1860, in which he endeavored to set forth the reasons why war with France was ultimately inevitable.

By its recent great successes, he reasoned, France had become "the head of the Romance world, resistlessly [*sic*] chaining to its policies the dispersed German states as well. It had vanquished Russia in the Crimean War and humiliated Austria in the Italian campaign. Hence "a standstill on the road to the *idées Napoléonnes* was no longer in prospect, a European coalition that might halt these advances" no longer possible. "Until now France has fought for others, now it will fight and acquire for itself. The theories of plebiscite, of nationality, of natural frontiers are expedients suitable for any purpose, and the French army and navy are the means for their realization. It is England's and Prussia's turn [*sic*], threatened by Cherbourg and Châlons."

But since the conquest of England offered little practical political advantage, "a real expansion of territory is feasible only along the Rhine. There Prussia stands, and probably it stands alone." Indeed, even now far greater dangers loomed in the background, for a more distant future: "A collaboration between the Slavic East and the Romance West against the center of Europe," which would then, to be sure, unite all the Germanic elements in resistance.[73]

Soon after 1871 these forebodings took on more serious form. The specter of a two-front war arose, and Russia's propinquity now appeared as menacing as that of France. In the long run conflict in the east became as inevitable as it had been earlier in the west. All the skills of diplomatic alliance could not alter this inexorable course. Hence the aged field marshal ended his official career with plans for a preventive war against Russia.

Such, then, was the way in which the political world was reflected in the eyes of soldiers. Political extrapolation moved into wide though often rather vague horizons. The complex interplay of forces and interests was oversimplified. The sole crucial point was the power hunger of states and peoples, suppressing nearly all personal elements, in almost Hegelian fashion. All that was envisaged was opposing national goals, conflicts of interests, while common factors were completely ignored. Will clashed with vital will and there could be no common ground.

Everything was brought down to the single denominator of possible war motives—an approach natural to military thinking, but in its one-sidedness dangerous to the political layman and dilettante historian who is likely to be taken in by its straightforwardness and seemingly objective *Realpolitik.* Its persuasiveness comes into force particularly with the educated classes who are fond of debating history and politics—especially foreign affairs and national interest—without ever coming into close contact with the day-to-day business of politics and diplomacy. It is a pastime engaged in from general cultural motives rather than from any sense of personal responsibility, an interest particularly fond of fastening on the climactic junctures of history, on war and all it entails.

In his capacity as chief of the General Staff Moltke had no particular occasion to concern himself with questions of history and politics other than those that created tensions among the great powers and might thereby lead to war. His jurisdiction did not extend to the evaluation of possible peaceful solutions. The limited historical perspective in his military writings thus derived from the contingencies of his work and its goals, and as such it is quite understandable. To create the kind of fighting morale that must inspire an army requires an appropriate view of history.

Those who credit Moltke with thinking through Bismarck's foreign policies on his own tend to overlook his narrow professionalism. They also ignore a fundamental distinction: the man who was here endeavoring to judge events of history and of the moment was not a diplomat with an intimate knowledge of the business of politics and its personalities. He was an outsider whose credentials for such a task were sketchy.

The files are not very informative on the subject of Moltke's communications with the German foreign office. Unlike Waldersee, there was no air of political hustle and bustle about Moltke's personality, and his character suggests that even in private life he was not very outgoing. The General Staff archives show that only a few of his numerous deployment plans, operational studies, and other designs were conceived in response to specific suggestions or requests by the war ministry of the foreign office.

Most of them seem to bear a completely academic character, so to speak—provisions against any conceivable contingency in foreign entanglements. There are many examples of the most careful attention given to highly unlikely and even thoroughly preposterous eventualities.[74] Moltke's mind was tireless. Plans and calculations were the very stuff of life to him, an indispensable form of exercise that had become his way of self-identification.

Only in times of outright crisis, such as especially 1865-1866,[75] can we spot intensive written and oral exchanges between Moltke, Roon, and Bismarck, and perhaps with the king and the military cabinet as well. On these occasions the statesmen usually made the welcome discovery that the chief of the General Staff was able to produce finished mobilization plans even against war contingencies that were still far on the horizon.

In but one point can we discern a consistently common element in the politico-historical views of Moltke and Bismarck. They shared the conviction that foreign policy always had precedence. Yet in the soldier this view was much more militaristic than in the diplomat. Bismarck could never have said, as did Clausewitz, that defense against the external enemy was the essence of the state, all else being no more than "frills"; but Moltke, disciple of Clausewitz, had no compunction in subscribing to this view.[76] To him the foreign policies of the great powers necessarily tended toward ever new conflicts on the battlefield, and the possibility of a peaceful balance did not even arise. This was in accord with the iron law of power once formulated by Ranke in these words: "Great powers move forward under their own impulse until they encounter resistance . . . [for] power, once established, must forever grow, since it cannot otherwise fathom whatever hostility it may encounter."

Part 4

Bismarck's Position — War as an Adjunct of Responsible Statesmanship

THE LAWS of power are inexorable, but they must be read aright. Ranke, as have seen, was overawed by the unending rivalry of the great powers which he saw as a contest among "tangible spiritual entities" *(realgeistige Wesenheiten)* and "units of moral energy." He described this contest as a creative life-begetting process, the "ideal core of mankind's history." Indeed, he rose to the brash formulation that the essence of a state was its basic hostility to other states. Yet even Ranke carefully avoided viewing history purely in terms of armed action.

Ranke always remained keenly aware that the great nations of Europe, beyond their shifting conflicts of interest, formed a higher community, a "Romanic-Germanic" family of peoples with common political and spiritual traditions, the origins of which he set forth in the famous introduction to his youthful work.

Here we touch on a second mainstream of political tradition, running counter to the ideological trends we have until now detailed, a current that is material to an understanding of the historical problem we have set ourselves. Side by side with the approach of neo-German nationalism with its emphasis on individualization, leading more and more to a militant political stance, there also lived on in nineteenth-century Germany the older approach of political universalism, still fully aware of the age-old common fabric of the Christian West. This tradition, persisting especially in the sphere of diplomacy, reaches across all the vicissitudes of time and personality from Metternich to Bismarck.

An essential part of this ideology is the notion of a European society of nations that blends the states of the Christian West into a moral union *(societas nexusque moralis)*. Voltaire had represented this European union, the late and secularized form of the medieval *res publica christiana*,[1] as a kind of republic. It imposed on its members a certain commitment to mutual consideration, above all the maintenance of the "balance of Europe."

The theory of such a balance formed a favorite theme of eighteenth-century historians and jurists who kept enlarging it into a body of international law that was not merely anti-imperialist but downright pacifist in character. Peace in Europe, they taught, could be secured only by a balance between special and general interest, contingent on no state being able to achieve such preponderance that it could vanquish one of its neighbors without instantly calling forth a superior alliance to which it would have to yield.

It is true that these hopes of the Enlighteners—as voiced, for example, by Count Ewald Friedrich von Hertzberg, minister under Frederic the Great, after the death of his lord and master—had soon proved illusory; but this did not disprove the theory of the balance, which took on renewed life during the Wars of the Revolution, when publicists like Friedrich von Gentz used it as a stick to beat French hegemony. Under the doctrine of the "natural law of nations," to prevent or redress upsets in the balance of Europe was the duty of the threatened powers, which must regularly combine to that end.

This was, in particular, the mission of the great peace congresses—at the conclusion of great upheavals they must redistribute power in such a way that as many participants as possible came into their own, none increasing excessively at the expense of others, nor any one being enfeebled in the same way. For Europe was to be maintained as a community of nations, large and small, living freely and peaceably side by side in a state of balance that would not countenance the overweening weight of any one power.

At the conclusion of his famous programmatic essay on the *Great Powers* Ranke, however, pointed out that the notion of a true community meant not only the duty to seek a common higher ground but the right of the member state to its separate, peculiar, and autonomous existence. To preserve the diversity of the European nations against the overwhelming encroachments of a superpower was indeed the ultimate goal of the "natural law of nations" of the Enlightenment; and in that respect Ranke's dynamic and individualizing approach to history represents the direct continuation and elaboration of the older mechanist doctrines of the balance of Europe with its "system of states."[2]

In the light of historical realities both these concepts appear pale, abstract and equivocal, and therefore dubious. Yet they are capable of expressing a genuine community awareness, the political significance of which can scarcely be overestimated, at least to the degree that such an awareness could prevail in the form of a true unity of interests. It was, after all, the only limit set to political chaos in the intercourse among European states.

For what is the ultimate meaning of the idea of a "European order," a *societas moralis?* It means to live and let live, to respect one another, even as an enemy, to set uttermost limits to might and main—at the point where the inviolable diversity of European life would otherwise be swamped in political and intellectual uniformity. Above all it means an awareness that there are peaceful as well as violent methods for settling conflicts of interest; it implies a basic preference for the diplomatic approach over the immediate use of force. It means, lastly, that every power struggle must have as its goal and end a durable new order of law in Europe; and that such an order can endure only if it be based on a real balance of opposing interests rather than on terms imposed on the vanquished by force.

From such a point of view the work of the Congress of Vienna, standing at the start of the most peaceful century recent European history has known, seems to have been particularly fruitful. In any event, one excellent measure of the European idea is to compare with the Versailles treaty of 1919 the generous treatment accorded France in 1815 after twenty-three years of war. Metternich, principally responsible for the treaties of 1814-1815, was, like his French counterpart Talleyrand, wholly a man of the eighteenth century and its intellectual heritage. Hence the dogmatic rigidity of his system of restorations, which left too little room for living political movements. Yet the principle of the balance of power and of European order for which he fought was still very much alive and viable, even in the age of the incipient nationalist movement. It may even be asserted that in no earlier century did the theory of the balance of power play such an important role in the practice of European diplomacy as in the century between 1815 and 1914.

In the first place, the European order brought into being at Vienna was firmly based on a single principle of political homogeneity—dynastic legitimacy and the preservation of the monarchial system. To maintain peace and order, a virtual Areopagus of the five main powers was created, a pentarchy that was to police all of Europe, so to speak, under the name of the "Concert of Europe." This, of course, ill accorded with the idea of a community of free peoples on which the diversity and creative mobility of European life rested.

But could not the basic notion of balance be reconciled with the nationality principle—indeed could it not in the process even be materially deepened and enriched? It was precisely in this way that a Europe of independent states could become the sought-after community of free peoples, each entitled to assert the right to develop in freedom all the creative cultural faculties that lay dormant in it. This would not necessarily exclude some form of political leadership by a stronger power—but it did rule out any form of political tyranny. The rigid concept of "balance" would be turned into a free marketplace for forces that were no longer trammeled by a power monopoly. The self-seeking nationalism to be expected would be limited by mutual respect for the other nation's right to exist.

The dangerous proposition of Hegel's philosophy of law that war, the living expression of the world spirit, always leads to a just issue is thus circumscribed.[3]

For in truth a preponderance of brute force can never be accepted as a criterion of a nation's historical worth. War carries moral meaning only in the degree that it represents a struggle of moral quality, among "units of moral energy." Elaborated in such fashion into a dynamic rather than a rigidly mechanical principle, allowing for the free competition of national forces that must never countenance contempt and brutality toward a rival, that shuns blind xenophobia—in this guise we find the principle of the balance of Europe to be a steady keynote in nineteenth-century German historiography, literature, and diplomacy.

This elaboration of the old theory of balance, of the notion of a European order, can be read into what Friedrich Meinecke viewed as the "universalist after-effects" of the Age of Enlightenment within the ideological framework of the awakening German nationalist movement.[4] Adam Müller, for another, was willing to countenance the theory of balance if it were meant to stand for "even growth and mutual enhancement among the states." For him national independence, the free individuality of the several European states and cultures, was as yet far from the supreme goal. Rather were these to form a higher community, a legal and cultural grouping based on the Christian faith. Insofar as this was a true community founded in law, it would not be abandoned even in time of war, since it was "of the essence of a true war that the belligerent states should have something in common . . . [namely] the notion of international law, as expressed in the great and extraordinary peace treaties of the sixteenth and seventeenth centuries."[5]

Men like Freiherr vom Stein and Barthold Georg Niebuhr, protagonists of a powerful and unified German state, always considered a European community of states to be a mandatory reality. Like Metternich, Stein based his constitutional and libertarian plans on the premise that Europe had an interest in maintaining a balance of forces.[6] It is true that in the later phases of the nationalist movement the European idea receded more and more within the political sphere of educated Germans, in curious contrast to the universality of their cultural interests, but it never vanished altogether. We find remarkable evidence of this scattered among the writings of even the most impassioned nationalist historians.[7]

A determining influence in shaping Bismarck's political views was the fact that his intellectual development took place entirely outside the great nationalist movement into which the German bourgeoisie was swept. Bismarck persisted in viewing Germany as the logical theater for Prussian power politics and so remained untouched by both the excesses of neo-German nationalism and its narrow-minded prejudices. The beginnings of his political career as a Prussian diplomat fell into the decade of the Crimean war, as an era of the purest cabinet diplomacy at the great courts of Europe, when the catchword of the balance of Europe played a central role in diplomatic exchanges and even more so in international treaties. Prussian policy under Otto von Manteuffel was entirely dominated by the endeavor to avoid issue on the field of battle by shrewd mediation, diplomatic pressure and expedient.

In his way Bismarck took a vigorous hand in securing peace and neutrality to Prussia by such means. Even then his opponents noted with consternation the fertility and boldness of his political vision, his inexhaustible store of ideas and alternatives, which perplexed his friends as well. It never occurred to him to see in France Germany's irredentist archenemy, a perpetual threat looming over Europe and fomenting revolution. Nor did he view Napoleon III as the most dangerous power politician of the age, any dealings with whom would necessarily be disastrous.

Bismarck was averse on principle to regarding any constellation of powers (like that in 1813-1814) as sacrosanct and mustered the courage to advocate a *rapprochement* with France as the most appropriate policy for Prussia as early as the era of reaction. He never succumbed in the least to an overestimate of French power, in contrast to public opinion in Europe, and to the views of nearly all the diplomats at the major courts and of professional soldiers like Moltke and Roon who were awed by the military achievements of Napoleon III's troopers in the Crimea and in Italy.

Unmatched by anyone in insight and objectivity, Bismarck early perceived the inner weakness of the Second French Empire, the inner insecurity and theatrical pose of the adventurer Louis Bonaparte.[8] He trusted his own ability to outwit the great gambler and intriguer on the diplomatic stage; but he preferred to resist Bonaparte's efforts at intimidation at the helm of a Prussia solidly founded on military power, and he was willing, if necessary, to summon up the full weight of nationalist passion against France.

Bismarck's writings display historical perspective and political insight as well, with individual issues viewed in broader contexts; but his arguments never stop at generalities or abstract dogmatism. He always speaks on the basis of concrete experience as a seasoned diplomat, of vivid appreciation of political realities, from an amazing knowledge of people and things and of the various contending parties, their foibles and weaknesses. His instinct for detecting the political repercussions of his every step was all but infallible, and his resourcefulness in devising new approaches to his goal inexhaustible.

To cite but one example, the mutations in Prussian foreign policy which he considered and tested during the Schleswig-Holstein affair and the years between the Schönbrunn conferences of 1864 and the outbreak of war in 1866 are almost infinite in their diversity. The diplomatic papers of that period are available to us today with virtually no single item missing; and the astonishment, not to say confusion, of historians is likely to grow in the measure that they immerse themselves in this abundance of documentation, which has given rise to the most diverse interpretations.[9]

Bismarck never moved an inch without sounding out the terrain on all sides with the greatest care, without considering every possible source of diplomatic intelligence, every expedient and even detour that might take him to his goal. He once explained his political approach to the historian Heinrich Friedjung, with special reference to the events that preceded the War of 1866:

> In politics you cannot fix on a long-range plan and then blindly proceed in accord with it. All you can do is to draw the broad outlines of the direction you seek to follow. This you must keep unswervingly in view, however, even though you may not know the precise route that will get you there. A statesman is like a wanderer in the woods who knows where he wants to go but does not know the precise point at which he will emerge from the forest. So too the statesman—unless he wants to lose his way—must follow the trails that are passable. It is true that war with Austria was hard to avoid, but anyone with the least sense of responsibility for the lives of millions will shrink from starting a war until every other resource has been exhausted. All or nothing has always been a peculiarly German vice, and we are quite pigheaded in sticking to one method, and one only. Personally, I always considered myself lucky to bring German unity nearer a step at a time, whatever the way. I should have embraced ardently any solution that would have led to the enlargement of Prussia and the unity of Germany without recourse to war. There were many roads that led to my goal, and I had to follow them one after another, *the most dangerous road last.* Action along a single line was never my forte.[10]

"The most dangerous road last"—the phrase strikingly characterizes the style of Bismarckian diplomacy, particularly the essence of his policy of alliances. Like Moltke, Bismarck knew that circumstances could force his hand, that war was sometimes inevitable. At the very outset of his ministry he said with the utmost *sang froid* that the German question could probably not be solved except by "blood and iron" and that powerful armaments were therefore indispensable to Prussia. To this day his liberal critics at home and abroad are fond of citing this term as though it meant that Bismarck favored a policy of brute force.

This is a profound misinterpretation. Bismarck was anything but an adventurer and opportunist. He took his responsibility for deciding on war with the utmost seriousness and never dreamed of fobbing it off on the "inexorable march of history." He was altogether lacking in the humanist faith that the universe is rational and comprehensible. ("I try to understand God's will," he was prone to say, "but I don't always understand it."[11]) He did not feel himself entitled to "sneak a look into destiny's cards" nor to "put my own judgment above historical developments by anticipating them."[12]

Politics is a sphere of incessant uncertainty and unpredictable chances. The statesman's plight is that he must grope about in a fog of doubt as to what the future may offer, swaying on flimsy footholds that may give way at any moment, yet compelled to go forward, his every act determining the future for a long time to come. Bismarck often voiced this predicament in striking imagery. It is perhaps the theme on which he dwells most often in his letters, speeches, and writings, for it touched the deepest layers of his character. He said more than once that only his Protestant faith in God enabled him to bear the burden of his responsibilities.[13]

It was a responsibility that grew most crushing when it came to war. "It is easy for a statesman," he said in his well-known Olmütz speech in December, 1850, ". . . to ride the popular wave and sound the trump of war by his cozy hearth, or to intone thunderous speeches from a platform such as this, leaving it to the musketeer bleeding in the snow to settle whether his policies win glory or end in failure. Nothing simpler—but woe unto the statesman who at such a time fails to cast about for a cause of war that will stand up once the war is over."[14] These words were uttered in deliberate opposition to the war fever of the parliament. But beyond question they were spoken from the heart.

He put his convictions into even plainer words in 1867, on the occasion of the Luxembourg crisis:

> Only a country's most vital interests justify its embarking on war—only its honor, not to be confused with what is called prestige. No statesman has the right to start a war merely because, in his subjective judgment, he believes it to be inevitable at the moment. Verily, history would record fewer wars if only foreign ministers had always followed their sovereigns or commanders-in-chief into the field. On the battlefield and, far worse, in the field hospitals I have seen the flower of our youth cut down by wounds and disease. Looking out of this window I can see many a cripple hobbling along the Wilhelmstrasse, looking up and thinking to himself, if it were not for that man up there who made this wicked war I would sit at home unharmed with Mom. Such memories and such sights would leave me not an hour of peace, had I to reproach myself with having started the war frivolously, or from personal ambition, or from vainglory on behalf of the nation. Aye, I made the war of 1866, fulfilling my harsh duty with a heavy heart, because without it the nation would have bogged down politically, soon to fall prey to avaricious neighbors; and if we stood in the same place where then we stood, I should resolutely make war again. Never, you may be sure, shall I counsel His Majesty to wage war unless the innermost interests of the fatherland require it.[15]

Bismarck often pledged himself never to challenge another country to war because it was weaker or might start a war itself later on. His responsibility "before the king, the fatherland, and God" weighed too heavily for that.[16] Perhaps the old Chancellor's most impressive words on the subject of preventive war were spoken in the most famous of his great Reichstag speeches, on February 6, 1888, after the General Staff under Waldersee and Moltke had pressed for a timely strike against Russia:

> If we in Germany wish to wage war with the full weight of our national power, it must be a war with which the whole nation is in agreement—all who fight in it, all who sacrifice for it. It will have to be a people's war.... Should we ultimately attack, [i.e., launch a preventative war], the full weight of the imponderables—which weigh far heavier in the balance than material factors—will be on the side of the enemies we have attacked.... It is not fear that makes us peaceable but rather awareness of our strength, awareness that even should we ourselves be attacked at a less favorable moment, we shall be strong enough to defend ourselves, meanwhile leaving it to divine providence whether it may not sweep aside the need for war.... We Germans fear God and nought else in the world; and it is the fear of God, and nought else, that causes us to love and cultivate peace.[17]

Bismarck research in the time before the First World War was intent on celebrating the hard and shrewd political realism of its hero and on depicting the Machiavellian cunning of his diplomacy in the most dramatic terms. Unwittingly this only served as grist for the mills of Bismarck's liberal-democratic accusers. The experiences of two consecutive world wars have deepened our understanding of the exaggerated saber-rattling of the time around 1900; and now that the original evidence of Bismarck's actions is spread out before us in such overwhelming abundance, we are likely to regard his statesmanship in a rather different light. Let us beware, however, of lapsing into the opposite error of denying the demoniac traits in the character of the great power politician, of watering down and trivializing the harsh cunning of his savage and grandiose militancy.

Bismarck was certainly no protagonist of peace in the sense of Anglo-Saxon pacifism, no partisan of peaceful agreement at any price like his great adversary Gladstone. His game was Continental power politics in the style of, say, Richelieu. Gladstone had little sympathy with Bismarck, who had no real understanding for the special conditions of insular liberal politics that formed the background for Gladstone's actions. To Bismarck the liberal Christian ethic of the Englishman seemed hypocritical, which was not really true. Yet on their side the opponents of Bismarck mistook—and indeed mistake to this day—the evidence that he too was inspired by Christian morality.

The main difference is that Bismarck was unwilling to allow himself to be pinned down to general principles of political action. His political morality was guided purely by the concrete situation with which he was dealing. It is quite true that Bismarck's political orientation was far more militant than was acceptable to English liberal thinking. Yet compared with the later militarism of the world war period it cannot really be said to have been truly militant. Preparedness and peaceableness are not mutually exclusive. In the true states-man—especially on the Continent—they could be as inseparably linked as per-sonal ambition and power drive with selfless service to the state.

For the rest, Bismarck's thinking unfolded before a historical background from which there was as yet no looking back on the phenomenon of total war in the style of the twentieth century. Bismarck did not shun war as such, as a means of power politics. On the contrary, as was common throughout the nine-teenth century, he looked on war as morally justifiable when vital reasons of state demanded it, when there was no other way of breaking out of a situation that was felt to be untenable. In other words, the limits of what Bismarck con-sidered permissable did not end with purely defensive warfare but extended to war waged for the purpose of enhancing state power.

Yet Bismarck did not take this to mean carte blanche for a policy of unrestrained conquest.[18] He was willing to go to war only in the "innermost interests" of his country. Unfortunately this is a very elastic concept. As was said in our introduction, there is no rational dividing line between power struggle and peaceful order. All depends on how scrupulous the statesman in point interprets it, on his basing his decisions on conscience and a true sense of responsibility. Few people today would deny that Bismarck's character was indeed pervaded with such a sense of responsibility. His whole policy of alliance has been rightly described as a skillful balancing act. It was certainly not designed to support a policy of unlimited war. On the contrary, Bismarck wanted to include the other powers in a system of peaceful settlements in order to lay the basis for a sound order secured in international law.[19] Until the time of the founding of the Reich in 1871 this Bismarckian policy was actively constructive in character. In the two final decades of his career its main goal was to preserve the status quo.

But for the three wars of unification the in-gathering of the German states under Prussian hegemony would have been impossible and Germany could not have risen from the dust of political impotence. No state that shared in the great nationalist movement of the nineteenth century achieved national unity with-out bloody struggle. Not even Switzerland and America were spared such ordeals. Bismarck, a true heir of Frederic the Great, deliberately calculated this risk. Prussia was to keep the peace, not from fear, but from a position of sufficient power to command it.

Yet Bismarck's war policy was very different from Frederic's adventurism in the Silesian conquest. In resolute opposition to united public opinion through-out Germany, he refused to embark on the Danish war as a campaign of conquest that would have invoked the "national interest" and provoked the rest of Europe. He launched it formally as an act of restoring international law, violated by Denmark. The annexation of Schleswig-Holstein was by no means his sole war aim, pursued blindly, but the result of a diplomatic campaign prepared with the greatest care and drawn out over many years, into which he even managed with consummate skill to introduce an international congress of the powers. Bismarck operated flexibly with a whole hierarchy of war aims and succeeded in saddling the Danish enemy with formal responsibility for the failure to reach a peaceful settlement.

Bismarck recognized at a very early stage that Prussia could not ascend to the leading position in Germany without a passage at arms with Austria. Yet he did not plan—as he was once generally charged with doing—the military alliance with Austria of 1864 as a trap for the dual monarchy from the outset, as a device for maneuvering Austria into an untenable situation. Source material that has recently become available shows conclusively that Bismarck made serious efforts over many years to crowd Austria from its position of leadership in Germany through peaceful diplomacy, by way of a dualist compromise. When these efforts failed, he expressly disdained—in Gastein in 1865—to exploit the quarrel over the Schleswig-Holstein prize as a pretext for war. Instead, to everyone's surprise, he openly proclaimed that the war was to be for the mastery of Germany. National interest alone was to justify this fratricidal war before the nation, not secondary issues in the style of old-fashioned cabinet politics. Once this second war was successfully concluded, Bismarck took the greatest care not to appear in the eyes of Europe as a heedless warmonger.

Undoubtedly concern for the international stature of his country played a major part in Bismarck's endeavors to postpone armed conflict with France, and indeed to avoid it altogether if possible.[20] In the long run, of course, that conflict became unavoidable, but the war of 1870-1871 was not a deliberately planned conflagration, the result of a skillfully staged act of provocation, as even some German historians have contended. Bismarck's basic orientation was truly defensive. It was in the vital national interest to put an end to Napoleon III's diplomatic intrigues, aimed at encircling Germany and paralyzing the progress toward unification. From the spring of 1870 on Bismarck tried to foil this design by means of an ambitious counterintrigue in which he exploited (and covertly supported) the Hohenzollern claims to the Spanish succession.

Were this diplomatic surprise attack to succeed, its diplomatic effects might embarrass the already tottering Bonapartist regime to the point of complete collapse. If it failed—as it did by an unhappy mischance—Napoleon could be expected to counterattack in the diplomatic sphere; and Bismarck trusted his ability to trump the great plunger's ace, at worst achieving a stalemate and at best forcing France to agree to a peaceful settlement on the German question.

It is true that the clash of two such diplomatic offensives was bound to create a serious danger of war, a war the German side had no reason to shun, provided the true relation between the two neighboring powers could be kept fully visible behind the diplomatic smokescreen. Ostensibly Prussian policy was peaceable, directed solely toward domestic power goals. Prussia was only unwillingly defending itself against French jealousy which begrudged its rise toward leadership in Germany, hence sought to humiliate it diplomatically. To clarify before all the world the true nature of this diplomatic contest—that was the true purpose of the notorious Ems telegram, carefully edited and highlighted from which Bismarck's "war guilt" was later constructed with such effort.[21]

All this is the more important within our context since it tends to show that Bismarck was ever reluctant to accept war as inevitable, to regard it as foreordained. This was true even when overriding national interests were at stake in which later historians, like Moltke the soldier at the time, thought they could plainly discern the workings of destiny. Even in such cases Bismarck thought it "folly if not a crime" to pursue one's goals on the battlefield so long as there was even the glimmer of hope for attaining them by peaceful means.[22]

While Moltke from 1859 onward kept pressing for war against France on a suitable occasion as the surest means of German unification, Bismarck rejected such a policy as irresponsible dilettantism, as "shaking down unripe fruit."[23] And what is true of his diplomatic preparations also applies to the execution of his wars. He resisted acknowledging that his hand could be forced, that circumstances could limit his freedom of action. He rejected the doctrine of "military necessity" to which Moltke, as we have seen, clung so stubbornly. Hence we face the anomaly that Bismarck, the born fighter, appears far more conciliatory than Moltke, the born humanist. Opposed to initiating any preventive war, Bismarck was always intent on restoring peace as swiftly as possible, once war had broken out, even at the cost of not exploiting military success to its fullest extent.[24]

Ultimately this attitude turned Bismarck more and more into the guardian of European peace, the responsible mediator and "honest broker." The second phase of his foreign policy after the founding of the Reich revolved entirely on preserving the status quo, exactly as in the case of Frederic the Great. On that account he has often been compared with Metternich, and beyond doubt he did deliberately follow in the footsteps of that statesman, taking his lead from the foreign policies of the Age of Restoration.[25]

But while Metternich's "pentarchy," his Holy Alliance, rigidly clung to the division of power reached in 1815 and for that reason soon began to crumble, Bismarck's policy of alliances displays an astonishing flexibility. Adapting itself to the ever-changing constellations of grand policy down to 1890 with ever new and often surprising modifications, it never wasted time on pursuing European order at a level above the national interests of the several states, let alone in contravention to them. On the contrary, the secret of Bismarck's success lay precisely in his skill in harmonizing conflicting interests by peaceful settlement, if at all possible, every pressure from one side being canceled out or at least balanced by counterpressure from another side.

Bismarck's convoluted interplay of dual and triple alliances, and later on of reinsurance treaties and Mediterranean and Balkan ententes, probably constitutes the most skillful system of groupings ever devised to maintain the balance of Europe. It could have succeeded only in the hands of a past master of European diplomacy who completely apprehended the "true interests" of the major courts, at home and abroad, and was always able to arrive at an accurate estimate of special interest in their relation to general European interests.

Bismarck refused to acknowledge that there were insoluble conflicts between national and European policy. He conceived of the European community of states as a vital cohabitation of great peer powers, always pervaded by tensions but also always impelled toward the achievement of a *modus vivendi.* Each country had the full right to live; none could be dispensed with. Bismarck asserted this repeatedly, not only in respect of Austria-Hungary, but also of Russia and even France. The survival of France as a great power, he said in St. Petersburg in 1887, "was as necessary to Germany as the survival of any other great power," if only to maintain a balance against Britain and a conceivable Anglo-Russian combination.[26]

A statesman willing to acknowledge so freely the right to existence of foreign nations[27] could scarcely be expected to look on war except in the light of power rivalry and nothing more. Bismarck allowed neither hate nor military ambition nor thirst for victory to keep him from concluding peace at such a time and on such terms as sober political judgment dictated. His was a wisdom of statesmanship inspired in equal parts by national and European interests, a rare blend of firm self-assertion and propitiation, of preparedness and a propensity for peace and order. To Moltke's military thinking, peace was inconceivable except by the security of powerful armaments, but Bismarck was always bent on basing durable peace on trust as well as fear.[28]

His utterances on the binding force of international treaties have been subject to colossal misinterpretation. "No great nation," he once said, "forced to choose between survival and foreign commitments, will ever be persuaded to sacrifice its life on the altar of treaty observance." But is this anything more than the realistic acceptance of the fact that there can be no unlimited reliance on the contractual pledges of others, a stricture of which Bismarck was ever mindful?

Part and parcel of the living dynamics of Bismarck's system of alliances was the necessity for adapting it to the ever-shifting constellations of power, but this was very far from a rejection of treaty obligations. It is true that Bismarck broke up the German League, but he replaced it at once with a vastly improved association. It is also true that in the process, in violation of the League constitution, he did not shrink from an alliance with a nonmember power against the member power Austria.

Yet as a rule the conscientious observance of international obligations was one of the major pillars of Bismarck's policy of alliances. It was a policy staked out with consummate mastery over so wide an area that enough room always remained for political action.[29] It is notable that after 1871 such action was no longer aimed at expanding the German frontiers in Europe. Indeed Bismarck time and again, expressly invoking the example of Metternich, declared that Germany was now "satiated"; and in the final phase of his policy he began once more to take into account the "solidarity of monarchial-conservative interests" which the youthful Bismarck had once derided as quixotic when his romantic conservative party friends had tried to turn it into a formal system of Prussian foreign policy.

Even now, however, Bismarck's true goal was not to elevate domestic partisan policy to the level of a guideline for European alliances. He simply wanted to maintain sober political reason in the face of the passions and ambitions of day-to-day politics abroad. In the case of Russia, particularly, much depended on helping the czarist government to keep the nationalist movement with its pan-Slavic dreams within reasonable bounds; and by virtue of common monarchial interest as well as sheer political reason that government was more inclined to seek support from the Prussian royal court than from republican Paris.

Austria-Hungary, Germany's main ally, was a multiracial state whose entire survival depended on maintaining the monarchial tradition, the authority of the Hapsburg-Lorraine dynasty, as the strongest bond of unity against the centrifugal tendencies of Slavic and Hungarian nationalism. Here nationalist ambitions posed the constant threat of precipitating a crisis in foreign affairs, with the clash Bismarck so greatly feared. The third ally, Italy, could be kept in line as a member of the alliance only so long as the monarchial governments were able to implement the shrewd policy of common interest that had driven Italy into the camp of the Central Powers, as a hedge against the irredentist movement's thirst for conquest and hatred of Germany.

Could such a policy of sober political reason be maintained in the long run in the face of the passions, ambitions, and power drives of increasingly politicized nations? Here lies the crucial question in respect of Bismarck's foreign policy. When we take a closer look at the peace treaties he negotiated, we come to see that Bismarck, unlike Frederic the Great and the cabinets of the eighteenth century, no longer had complete freedom of action in the sphere of *raison d'état,* could no longer ignore public opinion engendered by press and political parties and other opinion-making agencies not subject to control.

Bismarck tried very hard to bring about peace with Denmark swiftly and generously, without haggling over minor border regions and indemnities, at the cost of serious friction with King William who was much inclined to regard occupied Jutland as "conquered territory," to be returned only against special concessions by the Danes, over and above the handing over of the two duchies.[30] Once peace was made, Bismarck unhesitatingly accepted the obligation to conciliate the vanquished foe as soon as possible. This is shown quite impressively in his telegraphed directive to the press section of the Foreign Office of August 7, 1864:

> Hostile and resentful tone toward Denmark unworthy after victory. War waged for defense and regularization rather than from hatred. No harshness against Denmark intended, no terms of arrogant victor that would prevent future friendly relations by violating justified national sentiments. Separation of duchies completely achieved. This sufficient. If Denmark by definitive peace shows serious intent to put past behind, natural friendly relations restorable, which in interest both countries. Denmark faced with need to overcome sense of defeat. No occasion by victor to harbor or provoke bitterness.[31]

These words speak plainly enough, but there was still the question of drawing the border of northern Schleswig across marginal areas where the population was predominantly or entirely Danish. We have already seen that Moltke favored their return to Denmark. His sense of nationalism was so free of selfish chauvinism that he wished to see the nationalist principle strictly adhered to even at Germany's expense. His position was wholly at odds with neo-German nationalism—the great mass of Germans regarded Schleswig as an indivisible historical entity; and Article 5 of the Peace of Prague, which provided for a plebiscite in North Schleswig on the question of national allegiance, was taken as a highly unwelcome concession to French wishes. Bismarck was fond of relating that at headquarters in Nikolsburg Moltke alone had expressed sympathy for this concession.[32] But what were his own views on this matter?

The heart of his convictions is not immediately apparent from his many contradictory utterances—it can only be surmised. Outside Germany he always showed himself in a very conciliatory light, especially before 1870 when the conflict with France was still no more than a threat. Ambassador Count Vincent Benedetti was given to understand from a source close to Bismarck that the Chancellor would be personally prepared to return even Alsen and Düppel but for King William's absolute refusal.[33] Indeed, in a top-secret mediation effort in 1868 Bismarck had a suggestion conveyed to the Danes, to the effect that they should persuade the Czar of Russia to influence King William in the direction of dropping his objections to drawing the line for the plebiscite south of the Bay of Gjemmer.[34]

But Bismarck's statements for domestic consumption have an entirely different ring. Here the plebiscite in North Schleswig was made to appear simply as a French demand that could not readily be waved aside, for political reasons. Its practical execution was to be limited to the smallest possible area, and things should be arranged in such a way that if possible everything would remain with Prussia.[35]

Actually, Bismarck postponed the plebiscite again and again; and ultimately, in 1879, he had Article 5 of the Peace of Prague revoked by a treaty with Austria. On the other side this created the impression that he was never really serious about the whole plan and that his repeated diplomatic representations about the difficulties attending the plebiscite and border rectification were merely a pretext to avoid complying with an irksome requirement.

Now that we have access to the complete files, both on the Danish and the German side, we can see plainly that Bismarck spoke no more than the truth when he told the Reichstag, like the diet, that he had always held that foreign nationals who persistently and unequivocally wished to give their allegiance to a neighboring country never constituted a source of strength for the power from which they sought to separate themselves. We can see further that he was indeed sincerely eager to find a tenable solution to the question of North Schleswig, with the purpose of conciliating Denmark, winning over France, and lending strength to his European policy as one that never deliberately sought to evade its treaty obligations.[36]

The more deeply we look into the Chancellor's long-drawn-out negotiations on this issue, the plainer become the difficulties in its way. At bottom these difficulties all stemmed from a single source, national differences ingrained as deeply on the Danish side as on the German. They were differences that grew more acute with the years, rendering altogether impossible any objective settlement that would have accorded with the needs and desires of both parties.

It seemed impossible to reach agreement with Denmark along lines politically and militarily acceptable to Prussia, either on the question of the plebiscite area or on safeguarding German minority rights on Danish soil–a matter to which Bismarck had to give much weight, since a neat separation of Germans and Danes was virtually impossible. German public opinion followed every step with profound distrust and occasionally there were indignant demonstrations in the legislatures against Danish agitation and the surrender of the "border march." The German public generally, chiefly under the leadership of the National Liberals, but also the army and provincial officialdom, so vigorously resisted any "cession of German soil" that Bismarck could not dream of setting a plebiscite among the *up-ewig-Ungedeelten* (forever undivided) without manifest outward coercion—which no longer existed after 1870. In the face of the Danish attitude, Bismarck himself after 1868 no longer believed that any border settlement would have a conciliatory effect.[37]

Here, then, we have a point where Bismarck's diplomatic conduct was strongly affected by the pressure of public opinion, by neo-German nationalism. This was true of frontier issues in the west as well, Luxembourg and

Alsace-Lorraine. Bismarck personally drew Napoleon III's attention to the possibility of securing some recompense for his loss of prestige in 1866 by the acquisition of Luxembourg. There is no reason to doubt that he would have been prepared to acquiesce in a French annexation of the principality if it were carried out in a way that would not injure Prussia's prestige and if the events of 1866 would thereby have been rendered more palatable to the French—i.e., if they could have become more resigned to the appearance on German soil of a great national power that would no longer countenance foreign influence on German affairs.

Under the stimulus of nationalism, German public opinion in the spring of 1867 professed to look on Luxembourg too as "German soil," a view which Bismarck almost certainly did not share. The German right to maintain a garrison in the fortified capital had become invalid with the dissolution of the League, and in any event Bismarck set little store by the fortress. Even though he sometimes gave the appearance, he never for a moment really desired the kind of alliance offered by Napoleon and urgently recommended by Ambassador von der Goltz, which would have aimed at extending the French frontiers beyond Belgium while guaranteeing Germany's western frontier. This would have meant deliberately bringing the French menace to the Rhine by way of Belgium, to say nothing of alienating England and probably Russia too, for no good reason.

Yet Bismarck decided not to forego the effort to appease French jealousy for the time being, by means of the relatively trifling Luxembourg border rectification, thus gaining time and concentration for the work of German unification; and if his hopes were ultimately foiled and the Luxembourg crisis brought him to the brink of war, it was less the fault of King William's stubborn resistance than of frenzied German public opinion. Indeed, considerations of national prestige constrained Bismarck from the outset to adopt extremely devious ways in launching the Luxembourg plan, and Napoleon was neither willing nor able to meet him. Thus the whole project ended only in worsening rather than improving Franco-German relations.[38]

We see from all this how extraordinarily difficult it was to follow the dictates of political wisdom in an age when "national interest" had long become the leading catchword of the day and cabinet policy was being watched with jealous distrust by public opinion in the politicized nations. A cabinet politician like Bismarck who sought to exploit the powerful current of nationalism to carry along the ship of state toward the goals he envisaged was ever in danger of being swept away farther than he wished.

Only in the case of the Austrian conflict—a basically unpopular cabinet war—was Bismarck ever able to proceed and conclude in accord with his own original intentions. Even here there was a bitter struggle with the king and with the king's military and dynastic prejudices, but there was no intervention by public opinion. The upshot was a more moderate peace than anyone would have expected after the total victory of Prussian arms, a true preparatory step for an enduring peaceful order and for subsequent reconciliation with the Austrian enemy.

Things were different in the national war of 1870, which was meant to join all Germans in a national front in order to establish the "Little German" Reich. Bismarck himself therefore helped fan the flames of nationalist passions and proclaimed from the outset as one of the war aims—beyond the prevention of the French policy of intervention—the slogan that Alsace-Lorraine must become German. He thus blocked every possibility of reaching a peace until the enemy was finally and totally vanquished—which was not really what he wanted. Worse than that, in the eyes of the French and also of most of the neutral nations the peace took on a forcible character. The loss of the two provinces whose acquisition the French recorded among the proudest memories of their royal age put in the shade all of Bismarck's efforts to spare vanquished France the humiliation of a dictated peace. The question therefore remains whether the great statesman, at this crucial juncture of his career, did indeed allow himself to be diverted from the course of political reason by the onslaughts of frenzied nationalist passions.

Certainly Bismarck was aware of no such thing. In the very first week of the war the difference between his own thinking and the excessive nationalism of even educated Germans emerged with the greatest clarity. Neither in his private utterances nor in his official statements is there ever any mention of "regaining historic German soil" or "returning our kith and kin to the fatherland." He spoke exclusively of securing the frontiers against new incursions by the French, having long been convinced that this was essential if South Germany were ever to muster the courage to join in a close union with the north, based on mutual trust.

In support of this standpoint he was fond of citing a talk he had had with King William I of Württemberg during the Crimean War when he, Bismarck, had been a *Bundestag* envoy in Frankfurt, a discussion that must have made a deep impression on him.[39] Its substance was that South Germany would long have been occupied by the French from the direction of the strategic invasion base of Strasbourg by the time help could arrive from Berlin; hence that so long as Alsace remained in French hands South German policy would always in some measure have to take France into account. It was in this respect that Bismarck held the acquisition of Alsace to be virtually indispensable to any extension of the neo-German Reich beyond the line of the River Main. He was interested not so much in Alsace and the Alsatians as in control of the fortress of Strasbourg.[40]

The acquisition of Alsace for Germany had indeed been one of the demands even of the German patriots of 1814; and the fact that the Alsatians, ethnically and historically, belonged to the ancient German stock that inhabited the upper Rhine valley was quite incontestable. Alsace was full of historical memories and traditions that dated back to the most glorious times of the German-dominated Holy Roman Empire. It was at least conceivable that France might have become more readily reconciled to the cession of Alsace alone than to the loss of both provinces, particularly in the light of the fact that France was the pre-eminent champion of nationalism.

The course of the peace negotiations seemed to bear out this analysis. By the time Thiers arrived at Versailles, he had inwardly become reconciled to the severance of Alsace and the German-speaking sections of Lorraine.[41] What he was really fighting for was Metz, Belfort, and the border regions that were French in character. The loss of the great military staging area of Metz particularly he described as an intolerable act of humiliation that would stand in the way of a durable peace.

Why, then, did Bismarck insist on this cession? We have already seen, in Part 3, that certain generals at headquarters were greatly upset over the rumor that Bismarck might ultimately drop the acquisition of Metz. Was he swayed by this opposition in high military circles? Was he, further, afraid of letting down German public opinion after he himself, by means of his press statements and diplomatic round robins in the wake of the first great victory, had encouraged such exaggerated expectations?

For once his attitude displays a strange and uncharacteristic vacillation—at least in his private and confidential utterances, for after the official peace program of September 16, his official statements kept up the demand for Metz in addition to Strasbourg.[42] Above all, he had severed Lorraine from the administration of occupied France as early as August, 1870, placing it under the "Government General" at Strasbourg.

In late January, 1871, he rejected a Russian suggestion that he renounce Metz and annex neutral Luxembourg instead. He did not, he said, wish to appear in the light of a frivolous conqueror who failed to respect the neutral rights of the weak.[43] Even after the hard-fought winter campaign, he would not enlarge his original claims against France, but neither was he minded to retreat from them. Yet the question remains whether all these proclamations meant anything more than the formal assertion of German claims, with the secret reservation that some of these might be relinquished in appropriate circumstances.[44] The question is much to the point, for the new peace program he presented to King William on January 14, speaks only vaguely of a "cession of the present area of the Strasbourg Government General, with a number of modifications," without making any special reference to Lorraine and Metz.

From September on, in private conversations, Bismarck had voiced serious political reservations against the acquisition of the foreign-speaking areas of Lorraine; and on occasion he even expressed strong doubt that Metz was indeed indispensable in a military sense.[45] Early in November, when the cessation of operations seemed to make a swift peace desirable and the anti-German attitude of the people of Lorraine caused more and more concern to the German administration, Bismarck seems to have been not disinclined to negotiate with Thiers on the basis that Metz would stay French.[46]

His doubts about the acquisition of Lorraine must have grown when a final settlement of this question during the peace negotiations became a matter of immediate urgency after the Paris armistice. Many expedients were now considered, some of them recommended especially from English sources, in the interest of securing a durable peace. The idea given the greatest currency there was that Alsace-Lorraine should be neutralized under European guarantees, the fortresses of Strasbourg and Metz being dismantled.

This solution had the least appeal for Bismarck. He set no store by European and especially English guarantees which would be ineffective in the event of a crisis. The neutralization of Alsace, he felt, would confer much greater protection on France than on Germany. Germany would be virtually prevented from invading France, while the French might well land their troops on the German coast, or the coasts of their allies like Denmark and Russia, and thus launch an invasion.

Above all, the people of Alsace and Lorraine, French subjects for centuries, could not be counted on to defend their neutrality by force of arms, as might be expected of the Swiss, the Belgians, and the Dutch. There would be nothing to prevent the French from traversing the provinces, and even in peacetime this supposed buffer would be in effect a French satellite, and in any event a hotbed of anti-German intrigue. Razing the fortresses would confer no certain protection. In a crisis they could be rebuilt rapidly, and any injunction against such an eventuality even in peacetime could be enforced only by international control, which the French were bound to regard as a humiliating invasion of their sovereign rights.

The same reservations militated against an expedient which Bismarck himself seems to have conceived. After the razing of Metz a powerful new border fortification would be built in an appropriate location, most probably in German Lorraine or in the Saar region. A certain synthetic element attaches to this notion. It certainly would not have spared the French political humiliation, and one must doubt that Moltke would ever have assented to such a plan.

At the last moment the Chancellor seems to have given far more serious thought to the purchase of Luxembourg and the restoration of its fortifications, dismantled in 1867, as a substitute for Metz; but this would have meant sparing the vanquished foe at the expense of an uninvolved third party, while giving Germany a European reputation for unrestrained conquest.

Lastly, there was the idea of holding a plebiscite to determine where the people of Alsace-Lorraine wished to go, another plan advocated in English quarters; but the thought of entrusting the setting of Germany's southwest frontier to such an unpredictable device was so utterly at odds with the reasoning processes that governed Bismarck's policies that he never even mentioned it, so far as we know.[47]

There were thus arguments against every one of these possible solutions. It appears, nevertheless, that in the final days before Thiers's arrival Bismarck sought support from the grand-duke of Baden and from Crown Prince Frederic, the grand-duke's brother-in-law and sympathizer, to persuade the king to agree to forego Metz, against the voice of the military. Both the grand-duke and the Crown Prince were firmly opposed to annexation, especially of French-speaking regions. The generals, Bismarck told the grand-duke, gave too little thought to the future. "We cannot forever remain hostile to the French. . . . The question is, how can we conclude a peace that has any prospect of lasting? The incorporation of Lorraine would constitute an enormous complication."[48] We see again that Bismarck was not motivated merely by his repugnance to the acceptance of foreign-speaking elements into the Reich. The crucial factor to his mind was a durable peace. He shrank from taking a step that would poison Franco-German relations for a long time to come.

In the end Bismarck did take this step, not merely because the military insisted. True, Moltke's formal report strongly influenced him, as was discussed in Part 3, but it did not actually tip the balance. His thoughts emerge with considerable directness in a conversation at table during the crucial days of the peace negotiations: "I don't like to see so many Frenchmen in our house who don't want to be there . . . but the generals simply don't want to forego Metz, *and perhaps they are right.*"[49]

There was a good bit of the Prussian officer spirit in Bismarck. More importantly, however, he harbored deep doubts on whether Germany's French neighbors could ever be reconciled at all. He voiced these doubts quite plainly in his circular letters of September 13, and 16, to the German diplomatic missions in the neutral countries. France, he says there, forced the war on Germany, though Germany very much wished to avoid war, as the events of 1867 had shown. "In the face of this fact we cannot look to the French temper for our guarantees. We must not deceive ourselves that because of this war we need not be prepared for another attack by France at an early date; we must not expect a durable peace, regardless of any terms we may wish to put to France. What the French nation will never forgive us is their defeat as such, our victorious defense against their heinous attack. Even if we were now to depart France without any territorial cessions, without any indemnities, with no other advantage than the glory of our arms, the same hatred and vengefulness . . . would persist among the French people and they would but wait for the day when they dare hope to translate these sentiments into successful action. . . .

"Any peace we may now conclude, even without territory changing hands, will be but an armistice. We shall demand Alsace and Lorraine not to vindicate old property rights . . . but merely to protect ourselves against the next attack. . . . In German hands Strasbourg and Metz will take on purely defensive character. In more than twenty wars with France we have never been the aggressors."

The French, on the other hand, he went on, would again attack the Germans as soon as they felt strong enough, by their own resources or by foreign alliances.[50] The ambitions of that nation had always sowed disquiet in Europe. For three hundred years there had scarcely been a generation in Germany that had not seen itself compelled to unsheathe the sword against France (this was a theme Bismarck was fond of putting forward in several versions).[51] The French had always shown the same aggressive spirit, no matter what their form of government. The guarantees and alliances of 1815 had long since lost their force. Germany must now protect itself alone, by material rather than purely moral guarantees.

Plainly, the Bismarck who speaks here is not the shrewd diplomat of the 1850's and 1860's who did not share the general overestimate in Germany of the French menace, who pointedly ignored the prejudices of his romantic conservative party friends as well as the patriotic traditions of the Wars of Liberation we still see ghosting about in Moltke's head. Then he had thought himself capable of laying the specter of war with France by diplomatic means, indeed of outgambling that great plunger, Napoleon III, and of using him as a pawn in his own game.

What speaks to us here is, first of all, simply the innate militant nationalism which Bismarck himself, in his memoirs, not without a certain irony, described as the first political response of his youth, attributable to the influence of the Plamann school he had attended and the student corporation to which he had belonged. "Any thoughts on foreign affairs I may have had were along the lines of the Wars of Liberation, from the point of view of a Prussian officer. When I looked at the map, I was irked that the French owned Strasbourg, and visits to Heidelberg, Spires, and the Palatinate rendered me vengeful and bellicose."

It is only natural that such primitive sentiments should have revived under the impact of a national war. Yet the facts show that their revival did not impair his calm insight when peace was at stake, that they did not engender a vengeful spirit within him. His bearing during the peace negotiations was generous and broad-minded, and he displayed a spirit of chivalry despite the firmness dictated by the circumstances.[52] His frankness, not devoid of a sense of humor, deeply impressed and occasionally confounded the French. There is also his protracted reluctance to ask for the cession of Lorraine, his efforts to make the loss of Metz more palatable to the French by the return of Belfort and Nancy, the reduction of the war indemnity from six to five billion francs, the foregoing of the seizure of the French colonies desired by German colonialists, and above all the step that was to have ominous consequences, his refusal to insist on French disarmament and arms limitations, which even Thiers had anticipated.

Despite the aforementioned words about the irreconcilable French—words uttered in public justification of the German annexations—Bismarck beyond any doubt wished to see to it that the peace would be as durable as it was possible to make it, and thus at least acceptable to the vanquished French. But if Bismarck's conduct was free of hatred, he did entertain the deepest distrust; and he lived in an environment that was even more deeply distrustful and certainly not free of hatred. Thus Bismarck was constrained to expand the material guarantees Germany required by a step or two farther than had seemed suitable to him at an earlier time—and than was to appear suitable to him later on.[53]

Because of this, the peace with France took on a curiously ambivalent character. It was certainly not the kind of dictated peace Moltke would have wanted, for no arms limitations were imposed on the defeated nation; but neither was it a peace of reconciliation in Bismarck's 1866 style, for it did mortal injury to French pride. In 1866 Bismarck had made peace in the role of cabinet statesman. At Versailles and Frankfurt his role, while not precisely that of a nationalist, was certainly influenced by a conviction that unbridgeable national conflicts would inevitably remain.

Even before the war Bismarck had occasionally prophesied that the outbreak of a national war between Germany and France would necessarily unleash a whole chain of wars. Indeed, this was why he felt such a strong obligation to seek to prevent it by diplomatic means.[54] Now his reliance on such methods was severely shaken, for the national war had brought on the very effects he had feared, stirring up insensate passions and irreconcilable hatreds that diplomacy could not readily bring under control. It was for these reasons that Bismarck resorted to the strongest frontier guarantees available to him, without troubling too much that this might serve only to deepen the spirit of revenge.

Yet this was a long way from sinking down into the fatalist attitude of nationalism, as we know it from Moltke, which held that war represented the all-powerful forces of destiny, that it might be hastened or slowed but never altogether avoided. In the early years following 1871, especially during the *Kulturkampf*, Bismarck watched internal developments in France with the sharpest distrust, though refraining from any intervention in French constitutional issues. When the country's unexpectedly rapid economic recovery made it possible for France to advance the dates for paying the war indemnity, Bismarck unhesitatingly evacuated the German troops.[55]

It is true that the rapid rearmament instituted by the Third Republic caused Bismarck concern; in 1873 and again in 1875 he tried diplomatic intimidation to secure arms limitation and thus, in a manner of speaking, make up for the omissions in the Peace of 1871, as Moltke would have put it. Yet Bismarck, as we have already seen in Part 3, emphatically resisted the temptation to underscore the action by military means in order to precipitate at a favorable moment a conflict considered inevitable at a later date.

Indeed, when it turned out that not only did these diplomatic pressures remain unsuccessful but that they rallied the great powers of Europe against Germany, conjuring up the specter of political encirclement, Bismarck promptly dropped this approach. Instead of seeking further material guarantees, he was now concerned with adding ever new refinements to his system of alliances. Far from allowing himself to be deterred by the alleged inevitability of Franco-German war, he hoped throughout the 1880's that French bellicosity and revanchism would fade, and he fostered such tendencies as much as he could by giving vigorous support to French colonial aspirations, thereby seeking to divert their ambitions from the Rhine to overseas goals.

The Boulanger crisis of 1887 taught him that such a policy did not necessarily banish the specter of war for good. Somehow danger still flashed on the horizon, like distant lightning. Thus a continuous increase in German armaments, to hold pace with those of Germany's western neighbor, remained an indispensable part of Bismarck's peace policy. Yet to his last day in office, Bismarck was never at a loss for ideas of how each new European crisis might be mastered by peaceful diplomatic means.

The irrational belief of radical nationalists and imperialists—that the essence of diplomacy is exhausted in power struggles—which grew to be rife among Bismarck's successors was never really justified in invoking the Iron Chancellor himself. Despite the demoniac militancy that plays about his figure, posterity is inclined to believe that the ultimate goal of his life's work was the creation and maintenance of an enduring peaceful order, on the basis of unfolding German national power.

It is true that the unresolved tensions of national passions left behind by the most important of the peace treaties he concluded weighed as a heavy mortgage upon Germany's future. Even those who are reluctant to regard this burden as having been totally inescapable and to believe that it inexorably led to the disaster of 1914 will have to admit that the historical consequences were indeed fateful. Unquestionably the War of 1870-1871 for the first time signaled the sinister concatenations of modern national war, from which the great disasters of our own age have grown. And manifestly Bismarck's statesmanship was unable to cope successfully with the set of problems. His political wisdom, so brilliantly displayed in 1866, here reached its limits.[56]

The story of Bismarck, the last great cabinet statesman, at this point already verges on a new era.

Notes

Notes to the Introduction

1. On origin and usage of the term "militarism" in the various countries, see H. Herzfeld, "Der Militarismus als Problem der neuen Geschichte," in *Schola* Vol. 1, No. 1 (1946), pp. 41 ff.
2. E. Ludendorff, *Der totale Krieg* (1935), p. 10; General Alfred Krauss, "Die Wesenseinheit von Politik und Krieg als Ausgangspunkt einer deutschen Stretegie," in *Deutschlands Erneuerung*, Vol. 5, No. 6 (1921), p. 324.
3. See my book, *Machtstaat und Utopie. Vom Streit um die Dämonie der Macht seit Machiavelli und Morus* (3rd ed.; 1943), or more recent editions under the title: *Die Dämonie der Macht* (6th ed.; Munich, 1948); also my study, "Machiavelli und der Ursprung des modernen Nationalismus," in *Vom sittlichen Problem der Macht* (Berne, 1948), pp. 40-90.
4. I am here but opposing the two extreme cases. There are, of course, a thousand intermediate forms that preponderate numerically.
5. As is well known, Friedrich Meinecke made the internal dualism of the political sphere the subject of an important book, his *Idee der Staatsraison*. It may be useful to consider immediately whether and to what extent his conceptual distinctions overlap what is here discussed, the opposition of militant power concentration and enduring peaceful order, a contrast distilled from an analysis of concrete conflict situations rather than by theoretical abstraction. Meinecke views the history of states as an everlasting struggle between a "natural" or "nocturnal" side of politics, which he calls *Kratos,* and an "ideal" or "lighted" side, which he calls its *Ethos*. The latter is in essence dominated by "ideas," the former by base and selfish "brute" instinct. Meinecke presents in detail a highly colorful variety of polarities, based on moral, juridical, and metaphysical categories: selfishness and ethical standards, politics and morality, reality and idea, power and law, egotism and observance of commitments, nature and spirit, nature and culture, fate and reason, causality and freedom, existence and duty, darkness and light. (See C. Schmitt's critique, *Positionen und Begriffe im Kampf mit Weimar–Genf–Versailles*, 1940, pp. 45 ff.) There is a self-evident general relationship between these sets of concepts and our contrasting of power struggle and peaceful order; yet I am at pains to emphasize those points where I feel myself to be at odds with Meinecke. First: My distinction is not meant as a moral deprecation of militancy as such. The power struggle displays a true ethic in the same sense as does peaceful order, though the two ethics may come into sharp conflict. we have already outlined a catalog of the "virtues" of militancy. True, in my conviction, too, militancy must never become an end in itself; and true historic grandeur is attained only when power gained in struggle creates a new and better order, i.e., one better adapted to the living forces of the age; but neither, on the other hand, must a peaceful order, once established, be regarded as an absolute moral value, removed from all temporal contingencies. It is from the need for the destruction of obsolete orders and for the conquest or defense of true living orders that militancy receives its true ethic—not merely its peculiar moral pathos but its ultimate ethical justification. Second: My distinction has nothing in common with the Neo-Kantian conceptual doublets of existence and duty *(Sein und Sollen)*, causality and freedom, idea and reality, nor with such juxtapositions as spirit and nature, spirit and power. The drive for power and self-assertion is as "natural" to the individual and the nation as is their thirst for an enduring peaceful order, militancy as much as the drive for sociability and gregariousness. The restless urge for action (today often called "dynamics" or "activism") is as normal as is the need for continuity, perpetuity, outward and inward repose. In my view "spirit and power," so often contrasted in historical literature, do not constitute a real polarity at all. Historians need not be reminded that power struggles not only destroy but often recreate spiritual creations of the highest rank. Even Meinecke knows this, for he keeps on discussing the creative repercussions of political struggle. One might even say that great creative achievements have scarcely

ever come into being but for great ambitions, which always contain a modicum of the living power drive and self-assertion; and we can give credit to Ranke for the insight that great powers are not crudely primitive but "tangible spiritual entities" *(realgeistige Wesenheiten)* and that Europe's spiritual life was indeed kindled by the flames of their perpetual struggles. Third: I believe that the frequent references to political power struggles being "spiritualized," "purified," or "transfigured" by "ideas" is dangerous nonsense, because these terms are too easily misunderstood. Meinecke speaks of "primitive instinct burgeoning into ideas," of the "transition of a nation's instinctual will to life and power toward the idea of nationhood as an ethical concept, an idea that views the nation as the symbol of everlasting values" (p. 13), of "ennobling the primitive power state to the level of a higher ideality," the mere state becoming the *Kulturstaat,* investing power instincts with ethical values. It does not appear to me at all that a power struggle is made ethical simply by virtue of the fact that it is waged for some idea, true or false. The ethical character of such a struggle derives solely from an awareness of moral responsibility for the perpetuation or restoration of a truly ethical—which also means an enduring—community of those who conduct it and who aspire to replace a wrecked order with a new, better, and more durable one based on law; for it must not be based on mere force, since force without law always cancels out the individual and thus destroys the very basis of a true society. What matters is not the ideality of political aspirations but true *raison d'état,* that combination of practical insight into realities with moral reason of which we have spoken in our text. At bottom Frederic the Great already knew that; hence his *raison d'état* means much more to me than Meinecke's, as will be discussed further on. The self-discipline of power through the proper use of reason (to be secured by appropriate institutions, as circumstances dictate) is indubitably a most urgent task, morally as well as politically. The transfiguration of a power struggle by the agency of an idea to which the struggling power is supposed to give subservience seems to me a far more dubious matter. It is quite true that the greatest power struggles of history have always been related to some "idea"—the Greek wars against the Persians, the crusades, the imperial excursions into Italy, the struggle against the Slavs in the middle ages, the Turkish wars and revolutionary wars of modern times. Yet the character of these struggles, even viewed purely as power struggles, was not thereby changed in the least; and no reasonable self-limitation of power can be expected from that quarter, indeed less than from any other. The history of the wars of religion teaches us quite the contrary, as does even more eloquently the experience of our own generation. Or did by any chance the transition of "the nations' instinctual will to life and power toward the idea of nationhood as an ethical concept that views the nation as the symbol of everlasting values" do anything to impart an ethical character to the power struggles staged in the First World War? Were illusions ever more cruelly disappointed than was the idealistic faith of national liberalism which all the civilized countries of Europe reposed in the "national idea" or even the restraining influence of "European culture?" The serious question that always remains concerns the degree to which the contending power really subserved the "idea" to which it professes to give allegiance—whether, indeed, it is not merely using that idea as a pretext. Nothing appears to be simpler than to unearth a transfiguring "idea" for shifting power goals that are all-too-often omnivorous. The prophets of such ideas always seem to be "on tap," so to speak.

In this connection, a word on the dangers inherent in the modern "history of ideas" generally may be appropriate. It seems to me that modern German historians are in grave danger of overestimating the practical political importance of ideas in the power struggle. Otherwise it could scarcely happen that widely known recent historical works seek to persuade readers that futile and hopeless political adventures can be justified by reference to the grandeur, antiquity, and general significance of the ideas expressed or at least somehow perpetuated in them, no matter how abstract these ideas may be, how ineffective in the political sense, indeed, sometimes purely academic. Even so important and meritorious a work as H. von Srbik's *Deutsche Einheit* seems to me not free of such tendencies. In any event, political history must not be misled into a mere description of abstract "struggles of ideas." Unswerved by mere ideology, it must keep its eye on the concrete power conflicts that determine the course of political life beneath the coruscating surface of ideas that keep on emerging anew, flashing into view only to fade away soon afterward.

6. When C. Schmitt, in *Positionen und Begriffe*, p. 52, notes that "we are today far removed from *ratio* and *status* [in the sense of the seventeenth century] this does not argue against the need for true *raison d'état* in general. Without real political wisdom sound policy is impossible even in the age of modern mass democracy.

Notes to Chapter 1

1. *Ob Kriegsleute auch in seligem Stand sein können (Whether Soldier May Attain a State of Beatitude)* 1526 Wartburg ed., Vol. 19, pp. 648f.
2. Moltke, *Military Works*, iv, War Doctrines (Grand General Staff, 1911), p. 1.
3. Küntzel and Hass (eds.), *Die Politischen Testamente der Hohenzollern*, Vol. 1 (1911), pp. 88f.
4. This, of course, is not to say that only under Frederic the Great did Prussia first take part in the diplomatic deals of the great powers of Europe. The Great Elector had tried his hand in this sphere, as had Maximilian I and Maximilian II, Emanuel of Bavaria, Frederic Augustus II of Saxony-Poland, John Philip Schönborn of Mainz, and many other princes of the seventeenth century Holy Roman Empire, big and small. None of them, however, attained the measure of independence and big-power prestige that accrued to Frederic.
5. *Denkwürdigkeiten* (1792), Section: "Regierungsantritt." From the Works, in German translation, edited by Volz, Vol. 2, pp. 5f.
6. This was first shown by A. Berney in his *Friedrich der Grosse, Entwicklungsgeschichte eines Staatsmannes* (1934), p. 123, n. 74.
7. See my book, *Europe und die deutsche Frage* (Munich, 1948), Chapter 2; and R. Stadelmann, *Deutschland und Westeuropa* (1948), pp. 23, 26ff. Also St. Skalweit, *Frankreich und Friedrich der Grosse* (Bonn, 1952), and the bibliography there given.
8. *Collected Works*, Vol. 7, pp. 197ff.
9. Friedrich Meinecke, above all, has emphatically pointed this out—too emphatically for my taste *(Klassiker der Politik*, Vol. 8, pp. 27f., and *Idee der Staatsraison*, p. 44). See my book, *Die Dämonie der Macht* (6th ed., 1948), p. 190, n. 49 to Chapter 2; also my collection of essays, *Vom sittlichen Problem der Macht* (Berne, 1948), pp. 62f. and n. 50.
10. Meinecke, in *Idee der Staatsraison*, p. 357, remarks that Frederic never made the barbarous coercive system of Prussian recruitment the object of humanitarian consideration; but in the *Antimachiavelli*, Chapter 12, the imperfections of Prussian army replacement are expressly acknowledged. On later reform efforts, see C. Jany, *Geschichte der preussischen Armee*, Vol. 2, pp. 9f. Actually, this form of barbarism was part and parcel of the eighteenth-century way of life, and it was perhaps at its most barbarous in the British Navy—see, for example, the very vivid description of "eighteenth-century militarism" in the excellent book by the American Walter L. Dorn, *Competition for Empire 1740-1763* (New York, 1940), Chapter 3.
11. *Betrachtungen über den gegenwärtigen politischen Zustand Europas*, in the *Collected Works* (translation), Vol. 1, p. 234. He says on pp. 237 and 242: "Great power policy has scarcely ever varied. At all times its basic principle was to subjugate everything to the end of indefinitely expanding one's own power. Its skill consisted

in anticipating the enemy's tricks, to play with greater finesse. . . . The stronger is like a raging torrent. He overflows his banks, sweeps everything before him and brings about the most pernicious upheavals."

12. Preface to the *Denkwurdigkeiten* of 1742, in the *Collected Works* (translation), Vol. 2, p. 2.

13. Political Testament of 1752, in *Klassiker der Politik,* Vol. 5, p. 63; see also *ibid.* p. 55: "It is a great fault in politics always to appear arrogant and to seek to prevail by force, but it is equally a fault always to show oneself gentle and yielding." Meinecke, in *Idee der Staatsraison,* takes the passage cited in the text to mean that Frederic was "more intent on rationalizing power politics than in investing it with an ethical character." The word reason here did not mean moral reason to Frederic, according to Meinecke, but rather appropriateness of political action. I find this surmise baseless. In the case of Frederic the Great there was always a humanitarian component whenever he acted from reason rather than passion. To have recommended to his successor that he should combine ambition with shrewdness in his choice of methods—this Frederic would have considered either banal or "Machiavellian." The whole passage in question plainly deals with the moral problem of the proper use of power. Frederic's concept of *raison d'état* is discussed in a dissertation which I sponsored: Marianne Melcher, "Vernunftideal und Staatsraison bei Friedrich dem Grossen" (University of Berlin, 1944).

14. *Collected Works,* Vol. 2, p. 2, preface of 1742.

15. "Cet homme extraordinaire, ce roi aventurier digne de l'ancienne chevalerie, ce héros vagabond dont tous les vertus, poussées à un certain excès, dégénéraient en vices. . . . " *Antimachiavelli, Oeuvres,* Vol. 8, Chapter 8, p. 197, *Collected Works* [German], Vol. 7, p. 33. See also "Betrachtungen über die militärischen Talente und den Charakter Karls XII," written in 1759, *Collected Works,* Vol. 6, pp. 367ff., especially pp. 369 and 380.

16. Friedrich Meinecke, in his *Idee der Staatsraison,* sharply brings out the coexistence of two trends in Frederic's thinking (e.g., on p. 355), repeatedly contrasting the humanitarian "ideal of enlightenment" and *"raison d'état."* To my mind it is not clear that for Frederic *raison d'état* fulfilled a similar function to humanitarianism: the curbing of blind passion. Unlike Meinecke, Frederic did not view the "state-as-power," let alone *raison d'état* as such, as a demoniac menace to be contended with. What did seem dangerous to him was power politics impelled by blind affect rather than calm reason. *Vernunft (raison)* must, in this context, always be read as moral reason, which is indeed true for the whole eighteenth century. Once the problem of taming the daimon of power is conceived in these terms, one is scarcely entitled to say (as Meinecke does on p. 344) that this problem was "not yet" soluble within the framework of the philosophy of the Enlightenment. It is no doubt true that Frederic as a functioning statesman always followed the "imperative of reasons of state" which commonly prevailed over the "demands of [pure] humanitarianism" (p. 354); but that does not at all mean that his course of action was "always quite clear and unproblematical"; for it was never known in advance whether reasons of state, in the individual case, would require military or political means, boldness of caution, ruthless sacrifice of humanitarian consideration; and even the triumph of *raison d'état* over natural passions never proceeded without inner struggle.

Frederic's statements on the breaching of treaties as a means of grand policy show with particular succinctness how he conceived of the moderating effect of political wisdom in practice. Unfortunately such breaches are often indispensable, not because they are universally practiced, thus leaving every ally in danger of being deceived by the other, and also because conscientious observance of treaties sometimes exceeds the strength of those legally obliged to such observance. Even so, breach of treaty is not politically dubious because it risks the foreign prestige of the breaker, but is morally reprehensible as a violation of "honorable conduct." Contrary to Meinecke's view (p. 382), this notion is steadfastly clung to by Frederic, though after 1752 the concept of "reasons of state" was added as a consideration. In certain circumstances, therefore, the moral law must be violated in the interest of the state. Yet it remains the task of political reason to see to it that the statesman "departs as rarely as possible from the honorable course." He will seek to preserve "purity of heart" by violating his treaty obligations only when he is compelled to do so by forces beyond his control, never from roguery, whim, instinctive hatred, or base selfishness. The power drive that impels him to break international law must never be blind–it must always be informed with insight into the higher reasons of state. We evidently have here a special case of the conflict between enlightened moral reason and the blind power drive.

17. Here and elsewhere, see also my biography, *Friedrich der Grosse. Ein historisches Profil* (3rd ed.; 1953).

18. Political Testament of 1752, translation in *Klassiker der Politik,* Vol. 5, pp. 28f., 32f., 37, 42, 52; Political Testament of 1768, *ibid.* p. 240. For the French original, compare the edition by B. Volz, supplementary volume to the Political Correspondence, 1920.

19. This runs counter to the view of G. B. Volz, in his introduction to Vol. 8. of *Klassiker der Politik,* pp. 18f.

20. Political Testament of 1768, translation in *Klassiker der Politik,* Vol. 5, pp. 129 and 169. In the last-cited passage, Frederic defends the soldier's calling against attacks by pacifist Frenchmen of the Encyclopedist circle: "There is no finer nor more useful art than the art of war, when it is practiced by men of decency"–men, that is to say, who seek to protect the peace of the land. In this context it is appropriate to mention the very great importance to the eighteenth-century Prussian armies of popular education under religious auspices, the effect of which continued into the Wars of Liberation. See R. Höhn, *Revolution, Heer, Kriegsbild* (1944), pp. 392ff.

21. There was, of course, even then no dearth of conflicts between generals and statesmen, and sometimes these were of great severity. Perhaps the best known are associated with Marlborough and Prince Eugene. For the most part these quarrels stemmed from government reluctance to risk sufficient resources in wartime; but there are also instances when civilian government pressed for more intense military action, while the general hesitated, preferring careful maneuvering to pitched battles (e.g., Maria Theresa and Field Marshal Daun). Yet what was still almost altogether missing in such conflicts was the basic claim by the military experts, put forward later by Moltke, to be left entirely free from political intervention in the sphere of operational decisions. Indeed, there was not yet a sharp jurisdictional delimitation between politics and the army. The story of Prince Eugene provides a particularly illuminating demonstration of the accepted interplay between the two spheres. See Eberhard Ritter's careful study, *Politik und Kriegführung. Ihre Beherrschung durch Prinz Eugen 1704* (Monograph No. 10 of the Section on Military History of the Historical Seminary, Berlin, 1934).

22. The controversy initiated by Hans Delbrück on whether Frederic the Great was a "strategist of annihilation" or a "strategist of attrition" must be considered passé today, since it is generally agreed that the expression "strategy of attrition," understood in the sense of a pure strategy of maneuver, is simply not appropriate to the strategy of Frederic the Great. I do not wish to rekindle this discussion here, my views being stated in Chapter 8 of my biography of Frederic the Great. It does seem to me that the controversy might have been more fruitful, if at the outset it had not limited itself so much to the sphere of military techniques, taking more account of the relation of sword and scepter, as it is here envisaged.

23. Political Testaments, *loc. cit.,* p. 169.

24. Political Testament of 1752, *ibid.,* p. 58.

25. That Frederic intended this to be a main blow, indeed a decisive battle, is clear from his letter to Algarotti of December 27, 1757 (Political Correspondence, Vol. 14, p. 172; *Oeuvres,* Vol. 18, p. 103). "We shall have done nothing," Frederick wrote, "until we have emulated Caesar on the day after Pharsalus. It is on this passage and similar ones that W. Elze, in his *Friedrich der Grosse* (2nd ed.; 1939), pp. 104ff., 123f., bases his assertion that Frederic, in Bohemia in 1757, sought to fight a "battle of German unification." The defeat of the Austrian army was to be the

prelude to Frederic being appointed "lieutenant general or imperial field marshal in perpetuity" by Maria Theresa. At the head of the Prussian army, the imperial army, and the armies of the several princes of the empire, and the Austro-Hungarian army, he would then have addressed himself to the empire as a whole, driving out all foreigners, especially the French. Elze makes this fanciful "unification plan," which supposedly came to grief at Kolin, virtually the main thesis of his book. This would require very convincing evidence, since it flies in the face of everything we know about Frederic's policy of alliances and especially his relationship with France—indeed, anything ever the boldest flights of fancy could dream up. The source material Elze adduces (from the Political Correspondence, the dispatches, Mitchell's diary, and the letters exchanged between the king and his sister) tends to show only that Frederic, in his precarious situation in the spring of 1757, hoped for relief in a great decisive battle, as Caesar once did in his seemingly hopeless situation at Pharsalus, or the French in 1712 at Denain, or the Austrians in 1683 at the Kahlenberg near Vienna. As Plutarch related of Caesar, Frederic's "Pharsalus" was to bring the great miraculous turn. The very extrapolation of ancient Pharsalus as a "battle of unification" appears labored and arbitrary.

The meaning of Frederic's letters to his sister Wilhelmina in Bayreuth is quite plain. He was indirectly warning the petty princes of the Holy Roman Empire against joining its anti-Prussian measures, especially the establishment of an imperial army aimed at Prussia, which was decided in January, 1757. He commended himself (at the same time reassuring his anxious sister) as the protector of their liberty against Austrian servitude. All this has nothing whatever to do with plans for imperial reform or with a rising against France. See *inter alia* the letter to the margrave of February 26, 1757, Political Correspondence, Vol. 14, No. 8656. Elze might have cited still another utterance by Frederic with the Pharsalus simile, made to Prince Henry in April, 1757 (diary of Henckel von Donnersmarck, May 2, 1757, cited by Koser, *Historische Zeitschrift*, Vol. 93, p. 73). Even here, however, Frederick speaks only of a battle that is to "settle the fate of the empire." On December 27, 1756, by the way, when the name Pharsalus first appeared, the campaign plans for 1757 were not yet by any means fixed; and as late as May 2, 1757, the King contemplated dividing his forces between Austria and France, once the main battle was won (Political Correspondence, Vol. 15, p. 2, letter to Schwerin).

As for the statement to the British envoy Mitchell, to the effect that he wished he might reduce the Austrians to the point that they might subsequently be prepared to dissolve their connection with France, indeed to make their troops available for the fight against France (see Bisset [ed.], *Memoirs and Papers of Sir Andrew Mitchell* [1850], Vol. 1, p. 334), its political bias emerges clearly from the context. It was all important to encourage George II to engage in active resistance against France, and through him to sweep along the neutralist Hanoverian government as well. The King did not trouble to conceal even from the Englishman that these were far-fetched flights of fancy. For in the passage cited by Ranke (*Complete Works*, Vol. 30, p. 299, n. 4; see also Political Correspondence, Vol. 15, p. 62) Frederic continues: "But this from their pride was hardly to be expected." Ranke's quotation is thus misleading. There is not a single word about an imperial field marshalcy by means of which Prussia would liberate Germany, as envisaged by Elze. Ranke, whom Elze cites as his star witness, knew nothing about this. He was, however, whenever he came to a dramatic climax in his story given to pondering "what might have happened if . . ."; and in this connection he did emphasize the possibility that the two German-speaking countries might have coalesced, though he never took this quite seriously.

Nor is it at all surprising that Wilhelmina, in mid-June, 1757, reported that the French feared the King might again (as in 1742 and 1745) reach a swift reconciliation with Austria, at their expense. Actually, to drive the point home, we have utterances by the King in which he declares an alliance between Prussia and Austria to be as impossible as the union of fire and water (June 24, 1748, Political Correspondence, Vol. 6, p. 150). Statements from the other side are equally unequivocal. At the last audience granted the English ambassador, Keith, on May 13, 1756, Maria Theresa declared: "She would own freely to me, that She and the King of Prussia were incompatible together, and that no consideration upon earth should ever make her enter into an alliance, where he was a Party" (letter to Holdernesse of May 16, 1756, marked "most secret," personal communication by courtesy of W. Michael, from the papers of the Record Office).

Notes to Chapter 2

1. See my biography of Freiherr vom Stein (1931), Vol. 1, pp. 187ff., 210ff.
2. *Der Herr und der Diener, geschildert mit patriotischer Freyheit* (Frankfurt, 1759), pp. 19-20. Here and for the following, see also H. H. Kaufmann, "Friedrich Carl von Moser als Politiker und Publizist," *Quellen und Forschungen zur hessischen Geschichte*, Vol. 12 (1931), pp. 19ff.
3. A. W. Rehberg, *Über die Staatsverwaltung deutscher Länder und die Dienerschaft des Regenten* (Hanover, 1807), p. 29. While this pamphlet already falls into the period of Romanticism and the reforms of Freiherr vom Stein, the corporate spirit it reflects dates back much farther.
4. *Loc. cit.*, p. 239f.
5. Friedrich Carl von Moser, *Beherzigungen* (1763), p. 131.
6. *On Patriotism* (1777), cited after R. Höhn, "Der Soldat und das Vaterland während und nach dem Siebenjährigen Krieg," in *Festschrift für Ernst Heymann, 1, Rechtsgeschichte* (Weimar, 1940), p. 282. Höhn's interesting source study cites other instances of the change in the political atmosphere in Prussia toward the end of the reign of Frederic the Great.
7. Broadsheet: *Meine Antwort auf die Danksagungen den Landes nach der Aufhebung der Leibeigenschaft und einiger Abgaben* (Karlsruhe, September 19, 1785).
8. See the final paragraph of *Zum ewigen Frieden, Philosophische Bibliothek*, Vol. 47 (1913), I, p. 169. J. Ebbinghaus in "Kants Lehre vom Ewigen Frieden und die Kriegsschuldfrage," *Philosophie und Geschichte*, No. 23 (1929), emphasizes the austerely legal-philosophical character of Kant's writings on peace. This character emerges particularly impressively in *Metaphysische Anfangsgründe der Rechtslehre*, Paragraph 57, *Philosophische Bibliothek*, Vol. 42, pp. 176ff. In very clear words, "the future establishment of an enduring peace" is here designated as the only legitimate purpose of war. On the "sublimity" of war, see Kant's *Kritik der Urteilskraft*, Paragraph 28.
9. Berenhorst, *Betrachtungen über die Kriegskunst*, Section 1, (1798), p. 203, cited after H. Rothfels, *Carl von Clausewitz* (1920), p. 37, n. 27.
10. A particularly nice example is given by Bertrand de Jouvenel in *Après la defaite* (1941), p. 65, from the memoirs of Marshal Villars, who describes his encounter with Prince Eugene on November 26, 1713, in Rastatt to negotiate peace after eleven years of war: "As soon as I knew the Prince of Savoy to be in the palace courtyard, I went outside the palace to the top of the flight of steps, excusing myself from descending, on account of my crippled state. We embraced, with sentiments of an old and true friendship, which remained unaltered by the long wars and our opposed undertakings. . . . We settled the agenda in common. It was agreed that we should dine alternately, the one with the other, in company of the major members of our entourage, and that in the evening there should be a game in my suite, which was the more comfortable. . . ." De Jouvenel compares this with certain youthful recollections of his own—how he saw the German representatives, like caged beasts, walk to and fro behind the iron fence of the park in Versailles, waiting to be produced, so to speak, to receive the imposed terms. Johann Jakob von Moser, in *Versuch des neuesten europäischen Völkerrechts*, ix, 1 (1779), p. 145, reports that in 1756 the Austrian court had complained that the Prussians were cutting off the food supply

for the king of Poland-Saxony in the fortified camp at Pirna. The Prussians, however, gave assurances that they allowed free passage to supplies intended for the royal table.

11. We may here particularly call to mind the not infrequent instances of chivalrous conduct, in which aristocratic French officers hesitated to carry out harsh reprisals ordered by the emperor against the occupants of hostile territory; or of the curious notion that it was not altogether honorable for an officer to escape without ransom, even when he had not given his word of honor and was being guarded. Max Jähn, in *Über Krieg, Frieden und Kultur* (1893), p. 280, reports a case in which the English government later voluntarily paid the ransom for a naval officer who had escaped from Paris in this fashion, in fear of the guillotine.

12. See for example the Electoral-Saxon service regulation of 1752, cited by R. Koser, *Historische Zeitschrift*, Vol. 93 (1904), p. 240: "A battle is the most important and dangerous war operation. In open country without fortifications the loss of a battle may be so decisive that it should be seldom dared and is never advisable. . . . The skill of a great general consists in maintaining the ultimate purpose of a campaign through astute and sure maneuvers without danger." Or compare Massenbach's praise for Prince Henry: "By bold marches he won the favors of Lady Luck . . . more fortunate than Caesar at Dyrrhachium, greater than Condé at Rocroi, the equal of the immortal Berwick, he won victory without battle." Cited after von der Goltz, *Von Rossbach bis Jena* (2nd ed.; 1906), p. 375.

13. Tempelhoff (trans.), *Abhandlung über die allgemeinen Grundsätze der Kriegskunst* (Münster, Frankfurt and Leipzig, 1783), Introduction, p. xviii, cited after Rothfels, *loc cit.*, p. 41.

14. Vol. 1, Paragraph 10, p. 10, cited after M. Lehmann, *Scharnhorst*, Vol. 1 (1886), p. 17.

15. *Von Rossbach bis Jena* (2nd ed.; 1906), p. 361. An abundance of source material exemplifying Rococo strategy is found in the work by R. Jöhn, *Revolution, Heer, Kriegsbild* (1944), especially pp. 46ff. The same work, pp. 237ff., carries a detailed (but to my mind somewhat fulsome) appreciation of von Bülow's military teachings. In his new book, *Scharnhorsts Vermächtnis* (1952), Berenhorst and Bülow are represented almost as revolutionaries of the art of war and precursors of Scharnhorst's reformist ideas. This does not convince me. See also E. Hagemann, *Die deutsche Lehre vom Kriege*, Vol. I: "Von Berenhorst bis Clausewitz" (1940).

Notes to Chapter 3

1. A graceful presentation of this much-discussed subject, drawing on hitherto unknown material from Viennese archives, is given by E. Dard in *Napoléon et Talleyrand* (Paris, 1935; German edition, 1938). A more searching work is the two-volume biography of Talleyrand by G. Lacour-Gayet, 1930, compared with which Duff-Cooper's life, much-read in Germany, appears as a hasty and uncritical journalistic confection. Talleyrand was Europe's self-styled man of peace, as he proclaimed as early as 1792; but as I can only suggest here, when one examines the sources in detail, he did not always put this role into practice—neither in 1797 during the time when the conquest of Egypt was planned, nor in 1803 in the Enghien affair, nor in 1808 in the surprise attack on the Spanish Bourbons. His was a flawed mind, and his private ambitions repeatedly ran counter to his historic mission. His efforts at peace, moreover, were severely compromised by the now well-established fact that he was in the pay of his country's enemies. See also Louis Madelin, *Talleyrand* (1944).

2. See my book, *Die Dämonie der Macht* (6th ed.; 1948), pp. 32ff., 127f.

3. Directly after the signing of the peace of Campoformio, on October 18, 1797, Napoleon wrote Talleyrand: "Le moment actuel nous offre un beau jeu. Concentrons toute notre activité du côté de la marine et détruisons l'Angleterre. Cela fait, l'Europe est à nos pieds." Correspondence, Vol. 3, p. 392. In his St. Helena memoirs (Paris, 1823), Vol. 1., p. 46, Napoleon himself said that the goal of his ambitions

was "s'emparer de l'autorité, rendre à la France ses jours de gloire en donnant une direction forte aux affairs publiques." By contrast Talleyrand described his life's aim as "essayer de faire rentrer la France dans la société Européenne," *Mémoires* (Duc de Broglie, 1891), Vol. 1, p. 254.

4. Napoleon in his famous talk with Metternich on July 26, 1813, at Dresden, according to the report in Metternich's memoirs, written very much later. From the papers of Metternich, Vol. 1 (1880), p. 155.

5. As late as 1802 even Scharnhorst described the Napoleonic principle of headlong concentrated attack as "a desperate decision in which all strategy ceases"— *Denkwürdigkeiten der Berliner Militärischen Gesellschaft* (1802), Vol. 1, p. 56; the military writings of Scharnhorst, edited by H. Goltz, p. 262. See also Rothfels, *Carl von Clausewitz, Politik und Krieg* (1921); von der Goltz, *Von Rossbach bis Jena und Auerstädt* (2nd ed.; 1906), p. 369.

6. See the careful presentation, still the best, by Colmar Freiherr von der Goltz, *Von Rossbach bis Jena und Auerstädt* (2nd ed.; 1906). The novel elements in Napoleon's strategy were first comprehended and discussed by Clausewitz and Jomini, *Traité des grandes opérations militaires contenant l'histoire des campagnes de Frédéric II comparées avec celles de l'Empereur Napoléon* (2nd ed.; 1811).

7. *Vom Kriege,* sketches to Book 8, Vol. 6b.

8. Letter to his fiancée, October 3, 1807, in K. Linnebach, *Karl und Marie von Clausewitz,* (1916), p. 139; also in C. Schwartz, *Leben des Generals Carl von Clausewitz* (1878), Vol. 1, p. 292; and the collection, Rothfels (ed.), *Politische Schriften und Briefe* (1922), p. 21.

9. Rothfels, *Carl von Clausewitz, Politik und Krieg* (1920), Supplement, p. 201 (note from 1803).

10. See for example the letter to his fiancée of October 20, 1807, in Schwartz, Vol. 1, 296, in which he bemoans "the decline of European humanity," which he sees solely in the fact that the nations of Europe were losing the national freedom they had won over so many centuries since the destruction of the Roman empire.

11. Especially significant in this connection is the essay on Germans and Frenchmen in Schwartz, Vol. 1, pp. 73 ff.; *Politische Schriften* (selection), pp. 35 ff.

12. Rothfels, *loc. cit.,* p. 76.

13. *Ibid.,* pp. 206, 211.

14. Schwartz, Vol. 1, p. 293.

15. Hegel, *Die Verfassung Deutschlands* (1802), Section "Begriff des Staates."

16. Rothfels, *loc. cit.,* p. 198,

17. *Ibid.,* p. 212; for the following, *ibid.,* pp. 216, 211 ff.

18. Operational plan of 1806, in Schwartz, Vol. 1, pp. 221f.

19. Rothfels, *loc. cit.,* Appendix, p. 217.

20. Travel diary, August 25, 1807, in Schwartz, Vol. 1, p. 109; also in the selection, *Politische Schriften und Briefe,* pp. 24 ff.

21. "Historische Briefe über die grossen Kriegsereignisse im Oktober 1806," *Minerva,* Vol. 2 (1807), pp. 1ff.; in Schwartz, Vol. 2, p. 483.

22. Letters to his fiancée (1807), Schwartz, Vol. 1, pp. 230, 288f. In the "Nachrichten über Preussen in seiner grossen Katastrophe," *loc. cit.,* p. 430; Rothfels (ed.), *Politische Schriften,* p. 216, we still read: "A simple monarchy in which citizens are not motivated to political action by participation in the established institutions must have war from time to time, or at least the government must strike out boldly from a militant stance, must always move with honor and success, feared, honored, commanding the trust of its followers, so that the pride and integrity of the citizen are flattered."

23. Machiavelli could not have been familiar with these purposes, for the simple reason that he was as yet operating without the concept of the nation as a political community. He did know—and emphasize—that war brings great talent to light—*Discorsi,* Vol. 3, p. 16.

24. *Kritik der Urteilskraft,* Paragraph 28.

25. The same Kant, in his *Metaphysische Anfangsgründe der Rechtslehre*, Main Section 2, Paragraph 62 (Vorländer edition, in *Philosophische Bibliothek*, 4th ed., 1922), Vol. 42, p. 185, speaks of the irrevocable veto of moral-practical reason—"There shall be no war"; and in his treatise *Vom Ewigen Frieden (Philosophische Bibliothek*, i, 2nd ed.; 1922), Vol. 47, p. 146, he speaks of nature's irresistible will "that law ultimately gain the upper hand." *Ibid.*, p. 148, the "commercial spirit" is praised as nature's auxiliary to that end; and on p. 144 critical judgment is passed on philosophers who acknowledge "an inner dignity of war as such, leading to the ennoblement of mankind."

26. "Die Deutschen und die Franzosen" (1807), in Schwartz, Vol. 1, pp. 73ff. and especially p. 86; also in *Politische Schriften*, pp. 35ff.

27. Further proof of this argument in Rothfels, *loc. cit.*, pp. 114ff. On Clausewitz's relationship to Fichte, see *ibid.*, pp. 132f.

28. In a later context it will be shown that it was precisely the rigid consistency of his views on power politics that kept Clausewitz from lapsing into the moralizing approach to struggle usually seen in the patriots of the resurgence.

29. Note the close kinship with Humboldt's famous formulation (as well as the differences), in his memorial of December, 1813, on the German constitution : "Germany must be free and strong, not merely to defend itself against this neighbor or that, or indeed against any enemy, but because only a nation that is strong externally can preserve its spirit, from which all internal blessings flow. It must be free and strong, to nourish its essential self-confidence, even though it may never come to the test; to pursue its national development calm and unhindered; and to maintain for good the beneficent place it occupies amid the nations of Europe." See also my book, *Europa und die deutsche Frage*, pp. 57ff.

30. Pertz, *Gneisenau*, Vol. 3, Supplement 1, pp. 623ff.; excerpts also in *Politische Schriften und Briefe*, pp. 80ff.

31. "It is true that the likelihood of success is against us, but under what political system would that not be the case? . . . This is precisely our misfortune, that we are surrounded by abysses on all sides. How can one demand the likelihood of a successful outcome? Enough that it not be impossible. Whoever demands more contradicts himself. . . . One cannot take a single step forward in the kind of argument that likes to call itself calm consideration, without being caught up in the most extreme contradictions. Reason alone shall decide, we hear everyone cry. As though fear were not an expression of the mind as though there a free judgment on the part of reason could be admitted! All one can admit is that both professions of faith—on behalf of resistance as on behalf of submission—stem in equal measure from the mind. Yet courage is but one aspect of the mind, fear another. Fear paralyzes reason, courage invigorates it." Pert, *loc. cit.*, p. 642.

32. See also Gneisenau's characteristic marginal note to Clausewitz's second Protestation, Pert, *Gneisenau*, Vol. 3, p. 641.

33. Alfred Stern, *Abhandlungen und Aktenstücke zur Geschichte der preussischen Reformzeit* (1885), pp. 93ff.; Max Lenz, *Napoleon I. und Preussen. Kleine historische Schriften* (1910), pp. 315ff.

34. The line of thinking here detailed was published as early as 1943 in the special issue of the *Historische Zeitschrift* dedicated to Friedrich Meinecke, Vol. 167, pp. 41-65. On the highly complex genesis of *On War* and the sequence and meaning of its various versions see H. Rosinski, "Die Entwicklung von Clausewitz' Werk 'Vom Kriege,' " *Historische Zeitschrift*, Vol. 151 (1935); Eberhard Kessel. "Zur Entstehungsgeschichte von Clausewitz' Werk 'Vom Kriege' " *ibid.*, Vol. 152 (1935): *idem:* "Zur Genesis der modernen Kriegslehre. Die Entstehungsgeschichte von Clausewitz' Werk 'Vom Krieg,' " *Wehrwissenschaftliche Rundschau*, Vol. 3 (1953), No. 9. A kind of Clausewitz philology seems to be gradually developing. On the influence of the work and its changing misinterpretations see the new edition by W. Hohlweg (16th ed.; Dümmler, Bonn, 1952), the introduction to which contains complete references down to the present.

35. *Vom Kriege,* Book 3, vi, "Grundsätze der Kriegführung für den Kronprinzen" (supplement to *Vom Kriege*), Vol. 1, p. 1.

36. In his famous letter to Talleyrand of October 7, 1797 (Correspondence, Vol. 3, p. 490), Napoleon describes his ideal as a combination of "fervent and enthusiastic imagination with the coldest, most enduring and calculating reason." He had already voiced similar sentiments in his *Discours de Lyon.* There is a similarity to the ideas of Clausewitz (*Vom Kriege,* edition by W. von Scherff, *Militärische Klassiker,* Vol. 1 [1880], p. 50), who saw mere reason stimulated to creative achievement only by powerful sentiment and demanded an "amalgam of emotion and reason" for the great captain. Yet the marked reserve with which Clausewitz evaluates the role of imagination, of the inspired hunch, in military achievement (*ibid.,* p. 48, Paragraphs 4 and 7), and his marked preference for cool rather than hot heads (p. 51, Paragraph 2) is highly characteristic of the difference between Romance and Teutonic thinking.

37. See his famous account, *Nachrichten über Preussen in seiner grossen Katastrophe,* Monograph No. 10 in the series on the history of war (General Staff: Berlin, 1888). It is mercilessly sharp in its characterization of the military leaders.

38. This becomes particularly plain from his letters to General Staff Major von Roeder of December 22, 24, 1827 (published as a special issue of the *Militärwissenschaftliche Rundschau,* March, 1937). Having just finished his *chef d'oeuvre* and still entirely pervaded by its basic thoughts, he here criticizes certain operational tasks the chief of staff, von Müffling, had set Roeder. His propensity for considering everything on its own goes so far here that he virtually challenges the practical value of generalized operational problems. In Clausewitz's view, the abundance of possible political situations could not be calculated in advance, yet the particular situation would be crucial for the operational task in hand. "Every great military design stems from such a mass of individual circumstances—which make it what it is rather than something else—that it is impossible to devise a fictitious case that would resemble the actual. . . . War is not an independent thing, but the continuation of politics by other means, hence the main lineaments of great strategic designs are in large part political in nature. This is true in the proportion that they embrace the totality of war and the state" (p. 6). Of any fifty historical wars, something like forty-nine were not wars of subjection or annihilation, but rather wars of limited aim. Even a war of annihilation looked "nonpolitical," though it was neither a "normal" war, nor lacked a political element—except that that element here happened to be the enemy's destruction.

39. It is developed with complete consistency in Chapter 1 of Book 1, which Clausewitz shortly before his death described as the only one he regarded as being finished. He himself regarded the distinction, there elaborated, between absolute war (war of subjugation) and war of limited aim as basic—even though he seems to have appreciated it fully only during his work on the first six Books. In the sketches for Book 8, apparently unfinished, he reverts to it at great length, adding certain considerations that are especially important to our theme. My analysis in the text adheres primarily to the presentation in Book 1, but then does bring in Book 8 in supplementary fashion. Book 8, by the way, originally meant to deal only with the subject of war plans, summarizes the basic thoughts of the whole work in such magnificently impressive form that it may be called the most important and mature, despite its fragmentary character.

40. The point is argued in thoroughgoing fashion in Book 3, Chapter 16.

41. This seems to have been always sensed quite strongly in the Prussian general staff school—see preface and commentary in the Scherff Edition, *Militärische Klassiker des In- und Auslandes* (Berlin, 1880), which calls the work at best a handbook for student strategists, but certainly not suitable for commanding generals (p. v), and complains that it contains no handy lessons and directions for tactical combat.

42. Book 1, Chapter 2; more on defense and attack of theaters of war where no great decision is sought, in Book 6, Chapter 30, and Book 7, Chapter 16.

43. We know that Hans Delbrück in many of his books took this view, basing his ideas in the main on the *Nachricht* of 1827, printed in the preface. See his report on the controversy that arose over this, in his *Geschichte der Kriegskunst,* Vol. 4, pp. 439ff. The best refutation is found in the excellent study by von Caemmerer, "Die Entwicklung der strategischen Wissenschaft im 19. Jahrhundert" (*Bibliothek der Politik und Volkswirtschaft,* 1904), No. 15, pp. 71f.

44. Scherff edition, p. 32, which relates to what follows. I shall continue to give page references from Scherff.

45. Book 1, Chapters 1, 8, p. 7; see also Book 6, Chapter 30, p. 479, where there is a warning against overestimating the strategy of maneuver. *Ibid.,* p. 481: "War of great decisions is not only much simpler but also much more natural, freer of inner contradictions, more objective," etc. In Book 8, Chapter 2, p. 540, he says that mass inertia is hard to overcome. Book 3, Chapter 16, pp. 157f.: "Why put forward such immense effort in wartime, when the only purpose is to engender similar effort on the part of the enemy?" Only pusillanimity, indecision, lack of insight, a petty approach to things can rest content with a half-hearted effort. See also the sources cited by von Caemmerer, *loc. cit.* Book 4, Chapters 3 and 11; Book 6, Chapters 14 and 20; Book 8, Chapters 3 (note to B) and 9.

46. Book 8, Chapter 6a, p. 564.

47. Book 8, Chapter 3a, p. 543; Chapter 2, p. 541.

48. In many places in *On War,* and in the very large number of historical and strategic studies in the *Hinterlassene Werke.*

49. Book 8, Chapter 3b, p. 554; Chapter 2, p. 540f.

50. Book 8, Chapter 3b, p. 545; similarly in Book 1, 27, p. 18.

51. See p. 60.

52. Moltke's military correspondence (General Staff: 1902), Vol. 4, p. 188.

53. See p. 60.

54. Book 8, Chapter 6b, p. 566. A more detailed elucidation, *ibid.,* p. 567: "It is true that the political element does not descend deeply into the details of war. One does not mount guards and conduct patrols by political considerations, but the influence of the political element is all the more decisive in the design of the whole war, of individual campaigns and even battles."

55. In Book 1, Chapters 1, 8, p. 7, war potential is briefly mentioned in these terms: "The land with its area and population"; but the former is viewed only as a theater of war, the latter as a source of recruitment.

56. Ludendorff too noted this neglect, in *Der totale Krieg* (1935), pp. 27f. This is in accord with the utter failure to offer any moral-political justification for war, and it is in this respect that the book differs most conspicuously from all earlier philosophies of war. At the very outset (Chapter 1, p. 2) the question of the purpose of war is coolly consigned to the responsibility of politics as "something that does not belong to war proper." There is only one hint of the educational mission of war, which was once praised so highly in Clausewitz's early notes and letters. In Book 3, Chapter 6, near the end, he says that bold strategy is today the only possible means to educate the people to militancy and soldierly dash.

57. Only once does he casually mention that "political mass agitation may engender such tension in two nations or states, such an accumulation of hostile elements, that a very slight political motive may bring forth an effect far beyond its natural scope, indeed a veritable explosion" (Book 4, Chapter 1, p. 11). For the rest, as far as I can see, there is talk of only the "natural sloth" *(Inertie)* of the masses.

58. Book 1, Chapter 1, pp. 23-24. The expression is so vague and general that one cannot be certain of the justice of later interpretations, for example by the General Staff under Moltke, namely to the effect that politics must make no demands that conflict with military needs (i.e., continuation of a victorious campaign until the enemy forces are destroyed). A later passage, referring to the campaigns of 1799, *Hinterlassene Werke* (2nd ed.; 1858), Part 2, Chapter 6, p. 326 goes somewhat further: "In no field other than warfare are means and end so constantly and mutually interdependent. No matter how appropriately political intent may lend

things their initial direction, the means—that is to say combat—can never be regarded as a total instrument. A thousand motives may shoot out from its abundant vitality, and these may become more important and imperious than the original political motives ever were." Yet this is merely meant to establish that wars cannot be conducted by a remote civilian cabinet (as was the case from Vienna in 1799), but only from the headquarters of the commanding general. This point is already made in *On War,* Book 8, Chapter 6b, p. 570, Paragraph 1.

59. Book 8, Chapter 6b, p. 569. The words here put in quotation marks were emphasized by Clausewitz himself.

60. These are Clausewitz's own words—Book 8, Chapter 3b, pp. 551ff.

61. This original wording of the first edition (Book 8, Chapter 6b) was restored in the first Hahlweg edition, contrary to the following version in all subsequent editions (since the 2nd, undertaken by Count Brühl, Clausewitz's brother-in-law): ". . . enabling him to participate in its deliberations and decisions at crucial moments." Gisb. Beyerhaus, in "Der ursprüngliche Clausewitz," *Wehrwissenschaftliche Rundschau* (March, 1953), views this as a fundamental alteration, to which he devotes an entire essay!

62. See next chapter, on the war of 1815.

63. See the essay, "Umtriebe" (1819-1823?), in H. Rothfels (ed.), *Politische Schriften und Briefe,* pp. 194f.

64. *Vom Kriege,* Book 8, Chapter 6b, pp. 570ff.

65. Letter to Gneisenau, September 9, 1824 (Pertz-Delbrück: *Gneisenau,* v. 504): "The main notion underlying the state is defense against the external enemy. All else can be, strictly speaking, regarded as *faux frais.*" Clausewitz was able to envisage the unification of Germany as achievable only by the sword—" . . . when one of its states subjugates all the others" ("Umtriebe," *loc. cit.,* p. 171). His opinion concerning the efforts to politicalize the nation was scathing. He thought it downright pathological to invest a country with the kind of restless spirit that "will not allow citizens to sleep at night for worry of what the government did yesterday, does today, and will do tomorrow." This would only encourage government by cliques, while "the mass of the people will always remain no more than gawking spectators" (*ibid.,* p. 176).

66. See p. 60.

Notes to Chapter 4

1. Further details about Gneisenau's political ideology and secret political ambitions will be found in my essay, "Gneisenau und die deutsche Freiheitsidee," in the collection *Philosophie und Geschichte* (Tübingen, 1932), No. 37, from which I quote passages in the following. References will be found there.

2. For the historical context of the plans for the patriotic resurgence of 1808 and the attitude of Stein, see my biography of him, Vol. 2, Chapter 11.

3. An unpublished dissertation by a student of mine, Ulrich Meurer, "Die Rolle nationaler Leidenschaft der Massen in der Erhebung von 1813 gegen Napoleon" (Freiburg, 1953), uses abundant source material to demonstrate that the vaunted spontaneous "resurgence" of 1813 actually drew on only relatively insignificant military forces; and that so far as the masses were concerned there was no question of "popular hatred" of Napoleonic rule, in effective political or military terms.

4. See p. 53.

5. H. von Srbik: *Metternich, der Staatsmann und der Mensch* (1925), Vol. 1, Book 3.

6. W. von Unger, *Blücher* (1908), Vol. 2, pp. 139, 155; Pertz-Delbrück, *Gneisenau* (1880), Vol. 4, p. 146 and *passim.*

7. See the correspondence between Metternich and Schwarzenberg in *Österreichs Teilnahme an den Befreiungskriegen,* edited by Prince Richard Metternich-Winneburg and Freiherr Alfons von Klinkowström (1887), Appendix: "From Allied Army Headquarters," pp. 768-834; also G. Roloff, *Politik und Kriegführung während des Feldzuges von 1814* (1891). For Stein's attitude, see my biography of him, Vol. 2, pp. 239ff.

8. See my biography of Stein, Vol. 2, Chapters 16 and 17.

9. See my biography of Stein, Vol. 1, pp. 445ff. and Vol. 1, *passim*. Also the unpublished dissertation by my student K. Kindler, "Die Entstehung des neudeutschen Nationalismus in den Befreiungskriegen" (Freiburg, 1950).

10. Pertz-Delbrück, Vol. 4, p. 169.

11. *Ibid.*, p. 150, letter to Stein, January 9, 1814; and p. 289, letter to Gibson, November 19, 1814.

12. Correspondence with Clausewitz, February 18, 27, 1815, in Pertz-Delbrück, Vol. 4, p. 322. On the historical-political context of these plans, see Friedrich Meinecke, *Hermann von Boyen*, Vol. 2, pp. 17f.

13. Letter to Hardenberg, May 15, 1814, *loc cit.*, Vol. 4, pp. 254f.

14. See Blücher's letter to his cousin Blücher-Altona of April 26, 1815, in the letters of Blücher, edited by W. von Unger (1913), p. 269. The famous phrase recurs again and again, for example in the petition to the King of June 24, 1815, drafted by Grolman–von Conrady, *Grolman* (1895), Vol. 2, p. 318; and also in Blücher's well-known Paris toast, about which von Nostitz tells in his diary (*Kriegsgeschichtliche Einzelschriften*, Vol. 6, p. 70). See also Varnhagen van Ense, *Denkwürdigkeiten und vermischte Schriften* (1864), Vol. 7, pp. 169f.–though the account given there is rather confused. The outward events of the conflict are described, without any proper effort at analysis or interpretation, in a disseration by W. Petonke: *Der Konflikt zwischen Preussens Staats- und Heeresleitung... Juli-November 1815* (Greifswald, 1906). G. Wohlers, in *Die staatsrechtliche Stellung des Generalstabs in Preussen und dem Deutschen Reich* (1921), pp. 22ff., seeks to explain the bitterness of the conflict from the fact that Blücher's general staff was not under firm leadership by the war minister. Actually, this was not a case of organizational flaws, but of differences that went far deeper. Boyen, the war minister, apparently regarded Blücher as an ally and sympathizer in the struggle against the diplomats–see Grolman's letter to Boyen of July 17, 1815, in Conrady's *Grolman*, p. 341.

15. Nostitz's account in von Ollech, *Geschichte des Feldzugs von 1815* (1876), p. 298; see also von Müffling: *Aus meinem Leben* (1885), p. 237.

16. Blücher's letters, edited by W. von Unger (1913), p. 289, letter to his wife of June 26, 1815.

17. Letter to Gibson, November 19, 1814, Pertz-Delbrück, Vol. 4, p. 289. See also the interesting critical remarks on Castlereagh's Note of September 2, 1815, *ibid.*, pp. 464ff., and the petition to the King of July 8, 1815, *ibid.*, pp. 574ff.

18. Letter to Müffling, June 29, 1815, Pertz-Delbrück, Vol. 4, p. 544. Young E. L. von Gerlach's profoundly held Christian convictions are shown by his bitter struggle against the patriots' mood of hate and vengeance, as entertained especially by Grolman–see *Aufzeichnungen*, Vol. 1, pp. 86ff., and Leonie von Keyserling, *Studien zu den Entwicklungsjahren der Brüder Gerlach* (Monograph No. 36; Heidelberg, 1913), pp. 56ff.

19. Conrady, *Grolman*, Vol. 2, p. 344; *ibid.*, p. 341.

20. *Ibid.*, pp. 367f. The italics are mine. This memorial is found also in Nostitz's diary, *loc. cit.*, p. 92; and in the letters of Blücher, edited by von Unger (1933) pp. 320f.

21. Reported by H. Ulmann, "Die Anklage des Jacobinismus in Preussen im Jahre 1815," *Historische Zeitschrift*, Vol. 95, p. 442.

22. See, however, Chapter 5 on the beginning of reaction in the army.

23. This apparently also explains his reassuring letter to Blücher on July 29, 1815, Pertz-Delbrück, Vol. 4, p. 595.

24. Pertz-Delbrück, *Gneisenau*, Vol. 4, pp. 581f.

25. See von Müffling, *Aus meinem Leben* (1855), pp. 219, 225ff., 231. These rather disgruntled memoirs are among the most interesting reports from the time of the Wars of Liberation. They display with surprising candor the contrast between a general staff officer of consistently calculating objectivity, trained in the school of Scharnhorst, to weigh all the circumstances with the greatest care, yet possessing

personal dash and always willing to take the initiative; and the imaginative optimist and enthusiast Gneisenau, whose temper was easily aroused but who also tended to become confused and uncertain. Gneisenau is here characterized with all his virtues as well as his weaknesses–his disinclination to allow "sober truth to destroy comfortable self-deception"; the excesses in his demands as in his temperament; a certain lack of strict objectivity and self-control. Müffling had no sympathy whatever for Gneisenau's penchant for journalistic effect, describing his style as too flowery and his patriotic passion and political bent as strange and disturbing. To Müffling Gneisenau was "the head of a party [the *Tugendbündler*] that had its seat in the army" (p. 47). Withal Müffling himself was by no means untouched by the spirit of the resurgence–quite the contrary. In his memorial of July 5, 1821, he defended the institution of the *Landwehr* against reactionary designs (*Historische Zeitschrift,* Vol. 70 [1893], pp. 282ff.); and this document is one of the most impressive testimonials *sui generis*–although, or perhaps because, Müffling does not close his eyes to the *Landwehr*'s technical deficiencies. It seems to me that the essence of Müffling's criticism of Gneisenau and the spirit at Blücher's headquarters has been completely missed in the literature to date, including in essence E. Weniger's most recent characterization, "Goethe und die Generäle," *Jahrbuch des Freien Deutschen Hochstifts* (Frankfurt, 1936-1940), pp. 479ff., with an interesting supplement on pp. 532ff. The parallelism Weniger finds with Knesebeck completely misses the point, to my mind. From the general staff files I have studied, I conclude that Müffling's term as chief (1821-1829) was of the greatest importance for the further development of the general staff. Unlike even Clausewitz, Müffling was the first to regard general staff officers not merely as executive organs but as advisers who shared responsibility with their commanders. This is shown in his key directive of January 14, 1822, though this was not fully implemented until Moltke succeeded in doing so during the wars of unification. Moltke himself entertained a highly favorable opinion of this predecessor of his–see Kessel (ed.), *Gespräche,* p. 89, after A. Mels, *Erlebtes und Erdachtes* (1885), Vol. 2, pp. 190ff.

Grolman, whom Gneisenau finally chose as quartermaster in 1815, was an altogether different type–one in whom political passion was really driven to its extreme. He apparently bears the brunt of the responsibility for exacerbating the conflict in Paris in 1815–see *Tagebuch des Generals Grafen Nostitz,* Vol. 2, pp. 68ff, 80, 87 and *passim* (General Staff monographs on war history, 1885), Vol. 6.

26. It is quite remarkable in this context that when Gneisenau and Clausewitz in 1831 entered into a direct professional relationship as commander-in-chief and chief of staff, differences arose between them not unlike those that once existed between Gneisenau and Müffling. Clausewitz speaks of a lack of logic in the thinking of Gneisenau, while the latter found his adviser too critical and "lacking in faith." See the correspondence between Carl and Marie von Clausewitz, edited by Linnebach (1916), pp. 455, 461, 478.

27. "In the light of history, the English will have played the finest role in this disaster. They do not seem to have come here with a passion for vengeance and retribution, but rather like chastising masters, with a chilly pride and with absolute integrity–in sum, they are of higher mind than we." Clausewitz to his wife, July 12, 1815–see also diary entries of July, 1815, both in K. Linnebach (ed.), *Carl und Marie von Clausewitz–Ein Lebensbild* (1916), pp. 395ff. Also Schwartz; *Clausewitz,* Vol. 2, pp. 158ff., and the collection, Rothfels (ed.), *Politische Schriften und Briefe* (1922), pp. 121ff.

28. Pertz-Delbrück, Vol. 4, p. 544; Müffling, *Aus meinem Leben* (1855), p. 239.

29. Letter to Countess Voss, August 2, 1815, Pertz-Delbrück, Vol. 4, p. 599.

Notes to Chapter 5

1. This is especially well formulated in an opinion of Müffling of 1821, published by Friedrich Meinecke in the *Historische Zeitschrift,* Vol. 70, p. 284: "When the same

278 *Notes to pp. 93-119*

danger fails to exact the same contributions from the great and the lowly, when there are castes that must do everything for the common good and castes required to do nothing, no pure concept of a fatherland can develop; and when there is no such concept, love of king remains a mere article of faith." On Müffling's conservative but moderately progressive political attitude see the documentary notes by L. Dehio in "Wittgenstein und das letzte Jahrzehnt Friedrich Wilhelms III," *Forschungen zur brandenburgisch-preussischen Geschichte,* Vol. 35 (1923), pp. 216ff.

2. A study on military law by Erich Schwinge, "Gehorsam und Verantwortung," in *Mitteilungen des Universitäts-Bundes Marburg* (1939), No. 3, deals insightfully with the perpetual antinomy between unconditional obedience in the middle and lower command echelons and the virtually unlimited freedom of decision at the highest level. Readers may sense that the section that follows bears the mark of its time of origin, 1943.

3. See General von Rabenau, *Von Geist und Seele des Soldaten* (1941).

4. See Hegel, *Grundlinien der Philosophie des Rechts,* Paragraph 328: "True, to stake one's life means more than merely to fear death, yet it is purely negative, hence lacks goal and value on its own. What gives meaning to valor are the positive elements of purpose and content. Robbers and murderers too have the courage to stake their lives, for the purpose of committing crimes, as have adventurers for purposes sufficient to themselves, and still others." According to Hegel, only dedication to the common good "invests valor with a higher spirit."

5. Part 3 of Chapter 8 will deal with the repercussions of the Wars of Liberation on nineteenth-century German philosophy of history and war.

6. Rühle von Lilienstern, *Aufsätze über Gegenstände und Ereignisse des Kriegswesens* (Mittler, Berlin, 1818), Vol. 1. Essay No. 4 is entitled "An Apologia for War"; No. 5 "The Relationship between War and Politics." Both essays formed part of a book, *Vom Kriege,* published in 1814. No. 4 is also found in Schlegel's *Deutsches Museum* (1813), Vol. 3, pp. 158-173 and 177-192, there signed Colonel von Rühl. A dissertation by Gertrud Köhler (Berlin, 1922), sponsored by Friedrich Meinecke, has demonstrated that Rühle's remarks were by no means original, and followed Adam Müller's *Elemente der Staatskunst* almost slavishly, a good deal of the time word for word. Yet beyond these parts, especially in the sections on popular military education, the common intellectual concerns of the resurgence are reflected quite well. Essay No. 5, for example, contends that war provides as much sinful temptation as it offers occasion to display heroism and a sense of duty. "Whoever survives this dual ordeal by fire is consecrated for life; and a nation that keeps its honor and moral dignity inviolate in war gives unequivocal testimony of its inner nobility and national integrity." Only under the lash of war, moreover, "are the indissoluble bonds of a nationhood engendered. The rot and poison of peace evaporate in its flames, the savage is tamed, the soft are steeled. Only deprivation teaches enjoyment." Superficially these formulations are reminiscent of the youthful Clausewitz who would "lash this lazy brute" by means of war (p. 50). Yet Clausewitz is far more concerned with the mere acquisition of purely military virtues, while Rühle von Lilienstern wants the ordeal of war to train people also for peace, i.e., civic virtue. "It is up to national policies of education to see to it that war really exerts this fortunate effect on the character of the people, instead of leading to brutalization and alienation from the virtues of peace." In war destiny itself is the great taskmaster, and it is the duty of popular education to clip the savage urges that sprout in wartime, while fostering the virtues that likewise burgeon then. Military and civil virtues must supplement and balance each other. "As a nation is trained for war in peacetime, so must it be trained for peace in wartime." Rühle von Lilienstern still takes it for granted that the church will share the army's educational mission, for "without religion there can be no truly mandatory community for man. All national sentiment must be based on religion" (p. 192). This is a highly characteristic trait of the freedom fighters around Freiherr vom Stein, to whose circle Rühle belonged. Equally noteworthy and characteristic is the blend of

political morality with its military counterpart, projecting common goals in education, the inculcation of courage, obedience, and honor. "Courage—let us understand one another—is the soul's clear and ever-present disposition to freedom in all her forms. A sense of triumph befalls man when stalwart habit has persuaded him to love the limits imposed on him by law, and to acknowledge them freely, aware of his power to overturn them." This would seem to be the very opposite of "blind discipline."

In 1813 Rühle von Lilienstern was a member of Blücher's staff, after which he became the highly successful organizer of all the German armed forces, in Stein's administrative council. From 1821 to 1837 he was chief of the Prussian general staff, under Müffling as chief of the army general staff. He concluded his career as director of the war academy in Berlin and inspector general of military training. His writings are of amazing versatility, though largely unoriginal. The *Militärwochenblatt*, which he founded in 1816, in its supplement for October-December, 1947, carried, by way of an obituary, an anonymous biography and incomplete bibliography. Heinrich von Treitschke, who praises the book *Vom Krieg* in rather hyperbolic terms as "the scientific program of the modern German army system" (*Deutsche Geschichte,* Vol. 1, pp. 589f.) characteristically cites from Clausewitz only those passages directed against Kant's doctrine of peace everlasting, together with a few programmatic sentences, in which there is mention of the "militarization of the nations." Rühle was on friendly terms with Heinrich von Kleist, Adam Müller, and Friedrich von Gentz. He was for years in the Weimar service and belonged to Goethe's circle. He embodied perhaps most strikingly the combination of military training and general education in the liberal arts that was so characteristic of the resurgence. See also his latest characterization by the pen of Erich Weniger, in *Jahrbuch des Freien Deutschen Hochstifts* (Frankfurt, 1936-1940), pp. 481ff., 532ff. The book by L. Sauzin, *Rühle von Lilienstern et son Apologie de la Guerre,* was not accessible to me.

7. Conversation with Steffens, according to an official report to Hardenberg of April 19, 1813, in Lehmann, *Scharnhorst,* Vol. 2, p. 560. Steffen's memoirs (*Was ich erlebte,* 1840 to 1844) particularly exemplify the initial remoteness from the military system of the educated German of the age of Goethe, as do many memoirs from the time of the resurgence. Oddly enough, opposition to standing armies is found in Gneisenau too—their immense cost which serves only to "unnerve and corrupt the people," while helping to destroy their social consciousness and militant spirit. See his memorial of August, 1808, *Historische Zeitschrift,* Vol. 86, pp. 92f.; also Pertz, *Gneisenau,* Vol. 1, p. 320 (note from 1807). This passage was already being exploited by the liberal opposition during the time of the conflict.

8. See Friedrich Meinecke, *Boyen,* Vol. 2, pp. 143ff. This included the University of Breslau, where the uprising of the young students had begun in 1813.

9. *Loc. cit.,* pp. 53, 106. This basic attitude is not discernible in the detailed discussion of Rotteck's thinking by R. Höhn, *Verfassungskampf und Heereseid. Der Kampf des Bürgertums um das Heer 1815-1850,*pp. 19ff. I received much help and stimulation from this valuable work of scholarship with its rich harvest from forgotten publications and archives. Rotteck's protest, by the way, had its precursor in the writings of Benjamin Constant, *Über die Gewalt,* trans. by H. Zbinden (Berne, 1942), pp. 37ff., Chapter 1, p. 10; and *Cours de politique constitutionelle, esquisse de constitution* (1814), German translation by von Buss in the complete political works of Constant, Vol. 4.

10. *Ibid.,* p. 54.

11. *Loc. cit.,* pp. 86ff.

12. *Ibid.,* p. 69.

13. The militiaman was to retain the franchise, but the professional soldier was not to exercise it (p. 116).

14. Yet, significantly, Rotteck hoped the people's representatives would send professional men to the front only in the event of "extreme emergency," since their services

were particularly hard to replace. See pp. 131f., note.

15. *Loc. cit.,* pp. 190f.

16. It is highly significant that Scharnhorst's first drafts of 1807-1808 for the creation of a militia *(Provinzialtruppe)* in addition to the standing army still bear a close resemblance to Rotteck's proposals. The new formation was to be composed expressly, not of standing army veterans, but solely of the prosperous classes, in complete autonomy, and these were to provide their own equipment and maintenance. It was to serve under elected officers of the educated bourgeoisie rather than under regular army officers. It was, in other words, to be a true civilian militia. This is in part motivated by the need to lend the new units the semblance of being mere police formations, but the main reason was undoubtedly the desire to establish them in the spirit of patriotic volunteers. The militia would never attain this spirit, we read, "if it must first run the gauntlet of the regular army, if its autonomy is paralyzed by presumptuous pressures." Scharnhorst was not yet able to envisage that the educated citizen might pass through the constraints of the despised traditional army. Also highly significant is this passage, suppressed in earlier publications: "No fears need be entertained that such a militia, formed from the propertied classes, might become dangerous. ... Only a militia formed from the lower classes might give cause for anxiety." These latter classes, therefore, were to provide the recruits for the standing army, as before! This was almost certainly aimed at the prejudices of Frederic William III. Still, it confirms anew how the corporate pride of the upper classes was taken for granted even in reform circles. Draft of a report for the king by the commission on military reorganization of March 15, 1803: *Die Reorganisation des Preussischen Staates unter Stein und Hardenberg,* Part 2: *Das Preussische Heer vom Tilsiter Frieden bis zur Befreiung 1807-1814,* Vol. 1, edited by Vaupel (1938), in Prussian State Archives, Vol. 94, p. 321; see also Lehmann, *Scharnhorst,* Vol. 2, pp. 91f.

17. See the account by Freiherr Colmar von der Goltz, *Kriegsgeschichte Deutschlands im 19. Jahrhundert* (1914), Vol. 2, pp. 18ff.; and, for the following, especially Friedrich Meinecke, *Boyen,* Vol. 2. An excellent account, distinguished by the precision of its data, of the slow obsolescence of the institutions of 1814 is given by Rudolf von Gneist, *Die Militärvorlage von 1892 und der preussische Verfassungskonflikt von 1862-1866* (1893). The memoirs of Julius von Hartmann (1882), Vol. 1, especially pp. 140ff., give a particularly graphic account of the increasing ossification of the army, including the war academy, and of the growing sterility of intellectual life in Berlin in the final decades of Frederic William III.

18. Sir Robert Wilson, *Private Diary of Travels . . . with the European Armies, 1812-1814* edited by H. Randolph (London, 1861), Vol. 2, p. 229. No date is given for the conversation, but it is mentioned in connection with a discussion with Czar Alexander, which took place on November 17, 1813. Pertz-Delbrück, *Gneisenau,* Vol. 4, p. 162, reproduces the quotation in a somewhat exaggerated translation by Th. Bernhardi.

19. Müffling's own attitude is best exemplified in his letter to Gneisenau from Paris on February 15, 1816. Pertz-Delbrück, *Gneisenau,* Vol. 5, pp. 84ff. It is anything but reactionary, but plainly shows an aversion to propagandists like Arndt, Jahn, and Görres, and concern for their influence on army morale. In his memoirs Müffling repeatedly refers to Gneisenau as a "party chief " (e.g., pp. 47, 195).

20. *Correspondance diplomatique du Comte Pozzo di Borgo et du Comte de Nesselrode* (1890), 219ff. This was on October 5, 17, 1815.

21. Gneisenau reported this to Boyen on September 16, 1815–Pertz-Delbrück, Vol. 4, p. 631. See also *ibid.,* Vol. 4, p. 612; further Vol. 5, p. 85 (Clausewitz). According to Stein's notes (in Botzenhart, *Nachlasswerk,* Vol. 5, p. 273), the statement was made in the presence of the adjutants general, especially Repnin. According to Nostitz's diary *(loc. cit.,* Vol. 6, p. 71), it was made by the Grand Duke Constantine rather than the czar himself.

22. Documentation in Pertz-Delbrück, Vol. 5, pp. 22f.

23. Precisely because its detached criticism of the ideology of early liberalism is based purely on considerations of power politics, the account by Clausewitz is the most impressive of all. See especially his essay *Umtriebe* in Schwartz, *loc. cit.,* Vol. 2, pp. 200ff.; in the collection by Rothfels, pp. 153ff. Rothfels rightly rejects the older dating of 1819, on which Rothfels reports *ibid.,* p. 242. See also Schwartz, Vol. 2, pp. 288-293.

24. This was precisely what Freiherr vom Stein had in mind when he wrote in his memorial of November 5, 1822 (plan for a provincial-corporate constitution): "What mainly renders pure bureaucracy pernicious is the fact that it paralyzes the social spirit, which arises only from direct participation in public life, growing in the first instance from a penchant for association and local patriotism, and thence step by step to the level of true patriotism. At present, moreover, military and civil institutions are at odds. The latter paralyze the social spirit, the former are based on it, for they demand, above all, the sacrifice of life and fortune for national defense. The defects of the bureaucracy can be eliminated, or at least mitigated by constitutions on a local, county, and provincial basis. . . ." Botzenhart, *Freiherr vom Stein—Briefwechsel, Denkschriften und Aufzeichnungen,* Vol. 6, pp. 120f. It is not immediately clear how C. Schmitt in *Staatsgefüge und Zusammenbruch des Zweiten Reichs* (1934) could have invoked this quotation in support of his contentions. See also F. Hartung, *Historische Zeitschrift,* Vol. 151, p. 531.

25. For the crisis in the autumn of 1862 see Zechlin, *Bismarck und die Grundlegung der deutschen Grossmacht* (1930), pp. 291 ff., 324 ff., as well as the next chapter. For William's position after 1833, see *Militärische Schriften weiland Kaiser Wilhelms des Grossen* (1897), Vol. 1, pp. 152ff., 176ff.; Vol. 2, pp. 175ff., 453, and many other passages (see index under *Dienstzeit*); also E. Berner (ed.), *Kaiser Wilhelms des Grossen Briefe, Reden und Schriften,* Vol. 1, pp. 85, 110 and *passim*.

26. *Militärische Schriften,* Vol. 1, p. 366. The italics are mine.

27. *Militärische Schriften,* Vol. 1, pp. 337, 351. Boyen's memorial of 1841 on the *Landwehr* has an archaic and often purely rhetorical ring, and in objective respects it simply flounders about.

28. In 1833 he reproached the victors of 1815 with having gravely compromised the future of the monarchies of Europe by acknowledging the revolution rather than extirpating it—letter to Natzmer, April 1, 1833, in *Briefe, Reden und Schriften,* Vol. 1, p. 113; letter to Schöne, September 7, 1840, *ibid.,* p. 145 (see also Gerlach's diary, Vol. 1, p. 105); political memorial of 1845, *ibid.,* Vol. 1, pp. 148ff. (after Treitschke's excerpt).

29. Here too I make reference, for all pertinent details, to the excellent account by R. Höhn with its many original sources, *Verfassungskampf und Heereseid* (1938).

30. This was true, for example, of Moltke—see his letter to his brother Adolf of November 17, 1848, in the selection of Moltke's letters by W. Andreas, Vol. 2, p. 28. Initially even Prince William had generous praise for the loyal stand of the *Landwehr—Militärische Schriften,* Vol. 2, p. 15. Both quotations are also found in E. R. Huber, *Heer und Staat* (1938), p. 174.

31. Deputy Schwenzner, May 29, 1861, stenographic transcript for 1861, p. 1485. For a more extended quotation see G. Wohlers, *Die staatsrechtliche Stellung des Generalstabs* (1921), p. 76, n. 75.

32. A recent compilation of such cases, in part from unpublished documents, will be found in Höhn, *loc. cit.,* pp. 311ff.

33. The following is after Höhn, *loc. cit.,* pp. 222ff., 230ff., K. G. von Rudloff, *Handbuch des preussischen Militärrechts* (1826), Part 1, expecially Paragraphs 478ff., 538ff.

34. Rudloff acknowledges no interposition of moral conscience upon the duty to obey. He mentions "natural, or rather divine law" only in connection with the right of the sovereign state power to mobilize every means for maintaining public order "compatible with the inalienable precepts of natural law" (Paragraph 479).

35. In 1859 aristocrats made up 65 percent of the second lieutenants, 78 percent of the staff officers, and 91 percent of the generals, according to L. Simon, "Der

preussische Konstitutionalismus," in *Demokratische Studien,* edited by Walesrode (1861), p. 8, cited by Zechlin, *loc. cit.,* p. 180. The seniority list of 1861, cited in the stenographic transcript of the chamber of deputies for 1862, Vol. 7 (Appendix 3), p. 1203, names 750 aristocrats and 91 commoners among higher officers of the infantry and calvary, 50 aristocrats and 107 commoners among those of the artillery, engineers, and supply services.

36. Quotations in Höhn, *loc. cit.,* pp. 254 ff., from a work by O. von Platen, 1843, and the *Militär-Literatur-Zeitung* of 1831. See also the liberal criticism, *ibid.,* p. 276, n. 2: "Here no spirit is the finest spirit. It is called discipline."

37. *Militärische Schriften Kaiser Wilhelms,* Vol. 2, pp. 344 ff.; also in *Denkwürdigkeiten aus dem Leben Roons* (5th ed.; 1905), Vol. 1, pp. 521 ff.

38. See the book by Hermann Witte, still the best, *Die Reorganisation des preussischen Heeres durch Wilhelm I* (1910).

39. To investigate the attitude of the officers' corps on the question of national unification prior to 1866 would be indeed a rewarding task. See a dissertation which I sponsored, by Ursula Tempel, "Preussentum und Deutschtum im politischen Empfinden des preussischen Offizierskorps von Jena bis Sedan" (Freiburg, 1945). On the ideological changes within the Prussian officer caste and the struggle for reform of military education, especially in the cadet schools, see Friedrich Meinecke, *Boyen,* Vol. 2, pp. 110 ff., 467 ff., 510 ff., and *passim.*

40. Details in Höhn, *loc. cit.,* pp. 263 ff.

41. Roon's extraordinarily wide learning—contrary to the common oversimplification of his character—is fortunately recognized in Andrea von Harbou: "Dienst und Glauben in der Staatsauffassung Albrecht von Roons," *Neue deutsche Forschungen* (Berlin, 1936), Vol. 95.

42. *Roon als Redner* (1895), Vol. 1, p. 25.

43. This notion too antedates the revolution of 1848—see Höhn, *loc. cit.,* pp. 275 ff. For Roon's view of the army as "a great popular school" and "national academy in general," see *Roon als Redner,* Vol. 1, p. 70 (May 27, 1861), p. 296 (September 16, 1862), Vol. 2, pp. 150 ff. (March 20, 1865), p. 182 (March 23, 1865).

Notes to Chapter 6

1. A tendency to represent them both as closely akin in an ideological sense and to blur the differences between them also emerges from Ad. Wahl, *Studien zur Geschichte der Konfliktszeit* (1914).

2. A cousin of Georg von Vincke and a former general staff officer, personally close to the prince regent.

3. Stenographic transcript of the chamber of deputies for 1859, Vol. 1, pp. 621 ff. (April 2, 1859), and Vol. 3 (Appendix No. 56), p. 378. In the plenary session, von Bockum-Dolffs presented the concern of the liberals at greater length, Vol. 1, p. 626.

4. Stenographic transcript for 1859, Vol. 1, p. 623. This passage went unnoticed by H. Witte, *loc. cit.,* pp. 74 ff. See the alleged statement reported by Leopold von Gerlach, *Denkwürdigkeiten,* Vol. 2, p. 655.

5. Leopold von Gerlach, *Denkwürdigkeiten,* Vol. 2, p. 712. In the military committee of 1860 the contradiction between the military bill and the "binding" assurances of Bonim was sharply criticized.

6. The most important source is the stenographic transcript for 1860, Vol. 5, Appendices, Part 3, No. 171, pp. 1236 ff., report of April 30, 1860, by Stavenhagen. This report is also found in the complete collection of documents of the chamber of deputies (1860), Vol. 5, No. 204. Another report, on the cuts made by the committee in the government bill on May 5, 1860, is found in the Appendices, Part 3, No. 173, pp. 1263 ff., and in the document collection, Vol. 6, No. 229. Also to be consulted is the report of the budget committee of 1860, on the interim appropriation for reorganization (the "stopgap"), on May 9, 1860—Appendix No. 132, pp. 937 ff.

The deliberations of the military committee of 1860 are treated quite thoroughly by Parisius, *Hoverbeck,* Vol. 1, pp. 173ff. The most zealous advocate of the preservation of the *Landwehr* was the aged Harkort, a veteran of 1813-1814. I have also examined the manuscript protocols, some of them extremely detailed, prepared by the Prussian general staff, Arch. Rep. 169 C, Section 52 m 9.

7. See especially the report of the budget committee of May 9, 1860, Appendix 3, p. 937; and Vincke's speech of May 15, 1860, stenographic transcript, Vol. 2, pp. 1122ff.

8. "This was greeted with general approbation," says the report of the budget committee of May 9, 1860–Appendix 3, No. 132, p. 938.

9. Oddly enough, this debate is not mentioned in the manuscript protocols of the sessions, only in Stavenhagen's final report. On March 6, 1860, however, protests by several members against the substitute system are reported (Sheet 101f.). On March 20, Roon spoke of the need for a three-year term "so long as we cannot have a professional army, which is impossible with us" (Sheet 138). On March 24, Lieutenant Colonel von Hartmann, criticizing Stavenhagen's final report, pointed to the French army institutions with their *caisse de dotation* and the strong core of re-enlistees and veteran *troupiers* thus created. "Reduction of the three-year term to two years would lead to a similar institution, the acceptance of substitute service" (Sheet 158). Similar considerations seem to have been in Roon's mind (i.e., replacement of the third year of service by professional soldiers), when he occasionally remarked: "The decision on whether we shall be able to retreat from the three-year term to two years is essentially one of finances" (Sheet 186).

10. In place of 243 battalions of the line, there were to be 162 line and 81 *Landwehr* battalions. In the event of mobilization, the mobile *Landwehr* battalions were to be attached to the infantry as third battalions. In addition, it should be possible to organize one garrison battalion each from the original muster–committee report (Appendices, 3) p. 1242. Apparently there is a typographical error in the text of the report (p. 1242b). Line 14 reads to the effect that each regiment is to consist of three (rather than two) battalions of the line. That only two were meant is already clear from Vincke's speeches in the Prussian chamber of deputies on May 15, 1860 (stenographic transcript, Vol. 2, p. 1123) and September 12, 1862 (stenographic transcript, Vol. 3, p. 1620), as well as from the whole context.

11. To understand this attitude it is useful to bear in mind how small–in comparison to the situation today–was the share of the reserve and *Landwehr* officers. In the mobilization of 1870, 1,990 reserve and 4,279 *Landwehr* officers were called up. They joined a peacetime strength of 13,000 officers on active duty in the North German federal army. Officer losses were greatest in the battles of August, 1870, but by late September replacements still numbered only 574. By May 9, 1871, total officer replacements in the field army ran to 165 reserve, 164 *Landwehr,* and 835 regular. Most of the officers not on active duty belonged to the *Landwehr* battalions, and in 1864 none of these saw front-line service, while in 1870-1871 it was only during the winter battles that some of them were committed. Of the Prussian *Landwehr* battalions, 17 then remained completely immobile, and Moltke had a good deal of trouble in getting Roon to provide a sufficient flow of occupation troops. The lopsided army reorganization of 1860 made itself felt here, and this would have become much more critical had the war lasted longer. The emphasis had been entirely on strengthening the active formations of the standing army, and the *Landwehr* formations had not at all been conceived of as field forces. For that reason too they lacked replacement battalions of their own, which caused considerable trouble when casualties were incurred. The age limit for *Landwehr* service had also been set far too low (at age thirty-two in the Defense Act of 1867), and Roon was reluctant to exceed it by conscription. See Gustaf Lehmann, *Die Mobilmachungen 1870-1871* (1905), pp. 105ff., 158ff. It is virtually certain that the type of organization proposed by Stavenhagen in 1860 would have been far better suited to a mass war, or could have been more easily adapted to it. In the military committee of 1860, the government representative had to cope with

repeated doubts that there would be appropriate use for *Landwehr* officers. He had contemplated a muster of 1,200 officers from the furloughed class for the mobile army, 1,900 for the replacements, and 3,000 for the new *Landwehr* proper, a total of more than 6,000 (manuscript protocols, pp. 83ff.).

12. Leopold von Gerlach, *Denkwürdigkeiten,* Vol. 2, pp. 710ff. Gerlach was downright distressed over the attitude of the liberals. This was scarcely the conflict that had been so ardently anticipated! Gerlach himself regarded the *Landwehr* as a main weapon of liberalism. "The elimination of the standing army was a main axiom of the *Tugendbund,* and Boyen labored manfully to bring it about" (Vol. 2, p. 709). We see that the generation of the Wars of Liberation (Gerlach, Harkort) continued to nurse the old basic conflicts in all their traditional fervor, while these conflicts had long ceased to have much meaning for the younger generation. Roon told Gerlach that the feeble opposition offered by the liberals to the abolition of the *Landwehr* was "soft-hearted humanitarianism" (Did he perhaps mean a desire to spare the older men?). Perhaps the following conversation between Bernhardi and Max Duncker of June 12, 1861, belongs in this context. Duncker: "The new army reorganization could be pushed through with ease ... if some concessions were made in minor respects. The 81 replacement battalions that must be organized could be easily called *Landwehr,* and that would satisfy those people." Bernhardi: "Do you really think they are as stupid as that?" Duncker (with conviction): "Yes, I do! " Bernhardi, Vol. 4, pp. 139f.

13. Stenographic transcript (1860), Vol. 3, pp. 1576f.

14. *Ibid.,* pp. 1636f.: "The creators of our *Landwehr* based themselves on the words of our Johannes Müller, who said that true freedom rests on two pillars—that citizens are soldiers, and that soldiers are good citizens." Here indeed was a last genuine echo of the ideas of 1813!

15. George von Vincke, September 12, 1862, stenographic transcript, Vol. 3, p. 1620. Vincke expressly declared that it had not been the objections by the government— which indeed carried little conviction—that had persuaded him that the committee proposal was impractical. For the mood of the country see also Sybel's statements in Bernhardi, *Tagebücher,* Vol. 3, p. 321 (April 17, 1860). Discussions recorded by Bernhardi (Vol. 4, pp. 26, 66 and *passim*) tend to show that even in the provinces there was much regret over the passing of the *Landwehr.*

16. Stenographic transcript (1862), Vol. 3, pp. 1567, 1586, 1662f., 1696. Georg von Vincke, in the military committee of 1860, similarly disapproved of describing the *Landwehr* as a "bastion of freedom." The army must at all costs be kept above politics, he said (manuscript protocols, March 20, 1860, Sheet 140).

17. This was made particularly plain by Max Duncker and Sybel on November 18, 1861—Heyderhoff-Wentzcke, *Deutscher Liberalismus,* Vol. 1, p. 70. I fail to understand the distinction between people's army of the resurgence and citizens' army of the 1860's drawn by E. R. Huber in *Heer und Staat* (1938), p. 202. Gneist's speech in the diet makes the ideals he envisaged clear—a free, militant people on the ancient Germanic model. His essay of 1893 on the army bill of 1892 is, in its historical part, far removed from any glorification of the old *Landwehr.* Most of the Old Liberals can be viewed as the intellectual heirs of Dahlmann, whose view emerges with particular clarity from this sentence in his *Politik* (1835): "A parliament that commands the armed forces spells the crown's downfall" (*Klassiker der Politik,* Vol. 12, p. 111).

18. They included Grolman, Krauseneck, Müffling, Witzleben, Prittwitz (who wrote a pamphlet on the subject—see *Militärische Schriften Kaiser Wilhelms,* Vol. 2, pp. 1867f., where it is given anonymously, and also L. Schneider, *Kaiser Wilhelm I,* Vol. 1, p. 113), Peucker, Webern (Bernhardi, Vol. 5, p. 13) *et al.* As late as 1862 a commission of general officers, with Moltke as a member, favored the possibility of shortening the service term in practice to two-and-a-half years, together with a generous furlough policy *(Militärische Schriften Kaiser Wilhelms,* Vol. 2, pp. 467-469). For the liberal motivation, see Bernhardi, Vol. 3, p. 318.

In this connection I cite a passage from an unpublished letter in my possession, which Moritz von Blanckenburg, leader of the parliamentary conservative party, wrote to Roon in March, 1862: "Your most vulnerable spot is money! It is not true at all that the patriots burn with the desire to vote more taxes for the army budget—this will be done only if there is no alternative. On the whole, army appropriations are unpopular. The new formations are even more unpopular, on account of the 25 percent surtax. I should think that you new ministers [Roon and von der Heydt] would win the game for good if you succeeded, first, in showing the country you mean real improvement rather than to bring back servility, whip, and truncheon; and second, in presenting the defense budget as a single appropriation. Bits and pieces make only for mischief. They are an irresistible temptation to the conscientious deputy to keep his hands on the purse strings and examine the urgency of each item. I remember how I myself almost gagged at having to vote half a million for, of all things, your little toys and playthings, frills that bring a smile to the face of almost any soldier! Third, if you make your bow by eliminating the 25 percent surtax. The liberals have always brought more taxes, while the conservatives were the first to abolish the 25 percent surtax (this goes specifically to my credit), and if the conservative government now were to start out with such an abolition, it would have an enormous effect; and apart from the intrinsic merits of such a measure, it would grease the ways for the defense budget."

19. Instead of 243 battalions discharging 170 men each year, there would have been 162 with 255 each. Both rates would yield 41,310 each year. Total battalion strength in either case would have been 510.

20. He simply cited the Defense Act of 1814, which provided for a three-year term, or disputed the competence of the deputies to deal with questions of military organization. He also put his own interpretation on the statements by the military experts adduced by the liberals, or simply hinted that the last word had not been said in this much-disputed question, which did not even touch the heart of the reorganization problem, etc., etc. In judging the actual value of the three-year term it should be borne in mind that in the three wars of unification most of the infantrymen had undergone only two-and-a-half years of training, for since 1862 there had been an extensive policy of winter furloughs during the third service year, for reasons of economy.

21. See Note 17, above, and Bernhardi's criticism, in his diary, Vol. 3, p. 263 (February 15, 1860); for the cuts by the military committee, Appendix 3, No. 173. Very dubious were the cuts in the peacetime supply services, for their absence had been extremely harmful in 1849 and 1859. This error was corrected by the committee itself in 1861.

22. Vincke-Olbendorf to Bernhardi, March 11, 1860, diary, Vol. 3, pp. 284f. This was partly confirmed by Voigts-Rhetz, head of the "general war department" in the war ministry, March 16, 1860 (*ibid.*, pp. 295f.), and even more plainly, on April 4, 1860, by Lieutenant Colonel Hartmann (*ibid.*, pp. 309f.). Similar concern was voiced by General Etzel on April 28, 1860 (*ibid.*, p. 325).

23. Bernhardi, Vol. 3, p. 276 and *passim.* By the time the diet assembled, the ministry itself had prepared public opinion for a defense budget of only six rather than nine million thalers.

24. Stenographic transcript for 1860, Vol. 2, pp. 1113ff., May 15, 1860.

25. See Bernhardi, Vol. 3, pp. 326f. Lieutenant Colonel Hartmann insisted that Manteuffel was systematically sabotaging the acceptance of *Landwehr* officers who were commoners into the officers' corps when its strength was being increased. *Ibid.*, p. 331: Discrimination against officer candidates from liberal commoner families (also Vol. 4, pp. 67f.). Moltke too held the view that care needed to be exercised in the acceptance of commoner candidates unless "they had the kind of convictions that must be preserved in the army" (*ibid.*, Vol. 4, p. 166).

26. Bernhardi, Vol. 3, p. 272 (February 27, 1860), and p. 290 (March 15, 1860).

27. *Ibid.*, p. 281.

28. For Heinrich von Sybel, see Bernhardi, Vol. 3, pp. 313, 320f.; for Max Duncker, *ibid.*, pp. 321f., and Johann Schultze (ed.), *Politischer Briefwechsel* (1923). For Ludwig Häusser, see Bernhardi, Vol. 3, p. 308. For Johann Gustav Droysen, see his letters, edited by Hübner; for Hermann Baumgarten, see his famous essay, "Der deutsche Liberalismus. Eine Selbstkritik," 1860, in *Historisch-politische Aufsätze und Reden* (1894), pp. 128ff. Baumgarten's spirited "self-criticism" evidently underrated the opposition of the regent and his entourage against any consistently liberal course. Yet many of the questions he put have not been answered to this day. The attitude of the Auerswald ministry toward the regent and the Old Liberals, in particular, still required documentary clarification.

29. Bernhardi, Vol. 3, p. 320.

30. In addition to the parliamentary debates, compare what Bernhardi (Vol. 4, pp. 320f., 323) has to say on the subject of a conservative declaration of loyalty to the king, April, 1860.

31. President Wentzel, Bernhardi, Vol. 3, p. 331. Bernhardi himself said that the proposals of the Stavenhagen committee were impractical "adventurism," though he gave no particular reasons. He apparently thought they simply meant a return to the system of 1815-1859 (*ibid.*, pp. 306, 330f.—see also Vol. 4, pp. 110f., where there is talk of "silly opposition").

32. Andrea von Harbou, *Dienst und Glaube in der Staatsauffassung Roons* (1936), p. 67, and other authorities suggest that the liberal ministers introduced the defense bill in the house at the last moment before Roon was appointed war minister, but this is wrong. Roon was appointed on December 4, 1859, while the bill was introduced on February 10, 1860. Because of war contingencies I was unfortunately unable to examine the protocols of the ministry.

33. Stenographic transcript for 1860, Vol. 2, pp. 1122ff., June 15, 1860. If such control was to be more than a mere formality, it should certainly have included a voice in the matter of the volume of recruitment and thus service liability generally. E. R. Huber, *Heer und Staat*, pp. 207f., remarks: "Had the chamber of deputies prevailed with its demand for a two-year term, it rather than the king would have set the trend and substance of the army reorganization. Military command power would have been 'parliamentarized' and a parliamentary system would have succeeded the independent power of the crown." This had been precisely the viewpoint of the military cabinet since mid-summer 1860. It felt that any participation in organizational matters would mean "parliamentarizing" the command power. If this view were correct, the royal government should never have offered a service bill in the diet, either in 1860 or on the four subsequent occasions down to 1866—nor, for that matter, should have Bismarck in the North German Reichstag in 1867. The fact that this nevertheless was done certainly did not bespeak any softness in the face of a power challenge by the parliament. It was the expression of a genuine constitutional desire, voiced also by the liberals (and especially the jurist Rudolf von Gneist), to provide a legislative anchorage for the basic questions of army reorganization rather than have them debated year after year. Manifestly there was a paradox in the request to the diet for express participation in the army reorganization by the approval of a bill, while at the same time the right of the diet to participate in that reorganization was challenged.

34. Stenographic transcript, Appendix 3, p. 1244, report of April 30, 1860.

35. Stenographic transcript, 1860, Vol. 2, p. 1127, May 15, 1860. Liberal circles suspected that the precipitate formation of the new regiments was intended to provoke the house into an open rupture, an outright rejection of the nine-million-thaler appropriation. Vincke's reproachful remarks were meant to "blow off steam" in the general atmosphere of resentment (Bernhardi, Vol. 3, p. 338). In his initial outrage Roon, nevertheless, was minded to challenge Vincke to a duel with pistols, a design from which Alvensleben and Manteuffel dissuaded him only with difficulty. Instead, he insisted that the Old Liberal ministers should make brusque demands of the chamber president (in the form of a government declaration), so that he would

be protected against insult in the future. At the same time Roon perceived the predicament into which he was placing the Old Liberal ministers, and he wanted to exploit this, with the aid of Manteuffel and Alvensleben, in order to undermine further their position with the regent. Manteuffel asked the regent's help—ministers would have to be properly protected in the exercise of their office. It was not really Roon who had been insulted but the regent himself. Vincke had described an act in matters of army command as "ill-considered," an act "going back directly to Your Royal Highness—unless the king is no longer regarded as being in direct supreme command of the army but wields such command only under war-ministerial responsibility" (draft by Manteuffel, May 15, 1860; Roon to Manteuffel, May 16, 1860). I have these data from Manteuffel's own papers which repose in part in the Hohenzollern Family Archives in Charlottenburg (*Hohenzollerisches Hausarchiv* Rep. 192 M), in part in the Secret Prussian State Archives in Dahlem (*Geheimes Preussisches Staatsarchiv,* Rep. 92, Edwin Manteuffel). I had hoped to publish an extensive series of items from these sources relating to the army conflict, as soon as the papers of King William and Manteuffel's letters in the papers of Roon were once again accessible—which they were not during the war. Meanwhile the latter letters, 120 of them, have turned up in the National Archives of the United States, together with all of Roon's papers; and Gordon A. Craig has used them as the basis for a piece that appeared in the *Political Science Quarterly,* Vol. 66 (1951), No. 1: "Portrait of a Political General—Edwin von Manteuffel and the Constitutional Conflict in Prussia." Craig's excerpts confirm my account, without adding anything essential to it. A more comprehensive work on a subject closely related to the theme of the present book is to be expected from Craig's pen. Hereinafter, the Manteuffel papers will be briefly identified as H.F.A. (Hohenzollern Family Archives) and S.P.S.A. (Secret Prussian State Archives).

36. It remains an open question who originally proposed that the government bill be withdrawn and that the whole reorganization matter be turned into a budgetary question. According to Bernhardi, it would seem that the liberals at least hoped for such an eventuality. On the other hand, Leopold Gerlach (*Denkwürdigkeiten,* Vol. 2, p. 729) thought he might have had an influence in the matter, through Roon and Manteuffel. He was probably mistaken. On March 6, Manteuffel pressed the regent to appear before both houses in person to demand prompt passage, unless the ministers managed to secure a vote on the defense bill within the week. "No Prussian popular assembly would disobey such a challenge from the king . . . for the Prussians desire a personal, not a pseudo king." On April 21, Manteuffel heard through Alvensleben that there was talk of accepting Kühn's amendment and withdrawing the bill for the time being. He was horrified at the prospect of any form of compromise in the reorganization question, warned the king against indecision in the style of his brother, Frederic William IV, and counseled a totally unyielding attitude, which should bring the ministers round and cause them to put an end to the crisis. "In Prussia, things flourish only when the king commands and the ministers obey." Since William had repeatedly asserted staunch adherence to his plans before the generals, any compromise would only "give the army the impression that Your Royal Highness no longer has matters in hand but are ceding your royal prerogatives to the chambers" (H.F.A.). This was an argument Manteuffel was to repeat on countless occasions, always with the greatest success. In a comprehensive review of November 14, 1862 (H.F.A.), intended for Roon, Manteuffel maintained that the king had accepted the stopgap compromise only after repeated and clear-cut appeals from the entire government.

37. Hence, probably, his strong antipathy to Bonin, the mediator (*Denkwürdigkeiten,* 5th ed., Vol. 1, pp. 363ff., 388f.).

38. K. H. Keck, *Das Leben des Generals Edwin von Manteuffel* (1890), p. 119, cited after W. Gradmann, *Die politischen Ideen Edwin von Manteuffels und ihre Auswirkungen auf seine Laufbahn* (philosophy dissertation, Tübingen, 1932), p. 79—see also Bernhardi, Vol. 3, p. 309, Vol. 4, p. 286. A marked contrast is provided by what

Manteuffel himself related to Ranke—see A. Dove, *Ausgewählte Schriftchen* (1898), pp. 243f. Manteuffel, by the way, did not long play the role of nonpolitical military adviser. By 1860-1861 at the latest he discarded all restraint in exploiting every possible occasion for bringing about the fall of the Old Liberal cabinet.

39. Leopold Gerlach, *Denkwürdigkeiten,* Vol. 2, p. 716; also Roon, *Denkwürdigkeiten,* Vol. 2, pp. 385f. (February 8, 1859). Manteuffel's own comprehensive review of the history of the army reforms, which he wrote after the break with Roon on February 2, 1865, to exculpate himself (H.F.A.), states that after he saw Bonin's draft he put down on paper his own ideas on reorganization. These the prince regent rejected; and ever afterward Manteuffel had represented only the regent's views at all stages of the negotiations, defending them against all weakening amendments. Evidently this is a reference to a memorial Manteuffel wrote in Baden in October, 1859. Roon praised it highly in a letter of October 7, 1859, while Manteuffel himself mentioned it in a letter to Roon as late as October 4, 1862 (H.F.A.), in the context of discussing the difficulty of convincing the parliament of military needs. Unfortunately a wartime search for this memorial was unsuccessful.

40. Leopold Gerlach, *Denkwürdigkeiten,* Vol. 2, p. 729. Lieutenant Colonel Hartmann told Bernhardi (Vol. 3, p. 310): "It is General Manteuffel who has driven the military budget requests to their present level. General Manteuffel could not bear not being involved in the matter, and since he originally had no part in it, he simply went ahead and put in his oar. Well, he succeeded, and now the whole thing is in a muddle" (April 4, 1869). Hartmann and Voigts-Rhetz, who worked on the bill in the war ministry, were witnesses to how the regent continued to increase the requests. It is a moot point whether their assurances that Manteuffel was actually behind it all were anything more than conjecture, but Manteuffel's meddling is rendered highly probable from Roon's letter of November 8, 1859 (*Denkwürdigkeiten,* Vol. 1, pp. 395f.). What is alone documented is that Manteuffel fought relentlessly by every means against any compromise on the part of the king. The liberal camp was convinced by 1862 that "Manteuffel had from the beginning managed the army bill in such a way that it would become the instrument for toppling the government" (Bernhardi, Vol. 4, p. 184). The documentary evidence shows these apprehensions to have been well founded.

41. *Denkwürdigkeiten,* 5th ed., Vol. 1, p. 390 (December 1, 1859). The "bureaucrats" allegedly standing behind Bonin were probably Voigts-Rhetz and Hartmann—see also Leopold Gerlach, *Denkwürdigkeiten,* Vol. 2, p. 702. In the summer of 1860, both men were removed from the ministry. Roon ostentatiously absented himself from the farewell given them by their colleagues (Roon to Manteuffel, June 20, 1860). It is beyond me how Andrea von Harbou, *loc. cit.,* p. 65, can say that Roon had not the slightest political ambition as a minister. It is true that he probably had no direct part in the intrigue against Bonin—see *Denkwürdigkeiten,* Vol. 1, pp. 364, 387, 395f. But from 1859 onward his letters show him in constant and intimate touch with Manteuffel and participating in Manteuffel's fight with the liberal "playmates." Time and again he communicated details from cabinet meetings, etc., for the adjutant general to use in his audiences with the king. See also Friedrich Hartung, *Forschungen zur brandenburgisch-preussischen Geschichte,* Vol. 44, No. 4, p. 24.

42. Manteuffel to Roon, May 29, 1860, in R. Schmidt-Bückeburg, *Das Militärkabinett der preussischen Könige und deutschen Kaiser* (1933), p. 72.

43. Conversation with Leopold von Gerlach, December 6, 1860, in his *Denkwürdigkeiten,* Vol. 2, p. 760; see also *ibid.,* pp. 738f.

44. Stenographic transcript, 1861, Vol. 7, Appendix No. 176. Finance Minister Patow went much further, holding out the prospect of a shortened term of service in the event of inadequate financing (p. 1360).

45. Stenographic transcript, 1861, Vol. 3, pp. 1410ff. (May 27, 1861).

46. Stenographic transcript, 1861, Vol. 3, pp. 1431ff. (May 28, 1861).

47. During these months, when they were in the same place, there is naturally a gap in their

correspondence, of which I was allowed to prepare a copy in 1919, after a visit at Zimmerhausen. (The originals were later deposited in the S.P.S.A.) In the years of struggle immediately preceding Bismarck's entry into the government, however, this correspondence flourished mightily, taking on the character of a mutual consultation in matters of conscience. After Bismarck's rise to power, Blancken-burg, an old and trusted friend of the great man, was repeatedly called in for consultation on how his difficult personality was best dealt with.

48. *Denkwürdigkeiten*, Vol. 2, p. 24 (June 18, 1861).
49. "Was uns noch retten kann," reprinted in H. Rosenberg, *Die nationalpolitische Publizistik Deutschlands.* . . . Vol. 1, No. 575. As shown on pp. 78f., Twe-sten, with his wonted clarity, saw quite plainly that the conflict among the parties over the military question revolved lately more and more around the limits of the royal command power. The military cabinet, especially, he said, "took the basic view that army matters must be kept separate from all the other organs of the state, that every extraneous influence, every other consider-ation must be ruthlessly interdicted." As we know, Manteuffel responded by challenging Twesten to a pistol duel, in which he wounded his opponent quite seriously. Before he departed for the dueling ground, he left a kind of political testament for the king, in the event of his death; and he dispatched it nevertheless, after the duel. "My destiny is catching up with me," he said. "One more cry from the heart to Your Majesty. If the laws do not afford the means for protecting government officials in their honor, then change the laws, even if ten cabinets must fall over it.   Let the King voice his disapproval of the government's failure to take action against Twesten's pamphlet. Let new laws be requested, if the existing ones were bad. [In other words, press censorship.]   Let Your Majesty consider the situation in Prussia. There is no government in accord with Your Majesty's intent. Public opinion rules from day to day. Corruption and factionalism are rife, and the army is being systematically represented as the enemy of the people. The only salvation is Your Majesty's wisdom, national trust rooted in the whole personality of Your Majesty. The people will affirm that trust if Your Majesty act in person. There is no time to be lost, Your Majesty. I entertain no hate of anyone in my heart, but Your Majesty's ministers are not equal to their task. Your Majesty should pick minister after minister, until a real man be found; but Your Majesty should not allow the present situation long to continue, else confusion of purposes will grow apace and trust in Your Majesty's person will be more and more undermined. A time will then come when even Your Majesty's personal qualities will no longer be sufficient." We see that this paladin of the crown continued to be haunted by the events of March, 1848. (Two letters of May 24, 1861, S.P.S.A.) My student Veronika Renner has written an unpublished dissertation on Karl Twesten, based on the original documentary sources, "Karl Twesten als Vorkämpfer des Rechts-staates" (Freiburg, 1954).
50. See Hartung, "Verantwortliche Regierung, Kabinette und Nebenregierungen im konsti-tutionellen Preussen," *Forschungen zur brandenburgisch-preussischen Geschichte*, Vol. 44, p. 24.
51. This view is apparently based on a legal opinion on the royal right of pardon, ministerial responsibility, and the question of countersignature, which Manteuffel had recent-ly placed before Roon, and which met Roon's fervent approbation (in a letter of February 24, 1861), on account of its contention that "the king of Prussia is a monarch under no limitations other than those imposed by himself—in other words, there is not external limitation to his inherent freedom" (H.F.A.).
52. Roon, *Denkwürdigkeiten*, Vol. 2, pp. 38ff.
53. *Denkwürdigkeiten*, Vol. 1, pp. 152ff. (March 25, 1848).
54. He notified Bernhardi of this measure at the same time that he was rallying political sentiment in the army against the liberal reform laws (Bernhardi, Vol. 4, p. 114, April 13, 1861). Manteuffel seems always to have been haunted by fear of the spread of the liberal *Zeitgeist*. For this reason he sought to prevent publication of

even a scholarly military journal. He would not countenance the argument that such a journal could be placed under prepublication censorship by the war ministry: "That would not do—it would turn the war minister into a political minister, which is precisely what he must not be!" (*ibid.*, Vol. 4, p. 220). He told the crown prince he regarded it as to the special credit of King William that he had kept the army out of politics. "That is the reason for its inner firmness and cohesion. Officers who meddle in politics [i.e., on the liberal side] have been summoned before honor courts or instantly discharged by His Majesty" (memorial of June 27, 1863, in H. O. Meisner, *Der preussische Kronprinz im Verfassungskampf 1863* [1931], p. 100, similarly p. 141). In 1863 Roon was insistent in his effort to persuade the king to abolish the franchise for members of the armed forces, without formal consultation with the government: "In my view this is not a ministerial but purely a military question, a question of what the army can tolerate, what is essential to its cohesion. A civilian minister can neither know nor judge that." The only aspect on which Bismarck and the government were to be consulted was the question of implementation, whether a change in the royal edict should be sanctioned by regular or imposed legislation. If the franchise were to continue in the army, Roon said, he would not be able to answer for its cohesion, and its confidence in a commander-in-chief who could not protect it from factionalism would inevitably decline, etc., etc. (September 15, 1863, S.P.S.A.). On September 28, 1863, after long deliberations within the government, Roon did extract an order which, while it did not formally abolish the franchise for officers and men, prohibited its exercise. This did not go nearly far enough to suit Roon—see E. Immel, *Albrecht von Roons Entwicklungsgang* (Dissertation; Berlin, 1936), pp. 57f. What the military franchise meant in practice is graphically illustrated in a royal note to Manteuffel of April 5, 1862, in which the king, responding to an inquiry from Prince Hohenlohe, granted the Potsdam military permission to vote for the Prince, if the only alternative were a democrat. "If the military have a third candidate, such as one of the present ministers, for example—in other words, not a reactionary [i.e., a democrat]—they may give him their vote" (copy in S.P.S.A.).

55. *Denkwürdigkeiten*, Vol. 2, pp. 55, 78. Bernhardi (Vol. 4, p. 339) describes the great pressure that was exerted on the crown prince too, invoking the problem of army morale, in order to turn him away from the liberals.

56. Sybel probably saw this most clearly at the time, and also put it in words; see his speech in the diet on May 11, 1863.

57. As a general Roon felt himself bound to unconditional obedience to the king, despite his ministerial office. Invoking this duty in December, 1861, he declined to take part in the cabinet's resistance to royal desires in the matter of ministerial responsibility—see Zechlin, *loc. cit.*, pp. 210f., based on ministry documents.

58. Report to the King of August 11, 1860, cited after Zechlin, *loc. cit.*, pp. 307f. See also the discussion with the crown prince, *ibid.*,

59. L. Dehio, *Deutsche Rundschau*, Vol. 213, p. 99. The aged Wrangel is supposed to have threatened the king even more bluntly with disaffection in the army, should he desert his royal office for fear of conflict with the democrats *(ibid.)*

60. *Denkwürdigkeiten*, Vol. 2, pp. 44ff.

61. Letters of July 9, 23, and August 24, 1861, at Zimmerhausen (unpublished). In the last one we read: "I merely thought you might have missed the proper moment to knock the stuffing out of them—that you might have won, if you had really stuck it out instead of signing this crude and wretched compromise. Personally, I could not have brought myself to sign it." His letters to Manteuffel during these weeks show how downcast Roon was over his failure, how seriously he thought of resigning. E. Immel, *loc. cit.*, p. 35, gives a few excerpts. Roon feared that if he continued for any length of time in the government "the army will begin to doubt me, and then I am undone." Here again we see the adjutant general busily at work in the background. On June 27-28, 1861, he told the king about the course of the negotiations, in a kind of memorial. Morally, he said, Roon could not maintain his position in the

government, if the king were to yield on the homage issue. It was a matter of "complete surrender of independent royalty in Prussia" and of "whether Your Majesty or a ministerial cabinet is to rule in Prussia. . . . Your majesty desires to maintain the sovereignty of the crown even under a parliamentary constitution, but the ministers wish to make the crown subordinate to parliament [because they insisted that the traditional homage was not possible without constitutional change]. The former is Prussian, the latter a repetition of Louis Philippe. The world knows whither that leads." If the ministers were to return to the path of obedience, the king must take the necessary steps (S.P.S.A.).

62. See Blanckenburg's letter to Roon on December 8, 1861, *Denkwürdigkeiten*, Vol. 2, pp. 56f., which I am able to complement from the original. P. 57 should read: "Augusta will be courting Waldeck even now and soon see . . . " etc. "The waves that have been raised will not be so easily calmed, by the way, some blood will have to flow—and whose fault is that?" etc.

63. *Denkwürdigkeiten*, Vol. 2, p. 52.

64. Letters to Manteuffel, in Immel, *loc. cit.,* p. 41. According to them, a regular campaign plan against the Old Liberals was hatched out with von der Heydt as early as February. Roon had decided to precipitate a conflict with the chamber as early as December (Bernhardi, Vol. 4, p. 172; see also pp. 208f., February 15,).

65. L. Dehio, "Die Pläne der Militärpartei und der Konflikt," *Deutsche Rundschau,* Vol. 213 (October-December, 1927), p. 99. Unfortunately Dehio did not give the dates of the documents he used. Apparently the military plans were prepared as early as November-December, 1861. The king signed the secret marching orders on January 15, though the diet had assembled on January 14. The congratulatory telegram which the commanding general, von Steinmetz, had the audacity to present at New Year's, 1862, belongs in the context of this civil war mood. In it he pressed quite boldly for dismissal of the liberal government. Things would have to return to the state in which the king himself ruled rather than the parliament, through a government identified with it! William I took the hint very graciously—see von Krosigk, *Generalfeldmarschall von Steinmetz* (1900), p. 190.

66. Twesten insisted in the chamber of deputies in September, 1862 that even after the elections of 1861 "agreement would have been extremely easy to achieve, except for the deliberate exacerbation of the quarrel" (stenographic transcript, 1862, Vol. 3, p. 1702).

67. The recent account by Zechlin (*loc. cit.,* pp. 225ff), based on ministry documents, shows that the conflict occasioned by the Hagen motion merely served to provide the conservative ministers with the much-sought-for occasion to end the New Era by force. As early as February, Roon entertained ardent hopes for a new election, which the government might influence favorably (Bernhardi, Vol. 4, pp. 208ff.). The old controversy between A. Wahl and L. Bergsträsser over the original purpose of the Hagen motion now retains only slight interest. If that pretext had not served, the dissolution would have come about by some other.

68. Stenographic transcript, 1861, Vol. 3. p. 1412 (May 27, 1861).

69. Letter to von Saucken-Julienfielde of August 30, 1862, reprinted in *Roon als Redner,* Vol. 1, pp. 317ff.; also in Parisius, *Hoverbeck,* Vol. 2, pp. 65ff.

70. Blanckenburg to Roon, April 7, 1862—see also the letter of March, 1862, cited below (Note 71).

71. Bernhardi, Vol. 4, pp. 172ff, 227. Blanckenburg kept Roon currently informed about the campaign organization of the conservatives and its success outside the aristocratic class as well. He remarked, among other things, that one great handicap to a favorable election outcome was that many conservative voters believed "the King does not want us," which meant that many would stay away from the polls (March, 1862). He repeatedly proposed that the 25 percent surtax be lifted (see Note 18, above), especially since it could not continue to be levied without a vote in the chamber, which would make the Roon-von der Heydt government dependent on parliamentary action (letter of April 7, 1862). Manteuffel began to distrust the

tendency to compromise of even this conservative minister at a surprisingly early stage. As early as March 25, he warned the king (S.P.S.A., Conc., exp. 26.3.) against von der Heydt's economy goals, which had transpired because a letter by the finance minister to Roon had reached the press. Manteuffel reminded the king that he had repeatedly and publicly asserted the minimal requirements of his reform program. "Not only the army knows this, but the whole nation and every cabinet in Europe." Any yielding would profoundly shake the army's confidence in the king. "The consequences to the inner fabric of the army would be incalculable. . . . The finance minister's letter takes the position that what matters is not the role of the king, his positive authority, maintenance of the army's striking power, but command of a majority in the chamber." At heart Roon certainly did not share this view, but the king must help him in his difficult stand, by reference to the decree of December 2, 1861, on the limits to the economies to be made, which strictly enjoined any lowering of cadre strength and service term. This the king must do swiftly, before there would be time to work out compromises. On April 6, Manteuffel once again goaded the King against von der Heydt *(ibid.).*

72. Stenographic transcript, 1862, Vol. 7, Appendix, Part 3, No. 126, report of the budget committee.

73. See p. 126.

74. Stenographic transcript, 1862, Vol. 3, p. 1567. He expressly declared that the reorganization did not materially violate the defense laws of 1814-1815. In other words, even then his views resembled his account of the founding of the Reich later on (Vol. 2, pp. 385f.), in which he glossed over his own militant stand during the conflict with consummate dissimulation, viewing the one-time disagreements solely in the light of the reorganized army's later successes and disposing—with something akin to irony—of liberal distrust of the reactionaries and liberal insistence on a two-year term.

75. Stenographic transcript (upper chamber), 1862, Appendix 1, p. 3.

76. Stenographic transcript (lower chamber), 1862, Vol. 3, p. 1565 (September 11, 1862). Von der Heydt's statement is emphasized.

77. Twesten to Lipke, September 9, 1862, in Heyderhoff, *Deutscher Liberalismus,* Vol. 1, p. 115. Droysen to Duncker, September 3, 1862, in his letters, edited by Hübner, Vol. 2, p. 796.

78. Stenographic transcript, 1862, Vol. 3, p. 1568. Sybel's speech memorably demonstrates how strongly this later Bismarckian official still clung to the notion of the army as a popular institution—or at least his willingness to emphasize that character for its effect on his constituents and progressives generally. The two-year term, he said, had to be accepted, even if it made little sense and was indeed "amateurish," for the Prussian people clung to this demand "heart and soul," and even in a military sense everything depended on maintaining the popular character of the army. With the popular will so unequivocally clear, no minister could be responsible to the people, nor any king to God, for the maintenance of an unpopular institution.

79. Twesten to Lipke, July 17, 1862, in Heyderhoff, *loc. cit.,* Vol. 1, p. 106; Philippson, *Max von Forckenbeck,* pp. 90ff. Roon himself wrote Bismarck as late as August 31, that he hoped to be able to postpone the issue until the spring of 1863 *(Denkwürdigkeiten,* Vol. 2, p. 111). A noteworthy passage appears in this letter (p. 110): "Ancient traditions of chivalry require us to come to the king's rescue, *even though he has deliberately risked his own neck."* Surely this can refer only to the king's rigid adherence to a three-year term. Droysen, too, thought he saw signs that there were efforts inside the government to delay the crisis until 1863 (letter to Duncker, September 3, 1862, in the volume edited by Hübner, Vol. 2, p. 797).

80. Manteuffel to Roon, August 1, 1862, in Schmidt-Bückeburg, *Das Militärkabinett,* p. 85.

81. Bernhardi, Vol. 4, p. 325.

82. *Denkwürdigkeiten,* Vol. 2, pp. 116f. Roon was here, not without qualms, mustering his

courage for the constitutional crisis that had now become inevitable. He tried to make it appear that his attempt at mediation had failed because of the stubbornness of the deputies rather than the king's recalcitrance.

83. The documentation was found in the Army Archives (War Ministry, Central Department, V, 4, 2, 1, Vol. 2;*adhibendum* to V, 4, 2, 1; unbound materials to V, 4, 2, 1). The genesis of the military service bill of 1863 can here be traced step by step. An added source are Manteuffel's papers in the S.P.S.A. and H.F.A. (correspondence with Roon, October-December, 1862, and letter to William I of December 14, 1862). Major items have been published in *Militärische Schriften Kaiser Wilhelms,* Vol. 2, pp. 479ff., and the war office documents have been used by L. Dehio in "Bismarck und die Heeresvorlagen der Konfliktszeit," *Historische Zeitschrift,* Vol. 144, pp. 31ff. Dehio's arguments in favor of Bismarck's authorship of this draft are by no means conclusive. See also Bernhardi, Vol. 4, pp. 330f, Vol. 5, pp. 4, 11, 19, 155, used by A. Wahl in *Beiträge zur Geschichte der Konfliktszeit,* pp. 93ff. The wording of the drafts seems to me to point to the situation in September, before the entire military budget was cut, rather than to October.

84. Stenographic transcript, 1860, Vol. 5, Appendix 3, No. 171, p. 1245, report of the military committee. Rudolf von Gneist recalled an extended discussion in which Roon expressed strong approval of the idea of levying a defense tax on those exempted from service by lottery, citing the Belgian envoy Nothomb (*Die Militärvorlage von 1892. . .* , p. 43).

85. See p. 125, above, and Note 9. An undated memorandum among Manteuffel's papers (H.F.A., sheet 231f.), by Alvensleben, judging from the handwriting, predicts that the chamber would "emphatically reject the whole deal, because it turns the honor of serving as a soldier into a burden, out of which one can buy one's way."

86. Letter to Samwer, September 26, 1862, in Philippson, *Leben Kaiser Friedrichs III* (1900), p. 423; letter to Bernhardi, December 26, 1862, in Bernhardi's diaries, Vol. 4, pp. 33f. A brief report on memorials by Duncker written shortly before November 9, with the same aim, is given by R. Haym in *Das Leben Max Dunckers* (1891), p. 274. In what has become known so far of Duncker's plans there is no mention of "stand-in payments" or anything of the kind. A letter by Droysen to Duncker of September 3, 1862 (in Droysen's letters, Vol. 2, p. 796) shows that Sybel too approved the increase in the number of re-enlistees (at double pay), hoping to win over even the left (Harkort) for such a plan. Georg von Vincke himself hinted in the diet on September 19, 1862, at certain mediation proposals he had suggested to the government (stenographic transcript, Vol. 3, p. 1754).

87. Bernhardi, Vol. 4, p. 331.

88. *Ibid.,* Vol. 5, pp. 19f. (January 15, 1863). Vincke proposed that those liable to military service who were not called up pay a proportion of their income or class tax into the army exchequer, being "unwilling to admit that such an arrangement would materially alter the character of our army." Introduction of the two-year term, he declared in the chamber, would make a sharp increase in the number of professional soldiers unavoidable. He proposed the creation of subaltern officer ranks (sergeant-lieutenant) for veteran re-enlistees, as a special inducement to long-time service (stenographic transcript, Vol. 3, p. 1591, September 11, 1862).

89. Stenographic transcript, 1862, Vol. 3, pp. 1638f., September 12, 1862. Gneist, in a pamphlet, *Die Lage der preussischen Heeresorganisation am 29. 9. 1862,* supported the same idea, namely that army organization proper was the exclusive province of the commander-in-chief and the current administration, but that the general basis of conscription and of service liability required legislative authorization. He pointed to the deterrent example of the English Parliament, quite unacceptable to continental countries with general conscription, of treating the strength of the professional army purely as a budgetary question. Later on Gneist was rightly able to take credit for having anticipated a principle of Bismarckian government. Roon's approval is shown in *Roon als Redner,* Vol. 1, pp. 222f. Sybel too proposed that annual legislative authorization of army strength be replaced by a fixed defense law.

In conflict with Roon's draft, however, he had in mind a fixed number of recruits—see Droysen's letters, Vol. 2, p. 796.

90. See his letter to Vincke-Olbendorf, April 13, 1857, in Dehio, *Historische Zeitschrift,* Vol. 144, p. 33.

91. See his words to the crown prince on September 19: "For thirty-three years he had opposed a term of less than three years, and he could not now answer for so great an inconsistency, either to himself or to the world. His mind was made up, before God and his conscience. He was bound by his declaration that the three-year term and the army reorganization represented a conviction on which he must stand or fall." H. O. Meisner (ed.), *Kaiser Friedrichs Tagebücher von 1840 bis 1866* (1929), p. 160.

92. The conservatives voiced the same objection. A letter of August 17, among Blancken-burg's letters to Roon, is followed by an undated "political memorandum," which cannot have been written before late fall, possibly November. We read there: "I don't like your plan for a percentage that is to rise and fall with the population. The King now has greater powers—he can conscript *all* able-bodied men. As for the money angle, this seems to me to be an illusion, for even if the percentage were to become law, the right to cut appropriations would be retained." Blanckenburg plainly preferred the king's theoretically unlimited right of conscription—even though it was purely theoretical—to legislative safeguards for the army budget, a prize example of stubborn party dogmatism. By contrast Moltke, in a discussion with Bernhardi in 1865, thought that fixing peacetime army strength by law at one percent of the population, with a standard lump-sum budget of 40 millions, was the best solution to the conflict (Bernhardi, Vol. 4, pp. 169f.).

93. *Kaiser Friedrichs Tagebücher, loc. cit.,* p. 161. Alvensleben added: "If Papa were to yield, the army would be done for, and he could no longer claim that it confidently looked to Papa. The king would remain firm. . . . The crown's sole supports were the upper chamber and the army, for the fathers of the officers sat in the former, which was not true of the lower chamber. The current chamber of deputies consisted of nothing but democratic scum. To yield would mean to topple every-thing that existed—he had studied revolutionary history and knew this well."

94. On the genesis of this view see E. Zechlin, *Bismarck und die Grundlagen der deutschen Grossmacht* (1930), p. 277. In an unpublished letter of April 7, 1862, Blancken-burg had already envisaged the possibility of carrying on the government on the basis of the old budget, without a new budget law, if only no new taxes needed to be levied. This, he contended, would be within the law. That the conservatives, by September, 1862, had already got well used to the idea that one could manage without a budget law is shown in a speech by von Gottberg in the chamber of deputies on September 11, 1862 (stenographic transcript, 1862, Vol. 3, p. 1581). In the upper chamber, von Below-Hohendorf reported on October 10, 1862, that Friedrich Stahl had long ago pointed out to him that Paragraph 109 of the constitution conferred the power to meet any dangers arising from excesses of the parliamentary power of the purse (stenographic transcript, 1862, p. 174). It is an odd spectacle to see the unlimited veneration in which conservative orators held the "mighty figure" of the jurist F. J. Stahl, to whom the Prussian constitution owed its Paragraph 109, considered so valuable by the conservatives. According to them, this paragraph had prevented Prussia from turning into a pseudo monarchy on the Belgian or English model.

95. Concern that King William might ultimately buckle under the conflict plays a major role in Roon's confidential correspondence with Blanckenburg. On details of Bismarck's appointment and the council session that preceded it, see Zechlin, *loc. cit.,* pp. 291ff.

96. In the fall months of 1862, Manteuffel and Alvensleben unmistakably invited the crisis, Manteuffel being convinced that "if it breaks out in earnest, it can be victoriously settled, for the good of the country" (passage cut in the draft of a memorandum for Roon of November 14, H.F.A.). He was willing, if necessary, "to see blood flow for

the King's unlimited personal command," for he no longer "believed in the possibility of a sound reconciliation by compromise. It is up to the King to interpret the constitution and to lead the nation through the crisis." The main thing now was to bring down the Old Liberals, the bitterest enemies of all, and to depart from the path of feeble concessions, which unfortunately even Roon had followed of late. It was high time, for even now the army believed there was no limit to the concessions that would be granted, now that the government, all the solemn declarations of the king to the contrary notwithstanding, had failed to display firmness in the matter of the three-year term of service (October 4, H.F.A.). Even Bismarck's first appearance was regarded with much distrust—would he redeem his pledge to solve the crisis by "blood and iron?" Was he not already showing a tendency to compromise? Some of his statements made a decidedly "dismal impression" (October 8, *ibid.*). If only Roon, "for God's sake, kept up his spirits for the inevitably impending struggle for legality!" Why was a reorganization law needed in the first place? Legislation that would extend active service was entirely sufficient. Thus every possible argument is brought forward against Roon's service bill. Manteuffel instantly and rightly saw that "the whole idea of a nation in arms is relinquished" (November 14, H.F.A.). Yet the fight against it was to continue, even after the "stand-in payments" by those serving only two years were cut—the whole thing "smacked of concessions!" There was unrelenting and dogmatic opposition to legislative regulation of the draft quota as an alleged curtailment of the king's freedom of action, in countless memorials to king and war minister, some of them of excessive length. As Manteuffel wrote to Roon on December 5, the quota would "turn the king, our natural-born and unlimited warlord, into an English commander-in-chief under the supervision and control of the popular assembly. . . . This is the very heart of the issue between royal and parliamentary army." Instead of postponing the fight over this issue, "we must stake everything." Roon immediately replied (December 7): "For my part, I am ready for that kind of gamble, and perhaps not altogether unsuited to carry it off. But like yourself and indeed all of us, the cards are simply not in our hand. They are held by another who thinks that to stake everything goes against the rules. . . . Self-preservation may induce us to play *va banque*, but despite the great service difficulties you emphasize, no matter how grave they are, the situation does not yet in my view jeopardize our survival. It is true that for these reasons there may have to be a *brumaire*—but where is our Bonaparte? "

In the course of the bitter controversies of those December weeks, with Manteuffel threatening his resignation, while Roon's attitude under Bismarck's influence grew more and more self-assured and unequivocal, as well as more and more autonomous in respect of the military cabinet, we can plainly see the growing estrangement between the two men, which, after a final, difficult clash in January, 1865, was to lead to the break between them. (I propose to give a more detailed account at a later date.) How deep the differences were even then is seen from the following hand-written note signed "v.A." (evidently Gustav von Alvensleben), accompanying the return to Manteuffel on December 31, 1862, of three documents, probably including Manteuffel's long memorandum of December 29 to the war minister: "The interesting enclosures are herewith returned with deep thanks. You are fighting vain and complacent self-righteousness, else how could you be answered, in a question of supreme importance, by such wretched and illogical arguments, indeed by sheer sophistry! He is a professor and a bureaucrat, not a general!" For parts of this correspondence, see Schmidt-Bückeburg, *Militärkabinett*, pp. 85f.: Immel, *Albrecht von Roons Entwicklungsgang*, p. 54; also L. Dehio, *Historische Zeitschrift*, Vol. 144, pp. 38ff.

97. Forckenbeck's amendments in the spring of 1863 plainly show this tendency: limitation of military jurisdiction; dissolution of military courts of honor and cadet schools; promotion of noncoms to officer rank; limitations on pensions for high military ranks; increases in pay for noncoms and men; line troops to be placed on

the same footing as guards units; easing of the garrison system, etc. For details of the continuing army conflict, see the carefully documented study by Fritz Löwenthal, *Der preussische Verfassungsstreit 1862-1866* (Dissertation; Munich, 1914).

98. See L. Dehio, *Historische Zeitschrift,* Vol. 144; Roon, *Denkwürdigkeiten,* Vol. 2, pp. 325, 331f. and *passim.* Roon's speech of May 9, 1863, shows that at the climax of the struggle, he personally would have accepted legislation covering the peacetime strength of the army and recruitment, although he held that the government was not required to do so by the constitution. He expressly acknowledged that the demand for legislative regulation of *Landwehr* organization was justified on the face of it–*Roon als Redner,* Vol. 1, pp. 476ff.

99. See his letter to von Saucken-Julienfelde of August 30, 1862, in *Roon als Redner,* Vol. 1, pp. 317f., and his letter to Grand Duke Frederic of Baden of November 14, 1863, in Oncken, *Grossherzog Friedrich I. von Baden und die deutsche Politik von 1854 bis 1871* (1927), Vol. 1, pp. 452ff.

100. Stenographic transcript (upper chamber), October 11, 1862, pp. 200ff.

101. Bernhardi, Vol. 4, pp. 338f.

102. Around 1860 the number of men who each year were liable to military service ran to about 180,000, of whom some 110,000 were rated fit for service, though only 63,000, or about 60 percent, were actually mustered in–Ziekursch, *Politische Geschichte des neuen deutschen Kaiserreichs* (1925), Vol. 1, p. 40. G. Lehmann, *Die Mobilmachung von 1870-1871* (1905), in his Appendix 12, "Summary of the composition of the mobile formation as a result of the mobilization of 1870," lists a total of only 1,124 volunteers in the entire army of the North German League (pp. 287f.). When a large contingent of one-year volunteers reached France with the first replacements, after the bloody August battles, King William expressed dissatisfaction, because these men did not seem up to the hardships of war and showed more zeal and good will than combat efficiency. "It was irresponsible to yield to the desires . . . of the young people and even their parents and send them into the theater of war before they had reached physical maturity." No matter how heartening the spirit of these young men, "one should not deal so carelessly with material so precious as the educated youth of the country"–L. Schneider, *Aus dem Leben Kaiser Wilhelms,* Vol. 2, p. 233.

103. See Note 11, above.

104. For further details, see my documentary study, "Die Entstehung der Indemnitätsvorlage von 1866," *Historische Zeitschrift,* Vol. 144, pp. 17ff.

105. See p. 24 of my essay, just cited, which deals with Twesten's draft. Both the progressive opposition and the National Liberals, in committee as in the plenary session, noted that the question of legal authority was passed over. After the successes of 1864 and 1866, the National Liberals expressly declared they would accept the army reorganization but suggested that the North German Reichstag was the proper place.

106. That is to say, the fixing of army strength as a percentage of the population, together with a fixed expenditure per soldier. See L. Dehio, *Historische Zeitschrift,* Vol. 144. I thoroughly agree with R. A. Huber's judgment of the indemnity bill (as against C. Schmitt), in his *Heer und Staat* (pp. 224-238). He rightly emphasizes the separation of the legal from the budgetary question (p. 239), but in my view fails to perceive (pp. 239ff.) that Bismarck did not ask for absolutist command power in the army reorganization of 1866, reserving a legislative settlement to the North German Reichstag rather than the Prussian diet.

107. *Gedanken und Erinnerungen,* Book 2, Chapter 10, Section 5–Vol. 15 of the collected works, edited by myself–pp. 293ff.

Notes to Chapter 7

1. See p. 132, above.

2. Among other things, through the creation of a superordinate commission on military

organization, an extremely complex relationship to the directorate general, the newly created military cabinet, etc. For details see, for example, Marschall von Bieberstein, *Verantwortlichkeit und Gegenseichnung bei Anordnungen des Obersten Kriegsherren* (1911), pp. 127ff.

3. Bronsart von Schellendorf, *Der Dienst des Generalstabes* (1875), Vol. 1, pp. 14ff. Massenbach's basic writings are: *Die Reorganisation der preussischen Armee nach dem Tilsiter Frieden,* supplement to the *Militärwochenblatt,* 1858-1866, with documentation; Vaupel (ed.), *Die Reorganisation des preussischen Staats, unter Stein und Hardenberg,* Vol. 2, p. 1, published by the Prussian State Archives, 1938, Vol. 94. Massenbach's memorial of 1795 is found in his *Memoiren zur Geschichte des preussischen Staates unter den Regierungen Friedrich Wilhelm II. und Friedrich Wilhelm III.* (1809), Vol. 2, pp. 168ff., under the title: "Uber die Notwendigkeit der engeren Verbindung der Kriegs-und Staatskunde," In my Stein biography, Vol. 1, p. 492, Note 59, and p. 492, Note 70, I refer to a similar constitutional plan which Massenbach submitted to the king July 2-8, 1806. The biography of Massenbach by L. G. von der Knesebeck, *Das Leben des Obersten Christian L. A. Reichsfreiherrn von und zu Massenbach* (1924), is an amateurish job, though it did use Massenbach's personal papers. For the beginnings and later development of the general staff see, besides Bronsart, G. Wohlers, *Die staatsrechtliche Stellung des Generalstabes in Preussen und dem Deutschen Reich. Geschichtliche Entwicklung bis zum Versailler Frieden 1921;* and Max Jähn: *Feldmarschall Moltke* (1902), Vol. 2, 1, Chapter 9. The technical development of general staff work receives its best treatment in the excellent study by von Caemmerer, *Die Entwicklung der strategischen Wissenschaft im 19. Jahrhundert* (1904), Vol. 15 of the *Bibliothek der Politik und Volkswirtschaft.* Another source I found valuable is the service manual prepared by the section on military history of the German army high command, *Generalstabsdienstweg und Generalstabs-Verantwortlichkeit,* which is abundantly documented. On the development of the military cabinet and the cabinet system in general, see R. Schmidt-Bückeburg, *Das Militärkabinett der preussischen Könige und deutschen Kaiser. Seine geschichtliche Entwicklung und staatrechtliche Stellung 1787 bis 1918* (Berlin, 1933). Some important supplements and corrections are given by K. Jany in *Forschungen zur brandenburgisch-preussischen Geschichte,* Vol. 45 (1933), pp. 409-413. See H. O. Meisner, *Der Kriegsminister 1814-1914. Ein Beitrag zur militärischen Verfassungsgeschichte* (1940); and "Zur neueren Geschichte des preussischen Kabinetts," in *Forschungen zur brandenburgisch-preussischen Geschichte,* Vol. 36 (1924). Friedrich Hartung, "Verantwortliche Regierung. Kabinette und Nebenregierungen im konstitutionellen Preussen," in *Forschungen zur brandenburgisch-preussischen Geschichte,* Vol. 44 (1932). The role of the adjutant general under Frederic the Great and the beginnings of the military cabinet in 1787 are dealt with in the carefully documented study by R. Arnold in "Die Anfänge des preussischen Militärkabinetts," *Historische Aufsätze, Festgabe für Karl Zeumer* (1910), pp. 169ff. W. Görlitz's book, *Der deutsche Generalstab. Geschichte und Gestalt 1657-1945,* while containing much useful material, is more a compilation, nor is it free from serious errors.

4. Boyen says in his *Erinnerungen* Vol. 1, p. 272): "Campaigns can be conducted and countries governed well only when the skill of the general is combined with that of the statesman in a single person. When they are separate, we have only the technically trained soldier or the crafty, weak diplomat." Scharnhorst speaks even more plainly, in a historical sketch on the Italian campaign of 1800 given by S. Mette in *Vom Geist deutscher Feldherrn* (Zurich, 1938), p. 54: "The experiences of all ages have shown that great things are seldom achieved, unless political prospects and military possibilities, the estimation of military resources and the evaluation of their proper use in war—in other words, politics and the art of war—are closely integrated. . . . When privy cabinets proceed by purely military principles they will commit as many blunders as when they fail to be guided, in their political designs, by military considerations and a thorough knowledge of the military situation. Both must always be combined. This was the strength of the French during the time of

the Committee of Public Safety, so long as Carnot was one of the five directors. This is a subject of the greatest importance to the welfare and survival of a state." It is much more reminiscent of Clausewitz's central doctrines than D. von Bülow's empty phrase cited by R. Höhn in *Revolution, Heer, Kriegsbild* (1914), p. 270, which in my view gives no hint of Clausewitz's thinking.

5. In the essay, "The Relationship between War and Politics," already cited (Note 5, Chapter 5). Appended to this was the draft of a *Reichskriegsverfassung*, done "in accord with higher instructions" for Stein's central administrative council in 1814, which was intended to supplement another constitutional draft, probably by Stein himself. This essay shows such resemblance to Clausewitz's doctrine that it becomes virtually certain Rühle von Lilienstern knew it. Here are some passages in point: "The art of war is indubitably a component of the art of statesmanship in the broader sense." Diplomacy, which Rühle calls "the good manners of states," must in wartime be described as "the art of waging war." By their nature, both are intimately joined. Great political achievements come only "when diplomacy – or politics, as it is sometimes called – goes hand in hand with the art of war, when both spheres are directly joined in the person of the sovereign, when top leadership is left to the supreme commander, or when the foreign minister is sufficiently cognizant of the secrets of generalship to be equal to the planning of military operations and is able to judge the full import of the military situation of his country and its satellites." Unfortunately, as a rule, neither was the diplomat trained in a military sense, nor the general properly oriented in respect of politics. What Rühle called for was a "diplomatic art of war," for war too was in the main a political and diplomatic affair. He primarily had in mind that peace should always be formally terminated, allies recruited, and a war plan formulated with a view to both the interests of these allies and a favorable attitude on the part of neutral nations. Yet it was not merely that the original operational plan must be thoroughly political in orientation, but that throughout a war political events and conditions must influence the course of operations. "To imagine that warfare is, by and large, a purely military matter is a widespread fallacy that works much mischief." True, many estimable military writers had inveighed against diplomacy intervening in the conduct of war, for fear that it either paralyzed operations or initiated heightened action and experiments in combat at an unsuitable moment. "These men are correct, so long as they envisage war as such, but they fail to consider the state, whose purposes war is meant to serve." It was true that the stubborn military naivete of diplomats often did harm, but equally mischievous could be the vainglory of soldiers, their quarrelsome adventurism that was likely to carry the state to the brink of disaster. Napoleon had the knack of exploiting his diplomacy even more effectively than his victories. Political success rather than military triumph was always his ultimate goal. Every war, after all, had to end some time, and the fewer resources it required, the better. Yet to end a war was as much a diplomatic as a military task. Diplomacy and war not only supplemented each other, they overlapped. Hence, up to a certain point, diplomats and general staff officers should have the same kind of training. Every diplomatic corps and every war office should be staffed with a proper blend of political and military members. At this point Rühle von Lilienstern cited the *Ecole militaire* of Frederic the Great as well as Massenbach's projects.

Despite the many similarities, we note the sharp difference between Rühle von Lilienstern and Clausewitz. Rühle had no inkling as yet of the idea of absolute war, which appears to be Clausewitz's proper discovery; and Rühle is much closer to the spirit of eighteenth-century cabinet warfare. His basic convictions already emerge in his polemic with Kant ("Apologia for War," No. 4 in the essays here cited, reprinted in Schlegel's *Deutsches Museum* [1813], Vol. 3, pp. 158-173, 177-182). The state could not be simply regarded as the guardian of peace and law, as Kant saw it; for law itself undergoes a constant process of growth, requiring occasional regeneration, which could not be achieved without a power struggle. On the other hand, such a struggle must never become an end in itself. The militant and peaceful functions of the state are coequal. "The whole state is to be completely steeped in the spirit of both peace and war, in equal parts" (p. 180 in the essay, "The Relationship between War and Politics"), and this must be fully expressed in diplomacy, in war, in domestic politics, and in the education of the nation. In home affairs this means a proper balance between welfare and preparedness, in education a similar balance between religious training for civic virtue and military training to implant the virtues of courage, obedience, and honor. Army and church must collaborate in extricating the individual from his purely private life, motivating him to selfless dedication to the common good. In this context Rühle von Lilienstern saw with much greater clarity than Clausewitz that planned economic mobilization was needed. War ministry and treasury had to collaborate closely, for the economic capacity of a country was virtually the most important factor in the success of military operations.

6. Boyen describes this graphically in his *Erinnerungen,* Vol. 2, pp. 35 ff. When he was a very old man, Emperor William I was known on occasion to doze off when some of his councilors droned on with their reports.
7. Freiherr vom Stein, *Briefwechsel, Denkschriften und Aufzeichnungen,* edited by Botzenhart, Vol. 2, p. 374, February 18, 1808. Gneisenau believed the reforms could succeed only if the prime minister stood above all the other ministers, including the war minister; and Scharnhorst too put his hopes in full support to the prime minister. Beguelin: *Denkwürdigkeiten,* p. 16, August 29, 1807. Scharnhorst's letter of February 2, 1808, in Lehmann, *Scharnhorst,* Vol. 2, p. 26. See also my Stein biography, Vol. 1, p. 542, Note 29 to p. 460, and p. 521, Note 28 to p. 370. In connection with my Stein biography, another work now to be consulted is W. Döring, "Die Entwicklung der wehrpolitischen Ideen des Freiherrn vom Stein," in *Welt als Geschichte,* Vol. 6 (1940), pp. 15 ff.
8. Botzenhart, *loc. cit.,* Vol. 2, p. 452.
9. See my Stein biography, Vol. 1, p. 521, Note 28 to p. 370.
10. On the basis of the decrees of October 27, 1810, as pointed out by Marschall von Bieberstein, *loc. cit.,* p. 139; see also Boyen: *Erinnerungen,* Vol. 2, pp. 64 ff.
11. G. Wohlers, *loc. cit.,* pp. 22 f., thinks the error committed in 1815 was that the royal headquarters and army high command were not in the same geographic location. Another reason the quarrel grew so bitter was that war minister Boyen did not join Blücher's headquarters. If this be so, I still have failed to find any documentation for the contention that Boyen somehow tried to conciliate the conflict. In his capacity as war minister Boyen was less advantageously placed in respect of curbing the blustering field marshal than was the state chancellor, with the support of the king.
12. See Schmidt-Bückeburg, Wohlers, *loc. cit.;* H. O. Meisner, *Der Kriegsminister* (1940); E. R. Huber, *Heer und Staat in der deutschen Geschichte* (1938), pp. 118 ff.
13. As was the case in Austria from 1801 to 1809, under the Archduke Charles.
14. This was the argument put forward by Count Waldersee in his well-known challenge calling for the expansion of general staff jurisdiction even in peacetime. Unlike Schmidt-Bückeburg, I do not attribute this challenge solely to personal ambition, though Waldersee was certainly not lacking in that quality. Another pertinent example was when Falkenhayn, in 1915, combined the offices of war minister and chief of staff. See also K. L. von Oertzen: *Grundzüge der Wehrpolitik* (1933), pp. 132 f.
15. I doubt there is as yet enough light on the question of the extent to which Scharnhorst as a practicing strategist—and it should be borne in mind that his field services ceased after the battle of Gross Görschen—was able to surmount the prejudices of paper strategy, with which he had been indoctrinated in his youth at the war academy of Count William of Schaumburg-Lippe. There are some interesting contributions to this question, partly following Schlieffen's critique of the campaign of 1806, in R. Stadelmann's posthumous fragment, *Scharnhorst—Schicksal*

und geistige Welt (1952), but in its unfinished state this book fails to convey an unequivocal picture.

16. It was along such lines that Grolman drafted a kind of general service scheme as early as October, 1814—Conrady, Vol. 2, pp. 390ff.

17. Royal decree dated January 21, 1821, which retained for the second department custody and administration of charts, drawing, books, instruments, etc., as well as of the lithographic institute, but under the general direction of the chief of staff. Procurement had to be authorized by the war minister himself, but accounting and finance lay with the second department. When the war minister required military or technical advice, he had to go directly to the chief of staff. A regulation issued by Müffling on January 30, 1821, introduced what was called "general staff service channels" for correspondence between general staff officers and the chief of staff, freezing out the second department as well as the troop commanders as intermediate agencies.

18. H.F.A., Chief of the Army General Staff, file covering the organization of the general staff, 1814-1826, xii, 1, Vol. 2, unsigned and undated fair copy, from a registration note dating from the time from September 21, 1820, to January 25, 1821: report to War Minister von Hacke on the state of the general staff, as found in a recent review, no doubt by Müffling, who was appointed chief of surveys on September 21, 1820, and chief of the army general staff on January 11, 1821, while Rühle von Lilienstern was appointed chief of the "grand" general staff on January 25, 1821. Müffling explains that the general staff faces three tasks: 1. Service with the troop commands; 2. Procurement of matériel and war plans; 3. Teaching at the higher military academies. "There has been the contention that *one* head could attend to all these matters, but when it is considered that the general staff is concerned with the entire military educational establishment, the training of higher officers and the conduct of operations in wartime, it is soon seen that the only over-all chief of staff can be the war minister, in whose office all army affairs run together." Müffling advises that the planning room, historical section, terrain reconnaissance section, etc., be accommodated in the war ministry's second department, and to combine with it supervision of military training and the high commission of examiners, since the general staff was bound to know about all the good men among the officer candidates.

It will be seen that the idea that his agency should have direct access to the king beside the war ministry was still quite foreign to Müffling, who clung doggedly to Boyen's plan for centralized military organization.

19. Royal decree of January 11, 1821, reproduced in K. von Priesdorff, *Soldatisches Führertum*, Vol. 4, Part 7, p. 313. This is inaccurately cited in an opinion on the question of direct access to the king by the general staff, prepared by the general department on May 13, 1883 (H.F.A., War Ministry, Ministerial Section 5, 2, 1, No. 6), and even less precisely in a memorial of November 24, 1888, by Bronsart von Schellendorf (G. Wohlers, *loc. cit.*, p. 75, Note 48), which mentions only the war minister's assent in *major* orders and proposals. In his book, *Der Dienst des Generalstabes* (1875), Bronsart insists (p. 23) that the order of 1821 (which he wrongly dates January 25) formally established the general staff's right of direct access to the king, an interpretation quite typical of the trend of Moltke's time. Wohlers's opposite view that the chief of staff was entirely subordinate to the war minister seems to me to go too far. I can find no documentary support for the contention that down to 1859 the chief of staff could reach the war minister only by way of the general department of the ministry (p. 26), even though correspondence did in large part pass through this department. The second department of the war ministry was dissolved by royal decree dated August 31, 1824, Rühle von Lilienstern's appointment as liaison officer made effective by another dated February 3, 1825.

20. Full details in Marschall von Bieberstein, *loc. cit.*, pp. 84 ff.

21. Disproving Schmidt-Bückeburg, Jany has shown (*Forschungen zur brandenburgisch-preussischen Geschichte,* Vol. 45, pp. 410ff.) that this was true from the beginning, as early as 1809, under Scharnhorst.

22. Two memorials of December, 1888, in Schmidt-Bückeburg, *loc. cit.,* pp. 167ff.

23. Boyen too, on the basis of his long years of experience in reporting directly to the king, regarded a system under which a prime minister represented the government as a whole before the king, steering a fixed political course, as by far best adapted to the Prussian monarchy. (*Erinnerungen,* Vol. 2, p. 42.)

24. Still, the resignation of Boyen and Grolman in the constitutional crisis of 1819 shows the degree of political responsibility to the nation generals could feel. In both these men the ideals of the resurgence were still alive.

25. This was the situation after 1870, as described, for example, by Bronsart von Schellendorf, *loc. cit.,* pp. 70ff. For further details, see Vol. 2 of the present work.

26. See his letter to Roon of January 6, 1862, in Schmidt-Bückeburg, *loc. cit.,* p. 86. As Leopold von Gerlach reports in the spring of 1853 (*Denkwürdigkeiten,* Vol. 2, p. 28), Frederic William IV nevertheless on occasion considered excluding the war minister in practice and at the same time conferring extraordinary status on the army, by appointing a commander-in-chief who would be responsible solely to him. This would probably have been the Prince of Prussia (see also Hartung, *Forschungen zur brandenburgisch-preussischen Geschichte,* Vol. 44, pp. 20f.). This, however, would have been a deliberate breach of the constitutional system rather than its organic implementation. Such a commander-in-chief would, of course, have been under no political control whatever.

27. Zechlin, *loc. cit.,* p. 211, Note 1 (ministerial protocols).

28. It was different in the navy, which had no tradition reaching back to Frederic the Great. At least until the time of William II, there was no possibility of maintaining even a pretense that the king was able to assume personal charge in wartime. The navy, after all, was still so small that its chief ranked no higher than an army corps commander. What happened—though only after 1859—was that a separate high command was created, with a large degree of autonomy, the naval high command, whose command authority was quite separate from naval administration, which was handled by a "navy ministry" that was actually part of the war ministry. To end the ceaseless friction between the two naval authorities and bring naval affairs as a whole under his political control, Bismarck in 1870 merged command and ministry.

29. Decree to the government of July 1, 1849—see Schmidt-Bückeburg, pp. 40ff. (after *Deutsche Revue,* Vol. 32 [1907], pp. 155f.).

30. K. Jany, *Forschungen zur brandenburgisch-preussischen Geschichte,* Vol. 45, p. 412.

31. On the time of the restoration of the military cabinet, at first kept secret, see F. Hartung, *loc. cit.,* p. 21.

32. So unequivocal and well documented is this political intent that it remains unaffected by von Marschall's abstruse legal argumentation (*loc. cit.,* pp. 552 and especially 570-575), to the effect that the minister's constitutional responsibility was not lessened, let alone nullified by the absence of a countersignature on orders-in-council or by their being issued by some coordinate agency directly under the king.

33. In the former case I agree with Schmidt-Bückeburg (*loc. cit.,* pp. 73ff.), but in the latter I think he is mistaken. I think he overstates the view that upon promulgation of the constitution the king could no longer call on the adjutant general for direct advice in army matters (p. 81), which does not seem to me to flow from Article 44—not even when one holds, with von Marschall, that the exercise of the command power is a "government act," within the meaning of Article 44. I have already emphasized in the preceding chapter (p. 132, Paragraph 4 and *passim*) that there was no thought among the liberals in the 1860 diet to dispute the fact that the king did have a command power not subject to legislative control. Of importance is the finding by H. O. Meisner (*Der Kriegsminister,* p. 26) that Roon himself was responsible for the final wording of the royal decree of January 18, 1861.

34. Still, Bismarck tried as early as October, 1862, to remove Manteuffel from the scene by an appointment to an honorific diplomatic position abroad—see F. Hartung, *loc. cit.*, p. 30.
35. See for example the letter to William I of May 28, 1865, reproduced in R. Stadelmann, *Das Jahr 1865 und das Problem von Bismarcks deutscher Politik* (1933), appendix, pp. 79ff.
36. See Zechlin, *Bismarck und die Grundlegung der deutschen Grossmacht*, p. 319.
37. Correspondence between War Minister von Reyher and Chief of Staff von Krauseneck, April, 1848, in which von Reyher requested that all general staff reports to the king should pass through the war ministry. Von Krauseneck explained he had always presented the reports of troop staff chiefs directly through the military cabinet, and it was up to the king to inform the war minister. Further, it was the king's desire to leave it to the chief of staff himself to pick officers to carry out special royal missions. (Army archives of the War Ministry, Ministerial Division A.g., subject: general staff and adjutant's office, 1817 to 1886, V, 2, 1, 6.)
38. See Moltke's military correspondence, Vols. 1-4. The first of these memorials was requested by the war minister, not in 1859 (as believed by G. Wohlers, *loc. cit.*, p. 26, who probably had in mind the memorial of February 7, 1859, Vol. 4, pp. 1-35), but, at the behest of the general department of the war ministry, as early as November 24, 1857. It was submitted on November 28, 1857—see Vol. 3, pp. 1ff. of the military correspondence; also H.F.A., War Ministry, Army Section, Vol. 2, 2, pp. 1-2, and Vol. 3.
39. Report by the general department on May 13, 1883 (Army Archives, War Ministry, Ministerial Division V, 2, 1, No. 6), on the occasion of an opinion on granting the general staff the formal right of direct access to the king even in peacetime. It states that in practice the position of the chief of staff, in terms of access, was entirely like that of the commanding generals.
40. After 1852 there were repeated requests for the expansion and reorganization of the general staff, and on March 19, 1861, the war minister was presented with a memorandum from the general department (reporter: Colonel von Alvensleben) proposing better training for general staff officers and higher salaries for general staff officers. The AfdpA objected, fearing especially economies in other spheres of the army budget that might endanger the three-year term, as did the department of military economics. Roon penciled his decision, pressing chiefly for regular front-line service on the part of general staff officers and limiting academic training to a set level. "In the general staff," he remarked, "we have always made bricks with straw, even under Frederic William III." But before any further action was taken, he insisted that the reorganization plan be submitted to the chief of staff. A final note of July 19, 1861, states that His Majesty had assented to Roon's proposals, but the files show no further disposition or response from Moltke. (H.F.A., War Ministry, Ministerial Division V, 2, 1, 6.) Of course Moltke, on his part, did not relinquish the initiative in matters of general staff reform. As early as May 20, 1859, he applied to Bonin for a budget for scientifically trained officers, who were to remain with the general staff for extended terms without frequent front service, since otherwise the scientific work of the general staff, especially geographic and historical studies, would not make enough headway. On May 29, he put in a request for expanding the inadequate resources of the general staff, an application often repeated subsequently (Army Archives, Rep. 4, A 1). The application of May 20, in some measure contravenes the policies of his predecessor, von Krauseneck, who viewed general staff service as temporary duty (see his memorial of March 8, 1843, Rep. 4, Z 1).
41. Moltke's order to the chief of staff of the guards corps, March 6, 1861.
42. See memorial of December, 1864, by Major General Petersen, chief of staff of the second army corps, in the files of the military cabinet on the general staff, Vol. 1 (known to me from the service manual on general staff service channels and general staff responsibility). This interesting memorial points out that in all other European armies the responsibility of chiefs of staff serving with troop commanders was far

better regulated than in Prussia, where only Müffling, in his 1822 directive, had made any serious effort to turn general staff officers into something more than mere assistants to the commander. This directive, however, had not been communicated to the command agencies and was thus ignored in practice. It was left entirely to the commander's tact and discretion whether he consulted his staff chief. The fateful consequences of this neglect had now become apparent in the Danish war. "It may be boldly asserted that every moment of urgency was missed, every situation judged wrongly."

43. By an order of August 4, 1862, to all chiefs of corps staffs, placing general staff officers serving with troops both under the chief of the grand general staff and the troop commander. General staff posts with troop units were filled, in the event of mobilization, by the military cabinet, with Moltke's advice (see his military correspondence, Vol. 1, No. 17, p. 54; also Moltke's letter to Manteuffel, December 3, 1864).

Notes to Chapter 8, Part 1

1. See R. Stadelmann, "Moltke und das 19. Jahrhundert," *Historische Zeitschrift,* Vol. 166 (1942), and the posthumously published work, *Moltke und der Staat* (1950), to which I had access in manuscript as early as 1944. I regard it as a particular piece of good fortune that both in subject matter and time our studies of Moltke ran parallel. I owe much to Stadelmann's work, both in respect of the total personality of Moltke and of individual details and pointers—just how much is not always easy to say, since our studies were simultaneous. I shall not always expressly state where my view departs from his.
2. Stadelmann rightly emphasizes this and demonstrates it, in contrast to some older, rather shallow biographical characterizations. See, however, Note 8, below.
3. Collected Works, Vol. 5, p. 174.
4. Schiffers, *Bismarck als Christ* (4th ed.; 1915), p. 97.
5. Letter to Below-Hohendorf, May 16,.1864, Collected Works, Vol. 2, p. 667; letter to his wife, July 20, 1864, *ibid.,* p. 672.
6. Collected Works, Vol. 1, pp. 40ff.
7. After von Priesdorff, *Soldatisches Führertum,* Vol. 7, p. 380 (1852-1853). Farewell thoughts of 1855 in the Collected Works, Vol. 5, p. 152.
8. Carefully researched proof will be found in Stadelmann, *loc. cit.,* especially Chapter 4. I would emphasize the total absence of political ambition and power drive even more strongly than Stadelmann.
9. M. Busch, *Tagebuchblätter,* Vol. 1, p. 299.
10. "He was a very rare kind of man, wholly devoted to duty, an odd character, always prepared and utterly reliable, yet cold to the heart." Bismarck to a delegation from Leipzig on May 23, 1895, quoted in Stadelmann, p. 32, after H. von Poschinger, *Bismarck. Neue Tischgespräche und Interviews* (1899), Vol. 2, p. 256.

Notes to Chapter 8, Part 2

1. "Strategie," in the military works, Vol. 2, p. 2, "Taktisch-strategische Aufsätze" (1900), also reprinted as No. 13 of the monographs on military history, published by the General Staff, 1890. Quite useless as a historical source is the compilation of passages from Moltke's essays, memorials, historical studies, and letters which the General Staff inserted as Part 4 of the military works under the title, "Moltke's Kriegslehren. Die operativen Vorbereitungen zur Schlacht." By some obscure means, Moltke's thoughts are here blended with editorial additions. For example, nowhere in Moltke's writings in this phrase to be found (p. 13): "Unfortunately [*sic*], politics cannot be separated from strategy"; nor can this dubious sentence: "What politics does with his [i.e., the military leader's] victories or defeats is not his affair—their exploitation is solely up to politics." One can virtually see how

Moltke's followers hardened the master's thoughts into dogma. Von Haeften, in his well-known essay on Bismarck and Moltke (*Preussische Jahrbücher,* Vol. 177, p. 97), naively cites these passages as original.

2. Remarks on W. von Blume's *Strategie* (1882), in *Preussische Jahrbücher,* Vol. 111 (1903), p. 228. The italics are mine, to emphasize the anonymous distortion mentioned in Note 1.

3. Memorial on the bombardment of Paris, November 30, 1870, military correspondence, Vol. 3, p. 417.

4. This is stated even more plainly in a letter to General Hegemann-Lindencrone of November 9, 1874, on the war of 1864 published in *Dansk Historisk Tidsskrift* and subsequently in *Preussische Jahrbücher,* Vol. 181 (1919), p. 268: At the beginning of a campaign, "in my view only very general instructions can be given to a commanding general, and these should be political rather than military."

5. See Chapter 3, pp. 60, 65, 66. See also this sentence: "Hence politics permeates the entire act of war, exerting a continual influence on it, insofar as the nature of its explosive forces permit" (Book 1, Chapter 1, No. 23).

6. On pp. 68f. of his excellent work, distinguished by its clarity and independence of judgment, *Die Entwicklung der strategischen Wissenschaft im 19. Jahrhundert* (1904), *Bibliothek der Politik und Volkswirtschaft,* 15, von Caemmerer unequivocally supports Bismarck and Clausewitz against Moltke and his disciple Verdy. W. von Blume, in *Strategie* (1882), pp. 25f., follows Moltke's words quite closely, but stresses in addition that military considerations must play a part even in the decision on war or peace and acknowledges that when military success is indifferent politics must again come to the fore. In his memorial on the bombardment of Paris in 1870-1871 (1899, p. 12), Moltke goes so far as to acknowledge that "even in the course of military operations the command must concede influence on its decisions to political considerations." Nevertheless, "as free a hand as possible must be given to skilled technical army leadership"–surely a most reasonable formulation. In the third part, on strategy (No. 1, pp. 51ff.), of his *Studien über den Krieg* (1902), Verdy du Vernois carefully analyzes Clausewitz's words, only to disavow them cautiously. He prefers to see a "mutuality" between politics and war rather than a dependence of the latter on the former. He accepts the fact, moreover, that there are military-political questions that cannot be settled on military lines alone (like the question of Napoleon III's military-political role before Sedan and after); but he merely concludes that the army command itself should and must then engage in political analysis. He would "supplement" Moltke's words by adding, on the one hand, that strategic considerations must influence politics even before the outbreak of war, while on the other hand, in certain cases, political factors (like the response of third powers, for example) will affect the course of military operations. See also his interesting letters of January 27, and February 13, 1896, to the Austrian chief of staff, Count Beck, in von Glaise-Horstenau, *Franz Josefs Weggefährte* (1930), pp. 468ff.

7. See p. 65, above.

8. *Das Volk in Waffen* (1st ed.; 1883, quoted from the 5th ed., 1899), p. 129.

9. The notion that it was above all wars of coalition that forced a blending of military and political considerations recurs again and again in the military writings of the school of Moltke. W. von Blume, in *Die Beschiessung von Paris und die Ursachen ihrer Verzögerung* (1899), p. 17, thus rather naively concludes that since the Franco-Prussian war constituted a duel, pure and simple, its course required no particular political intervention.

10. Von der Goltz, *loc. cit.,* pp. 126ff., applying also to the following. On occasion Moltke too described a "position of power" as the ideal–see Collected Works, Vol. 3, p. 426.

11. The most recent treatment of this subject is found in von Srbik, *Deutsche Einheit,* Vol. 4, pp. 456ff.

12. On the so-called war council in the wars of King William I, see the Collected Works, Vol.

3, p. 426. On Bismarck's protest against it, see Penzler, *Fürst Bismarck nach seiner Entlassung,* Vol. 2, pp. 200, 209ff.

13. The question is raised by R. Stadelmann, *loc. cit.,* Chapter 4.

14. Among many of his statements to that effect, see his Reichstag speech of January 11, 1887, Collected Works, Vol. 13, pp. 209ff., and especially his directive to the press section of the foreign office of August 7, 1864, Collected Works, Vol. 4, p. 531.

15. One piece of evidence among many: In a letter of May 10, 1888, William II said it had been a military error not to have "truly destroyed" the enemy in 1870-1871, together with France's military resources. Bismarck made this note in the margin: "Forty million people! And what about Europe?" (*Gedanken und Erinnerungen,* Vol. 2, p. 141–Vol. 15, p. 555, in my edition of the Collected Works). See also the preceding letter to Crown Prince William of May 9, 1888, in which he said it would be impossible to destroy Russia's military resources. In 1871 the Germans had been unable to prevent French rearmament, despite their thoroughgoing destruction of the French army (*Grosse Politik,* Vol. 6, p. 304).

16. More on this in Part 3 of this chapter.

17. *Gedanken und Erinnerungen,* Collected Works, Vol. 15, pp. 315, 317; *Grosse Politik,* Vol. 2, p. 88, dictated note of January 9, 1871: "I always hear the word Europe on the lips of politicians who ask of other powers what they dare not demand in their own name."

18. *Gedanken und Erinnerungen,* Collected Works, Vol. 15, p. 422.

19. Collected Works, Vol. 15, pp. 313f., chapter on Versailles.

20. Moltke, complaining about Schleinitz, January 17, 1861, in R. Stadelmann, "Moltke und die deutsche Frage," *Festschrift für K.A. von Müller* (1943), p. 33. The deployment plan of October 10, 1879, is found in Schmerfeld, *Aufmarschpläne 1871 bis 1890,* No. 7, *Forschungen und Darstellungen aus dem Reichsarchiv,* p. 83. A similar reference of February 7, 1859, in the military correspondence, Vol. 4, p. 4 and *passim.*

21. Moltke to his brother Adolf, January 1, 1852, after reading Pertz's life of Stein: "Our diplomats have always hurled us into misfortune, our generals have always saved us" (cited by R. Stadelmann in "Moltke und die deutsche Frage," *Festschrift für K. A. von Müller,* p. 24). See also letter by General von Voigts-Rhetz, April 1, 1871, in his *Briefe aus den Kriegsjahren 1866 und 1870/71* (1906), p. 342.

22. Military works, Vol. 3, p. 2 ("Kriegsgeschichtliche Arbeiten 1899"), where Moltke is highly critical of Danish war leadership in the hands of a minister responsibile to parliament: "Under pressure of public opinion, impassioned speeches in the assembly, and partisan furor, a minister responsible to the nation will find it hard to proceed on purely military considerations. Once war is declared the supreme commander must be given full freedom to act by his own discretion. A heavy responsibility weighs on him, before God and his conscience, beside which his responsibility before the tribunal of the nation pales into insignificance. Hence the sovereign is always the proper commander-in-chief, not accountable in theory, but actually bearing the heaviest responsibility—for who has more at stake when it comes to crown and scepter?" This essay was written in 1875. Moltke repeatedly discussed the baneful influence of politics on Bazaine's operations—see the compilation of his war doctrines in the military works, Vol. 4, pp. 37ff.

23. *Vom Kriege,* Book 8, Chapter 6b, pp. 570ff.

24. For that reason he insisted—with much exaggeration—that no council of war was ever held in 1866 or 1870-1871 (Collected Works, Vol. 3, p. 427), occasionally emphasizing that the king invariably took his military advice. See also his report to the king of January 25, 1871, *Preussische Jahrbücher,* Vol. 177, p. 100, Paragraph 2, and the highly characteristic opinions of members of the general staff reported by L. Schneider in *Aus dem Leben Kaiser Wilhelms,* Vol. 2, p. 237 (September, 1870). Apparently "the presence of the federal chancellor at headquarters was regarded as not merely unnecessary but as downright harmful. . . . Indeed, continuous political consultation could only hinder the speed and force of military action, blunting

swift decision by means of slow deliberation." In wartime it behooved diplomacy to practice reserve and wait until the army delivered the enemy to it, bound and defenseless, etc., etc.

25. Note Bismarck's notorious intervention in the deployment plan of 1866 (leaving the eighth army corps at the Rhine, instructions to Falckenstein), the debate over the turning of the Floridsdorf lines, or Moltke's complaint about the long and pointless discussion of February 8, 1871, on reinforcing the second army during the armistice, which was finally settled as Moltke wished after all. Sources are enumerated in Klein-Wuttig, *Politik und Kriegführung in den deutschen Einigungskriegen* (1934), pp. 155f. The most important source is Bronsart's diary, used in the article, "Moltke in Versailles," *Militärisches Wochenblatt* (1902), Column 2972. In the question of the bombardment of Paris too it must be acknowledged that Moltke's weighty objections to a premature bombardment were not taken into proper account by Bismarck and Roon. To the modern mind it is hard to grasp why the war minister, if he did indeed regard the bombardment as so urgent, devoted no greater energy to the timely procurement of adequate rolling stock from home for the artillery transports. In a long memorial of November 30, 1870, requested by the king two days earlier (military cabinet files, xxiv, Vol. 1), Roon tried to put the full blame on "land transport not subject to my official authority," and to the overloading of the rail line to Nanteuil. In manifest conflict with Moltke's coincident memorial (military correspondence, Vol. 3, pp. 417ff.), Roon insisted that if a real effort had been made, another 14,000 service and 600 to 800 depot horses should have been available to the field army, and a great many horses might have been requisitioned through the cavalry. The general staff, moreover, had not applied to the war ministry for the procurement of land transport, though Roon had on his own arranged to purchase 500 heavy vehicles. When one compares the picture drawn by Moltke, one finds that this purchase was effected rather late in the day and apparently only at the suggestion of the third army high command. Roon, from traditional Prussian thrift, seems to have relied too long on the requisitioning of inadequate carts and horses. An echo of these financial considerations is found in Bismarck's Collected Works, Vol. 15, p. 322, lines 27-36. O. Bihler, in his dissertation, *Die Beschiessung von Paris 1870/71 und die Ursachen ihrer Verzögerung* (Tübingen, 1932), makes virtually no attempt at a fair evaluation of the technical obstacles and reservations, and his study amounts to little more than a biased indictment of Blumenthal and his indubitably dogmatic views.

26. Reports to the King of November 18, and December 5, 1870, Collected Works, Vol. 6b, Nos. 1920, 1950.

27. Reported by von Haeften, from the diary of an unnamed general staff officer (Bronsart von Schellendorf), *Preussische Jahrbücher*, Vol. 177, p. 96. If true, it would mean that Bronsart acknowledged the need for the military and political leadership to work together. The same diary alleges that Bronsart, as chief of the operations division, compelled the King, by a kind of letter of resignation, not to implement a directive under which Bismarck would have been invited to military briefings of political import and would have been personally briefed whenever he wished. (Hermann Hass, *Der Kanzler und das Heer* [1939], pp. 30f; Dr. Hass kindly communicated this passage to me.) Bronsart's diary treats of these matters at great length. According to the crown prince's diary, p. 319, January 8, 1871, Moltke himself was indignant that Bismarck asked for answers to purely strategic questions.

28. Complaint to the King, January 25-26, 1871, in Stadelmann, *Moltke und der Staat*, pp. 434ff. See also Note 45, to Part 3, below. The claim is also plainly stated in the work by von Blume, who counters Bismarck's claim to be invited to military briefings with the argument that Bismarck "had left it entirely to the chief of staff how and where he got the political information he needed" (von Blume, *Beschiessung von Paris*, p. 19). The complaint that the general staff lacked political

information dates back to 1866 (military correspondence, Vol. 2, pp. 351, 355f.).
29. The justice of one of these complaints, of December 5, 1870 (Collected Works, Vol. 6b, p. 1950), has been difficult to judge, from the documentary material hitherto known, but can now be clarified, from the military cabinet papers (xxiv, Vol. 1). On that day Bismarck wrote the king in his own hand: "I respectfully ask Your Majesty, before deciding on whether negotiations are to be started with the Paris regime, graciously to allow me to present my views on this question, which touch essentially on my sphere of responsibility—von Bismarck." The king's penciled marginal note: "Since Colonel von Bronsart brought along your consent to the dispatch of the letter by Chief of Staff von Moltke to Trochu, I approved such dispatch. If you wish to postpone it until after you have seen me, please let Moltke know at once. I shall expect you at three o'clock—W., December 5, 1870." Bismarck's complaint followed (Collected Works, 6b, 1950), being actually handed in on December 6. The king's marginal note reads: "General Moltke and the war minister are to report on this—V [ersailles], December 6, 1870, W." An added note reads: "Read, G [eneral] Moltke, December 7, 1870." Some further marginal notes to No. 1950: beside the words "would seem doubtful to me...": "Why didn't Bronsart say so?" (p. 616. line 4); beside the words "never seen by me...": a question mark (p. 616, line 10); beside the words "not at all in agreement...": "If I had been told this, instead of his *agreement,* the letter would not have been dispatched. Bronsart does not seem to have received such a message?" Beside the words "to direct my presence ....": "This will always be done, as before, whenever really political questions are to be discussed" (p. 617, line 2); beside the words "to direct questions on the military situation...": "This is understood—W.... A considered [*motiviert*] reply sent to Bismarck, in accord with these marginal notes and the report of Lieutenant Colonel von Bronsart—W., December 10, 1870."

Bronsart reported to Moltke at Versailles on December 7, 1870, that two days before at ten o'clock in the morning he had read the draft of the letter intended for Trochu word for word to the chancellor, asking him whether he had any political objections, and then reporting the victory over the army of the Loire at Orléans. Bismarck asked that the word *volontièrement* be cut, solely for stylistic reasons, he said, and this was done. Bismarck further questioned whether the letter might not give Trochu the impression that the Germans were in trouble and were simply trying to intimidate him. Bronsart denied this possibility. Bismarck then said he had no objection in principle to the letter being sent, but the fall of Orléans announced in it should be awaited. Bronsart assured him Moltke shared this view. Bismarck further remarked that if the letter led to further negotiations, these should not be limited to military surrender but at the same time be directed toward peace negotiations. In the king's antechamber Bronsart learned that Orléans had been occupied and then simply reported Bismarck's concent to the king. He immediately reported to the chief of staff on what had taken place.

Thus there can scarcely be any doubt that the officers behaved quite correctly. Apparently Bismarck's doubts returned only after his talk with Bronsart. He was irked over being too late with his request for an audience, for he had anticipated that the fall of Orléans would take longer.
30. M. Busch, *Tagebuchblätter,* Vol. 1, p. 371, November 9, 1870.
31. See the rather petty quarrel over the military administration of Rheims—though this emanated from Podbielski, the quartermaster general, rather than from Moltke (Collected Works, Vol. 6b, No. 1797, with sources there cited). See also L. Schneider, *Aus dem Leben Kaiser Wilhelms,* Vol. 2, pp. 233ff.
32. See Chapter 6, above.
33. See von Stosch's highly instructive and shrewd letter to the crown prince, January 24, 1871, to which Stadelmann drew my attention (appendix to the crown prince's war diary, p. 483).
34. This is the burden of the book by Hermann Hass, *Der Kanzler und das Heer* (1939).

Notes to Chapter 8, Part 3

1. In his Machiavelli piece of 1807, *Philosophische Bibliothek* (F. Meiner), Vol. 163d (2nd ed.; 1919, supplementary volume to the works). See Gerhard Ritter, *Die Dämonie der Macht* (6th ed.; 1948), p. 141; Friedrich Meinecke, *Die Idee der Staatsraison* (1924), Book 3, Chapter 2. Book 1, Chapter 6, of *Weltbürgertum und Nationalstaat* shows persuasively how alien in effect is this Machiavelli essay within the totality of Fichte's political philosophy.
2. The abruptness of this change and the powerful influence on it of Hölderlin's notions of destiny and his enthusiasm for Greece can be instructively followed in Hegel's manuscripts—see Franz Rosenzweig, *Hegel und der Staat* (1920), especially Vol. 1, pp. 86ff.
3. *Grundlinien der Philosophie des Rechtes* (1824), Paragraphs 257, 258, 270.
4. *Philosophie des Rechtes*, Paragraphs 321, 323-326, 331, 334-337—especially 335.
5. *Loc. cit.*, Paragraph 338. For the following see Paragraph 324.
6. "Whatever value man possesses, all his spiritual reality, is his through the state alone' (Lasson [ed.], *Philosophie der Weltgeschichte*, [*Philosophische Bibliothek*, Vol. 171a], Vol. 1, p. 90). The implications of this sentence are awesome!
7. It appears very early with Hegel, as early as the *Phänomenologie des Geistes* (1807). See also the unpublished dissertation (already cited) by K. Kindler, "Die Entstehung des neudeutschen Nationalismus in den Befreiungskriegen" (Freiburg, 1950).
8. There is a single addition, traceable to Gans (possibly from university notebooks), to Paragraph 339 of the *Rechtsphilosophie* (Lasson edition, *Philosophische Bibliothek*, Vol. 124, p. 371): "The European nations, by the general principle of their laws, their customs and their culture, form a family, and this tends to modify international conduct away from the prevailing mode of the mutual infliction of harm." A very tenuous bond of traditional mutual consideration is thus acknowledged after all, though this does not seem to imply a moral obligation. For Hegel the Holy Alliance was but a "relative and limited" union among states (supplement to Paragraph 259, *ibid.*, p. 350).
9. Hegel's influence has been described in detail, not without a measure of bias and exaggeration, by Hermann Heller in *Hegel und der nationale Machtstaatsgedanke in Deutschland* (1921). On the position of Ranke and the historical school within this ideological trend see my book, *Geschichte als Bildungmacht* (2nd ed.: 1947), pp. 51ff., and also my book, *Europa und die deutsche Frage* (1948), pp. 66ff.; also Part 4, below.
10. *Sendschrift an den Politiker der Zukunft* (not available to me, hence cited after Heller, *loc. cit.*, p. 186).
11. *System der Staatslehre. A: Allgemeine Staatslehre* (1857), p. 408. For the following, see *ibid.*, pp. 376, 380, 538, 547, 556.
12. *Prinzip und Zukunft des Völkerrechts* (1871), here cited after Heller, *loc. cit.*, pp. 199ff. For even more far-reaching expressions of militant nationalism see *Das Kulturideal und der Krieg* (1868).
13. These basic thoughts recur in much milder form in *System der Rechtsphilosophie* (1882), Paragraphs 36 and 37. Here the state's power interest appears as a fixed entity beyond regulation by man's will and drifting so to speak by necessity into power conflicts. "There is but one morality, a morality for humans, for reasonable beings who can freely set their own goals. There is no morality in respect of states, for states act neither rightly nor wrongly but solely in accord with their nature, by necessity and without choice. They puruse their interests with shrewd selfishness." To run counter to these interests for the sake of a hypothetical social morality would ill befit a sovereign state. "The highest duty of government is to carry out the will of the state unselfishly, i.e., to act as a government in the cause of the state's shrewd selfishness." Fixed law among states would be unreasonable, if only because any system of fixed law essentially treats the parties to it as equals. Individuals, however, are quite different from states, and this difference is of the greatest

importance to mankind. "It is only natural that a nation of greater stature and greater value to culture should have wider scope on the stage of history." This cannot be settled by legal codes, but only by "the march of history, which brings about a just issue with the inexorable certainty inherent in it." For the most part, this takes the form of war, of arbitrament by force. "In normal circumstances, it is neither the rulers nor the people who resort to force, but the states themselves, through those who represent their will [*sic*]." To settle the issue by war is just, because it is not brute violence that triumphs, but rather superior culture, expressed in higher forms of organization, more advanced moral strength and insight. It is not brute force that prevails, but order, harmony and reason. "A victorious nation becomes one that leads and serves as an example. The great cultural eras therefore follow in the wake of the issue in wars." The judgment of history is manifested in terms of victory and triumph, of defeat and humiliation. It is a just verdict, because neither victory nor defeat is final unless the will of man submit to it.

We see the cohesive grandeur of the Hegelian system once again come impressively to the fore here. Yet we also see that this view of history was an outgrowth of its age, for on p. 408 we read that militant *hubris* is naturally held in check by the balance of the powers that lends uncertainty to the issue of any war; and again on p. 411 that brief wars with narrowly limited destruction of cultural resources may be followed by the kind of blessed revitalization of culture Lasson expects from the grandeur of war.

14. Pertz-Delbrück, *Das Leben Gneisenaus*, Vol. 5, p. 504. There is no reason for assuming that Clausewitz was influenced by Hegel, directly or indirectly. H. Heller, on p. 203, cites a work by Lieutenant Colonel P. Creuzinger, *Hegels Einfluss auf Clausewitz* (1911), but this turns out to be no more than an eccentric notion by an amateur philosopher.

15. R. Stadelmann, in *Moltke und der Staat,* traces the development of Moltke's political ideology with great care and dedication. His impressive treatment of the subject renders all the older monographs obsolete—R. Peschke, "Moltke's Stellung zur Politik bis zum Jahre 1857" (Dissertation; Berlin, 1912), and the same author's article, "Moltke als Politiker," *Preussische Jahrbücher,* Vol. 158 (1914); and R. Rapp, "Moltke's politische Anschauungen" (Dissertation; Freiburg, 1925). Both these writers deny that Moltke had any real political sense. O. Schiff, on the other hand, in "Moltke als politischer Denker," *Preussische Jahrbücher,* Vol. 181 (1920), rightly disputes the charge that Moltke merely shared the views of the average Prussian officer. Stadelmann acknowledges that Moltke lacked certain qualities of political militancy, but seeks to show that he was nevertheless a political thinker of stature and strong independence. He dwells especially on Moltke's Great German and dualist notions of empire and on the related thoughts of the Swabian, Wolfgang Menzel. I am unable to follow him in these sympathies and believe he rather overestimates the practical significance of the Great German ideal in Moltke's political orientation. There seems no reason to question that for Moltke politics was an acquired interest rather than a congenial preoccupation and that he was deeply concerned with it only when it directly touched the military sphere.

16. Correspondence with Bluntschli and Goubareff, 1880-1881, Collected Works, Vol. 5, pp. 194ff—for the following as well.

17. *Loc. cit.,* p. 200. Similar sentiments are found in a letter of February 28, 1879, in Andreas (ed.), *Letters,* Vol. 2, p. 455: ". . . . that every war, even one that is victorious, represents a national misfortune."

18. Letters to his fiancée and wife and other relatives, *Letters* (1894), Vol. 2, p. 327. During the Crimean War he spoke of "human slaughter" (Collected Works, Vol. 4, p. 156). The national war of 1870 he described as "a step backward into barbarism" (to Adolf von Moltke, October 27, 1870, *ibid.,* p. 205). In October, 1870, he said it was "a pity for each and every one who might still fall, now that the fate of the war is decided" (Collected Works, Vol. 5, p. 178). In Moltke's earliest writings, dating back to the 1830's, an even more pacifist note is struck. Occasionally he even spoke

of war as an expression of "crude barbaric instincts" (Collected Works, Vol. 2, p. 225).

19. Moltke strongly emphasized the educational mission of universal military duty. The military estate trained men "to physical fitness and mental vigor, order and punctuality, loyalty and obedience, love of country, and manly virtue" – speech of February 16, 1874, Collected Works, Vol. 7, p. 108. Similar sentiments are found in the draft for a speech before the parliament of the customs union, *ibid.*, pp. 13f.

20. Collected Works, Vol. 5, p. 194; Andreas (ed.), *Letters*, Vol. 2, p. 455.

21. Last Reichstag speech of May 14, 1890, Collected Works, Vol. 7, p. 138. Similar sentiments as early as February 10, 1881, in a letter to Goubareff, Collected Works, Vol. 5, pp. 200f.: "If only governments everywhere were strong enough to control popular passions that clamor for war!' See also the introduction to *Die Geschichte des deutsch-französischen Krieges 1870/71*, Collected Works, Vol. 3.

22. Letters to fiancée and wife of September 16, 1864, *Letters*, 1894, Vol. 2, p. 173; the diaries of Emperor Frederic, 1848-1866, p. 359; and chiefly Platzhoff, Rheindorf and Tiedje (eds.), *Bismarck und die nordschleswigsche Frage* (1925), p. 397. To Ambassador von Schweinitz Moltke said in 1869: "Alsen we could surrender, except for Sonderburg" (Schweinitz, *Denkwürdigkeiten*, p. 249, also in Kessel, *Gespräche*, p. 125). By Benedetti's report, he told the Danish and Swedish envoys in April, 1868, that it would be sufficient if Prussia, instead of Alsen and Düppel, kept the Droacker peninsula, whence its guns could command Sonderburg and passage to the Alsen and Flensburg fjords. (*Origines Diplomatiques*, Vol. 21, No. 6632, pp. 153f.; also A. Friis, *De Nordslesvisk spørgsmall*, Vol. 2, pp. 8f., 53 72f.) It is interesting to compare these utterances with the fanciful notions of civil strategy developed by the nationalist Johannes Haller in *Bismarck's Friedens-schlüsse* (1916), pp. 21f.

23. Collected Works, Vol. 4, p. 181 (to his brother Adolf, May 20, 1866).

24. *Die auswärtige Politik Preussens*, Vol. 6, p. 180.

25. Unpublished directive to the military negotiators in Prague, August 22, 1866, after R. Stadelmann, *loc. cit.*, Chapter 2, Notes 262 and 265; letter to his wife, July 23, 1866, Collected Works, Vol. 6, p. 455; Friedjung, *Kampf um die Vorherrschaft*, Vol. 2, pp. 580f. For further details I make reference to the excellent study by my student Anneliese Klein-Wuttig: "Politik und Kriegführung in den deutschen Einigungskriegen 1864, 1866 und 1870/71," *Abhandlungen für mittlere und neuere Geschichte*, edited by G. Ritter *et al.* (Berlin, 1934), which deals exhaustively with the source material known up until that time; also to the very detailed work of R. Stadelmann, *loc. cit.*, enriched with more recent documentary findings. These references make it unnecessary for me to enter into another detailed account of the much-discussed quarrels at headquarters in 1870-1871. In his *Fragen des Präventivkriegs*, R. Stadelmann has dealt at such length also with the crises of 1867, 1875, and 1887 that I may here rest content with discussing his findings.

26. Military correspondence, Vol. 4, pp. 103f., May 19, 1859.

27. A carefully documented account of the negotiations is given in Stadelmann, "Moltke und die deutsche Frage," in *Stufen und Wandlungen der deutschen Einheit. Festschrift für K.A. von Müller* (1943). I do not understand how Stadelmann, in this objectively meritorious study, could have misread almost entirely Moltke's impossible political attitude, casting all the odium on Foreign Minister Schleinitz – who was indeed a man of no great stature – and thus reaching a highly favorable judgment of Moltke's political abilities. Moltke was convinced that war would automatically realize all Prussia's legitimate claims for power, which Stadelmann describes as a "profound and genuine belief in the organizing power of action." I hold a contrary view. Bismarck knew very well why he did not start the war against France until he had pledged the middle states to unconditional military and political allegiance in war.

28. R. Stadelmann, *Moltke und der Staat*, Chapter 3. Bismarck's disappointment speaks plainly from his telegrams to von der Goltz, A.P.P., Vol. 8, pp. 316, 332. But he

immediately used the opinion to increase the diplomatic pressure on France.

29. Letter to his brother Adolf, January 24, 1868, Collected Works, Vol. 4, pp. 188f.

30. Military correspondence, Vol. 3, p. 115 (winter of 1868-1869).

31. I originally held a contrary view, but Stadelmann's account and a careful check of his sources has convinced me otherwise.

32. Conversation with Bethusy-Huc, Collected Works, Vol. 5, p. 298; Kessel (ed.), *Gespräche*, p. 105. See also the highly significant talk with Ambassador von Schweinitz, of December 12, 1869, *Denkwürdigkeiten*, p. 249 (p. 125 in Kessel): "If Austria rearms, we should really declare war against France at once, so that we will have finished within the three months it will take Austria to be ready for war. Austrian rearmament would be a sure sign that Napoleon had agreed to it and planned to attack us, being too weak by himself."

33. This statement was made to the former minister of religious affairs von Mühler in 1872–see W. Reichle, *Zwischen Staat und Kirche. Das Leben und Wirken des preussischen Kultusministers Heinrich von Mühler* (1938), p. 427; also the unerring judgment of the French ambassador, Gontaut-Biron, in 1875: "Il a un horreur sincère de la guerre, quoique ce soit à elle qu'il doive sa position actuelle; mais il trouve les avantages possibles en écrasant l'adversaire" (P. Vasili: *La société de Berlin* [Paris, 1884], pp. 130f.). I owe both these references to R. Stadelmann.

34. Unlike Stadelmann (*Historische Zeitschrift*, Vol. 166, p. 305), I would not be inclined to say that Moltke was nationalist in political outlook*(nationalpolitischer Blick)*.

35. In a discussion with the crown prince on January 8, 1871, Moltke said: "We must fight this nation of liars to the end and subjugate it completely" (diaries of Grand Duke Friedrich I of Baden, edited by H. von Oncken, Vol. 2, p. 300). It must be noted, however, that he treated civilian snipers much less harshly than Bismarck would have wished!

36. Direct report to the King, December 28, 1870-January 8, 1871, Collected Works, Vol. 6b, pp. 648ff. Especially characteristic of Bismarck's thinking in this petition is the remark that "a situation has been created in which our progress toward the goal of peace ... is all out of proportion to the cost in men and money [*sic*]." Any eighteenth-century cabinet politician might have said these words!

37. This is also admitted in von Blume, *Die Beschiessung von Paris*, p. 44.

38. Memorial of December 14, 1870, Collected Works, Vol. 6b, p. 634.

39. See the memorial just cited. Remarks made in private conversation may be found in M. Busch, the diaries of Frederic III, Stosch, and many other memoirs. On the legal aspects, see Bluntschli, *Das moderne Völkerrecht* (3rd ed., 1878); on the behavior of the German troops, Gabriel Monod, *Allemands et Français* (1872). Vol. 2 of E. Eyck's Bismarck biography emphasizes its subject's harsh statement on the struggle with the civilian population, the Zouaves, etc., without distinguishing sufficiently between private and public statements, and without taking into account that sniper terror could be controlled only by counter-terror, within certain limitations imposed by international law, which Bismarck never exceeded, in his official directives and elsewhere. It should also be noted that the chancellor was not altogether wrong when he remarked that the drastic reprisals were often not put into effect by the army.

40. A. O. Meyer, "Bismarck und Moltke vor dem Fall von Paris und beim Friedensschluss," in *Stufen und Wandlungen der deutschen Einheit, Festschrift für Srbik* (1943).

41. Conversation with the crown prince, January 8, 1871, Grand Duke Frederic, *loc. cit.*, Vol. 2, p. 300. Stadelmann thinks this was a dogmatic application of Clausewitz's doctrine of true warfare–the strategy of subjugation. A. O. Meyer, *loc. cit.*, it seems to me, fails to refute this view when he observes that only in this special situation did Moltke see no other way to achieve peace.

42. Collected Works, Vol. 6b, No. 2005, pp. 665ff.

43. War diary of Emperor Frederic III, p. 325, January 8, 1871.

44. Stosch, *Denkwürdigkeiten*, p. 227; Grand Duke Frederic, Vol. 2, p. 328.

45. Von Haeften, in *Preussische Jahrbücher*, Vol. 177 (1919), gives a rather imprecise

account of the incident, as reflected in the documents. I myself first corrected this, from the files of the military cabinet, in a wartime lecture that appeared in mimeographed form and was subsequently reprinted in *Deutschland und Europa, Festschrift für Rothfels* (1951), pp. 69ff. This persuaded Stadelmann, in *Moltke und der Staat*, to reproduce Moltke's bill in facsimile, at various stages of its composition. See also the documentary study by W. Förster, *Moltke, Persönlichkeit und Werk* (1943), p. 34.

46. E. E. von Krause, *Ein deutsches Soldatenleben* (1901), p. 140. Similar sentiments appear in the Reichstag speech of April 14, 1874, Collected Works, Vol. 7, p. 117.

47. For example, General Alvensleben, who wished to retain French territory all the way to the Marne—M. Busch, *Tagebuchblätter*, Vol. 1, p. 103.

48. As early as 1867 Moltke had described the fortification work around Belfort as "totally irrelevant" (military correspondence, Vol. 3, p. 79). Even in the deployment plans of 1872-1873 Belfort plays only a subsidiary role (Schmerfeld [ed.], *Aufmarschpläne 1871-1890*, [1929], pp. 19-25). See also Moltke to his brother, March 11, 1871, Collected Works, Vol. 4, p. 29. Details in Stadelmann's book on Moltke.

49. He reaffirmed this time and again—see the crown prince's diary, p. 399; Grand Duke Frederic, Vol. 2, pp. 381, 383.

50. Diaries from the years 1866 and 1870-1871 (1902), pp. 263f. Of considerable interest is the conversation Blumenthal had two days earlier with the crown prince (*ibid.,* pp. 201f.). He did not then dare to oppose openly the prince's willingness to forego Metz, being content to see the fortress dismantled, if Metz was indeed "French through and through."

51. Fitzmaurice, *Life of the Second Earl Granville* (1905), Vol. 2, p. 49 (discussion with Odo Russell, March 1, 1873); Kessel (ed.), *Gespräche,* pp. 174ff. (discussion with Gontaut-Biron, April 25, 1872, according to Gontaut's memoirs).

52. Schmerfeld (ed.), *Aufmarschpläne 1871-1890* (1929), pp. 20, 25; *ibid.,* p. 23. "No matter who first declares war, the war will actually have been started by the French government" (*ibid.,* p. 23).

53. *Documents diplomatiques français, 1871-1914* (1929), I, 1, No. 406, p. 441—official report by Gontaut-Biron, from what Baron Nothomb told him. This passage is also reproduced, from Gontaut's memoirs, by von Kessel, *Gespräche Moltkes,* pp. 180f. Nothomb's report to Brussels is also reflected in *Documents diplomatiques français,* I, 1, No. 413, p. 450. On the significance of the Nothomb conversation, see also Stadelmann, *loc. cit.,* pp. 291f.

54. The French ambassador, Gontaut-Biron, on one occasion, put forward this argument to Manteuffel, when the latter kept talking about the "inevitability" of a revanchist war, given France's situation. "Inévitable dis-je? Je ne la crois pas telle, car je suis convaincu, qu'il y a d'autres moyens que la guerre pour réparer des désastres; mais si on la jugeait telle ice, il faudrait donc croire que l'Allemagne ne nous a imposé une paix aussi onereuse qu'avec la conviction que tôt ou tard la France, comme étouffée dans ses conditions, la violerait et serait invinciblement amenée à recommencer la guerre? " (*Documents diplomatiques francais,* Vol. I, 1, 431, April 30, 1875).

55. That it originated indirectly with Bismarck is now unequivocally proven by Aegidi's letter to Kruse, editor of the *Kölnische Zeitung*—see *Deutscher Liberalismus im Zeitalter Bismarcks,* edited by Wentzcke (1926), Vol. 2, p. 124. On Moltke's attitude and the latest status of the problem, see especially Stadelmann, *loc. cit.,* pp. 284ff.

56. In addition to the incident with Gontaut, there is evidence of a discussion with Odo Russell on May 2—Russell's dispatch was reprinted by W. Taffs in *Slavonic Review,* Vol. 9 (1930-1931), pp. 634ff., and in *Lord Odo Russell* (1938). The content is also given in Kurt Meine, "England und Deutschland, 1871-1876," *Eberings Historische Studien,* Vol. 306 (1937), p. 157. Moltke seems to have said that in his view peace would not be broken by the power that marched first, but by the power that made it necessary for another to defend itself. The effect on British policy was very strong, and Bismarck's perplexity at the British attitude is not altogether explained in the circumstances (*Grosse Politik,* Vol. 1, p. 281). On other statements about the

danger of war to Miguel, see Treitschke, letters, Vol. 4, p. 414; and to Mohl, Stadelmann, *loc. cit.*, p. 515, Note 81.

57. *Grosse Politik,* Vol. 1, p. 282, which records that Emperor William regarded preventive war as morally irresponsible among states. In addition it would alienate public opinion throughout the world.

58. War minister von Kameke evidently entertained similar thoughts—see *Grosse Politik,* Vol. 1, p. 295, note to a private letter by Hohenlohe to Bismarck of April 21, 1875. W. Kloster in *Der deutsche Generalstab und der Präventivkriegsgedanke* (1932), seeks to play down Moltke's bellicose statement of 1875 and even to deny it was ever made, but he does not succeed. What is correct, however, is that on this occasion no open political conflict took place between Moltke and Bismarck.

59. Schmerfeld (ed.), *Aufmarschpläne, 1871-1890* (1929). In the memorial of April 17, 1871, Russo-German hostility is described as rooted in ethnic differences (p. 5), while the Province of Prussia is described as a target much coveted by the Russians (p. 11). On February 3, 1877 (p. 65), and in April, 1879 (p. 77), this territory is again described as Russia's most immediate objective for conquest. In a note made in the early 1880's (p. 108), on the other hand, doubt is expressed that the Russians, in their current mood, would welcome such a major acquisition of German elements. The Pan-Slav movement would probably be more pleased with Galicia. Usually—e.g., on April 27, 1871 (p. 5)—Moltke pictured Turkey, Istanbul, and the Dardanelles as the Russian main targets. The 1871 memorial speaks of an inherent Russo-German conflict of interest, but an exposé of February 3, 1877, begins with these words (p. 65): "It is hard to see why Russia should have any good reason to ally itself with France. . . . The purpose of such a war would probably be no more than the expansion of its already limitless territory," to wit, the acquisition of the seaports of East and West Prussia. A similar statement appears in 1880 (p. 87): "There seems to be no valid reason why Russia should attack us alone." Russia's real enemy was Austria, Germany being of but secondary importance—the precise opposite of the text of April, 1871 (p. 5).

60. Conversation with Gorchakov, 1872. Moltke "faisait observer, que ces grandes armées de l'Europe étaient quelque chose d'effrayant"—report by Gontaut, from a communication by Gorchakov, September 13, 1872, *Documents diplomatiques français,* Vol. I, 1, p. 184.

61. In the west there was at best Belfort, but there was nothing of any use to the Germans in the east, where instead they might face the unwelcome prospect of having to restore Poland. For the rest, the Russians were "unpleasant neighbors, for they have absolutely nothing that could be taken away from them, even after the most resounding victory. They have no gold, and we have no use for land." Letter to Lucius von Ballhausen in his volume of recollections of Bismarck, p. 139. See also the concise review by P. Rassow, *Der Plan des Feldmarschalls Grafen Moltke für den Zweifrontenkrieg, 1871-1890* (Breslau, 1936). In my view Rassow fails to grasp the conflict between Bismarck and Moltke on the question of campaign plans, discussed in the following.

62. See his discussion with Ambassador von Schweinitz of October 28, 1881. In contrast to Moltke's new plans, he favored an offensive in the west rather than the east, for "in Russia there are no objectives, the capture of which might end the war" (Schweinitz, *Denkwürdigkeiten,* Vol. 2, p. 174). The secret journal of the General Staff in the Army Archives reveals that early in 1877 lively discussions on the danger of an east-west war took place between the chief of staff and the foreign office. W. Windelband, *Bismarck und die europäischen Grossmächte 1879-1885* (1940), pp. 49f., reports that Bismarck and Moltke joined in a common line of action on the war question in February, 1877. According to this version, both men, with the support of War Minister von Kameke, prevailed on William I, after a long struggle, to authorize reinforcement of the western border garrisons. Windelband's documentation, however, fails to demonstrate that Bismarck was actually aware of Moltke's deployment plan of February 3, 1877 (Schmerfeld [ed.], *Aufmarschpläne* pp. 65ff.), still less that he approved of the preventive war sentiments expressed in that

document. From his attitude in 1887, however, this is probable (see Note 64, below). In the east too, Bismarck sought to secure the border against Russian surprise attack by reinforcing the garrisons, while Moltke, for technical reasons, thought it better to anticipate the Russians by German mobilization, which was unpalatable to the Reich chancellor (Schmerfeld [ed.], *Aufmarschpläne*, pp. 109ff.).

63. Bismarck expressed himself quite openly–though in theoretical terms–in his Reichstag speech of November 4, 1871 (Collected Works, Vol. 11, p. 204). He described a timely strike in such situations as "aggressive defense," citing the example of Frederic the Great. In a country with Prussia-Germany's central location there were frequent cases in which enemy attack could be precluded only by a timely strike. It was "the government's duty . . . when a war becomes truly unavoidable, to choose a time for waging it at which it will exact the least sacrifice and hold the smallest danger for country and people." He seems to have remained unaware that in this formulation he contradicted in some measure his sharp rejection of preventive war stated elsewhere (see Part 4, below). On this point, as in all matters, Bismarck made up his mind on the basis of concrete situations rather than by fixed dogma. A similar phrase occurs in his directive to Arnim of October 30, 1873 (*Grosse Politik*, Vol. 1, p. 221): "Once a government, against its inclinations, is compelled to consider war unavoidable, it would be acting with the utmost folly to permit the enemy to pick time and occasion at his pleasure, to wait for the moment most suitable to the enemy."

64. This becomes quite plain from his attitude toward the danger of war in 1887. In the event of an Austro-Russian war, he was willing to attack France at once, if necessary with a German declaration of war, unless peace with France was "better safeguarded than it is now." If Austria were the aggressor in the east, he would make German participation dependent on the course of the French campaign; but even if Austria were not the aggressor, he would postpone German intervention in the east until the western border had been secured (*Grosse Politik*, Vol. 6, pp. 68, December, 1887).

65. To Count Hatzfeld–see the recipient's letter to Holstein, June 18, 1895, *Grosse Politik*, Vol. 9, p. 353.

66. Memorial and accompanying letter of November 30, 1887, see Schmerfeld (ed.), *Aufmarschpläne*. On Waldersee's authorship, see his *Denkwürdigkeiten*, Vol. 1, pp. 338f.; Hans Mohs (ed.), *Generalfeldmarschall Graf von Waldersee in seinem militärischen Wirken* (1929), Vol. 2, pp. 299ff.

67. There is much documentary evidence in the detailed account by H. Krausnick, *Holsteins Geheimpolitik in der Ära Bismarck, 1886-1890* (1942), especially on pp. 149ff. See also *Grosse Politik*, Vol. 6; von Glaise-Horstenau, *Franz Josefs Weggefährte. Das Leben des Generalstabschef Grafen Beck* (1930), pp. 306ff.; and other older accounts, in addition to the newer one in Stadelmann's book on Moltke.

68. In this process he was under the misapprehension that Waldersee had disputed the likelihood of a Russian attack in general to the Austrians. The real conflict was that Waldersee now did not regard as urgent the reinforcement of the Galician border garrisons, which Bismarck desired. Instead, Waldersee was pressing for offensive war on Russia as soon as possible. That was all Bismarck remembered in *Gedanken und Erinnerungen*, Vol. 3, p. 135 (Collected Works, Vol. 15, p. 554). On this misunderstanding, see Krausnick, *loc. cit.*, pp. 151ff. The Moltke-Waldersee memorial of November 30, was passed on to Vienna (on December 9–see Waldersee, *loc. cit.*, pp. 421f.) only to counteract the alleged "optimism" in Waldersee's statements on the war danger, and to encourage Austrian rearmament.

69. Von Glaise-Horstenau, *loc. cit.*, p. 463. The concession in Point 3 of the reply, pledging commitment of "more than half the German forces against Russia" in the event of French neutrality, was virtually meaningless, since no one counted on French neutrality.

70. *Gedanken und Erinnerungen*, Vol. 3, pp. 136ff.; Collected Works, Vol. 15, pp. 554ff.

71. See my essay, "Die Zusammenarbeit der Generalstäbe Deutschlands und Österreich-

Ungarns vor dem 1. Weltkrieg," in *Festschrift für H. Herzfeld* (1958), pp. 523ff. On the Moltke-Waldersee deployment plans after 1887, see also E. Kessel, *Moltke* (1958), pp. 713ff.

72. P. Rassow, *loc. cit.*, p. 5.

73. Military correspondence, Vol. 3, pp. 16ff., No. 3 (Spring, 1860). Similar deductions appear in many other places, e.g., the memorial of April 27, 1871, Schmerfeld (ed.), *Aufmarschpläne,* p. 5, Paragraph 3, where it is stated that Russia would one day have to turn on Germany.

74. Examples: memorial of December, 1859, on a two-front war against Russia and France, Schmerfeld (ed.), *Selected Works,* Vol. 4, pp. 20f. Deployment plans for war against France, Austria, and Russia (Spring, 1860), military correspondence, Vol. 2, No. 1; against Bavaria, Austria, and France, over the controversy in the Elector- ate of Hesse, *ibid.*, Vol. 3, No. 2; deployment plans against the eventuality of a Franco-Austrian war of aggression between 1877 and 1879, Schmerfeld (ed.), *Aufmarschpläne,* pp. 15, 17. The number of unpublished studies and drafts, for the most part in Moltke's own fine hand, is truly astonishing. At the Army Archives in Potsdam they reposed in the files for the most part without any further documenta- tion. My efforts to gain a clear picture of the chief of staff's dealings with the foreign office, with the help of the secret journal of the chief of staff (1869-1914), showed that in quiet times there was very little exchange, usually limited to the mutual transmission of information from abroad. A great deal was apparently discussed only by word of mouth between the two agencies. Unfortunately, the political archives of the foreign office were not accessible to me during the war.

75. This is vividly illustrated in Vol. A III, 1, I, war archives of the General Staff (Army Archives), also from a volume entitled *Vorbereitung zum Krieg 1864, ibid.,* Vol. 18Z 2314, III, II, 1, in which, however, Moltke appears in the role of full-fledged adviser to the war minister. On this question see also my lecture, "Kriegführung und Politik im Reiche Bismarcks," in *Deutschland und Europa. Festschrift für H. Rothfels* (1951).

76. See his speech of February 16, 1874, Collected Works, Vol. 7, p. 106: "The first requirement of a state is to exist and to see its survival outwardly secured. . . . As between states, the only outward security lies in power." In Vol. 2 of the Collected Works is an essay, "Die westliche Grenzfrage," which according to a study by E. Kessel in *Historische Zeitschrift,* Vol. 161 (1940), p. 436, is by Wolfgang Menzel rather than Moltke, It strongly emphasizes the primacy of foreign policy; and since both authors were on close terms, it undoubtedly accords with Moltke's views. Germany must learn (pp. 117f.) to examine all political questions "in the larger national context, and never to forget foreign policy over domestic discord. . . . Even in times of deepest peace, we must always look on ourselves as a great army, entrenched in a field camp within sight of a powerful enemy. . . . We must always form a front toward the foe from without."

Notes to Chapter 8, Part 4

1. See W. Fritzemeyer, *Christenheit und Europa. Zur Geschichte des europäischen Gemeinschaftsgefühls von Dante bis Leibniz,* Supplement No. 23, to the *His- torische Zeitschrift* (1931). It is significant that even medieval Christendom felt itself to be more a community than a federation of sovereign states in the form of the Holy Roman Empire.

2. Documentation in the excellent study of Hermann von Caemmerer, "Rankes grosse Mächte und die Geschichtsschreibung des 18. Jahrhunderts," in *Festschrift für Max Lenz: Studien und Versuche zur neueren Geschichte* (1910). Of special significance in our context is the demonstration that Ancillon as well as Gentz and Heeren regarded a balance as indispensable to the independence of free nations and a secure peace. As we know, the theory of the balance of Europe has been given the most diverse interpretations since the sixteenth century. It appears on the one hand as the guarantor of a "republic of states" against universal rule by one power, on the

other hand as equilibrium between two major powers, benefiting a neutral third power which actually holds the "balance of power." On this subject see H. Meisner, "Vom europäischen Gleichgewicht," *Preussische Jahrbücher*, Vol. 176 (1919).

3. See above. In a milder and more cautious form, this thought also occurs in Ranke, *Politisches Gespräch:* "You can name precious few wars of any consequence which cannot be shown to have ended in the victory of true moral energy."

4. Meinecke, *Weltbürgertum und Nationalstaat*, Book 1, *passim*. In keeping with the political mood of the pre-war era around 1907, these "universalist aftereffects" seem to this author a flaw that has not yet been removed. Such demonstrations may today have taken a rather different meaning, in the face of the exaggerated militant and imperialist traits in the ideology of awakening neo-German nationalism perpetuated by the latest English war propagandists. See for example Rohan d'O. Butler, *The Roots of National Socialism 1783-1933* (London, 1941). Eberhard von Vietsch's *Das europäische Gleichgewicht* (1942), seeks to show that the notion of the balance of Europe, while specifically the outgrowth of West European thought, always remained an alien intrusian on German soil. This proposition can be rendered plausible only by artificial exaggeration of national differences. On the other hand, I concur with the observation that the strong emphasis on the idea of balance in nineteenth-century West Europe somehow seems to be connected with the waning political spirit of the French and the British Empire's needs for security.

5. Adam Müller, *Elemente der Staatskunst* (1809), Lecture Nos. 4, 6, 10, 33. Heeren's doctrine of the unity of the "European system of states" should also be borne in mind in this connection.

6. On Niebuhr, see Meinecke, *loc. cit.,* pp. 216, 218ff. On Stein, see my biography, especially my critique of Meinecke, Vol. 2, pp. 366ff., 387f.

7. See for example J. G. Droysen, *Historik,* edited by Hübner (1937), p. 262: "The progressive development of international law suggests the idea that in certain aspects like trade, education, law, etc., states actually form a single great community, in which the sharp divisions contingent on the exercise of power are not entirely removed but inapplicable in respect of the most important matters and the orderly progress of affairs. This notion has been pursued in one form or another ever since the Roman Empire, to prevail at last in the form of the system of states. The church in its catholicity has not been able to bring this boon to mankind, nor the cabinet policy of alliances and counterpoises developed since the Thirty-Years' War, but only the insight springing from progressive philosophy that the great moral values men hold in common, while related to the state and its honor and safety, do not stem from it, nor exist for it, nor are confined within its borders." This is followed by a protest against the "exalted notion of the state projected by the doctrines of the last four generations," i.e., the blind worship of absolute state power, the frightful consequences of which were demonstrated by the Revolution of 1848, especially in France. "An abyss of danger to the highest moral values" had then opened up. We observe that this universalism feeds on the kind of progressive libertarianism that resisted narrow confinement within nationalist ties. This is also true of Heinrich von Treitschke's occasional protests against excessive nationalist "stupidity," compiled by Friedrich Meinecke, *loc. cit.,* p. 502.

8. See my study, "Bismarck und die Rheinpolitik Napoleons III," in *Vierteljahresblätter*, Vols. 15-16 (1950-1951).

9. See R. Stadelmann, *Das Jahr 1865 und das Problem von Bismarcks deutscher Politik*, Supplement No. 29 to the *Historische Zeitschrift*; and H. von Srbik, *Deutsche Einheit*, Vol. 4, especially Book 9, Chapters 3-7. At a later date, I plan to deal with Stadelmann's ideas, on the basis of the sources. Let me here suggest only that none of Bismarck's attempted dualist and conservative solutions to the German constitutional problems seems to me definitive, and that I think I can prove that every one of them deliberately kept the door open to a solution by force of arms. It was always no more than a question of undermining Austria's power in Germany—preferably, of course, in a way that would avoid or at least postpone war. Further indications are given in the following text.

10. H. Friedjung, *Kampf um die Vorherrschaft* (4th ed.), Vol. 2, pp. 545f., June 13, 1890 (Collected Works, Vol. 9, pp. 49f.).
11. Speech of April 1, 1895, Collected Works, Vol. 13, p. 556.
12. *Gedanken und Erinnerungen,* Vol. 2, p. 93.
13. See, for example, *Gedanken und Erinnerungen,* Vol. 2, pp. 157f.; M. Busch, *Tagebuch-blätter,* Vol. 1, pp. 447ff.; letters to his fiancée and wife, *passim;* A. O. Meyer, "Bismarcks Blaube im Spiegel der 'Losungen und Lehrtexte,' " *Münchner histo-rische Abhandlungen* Vol. 1 (1933), pp. 1 and especially 7ff.; as well as the older literature on Bismarck's attitude toward religion. Especially memorable is the discussion with R. von Keudell of November 30, 1863 (*Fürst und Fürstin Bismarck,* p. 136), at the moment of the first decision to make war: "That you who know me so long and so well should think I went into this big thing like an ensign, without realizing what lies ahead and what I must answer for before God – that is intolerable. It has cost me two nights' sleep."
14. Collected Works, Vol. 10, pp. 103f.
15. Collected Works, Vol. 7, pp. 186f., after Poschinger, *Bismarck und die Parlamentarier,* Vol. 3, p. 285. Similar sentiments were reported by the Württemberg envoy H. von Spitzemberg to Varnbüler on April 2, 1867: "Every foreign minister should be compelled to take the field and especially to witness the horror in the base hospitals. They would not take war so easily then." (*Die auswärtige Politik Preussens,* Vol. 8. p. 558, note.) A similar report comes from Grand Duke Frederic of Baden, on April 14, 1867. (Oncken, *Grossherzog Friedrich,* Vol. 2, p. 86.) See also his discussion with high school teachers in August, 1867 (Collected Works, Vol. 7, p. 219): "Anyone who has ever looked into the glazing eye of a dying soldier on the battlefield will think hard before he starts a war." Still other discussions in this vein took place with Völderndorff in May, 1868 (Collected Works, Vol. 7, p. 261) and Count Keyserling on October 10, 1868 (Collected Works, Vol. 7, p. 264). Manifestly the impressions Bismarck gathered in 1866 stayed with him for many years.
16. Collected Works, Vol. 7, p. 198, discussion with von Löw, June 4, 1867. For another, with Völderndorff in May, 1868, in which his Christian motivation was strongly emphasized, see *ibid.,* p. 261; also with des Houx on April 24, 1890 (Collected Works, Vol. 9, p. 14); and with H. Kleser on May 31, 1892 (*ibid.,* p. 207); and *passim.*
17. Bismarck's utterances on preventive war and its moral and political impossibility are many. Of special interest are the remarks of February 16, 1887 (edited by Herbert von Bismarck, *Grosse Politik,* Vol. 6, pp. 172ff.) in which Bismarck cites France's long peaceful record toward Germany and England after its defeat in 1815. See also *Grosse Politik,* Vol. 6, pp. 304ff., Collected Works, Vol. 7, p. 186. It is noteworthy that he did not regard a timely strike in the event of direct war danger immediately impending as irresponsible pre-emption – see his Reichstag speech of November 4, 1871 (Collected Works, Vol. 11, p. 204, already cited in Part 3). An unpublished dissertation by my student Rudolf Koop, "Bismarck und der Präventivkrieg" (Freiburg, 1953), seeks to elucidate this apparent contradiction on the basis of a careful study of the documents. He rightly emphasizes that theoretical considera-tions – not even whether preventive war is right or wrong in principle – never ultimately swayed Bismarck in his practical political decisions. What guided him were the political elements in the concrete situation. Yet these political require-ments were always influenced by an awareness of his moral responsibility.
18. See his speech to young students on April 1, 1895: "We Germans had no further reason [in 1875] to wage war. We had what we needed. To fight beyond that point, from a desire for conquest or territorial aggrandizement not needed for our satisfaction, seems to me particularly ruthless – indeed, a kind of Bonapartist, foreign ruthless-ness at odds with our German sense of justice" (Collected Works, Vol. 13, pp. 557f.). To appreciate properly this peace speech of the octogenarian, one should compare it with his Olmütz speech of 1850 – which showed some understanding for the possibility that "some would like to make war for the simple reason that king

and commander-in-chief say: I like that country and would like to have it" (Collected Works, Vol. 10, p. 106). The young Bismarck quite definitely displayed a propensity for conquest, but when he became a responsible statesman he yielded to it only within the sharply marked limits of clear-cut national needs.

19. See Count von Mandelsloh, "Politische Pakte und völkerrechtliche Ordnung," in *25 Jahre Kaiser-Wilhelm-Gesellschaft,* Vol. 3, pp. 230-234.

20. Conversation with Th. von Bernhardi of May 10, 1867, Vol. 7, p. 375. To Bernhardi's argument that France would certainly not surrender its position of hegemony in Europe without war, Bismarck replied simply and firmly: "Perhaps that is so, but that is no reason to provoke war." According to Bernhardi, Bismarck's main reason was that "Prussia would be charged with being Europe's perpetual mischief-maker and universally execrated." Bernhardi, the national liberal, characteristically added this note: "What harm would that do?"

21. The diplomatic background of the war of 1870-1871 has been thrown into deep confusion, because Bismarck afterward, notably in *Gedanken und Erinnerungen,* sought to conceal and even deny his role in the affair of the Spanish succession. When R. Fester uncovered his share, with the help of the documents in the case, Bismarck's "Machiavellianism" was greatly exaggerated. Bismarck's own pretexts, put forward as early as his memorials to William I, on behalf of Prussia's supposed realistic interest in seeing a Hohenzollern prince summoned to the throne in Madrid, led scholars still further astray. I cannot bring myself to believe that Bismarck seriously anticipated that such a succession would entail a political or military threat on the part of France. Still less could economic motives have weighed in the balance. Indeed, Bismarck was probably not greatly interested in whether the chaos in Spain was ended or not. He merely regarded it as a soft spot in the underbelly of the French empire that helped to keep down French ambitions. Fester theorized that his main purpose was to prevent Franco-Italian unity on the basis of relieving French troops in Rome with Spanish, but this is highly artificial and rather refuted by subsequent events. France withdrew its troops even when there was no Spanish relief. Thimme's conjecture (Bismarck's Collected Works, Vol. 6b, p. 269), to the effect that Bismarck wished to enhance the prestige of the Hohenzollern dynasty to the point that it would appear to be qualified to head an empire, also seems to me poorly documented, besides being inherently improbable. Completely untenable, as already emphasized by Thimme, *loc. cit.,* is Delbrück's theory that Bismarck wanted to provoke preventive war. There would have been other and far more favorable opportunities for that. H. Oncken, in *Die Rheinpolitik Napoleons III,* Vol. 1, pp. 100ff., points persuasively to Napoleon's policy of encirclement as the background for the whole Spanish affair, which seems to hit the mark in a political sense; but in my view Oncken goes too far in assuming that Napoleon and Ollivier deliberately sought war after July 6, 1870. I think I can show clearly that here again no more than a diplomatic triumph was intended, which to the horror of the emperor and his liberal minister president turned into the alternatives of diplomatic defeat or war. Bismarck, too, initially counted heavily on Napoleon's reluctance to become embroiled in war. These brief remarks must suffice here. My student, Jochen Dittrich, in 1948, in a voluminous dissertation at Freiburg University, presented a thoroughgoing study of the subject, based on all the source material, expanded by material from the Hohenzollern archives. Unfortunately it remains unpublished, though Dittrich summarized his major findings in an article in *Welt als Geschichte,* Vol. 53, No. 1. E. Marck, in *Der Aufstieg des Reichs,* Vol. 2, pp. 420ff., a carefully balanced account, scarcely transcends a tentative evaluation of the various ways—some of them extremely improbable—in which Bismarck's intentions might possibly be interpreted. E. Eyck, in the second volume of his Bismarck biography, discusses the genesis of the war of 1870-1871, but as a special pleader rather than an analytical historian.

22. M. Busch, *Tagebuchblätter,* Vol. 1, p. 7, February 27, 1870. Compare Stosch's judgment in his *Denkwürdigkeiten,* p. 181, from a letter to Freytag of April 5, 1870: "Bismarck keeps on pursuing his great goal, the unification of Germany,

which he would like to gain without war." The statements to Keudell in December, 1869, are in a similar vein: Bismarck refused to go after war with France. "One must continue to remove the reasons for a possible war and trust in the calming effect of time," etc., etc. He was then staking his hopes in Napoleon's worsening illness and the peaceful orientation of the new, liberal Ollivier government (Collected Works, Vol. 7, p. 302; Keudell, *Fürst und Fürstin Bismarck,* B. 419). On other occasions the possibility of Napoleon's impending death or the fall of his throne was taken into account. See also a conversation with Völderndorff in mid-May, 1868: "After all, there is always the possibility that we may reach our goal without war. . . . One would have to be a poor Christian and a man bereft of conscience not to try everything to spare one's fellow citizens a war, even it it should end in victory." (Collected Works, Vol. 7, p. 261.)

23. Directive to Freiherr von Werther, Collected Works, Vol. 6b, pp. 2, February 26, 1869: "I too think it likely that German unification can be helped only by forcible action. But it is an altogether different question whether there is any call to bring about a violent catastrophe, and who should be responsible for choosing the time for such a thing. Arbitrary intervention in history, stemming from purely subjective motives always means no more than shaking down unripe fruit. . . . The garrulous bustle with which people not officially concerned keep searching for the philosopher's stone by which German unification might be accomplished usually conceals a shallow and in any event impotent ignorance of the realities and their consequences. . . . We may advance the clocks, but this does not speed up time; and the ability to await developments is one of the prerequisites of practical politics."

24. See Part 2, above.

25. For details see von Srbik, *Metternich,* Vol. 2, pp. 531ff. On the role of the notion of balance in Bismarck's policy, see Ewald Kleisinger, *Bismarck und der Gedanke der europäischen Ordnung* (Legal dissertation; Jena, 1938, also published in book form by Triltsch, Würzburg). The peaceful objectives of Bismarck's policy after 1871 are misread to a surprising degree in the third volume of E. Eyck's major biography.

26. To Schweinitz, February 25, 1887, *Grosse Politik,* Vol. 6, pp. 177f. Even France's current hostility could not swerve long-range German policy from this course. "Even in the event of war, we would still hold out the hand of peace." Naturally all this was said for the benefit of the Russians, yet it holds a core of conviction confirmed elsewhere. See, for example, the discussion with Henri des Houx on April 24-25, 1890 (Collected Works, Vol. 9, p. 16): The integrity of France was a European necessity, like the integrity of Austria; or the directive to von der Goltz of January 30, 1867 (Collected Works, Vol. 6, p. 251): Prussia had the greatest interest in a solution of the eastern question, "which would turn France into a satisfied and peace-loving member of the European community."

27. Directive to von der Goltz, February 20, 1865 (Collected Works, Vol. 5, p. 94): "We must not be alienated or hurt by it [France's ambiguous attitude]. France owes us nothing. It would be simply following the dictates of natural selfishness in exploiting us and its position toward us," etc., etc. There are numerous similar passages. Perhaps the best-known instance is Bismarck's rejection of a policy of prestige and intervention in his Reichstag speech of February 6, 1888 (Collected Works, Vol. 13, p. 331, Paragraph 2).

28. Collected Works, Vol. 15, pp. 364-365 and *passim; Gedanken und Erinnerungen,* Vol. 2, p. 175, Paragraph 3.

29. This is shown in classic form in the great Reichstag speech of February 6, 1888, Collected Works, Vol. 13, p. 340, Paragraph 3. Like all international treaties, the triple alliance applied only with the reservation that things remained as they were. If changed conditions made fulfillment of treaty obligations impossible, this would have to be openly declared, since no statesman could be compelled to lead his people to perdition on behalf of the letter of an agreement. Indeed, no treaty really exacted such self-sacrifice. The treaties were "no more than an expression of common purpose in the endeavors and dangers the powers faced." One wished to fend off danger jointly and "jointly protect the peace that is as dear to one as it is to

the other. . . . this endeavor, together with the mutual trust that the treaties will be kept and that they will not make one dependent on the other in greater measure than his own interest can bear – that is what makes these treaties firm and durable."

30. Collected Works, Vol. 4, pp. 516ff.: *Die auswärtige Politik Preussens,* Vol. 5, pp. 230, 237.

31. Collected Works, Vol. 4, p. 531.

32. Count Friis to Quaade, June 27, 1869, *Det Nordslesvigske Spørgsmall,* Vol. 2, 588, p. 259; repeated in F. Hähnsen, *Ursprung und Geschichte des Artikels V des Prager Friedens,* Vol. 2 (1929), p. 257.

33. Report by Benedetti, February 8, 1868, *Origines diplomatiques,* Vol. 20, pp. 353f.

34. Quaade's report of March 27, and April 3, 1868, *Det Nordslesvigske Spørgsmall,* Vol. 1, pp. 430-32, Vol. 2, p. 446; also in Hähnsen, *loc. cit.,* Vol. 2, pp. 213f.

35. See for example the directive to Freiherr von Scheel-Plessen of July 31, 1866, in Hähnsen, Vol. 2, pp. 6ff.

36. The demonstration to that effect by Platzhoff in the introduction to the documentation cited above does not seem to me to be invalidated by the critical examination that follows (though on most points that is fair enough) – indeed, the supplementary publication by Hähnsen only serves to confirm it. See also Bismarck's Reichstag speech of September 24, 1867, and his speech in the Prussian chamber of deputies of December 20, 1866.

37. The clearest picture of his reflections is found in Bülow's memorandum of April 28, 1875, and the letter to Moltke of May 1, 1875, in Platzhoff, *loc. cit.,* Nos. 307, 308, pp. 397ff.

38. In addition to to the Collected Works, Vol. 6, *Origines Diplomatiques,* Vols. 13-16, and Oncken's *Die Rheinpolitik Napoleons,* Vol. 2, valuable new source material on the Luxembourg crisis is presented in the documentary appendix to the book by Count Stolberg-Wernigerode *Robert H. Graf von der Goltz* (1941).

39. *Gedanken und Erinnerungen,* Vol. 1, p. 99 (Collected Works, Vol. 15, p. 73). See also the speeches of January 22, 1864, and May 2, 1871.

40. To M. Busch on September 5, 1870 (Vol. 2, p. 172): "What we need and propose to take is Metz and Strasbourg – the fortresses. As for Alsace . . . that is a notion of the professors."

41. "Comprenant qu'il serait inutile de revendiquer ce qui était déjà perdu. . . . " Thiers, *Notes et Souvenirs,* p. 118. Note also his confidential proposal made as early as August 8, 1870, to exchange Alsace for Walloon territory in Belgium – see Rheindorf, *England und der deutsch-französische Krieg 1870-1871* (1923), p. 137. Also Thier's discussion with the crown prince on February 22, 1871, in *Grossherzog Friedrich I von Baden,* Vol. 2, p. 390: "The cession of Alsace would be considered a severe blow throughout France, but it would be accepted with resignation, if only Metz and Lorraine were to remain French." See the war diary of Emperor Frederic III, p. 391; also Gontaut-Biron's assurances in 1875 that the people of France were likely to be reconciled with Germany if Lorraine were returned (*Grosse Politik,* Vol. 1, p. 276, notes by Radowitz).

42. Collected Works, Vol. 6b, p. 501.

43. Collected Works, Vol. 6b, 2015, pp. 678f.

44. It is only on this assumption that we can explain the displeasure he voiced in late September over the exhortations by certain German newspapers to practice moderation in the peace terms. He thought this limited his freedom of action, for he had wished to point to the rather stiff demands of German public opinion in the negotiations, from which he might retreat as the occasion dictated – M. Busch, *Tagebuchblätter,* Vol. 1, pp. 250, 253f. See also A. Klein-Wuttig, *loc. cit.,* p. 159.

45. L. Bamberger, *Bismarcks grosses Spiel* (1932), p. 206, discussion of November 4, 1870; M. Busch, Vol. 2, pp. 168f., table talk on February 21, 1871: With the help of the French billions, one might well build suitable fortifications elsewhere. Abeken made a similar report to the Grand Duke Frederic on February 10, 1871 – see the Grand Duke's diary, Vol. 2, p. 367.

46. Thiers, *Notes et Souvenirs,* pp. 96f., 118. See also the communication by F. Hirth, *Preussische Jahrbücher,* Vol. 183, pp. 179, 185, from Thiers' own papers, where the passage just cited is absent, but there is mention of the possibility of prompt peace at the cost of only one province; also Thiers' communication to Lord Lyons in January, 1871, in Newton, Vol. 1, p. 358. For a critique of Thiers' memoirs, see G. Küntzel, *Thiers und Bismarck* (1905), pp. 55f.; Rheindorf, *England und der deutsch-französische Krieg* (1923), p. 140; A. Klein-Wuttig, *loc. cit.,* p. 160. Still, the doubts concerning Thiers' veracity voiced by H. Herzfeld cannot be waved aside (*Deutschland und das geschlagene Frankreich 1871-1873* [1924] pp. 12f.). On the other hand, Favre too insists that during the meeting at Ferrières Bismarck at first laid claim only to Alsace—Jules Simon, *Le Gouvernement de M. Thiers* (1880), Vol. 1, p. 111.

47. For Bismarck's reflections on this matter see the war diary of Emperor Frederic III, pp. 396f., 388; *Grossherzog Friedrich,* Vol. 2, pp. 367, 389, 393; M. Busch, Vol. 2, pp. 168f.; Reichstag speech of May 2, 1871. For the English proposals and the efforts at intervention by Gladstone, see Rheindorf, *loc. cit.,* pp. 132f., 135, 139, 141f.

48. *Grossherzog Friedrich, loc. cit.,* Vol. 2, pp. 367, 389. The grand duke learned from Keudell that in September or October the chancellor had casually remarked that the accession of French elements and French deputies in the Reichstag would be most irksome. "Alsace is rather more German and is good enough for us; and that line would secure us against future French attack."

49. M. Busch, Vol. 2, p. 169, February 21, 1871. Similar sentiments in Waldersee, *Denkwürdigkeiten,* Vol. 1, p. 163: "When someone asked him during the negotiations what would happen with Metz, he replied: 'I am afraid we already have it round our neck.'"

50. Collected Works, Vol. 6b, 1801, 1806, 1808.

51. Especially well known is his formulation during the surrender negotiations at Sedan: "Over two centuries, France has declared war on Germany on thirty occasions" (Ducrot, *La Journée de Sedan* [1871], p. 60).

52. A significant remark occurs in a letter to his wife of February 27, 1871: "I found it difficult to be as hard with him [Thiers] as I had to be."

53. As early as February 27, 1871, he wrote his wife: "We finally signed yesterday, and got more than seems useful in my personal political calculation. But I must take into account sentiment both above and below, and there is no calculation in those quarters. We shall take Alsace and German Lorraine, also Metz, with some very indigestible element. . . . " He expressed himself on August 13, 1871, with remarkable candor to the French chargé d'affaires de Gabriac, whom he had not met before (*Documents diplomatiques français,* Vol. 1, 1, p. 62): " 'I am under no illusion but that it was absurd of us to take Metz, which is French, away from you. I did not wish to have to defend it for Germany. The general staff asked me if I could guarantee that France would not seek revenge. I replied that, on the contrary, I was quite convinced they would, and that this war was but the first of many that would erupt between Germany and France, that it would be followed by many more. In such an eventuality, they told me, Metz would be a staging area for 100,000 Frenchmen, and we shall have to hold it; but that is as true of Alsace and Lorraine. If we are to have enduring peace, it is a mistake for us to have taken them from you, for those provinces will only be an embarrassment to us.' 'A kind of Poland with France behind it,' I retorted. 'Yes,' said the chancellor, 'A Poland with France in its rear.'"

54. See also the directive to Count Münster of May 12, 1875, *Grosse Politik,* Vol. 1, p. 274: "War between two countries of such stature is not settled with a single campaign, but will give rise to a whole series of wars. That was the crucial element in our reticence in 1867."

55. See H. Herzfeld, *Deutschland und das geschlagene Frankreich, 1871-1873* (1924); and K. Linnebach, *Deutschland als Sieger im besetzten Frankreich* (1924).

56. Since the first edition of this book, the question of Bismarck's war aims in 1870-1871

has taken a new turn with publication, in August, 1964, of the carefully documented analysis by Walter Lipgen, "Bismarck, die öffentliche Meinung und die Annexion von Elsass und Lothringen 1870," *Historische Zeitschift,* Vol. 199. Lipgen shows that prior to the victory at Sedan surprisingly few voices supported the annexation of Alsace, that eminent national liberals offered objections to it, and that as early as August Bismarck began to whip up annexationist sentiment by inspired propaganda in the press. Lipgen examines both the motives for annexation and its political consequences, on which he passes severely critical judgment.

Afterword to the Second and Third Editions

A NEW PRINTING of the first volume of this work has become necessary at a time when publication of the second volume still lies in the future. I had hoped to complete it by 1959, but the date has had to be postponed much longer than I anticipated in 1954. Among the reasons have been conflicting projects, expecially the revision of my biography of Freiherr vom Stein, as well as time-consuming library and source research for the interior history of the First World War, and lastly the completion of certain special studies that were indispensable to lay the groundwork for the second volume. They included:

1. *Der Schlieffenplan. Kritik eines Mythos* (Oldenbourg, Munich, 1956).

2. "Die Zusammenarbeit det Generalstäbe Deutschlands und Osterreich-Ungarns vor dem Ersten Weltkrieg," in *Festschrift für Hans Hersfeld* (Berlin, 1958), pp. 523-549.

3. "Die deutschen Militärattachés und das Auswärtige Amt," in *Sitzungsberichte der Heidelberger Akademie der Wissenschaften* (1959), first report.

4. "Die Wehrmacht und der politische Widerstand gegen Hitler," in *Schicksalsfragen der Gegenwart* (West German Defense Ministry: 1957), Vol. 1, pp. 349-381, reprinted in *Lebendige Vergangenheit* (Oldenbourg, Munich, 1958), pp. 184-212.

The appearance of my work met with a wide international response. An Italian edition is already in preparation, to be published by Einaudi, Turin. Scholarly review was in some measure handicapped by the fact that the whole work is not yet in print; and I have seen no reason for revising this volume. Except for a few passages which I have corrected or supplemented, the second and third editions, therefore, simply are an exact reproduction of the first.

Among relevant works published since 1954 the most important is Eberhard

Kessel's comprehensive Moltke biography (1958). It completely ignores my own, which is not even listed in the bibliography, and thus offers me no occasion for corrections of any kind. I find myself unable to accept Kessel's view of the conflicts between Moltke and Bismarck, which I think in one sense he treats in far too offhand a fashion.

By far the most detailed and significant review of my book was presented in 1955 by Ludwig Dehio in the *Historische Zeitschrift*, Vol. 180, pp. 43-64. It is a most gratifying over-all appreciation, though in the main it is preoccupied only with the first chapter; but to respond to it in detail would take up much space, while, I fear, promising small profit.

If I understand him right, Dehio views Prusso-German history from Frederic the Great to Adolf Hitler as a single, essentially continuous concatenation of expressions of "military *raison d'état*," basically undifferentiated, despite certain nuances. This is so utterly at odds with my approach to history and my political concepts that detailed disputation is unlikely to bridge the gulf. If Dehio were right, i.e., if Adolph Hitler had been in any sense the heir and continuer of traditional Prussian "political wisdom" in the militarist vein, then my book, in its political aspects, would have been written in vain (see p. 20). But perhaps I can at least briefly endeavor to clear up a few misunderstandings that recur in part also in Herzfeld's review in the *Vierteljahreshefte für Zeitgeschichte* (1956), pp. 367ff.

1. It is not at all my view that the danger of militarism in the history of Prussia and Germany—i.e., of a policy of overweening militancy—grew virulent only in the twentieth century; nor do I simply acquit Prussian tradition since Frederic the Great of this fault; nor—at least of all—do I grant "general absolution" to Frederic, whose demoniac character I neither glossed over nor idealized in my biography. Still less, of course, do I dispute the important role which vainglory, military ambition, and the drive for power have always played in the political sphere—not even in the few sentences I devoted to the German princelings before the modern age, though perhaps I did not always choose my words with sufficient care.

I am surprised that the picture I have drawn should have been misread in this fashion, despite everything I say on Frederic's invasion of Silesia, Marshal Blücher's headquarters, William I's pigheadedness, Roon, Manteuffel, and even Moltke—above all, despite my careful account of the militarist strain in German intellectual life since Fichte and Hegel (pp. 206ff.). One would think every historian knew that neither virtue nor error are encountered unadulterated in the pages of history—perfection and defect are always a matter of degree. Even statesmanship, true or false, is not an absolute concept (see my introduction).

Everyone knows that militarism has existed throughout Prussian history in Dehio's sense. The rulers of Prussia have always pursued a militant power policy, basing themselves on a strong army, which played an inordinately large part in their state. My objective was to show that only in the post-Bismarck era was the natural relation of scepter and sword formally reversed, and why that happened.

2. The problem with which my book deals is political and historical rather than sociological. The German title is *Staatskunst und Kriegshandwerk*, "The Art of Statesmanship and the Craft of War." True, the expository subtitle speaks of the "problem of militarism," but this is meant only in the sense that militarism is a political problem. I am in a way sorry that I ever included the vague and equivocal term "militarism" in my title at all, for it has been nothing but a nuisance in the discussion of my book. Contrary to what Dehio seems to conclude, I am not concerned with the contrast between militarism and political wisdom, but with the contrast between true statesmanship and unbridled militancy, between the true "art" of statesmanship and the false—the kind that approaches its mission solely from the technical military side. I did not need my critics to teach me the lesson that this conflict is not susceptible to rational resolution, that there is no clear-cut conceptual definition of "true statesmanship." In my introduction I pointed out that a practical solution is always found, nevertheless, when the statesman's ultimate goal, in the inevitable power struggle, is not power on its own but the pursuit, by the use of power, of an enduring and reasonable order, to be achieved in awareness of moral responsibility.

Dehio seems to regard as utopian this goal of peaceful and enduring order—its success resting on a distribution of power that satisfies all the nations sharing in it or that will at least be tolerated by them. He sees grand policy as the field of inexorable and everlasting struggle for "hegemony." I refuse to accept this deep-dyed pessimism; and I know no other way to tell the responsible statesman from the unconscionable adventurer than the one I have tried to follow, by seeking to define general political goals, even though this can never be done unequivocally.

My first chapter is devoted to a demonstration that Frederic the Great, seen in the round, *was* a responsible statesman rather than an unconscionable adventurer. I have never claimed that Frederic's *raison d'état* is the outright equivalent of a formal system of ethics, but unlike Meinecke I assert that even when Frederic speaks of *Staatsräson,* he was always aware of an element of moral responsibility, that there was always a striving for reason seen in ethical perspective.

For the rest, as far as I can see, I have scarcely used the term *raison d'état* and its various circumlocutions elsewhere in my book. Dehio views it as a demoniac ambiguity and reproaches me for idealizing it as a thing of general ethical value. I can find no valid reason for this indictment.

Even stranger seems to me his suggestion that I credit a military state with political wisdom only so long as its rise is attended by good fortune, in other words, that my moral judgments are contingent on outward success (*loc. cit.,* pp. 58ff.). I must, furthermore, object to the attempt to pin me down arbitrarily to a few abstract concepts that can serve as no more than a kind of shorthand for historical realities.

3. I have been reproached in several quarters for drawing my definition of militarism too narrowly. I am charged with ignoring that militarism can also be found when a grossly swollen army overwhelms all civilian life with its way of life and mode of thinking—as for example in Prussia from the time of Frederic William I. I do not at all dispute that the concept of militarism may be expanded in this fashion, nor that bourgeois society in Prussia had been burdened with the social dominance of the military since Frederic William I, with the bureaucracy, particularly, steeped in the military spirit.

Indeed, later on, when universal military service was strictly enforced for upper-class youth, all German life was to a degree militarized. I discuss this on pp. 95 and 158ff. and *passim,* and in Chapter 5 of the second volume I revert to the social order established by Frederic William I. In the context of the task I set myself, however, all this becomes important only at the moment when militarization visibly reacts in a certain way on the course of foreign affairs, or at least on the attitude of leading statesmen. This, in my view, took place only in the Wilhelminian era.

Freiburg, October, 1964   *Gerhard Ritter*

Index